Authentic
Reconstruction

Authentic Reconstruction

Authenticity, Architecture and the Built Heritage

Edited by
John Bold, Peter Larkham
and Robert Pickard

Bloomsbury Academic
An imprint of Bloomsbury Publishing Plc

BLOOMSBURY
LONDON · OXFORD · NEW YORK · NEW DELHI · SYDNEY

Bloomsbury Academic

An imprint of Bloomsbury Publishing Plc

50 Bedford Square	1385 Broadway
London	New York
WC1B 3DP	NY 10018
UK	USA

www.bloomsbury.com

BLOOMSBURY and the Diana logo are trademarks of Bloomsbury Publishing Plc

First published 2018

British Library Cataloguing-in-Publication Data
A catalogue record for this book is available from the British Library.

ISBN:	HB:	978-1-4742-8406-6
	ePDF:	978-1-4742-8404-2
	ePub:	978-1-4742-8405-9

Library of Congress Cataloging-in-Publication Data
A catalog record for this book is available from the Library of Congress.

Cover design by Eleanor Rose
Cover image: The reconstructed bridge at Mostar, UNESCO World Heritage Site, Bosnia-Herzegovina, Europe © Getty Images

Typeset by Integra Software Services Pvt. Ltd.
Printed and bound in Great Britain

To find out more about our authors and books visit www.bloomsbury.com. Here you will find extracts, author interviews, details of forthcoming events and the option to sign up for our newsletters.

CONTENTS

NOTES ON CONTRIBUTORS

David Adams is Lecturer in Urban Planning at the University of Birmingham. He has a long-standing research interest in post-war reconstruction and how people have experienced it.

Ingrid Appelbom Karsten, an art historian, urban planner and architect, has academic affiliations in Warsaw and in Stockholm (where she was awarded a PhD in 1987 for her study of the reconstruction of historic towns and cities in Poland and Czechoslovakia). She has been working at the University in Gothenburg, dealing with Cultural Heritage and is Professor in Urban and Cultural Planning at Chalmers University of Technology, Gothenburg. Her affiliation to practice has been with the Municipality of Oslo as Urban Planner and Architect.

John Bold is Reader in Architecture at the University of Westminster and has worked for several years as a consultant to the Council of Europe on cultural heritage. He has published widely on English architecture, European heritage and data standards. He was Head of Architecture at the Royal Commission on the Historical Monuments of England. He is editor of the *Transactions of the Ancient Monuments Society*.

Martin Cherry is a historian who has published in the fields of medieval studies, vernacular and Victorian architecture and UK conservation policy. He was Head of Listing and Research Director at English Heritage and has been an advisor to the Council of Europe. He was a member of the Commission to Preserve National Monuments in Bosnia and Herzegovina and President of the Vernacular Architecture Group, UK.

Bujar Demjaha, an architect, is a professor in three universities in Kosovo and Macedonia. He holds master's degrees in architecture and in graphic design from the University of Prishtina and PhDs from the Vienna University of Technology (on spatial planning) and the University of Sarajevo (on bioclimatic architectural design). He recently published *The Role of Tourism in the Rural Development of the Dukagjini Region in Kosovo* (LAP LAMBERT Academic Publishing, Saarbrücken, Germany).

Eva von Engelberg-Dočkal is an art historian who has specialized in the history of architecture from the eighteenth century until the present. After receiving her PhD in 2001 she worked with the State Office for Monument

Preservation in Schleswig-Holstein, the Hafen City Universität, Hamburg, and is currently at the Bauhaus-Universität, Weimar, specializing in contemporary historicizing architecture.

David Johnson is a conservation architect in private practice in London. He has a particular interest in the reuse of industrial buildings and sites, and has both worked on and promoted the conservation and rehabilitation of historic buildings in the UK and in South-East Europe.

Marieke Kuipers is an art and architectural historian who has specialized in the identification, valuation and preservation of twentieth-century-built heritage. She holds the chair of Cultural Heritage at the Faculty of Architecture and the Built Environment at Delft University of Technology and is also affiliated with the Netherlands Agency for Cultural Heritage at Amersfoort as a senior specialist of modern heritage.

Peter J. Larkham is Professor of Planning at Birmingham City University. He has a long-standing record of research and publication on urban form and conservation, most recently specializing in the processes and impacts of replanning and rebuilding after the catastrophe of the Second World War. He has recently edited *The Blitz and Its Legacy* and *Alternative Visions of Post-War Reconstruction*.

Alberto Lemme is a freelance engineer with thirty-five years' experience in the field of design and construction management for the restoration and seismic improvement of masonry buildings of cultural heritage interest damaged by earthquakes. He has been involved with various studies, research and publications on the analysis of seismic vulnerability in collaboration with the Italian National Group for Defence against Earthquakes (GNDT) and the Institute for Construction Technologies (ITC) scientific facility of the National Research Council (CNR).

Hans-Rudolf Meier is an art historian who has specialized in the history of medieval and modern architecture and in the history and theory of architectural preservation. He holds the chair for the Preservation of Historical Monuments and Sites and the History of Architecture at the Faculty of Architecture of the Bauhaus-Universität, Weimar.

Olivia Muñoz-Rojas is an independent researcher and writer. She holds a PhD from the London School of Economics, and is currently affiliated to the University of Westminster. She has published extensively in academic journals, and writes regularly for non-academic media such as *El Pais*. She specializes in cities, and is the author of *Ashes and Granite*, on the Spanish Civil War and its aftermath.

Robert Pickard is Emeritus Professor in Built Environment and Heritage Conservation at Northumbria University. He has worked for several years as a consultant to the Council of Europe on cultural heritage, heading the Legal Task Force, and is the author of several reference volumes on European heritage policy and practice.

Gail Sansbury has a PhD in Urban Planning and has taught urban planning and American studies at Cal Poly Pomona, San José State University and the California College of the Arts. She was Director of the Archive and Research Center, Chevy Chase Historical Society, Maryland. She is currently writing about Nathan F. Barrett, a pioneer landscape architect who developed plans for communities in the late nineteenth century.

Jennie Sjöholm is a specialist in conservation of built environments. She is associate senior lecturer in Urban Design and Conservation at the division of Architecture and Water at Luleå University of Technology.

Julija Trichkovska is an art historian with an expertise in the protection of cultural heritage. She was formerly Head of Department for Identification and Protection of Cultural Heritage, Ministry of Culture, Skopje, Former Yugoslav Republic of Macedonia. She has worked as a consultant to the Council of Europe on cultural heritage and is currently Assistant Professor of Art History, University of St Cyril and Methodius, Skopje.

Danièle Voldman is a historian who has specialized in the social history of contemporary architecture and towns, in particular after the two world wars in Europe. She is directrice de recherche émérite at the CNRS, in the Centre d'histoire sociale at Paris Panthéon Sorbonne University. She has just published a history of housing in France since the end of the eighteenth century.

ACKNOWLEDGEMENTS

Many debts have been incurred. The editors are especially grateful to all the contributors to this volume who contributed essays in the midst of numerous other professional engagements. We are grateful also for the institutional support which has been provided by the University of Westminster and by the Council of Europe, where Mikhael de Thyse has been both inspirational and outstandingly supportive over many years. We thank also the national representatives of the countries involved in the Council of Europe/European Commission Regional Programme for South-East Europe, particularly Amra Hadžimuhamedović and Mirela Mulalić-Handan from Bosnia and Herzegovina.

We are grateful to the publisher, Taylor and Francis, and to the editor, Roger White, of the journal *The Historic Environment Policy & Practice*, for permission to draw on the essay 'Reconstructing Europe: The Need for Guidelines', by John Bold and Robert Pickard (4/2, 2013), particularly for the introductory chapter and conclusions of the present volume.

John Bold also wishes to thank Masters of Architecture dissertation students at the University of Westminster for numerous illuminating discussions on post-war rehabilitation and reconstruction, particularly Hannah Gaze (Croatia), Jonathan Oswald (Berlin), Leo Palmer (Bellotto in Warsaw) and Robert Percy (Balkans). He also wishes to acknowledge the contribution in spirit of his good friend and Council of Europe colleague, the late Dr Walter Wulf of the Niedersachsen Institut für Denkmalpflege.

Lastly we are grateful to James Thompson and Claire Constable at Bloomsbury for all their advice and work during the preparation of this volume.

ABBREVIATIONS

2D	Two Dimensional
3D	Three Dimensional
ACORN	Association of Community Organisations for Reform Now
BNOB	Bring New Orleans Back
BOS	*Biuro Odbudowy Stolicy* (Office for the Reconstruction of the Capital)
CAD	Computer-aided design
COST	European Cooperation in the field of Scientific and Technical Research
CCC	Civilian Conservation Corps
DOCOMOMO	International Committee for Documentation and Conservation of Buildings, Sites and Neighbourhoods of the Modern Movement
DOE	Department of the Environment
DNH	Department of National Heritage
DPCN	*Decreto del Presidente del Consiglio dei Ministri* (Decree of the President of Ministers)
EU	European Union
EUR-OPA	European and Mediterranean Major Hazards Agreement
FEMA	Federal Emergency Management Agency
FRG	Federal Republic of Germany (West Germany)
GBP	British Pound Sterling
GDR	German Democratic Republic (East Germany)
GSA	Glasgow School of Art
ICCROM	International Centre for the Study of Preservation and Restoration of Cultural Property
IDA	Institute of Digital Archaeology

ITC-CNR	*L'Istituto per le Tecnologie della Costruzione* and *Consiglio Nazionale delle Ricerche*
ICOMOS	International Council on Monuments and Sites
ICORP	International Scientific Committee on Risk Preparedness of ICOMOS
IDP	Internally displaced persons
IWPR	Institute for Women's Policy Research
ISIS	Islamic State of Iraq and Syria
LGBT	Lesbian, gay, bisexual and transgender
LKAB	Luossavaara Kiirunavara AB
LMDC	Lower Manhattan Development Corporation
MRU	Ministry for Reconstruction and Urban Planning, France
NOB	Nederlandsche Oudheidkundige Bond (Netherlands Archaeological Association)
PACE	Parliamentary Assembly of the Council of Europe
PKZ	Pracownie Konserwacji Zabytków (Atelier for the Conservation of Cultural Property)
PRC	Preservation Resource Center
PRG	*Piano Regolatore Generale* (Overall Development Plan)
SPAB	Society for the Protection of Ancient Buildings
UNESCO	United Nations Educational Scientific and Cultural Organisation
UK	United Kingdom
US	United States
VCC	*Vieux Carré* Commission

Introduction: Reconstruction: The Built Heritage Following War and Natural Disaster

John Bold

The background

The issue of how to reconstruct the built fabric of towns and cities, whether individual buildings, ensembles or entire districts, has been a major concern for all who have suffered war or natural disaster. Immediate responses have been remarkably consistent. Once the needs of the survivors have been met, attention turns to long-term habitation and the reconstruction of what has been lost (for the post-disaster sequence of activities see Haas et al. 1977: xxvii). Writing during the rule of the emperor Augustus, Livy tells the story of the Roman reaction to the systematic devastation of the city inflicted by the Gauls in 390 BC. Some wished to rebuild elsewhere but the unjustly exiled Camillus, recalled as dictator to lead the army, had first defeated the invaders and then in a noble piece of oratory dissuaded his fellow citizens from such moral and political weakness – 'must it be seen that Gauls could tumble Rome to the ground, while Romans are too weak to lift her up again?' – and such a sacrilegious abandonment of a site endorsed by gods and men – 'of all places in the world the best for a city destined to grow great'. But 'the work of reconstruction was ill-planned ... All work was hurried and nobody bothered to see that the streets were straight; individual property rights were ignored, and buildings went up wherever there was room for them. This explains why ... the general lay-out of Rome is more like a squatters' settlement than a properly planned city' (Livy 2002: 433–5). There is a political message here: this was the 'rambling jumble' of a city which Augustus was regularizing, ornamenting with new temples and classicizing in a style which implied 'dignity, authority and restraint' (Lane Fox 2006: 486).

An earthquake in south-east Sicily in 1693 destroyed the town of Noto, which was then completely rebuilt on a new site ten miles to the south. The opportunity was taken to lay out the new town on a geometrical grid with 'three parallel streets running horizontally along the slope of a gently rising hill and cut across at right angles by a series of narrower streets running up and down the hill'. Three squares, each with a church, were included, the whole making for 'a layout of great clarity which at the same time allows a series of effective vistas' (Blunt 1968: 25). The coherence of the plan and the consistent use of a beautiful yellow stone, soft enough for the carving of remarkable grotesque figures carrying balconies, render Noto a scenic highlight of the baroque (Figure 1). Much less ambitiously but also taking the opportunity to regularize following an earthquake in 1965, the population of the old village of Palia Alonnisos on the Greek island of Alonnisos was rehoused some years later (after a period of living among the ruins and living in tents) on top of the hill above the small coastal town of Patitiri in a new settlement (Neos Oikismos) (Keller and Tsoukanas 2006: 105). This comprises single-storey concrete and rendered-brick houses, laid out on a grid plan, with space for planting and with the running water and

FIGURE 1 *Noto, Sicily, a balcony in the reconstructed town. Source: John Bold, 2011.*

electricity which had been lacking in the old houses. Many of the traditional stone-built earthquake-damaged houses in the picturesque old village where electricity arrived in 1988 were recoverable and have now been restored and rebuilt as holiday homes.

The need to reconstruct after war or natural disaster, rehousing the people and rebuilding civil society, is clear, but that requirement does not prescribe how it should be done. Debates have tended to polarize around two alternatives: rebuilding in a contemporary style, signifying a new beginning, eradicating the errors and accretions of the past; or reinstating in a historicist style (replicating original appearances and materials) the buildings which have been lost, for reasons of continuity and identity. Between these two extremes, a third way – restoring traditional scale, massing and detailing (often simplified) within a modern setting – provides a compromise solution. Discussing post-war reconstruction in France, Nicholas Bullock has referred to the need 'to balance symbolic concerns with utilitarian priorities', in the case of Perret's architecture in Le Havre responding to 'the ambiguities of a reconstruction called upon to privilege both the ties of the past and the promise of the future' (Bullock 2014: 180, 185). Such discussions are once again germane within the context of the rebuilding of the countries of the former Yugoslavia after the wars of the 1990s in which historic buildings were specifically targeted, and after more recent natural disasters in Italy (earthquakes in L'Aquila, 2009 and Amatrice, 2016), Spain (earthquake at Lorca, 2011) and the United States (Hurricane Katrina, 2005; Hurricane Sandy, 2012; Hurricane Matthew, 2016).

In considering how to reconstruct, precedent and guidance are abundant but not definitive, so each case calls for a review of overall principles and local practicalities: 'there are no templates for postwar recovery. Each situation requires a tailored approach ...' (Barakat 2007: 38). Reviews will necessarily involve discussions of immediate needs, the significance of what has been lost and what might be reinstated or built anew. Considerations of the appropriate permanent form for newly built fabric inevitably will be informed by such elusive and contested concepts as heritage, reconstruction, authenticity, integrity, identity and cultural predispositions, all capable of an ever-widening range of meanings and applications in societies characterized by their diversity and attribution of values. Such considerations are central in the burgeoning reappraisals of urban reconstruction after the Second World War. Following the twentieth anniversary of the Nara Document on Authenticity (Nara 1994), discussion of these evolving concepts has been further reanimated (see also Bold and Pickard 2013).

Authenticity

Discussions cannot avoid, but are often disabled by, attempting to pin down the precise interpretation of the word 'authenticity', whose meaning has become ever more diluted, the more it has been used as an advertising hook for everything from real estate to handkerchiefs and from objects to experiences. Is it descriptive solely of fabric, of original or replacement materials, assembled in a traditional manner, or is it also vested in the feelings and values which that materiality embodies? Consideration of authenticity and its cultural meaning and resonances is not simply a post-war or post-disaster issue. It bears also on the recreation and management of sites for purposes of education, commerce and tourism, a practice notable in the United States (Boyer 1992) and highlighted recently in the United Arab Emirates, where extraordinarily rapid development has had profound impacts on both traditions and appearances. The draft text of the 'Dubai Document on Reconstruction in the Gulf Region' 'seeks to establish that the meticulous physical reconstruction of lost or destroyed heritage places can serve "as a cultural tool to reconnect people with their history and tradition"', so enhancing the liveability of urban areas, fostering economic development and social cohesion (Silberman 2015). This is a notion of reconstruction which acknowledges the socio-economic instrumentality of heritage, but how far can an authentic experience be recreated or conjured through the simulation of an absent original monument? Such reconstruction as proposed in Dubai of what has been lost is surely qualitatively and morally far removed from the demolition of a historic building in order to reconstruct a simulacrum, a malign feature of contemporary practice in Moscow where the creation of 'sham replicas', recreating deliberately demolished buildings in new materials with new proportions and modern features has been powerfully condemned by Clementine Cecil and Nataliya Dushkina (Cecil 2011, Dushkina 2009). Dushkina invokes Walter Benjamin, whose influential nostrum – 'The whole province of genuineness [authenticity] is beyond technological (and of course not only technological) reproducibility' – has helped shape all subsequent discussions on unique original art and mechanical reproduction. But Benjamin's position was more nuanced than quotation of this phrase alone would allow. He went on to undermine the notion of an absolute authenticity when he referred to the 'aura' of an object: 'the quintessence of everything about it since its creation that can be handed down, from its material duration to the historical witness that it bears' (Benjamin 2009: 232–3).

In deciding whether and how to reconstruct we must consider how we are going to judge success and, indeed, who judges it. Reconstruction is likely to divide both specialist and lay opinion, whether it is a reconstruction of what was there before in a manner inimical to perceptions of how places used to be, or to notions of how they ought to look; whether it is simply badly done, in terms of scale, materials or re-designated function; whether urban revitalization might itself be classed as a category of disaster. Heritage professionals have long relied on the Venice Charter (Venice 1964) on 'The Conservation and Restoration of Monuments and Sites' as a rather negative, default starting point for considerations of reconstruction. But we must also consider the built heritage in the context of later charters and conventions. The Nara Document on Authenticity sought to build on the Venice Charter and on the framework provided by the UNESCO World Heritage Committee's 'desire to apply the test of authenticity in ways which accord full respect to the social and cultural values of all societies' (Nara 1994: article 2): 'Conservation of cultural heritage in all its forms and historical periods is rooted in the values attributed to the heritage' and 'Authenticity … appears as the central qualifying factor concerning values.' But judgements about values are neither absolute nor universal, so it is 'not possible to base judgements of value and authenticity within fixed criteria' since heritage must be judged within its specific cultural context and authenticity sought in form and design, materials and substance, use and function, traditions and techniques, location and setting, spirit and feeling and 'other internal and external factors', an expansion in application of the word 'authenticity' which for Nobuko Inaba, reflecting on Nara fifteen years later, 'continuously gives rise to confusion' (Nara 1994: articles 9–13; Inaba 2009: 162; see also Bold and Pickard 2013: 121–3). So the interpretative window was opened very wide indeed onto a world of immense cultural and heritage diversity in which, notwithstanding the potential difficulties in mutual understanding, 'the cultural heritage of each is the cultural heritage of all' (Nara 1994: article 8). The notion of a 'common cultural heritage', affirmed by UNESCO, was enshrined in Article 1 of the European Cultural Convention of 1954 (Pickard 2002: 63) but in spirit it goes back to the end of the Second World War, carrying with it the burden of joint responsibility and shared guilt. In his elaboration of the Charter of Athens (1933), referring to the historic heritage of cities, 'precious witnesses of the past', in 1943 Le Corbusier acknowledged that 'whoever owns them or is entrusted with their protection has the responsibility and the obligation to do whatever he legitimately can to hand this noble heritage down intact to the centuries to come'. This obligation, however, did not extend to historicist reconstruction. The Charter, a modernist manifesto, condemned 'the re-use of past styles of building for new structures in historic areas', a point reinforced in Le Corbusier's commentary: 'never has a return to the past been recorded, never has man retraced his own steps … The mingling of the 'false' with the 'genuine', far from attaining an impression of unity … merely results in artificial reconstruction capable only of discrediting the authentic testimonies that we were most moved to preserve' (Le Corbusier 1973: paras 65 and 70). Here the proponents of modernism and the Ruskinian defenders of an authentic built heritage – 'Restoration, so called, is the worst manner of Destruction' (Ruskin 1988: 194) – would find themselves on common ground.

In a heritage climate in which historicist reconstruction is frowned upon by heritage specialists as inauthentic, hence the deliberately provocative title of this book, there is a need for greater clarity about what reconstruction connotes, when it is admissible to carry it out in a style and form reflecting so far as possible what has been lost, how it should be done and, indeed, what authenticity actually means in theory and practice: wherein does it reside? Deliberations in Japan leading up to the twentieth anniversary of the Nara Document highlighted the need for further discussion of the relationship between authenticity and ever-changing values, the attribution of which 'is a social rather than a scientific or a technical process involving multiple individuals and groups', and between authenticity and integrity (UNESCO 2012b). Five key issues were identified two years later at the ICOMOS meeting in Japan, 'Nara + 20', which marked the anniversary: the diversity of cultural heritage forms and processes (acknowledging authenticity as a culturally contingent quality); the evolution of cultural values (questioning the validity of universal conservation principles); the involvement of multiple stakeholders (including virtual global communities); conflicting claims and interpretations (calling for consensus-building between communities in conflict) and the role of cultural heritage in sustainable development (not addressed in 1994 but now widely recognized) (ICOMOS Japan 2014).

A common cultural heritage

The notion of responsibility for a common cultural heritage was developed and advanced in the Council of Europe's groundbreaking Faro Framework Convention on the Value of Cultural Heritage for Society (Faro 2005). This redrew the traditional heritage map by situating the built heritage in its social context rather than seeing it simply as something of value for its own sake as an inalienable set of artefacts. The heritage in this document is interpreted as a tool for managing cultural diversity, improving the living environment and quality of life and developing democratic participation (Council of Europe 2013). The heritage is thus seen as a catalyst for participation and social improvement. It is therefore not just something to be managed by specialists but concerns us all, and we all have responsibilities as well as rights. It is a profoundly political document, rooted in the core values of the Council of Europe: human rights, democracy and the rule of law.

If access to cultural heritage is seen as a function of human rights, decision-makers must heed the voices of individuals and communities: 'everyone, alone or collectively, has the right to benefit from the cultural heritage and to contribute towards its enrichment; everyone, alone or collectively, has the responsibility to respect the cultural heritage of others as much as their own heritage' (Faro 2005: article 4). In her report to the Human Rights Council of the United Nations, Farida Shaheed in 2011 recommended that

> concerned communities and relevant individuals should be consulted
> and invited to actively participate in the whole process of identification,

selection, classification, interpretation, preservation/safeguard, stewardship and development of cultural heritage; ... states should take measures to encourage professionals working in the field of cultural heritage to adopt a human rights-based approach and to develop rules and guidelines in this respect; professionals working in the field of cultural heritage and cultural institutions ... should build stronger relationships with the communities and peoples whose cultural heritage they are the repositories of..... (United Nations 2011: para 80)

There is more to this than questions of the appearance of mere fabric: what does that fabric signify and what, if destroyed, did it once embody? As Michael Petzet has noted: 'in the evaluation of a monument not only the oft-evoked historic fabric but also additional factors ranging from authentic form to authentic spirit play a role' (ICOMOS 2004: 21).

Approaches to reconstruction

Esther Charlesworth has referred to the two major alternative approaches to post-war reconstruction: transformative (Rotterdam and Coventry) and facsimile (Warsaw and Dresden) (Charlesworth 2006: 27). There are numerous examples of both, and there are also examples of compromise positions in which both approaches have been used, together with many examples noted by Gilles Plum in France of the approach identified above as the third way between two extremes, rebuilding after the Second World War in a local style, not replicating the past but restoring a harmony believed to have been lost through the introduction of discordant elements, accepting modernity while acknowledging the realities of society, urban culture, economy and materials: the regionalist reconstruction of the town of Beauvais, too destroyed to envisage restoration, is a good example (Plum 2011: 44–9) (Figure 2). Architecture, he points out, is not free expression, still less is it conceptual (Plum 2011: 283). Comparable compromises have been identified by Wim Denslagen in his review of approaches to reconstruction in Belgium after the First World War where, notwithstanding the views of modernists, regionalism and some wishful thinking prevailed: 'this did not mean wanting to regain what had been there before, so much as building what they thought *should* have been there ... an architecture that was supposedly typical of the local, traditional style of construction' (Denslagen 2009: 99).

In reconstructing the monuments of the past it is necessary to decide which part of that past should be recreated. Although in the countries of the former Yugoslavia where new buildings express a fresh start and the embrace of the market economy, great emphasis also is placed on the reconstruction of buildings which are considered to be emblematic of identity or religious faith, and which also serve to demonstrate that deliberate destruction as an act of war should not be allowed to prevail. Historicist reconstruction

FIGURE 2 *Beauvais, France: the town centre reconstructed. Source: John Bold, 2014.*

is designed to send a message of continuity, a return to normal after exceptional events, together with the assertion of national cultural identity: an encouragement of those dispersed by war to return home. In Bosnia and Herzegovina there was massive systematic destruction: 1,180 mosques, 580 Roman Catholic and 290 Orthodox churches were destroyed or damaged in the wars of the 1990s (Walasek et al. 2015: 153–4), along with 78 per cent of the housing stock (Zetter 2010: 156). Here the reconstruction of the Town Hall, Sarajevo (completed with hardly any trace of its history preserved in the fabric, but with a less than conciliatory plaque outside detailing the responsibility for its destruction) and the ongoing work on the Aladza Mosque at Foca, one of more than twenty to be destroyed in the town as part of a deliberate 'policy of erasure' (Bevan 2006: 42–3), have been conducted with these sentiments of continuity and identity in mind. Public opinion on these sentiments was tested in a survey of residents carried out in Stolac, Bosnia and Herzegovina, following the beginning of their return in 1998 to a town from which they had been driven five years before. Results confirmed their strong identification with the built heritage and their desire to see it reinstated after catastrophic destruction, notwithstanding the resistance of local political leaders (Hadzimuhamedovic 2015: 259–84): 'the intangible expression of the heritage takes precedence when its material factors have been destroyed. The heirs to the heritage do not regard it as lost by virtue of its mere physical destruction, and they see its reconstruction as the essential bestowal of form on the intangible content that it retains' (Hadzimuhamedovic 2008: 328–45).

In Kosovo, 'art and architecture have become proxies through which ideological, ethnic and nationalist conflicts have been fought out … A mosque or a church is no longer a place of worship, but a token of the presence of a community marked for erasure' (Morel 2013: 4). Churches and mosques presented obvious targets as emblematic of the beliefs and heritage of the 'other'. The repair or reconstruction of the two hundred mosques damaged or destroyed in 1998–9, one-third of the overall total, has raised serious questions on how to restore and how far the intentions of the international funding bodies may be regulated. The Saudi Joint Committee for the Relief of Kosovo and Chechnya, 'the largest and most prominent Arab aid organisation in Kosovo' (Morel 2013: 7), favours the austere architecture and decoration of Wahhabi Islam over the richly decorated interiors of the Balkans. International donors tend to hold sway in the immediate aftermath of disaster, necessarily fulfilling the requirements of their own agenda as well as the needs of the recipients. Very few people have the will to refuse apparently well-meaning intervention or the confidence to direct it, particularly since aid tends to arrive in the immediate aftermath of war, which is, as Sultan Barakat has observed, 'precisely the time when the recipient nation lacks the capacity to absorb this high level of funding usefully' (Barakat 2010: 269). Great emphasis has been placed also in Kosovo on the reconstruction of many deliberately targeted traditional tower houses (*kullas*), 90 per cent of which were destroyed or damaged in the attack on the Kosovar Albanian heritage. For reasons of cultural affirmation, the *kulla* form has also been used in the construction of wholly new buildings, sometimes in new contexts, an act of political self-assertion.

Following attacks on the Serbian Orthodox heritage in Kosovo, notably in riots in 2004 in which thirty-five cultural and religious sites were damaged or destroyed, works of reconstruction were carried out by the Council of Europe–led Reconstruction Implementation Commission and the long-term protection of major Orthodox sites was written into the 'Ahtisaari Plan' (2007). This, the 'Comprehensive Proposal for Kosovo Status Settlement', established forty-five Serbian 'protective zones', whose integrity was to be maintained within the newly independent territory. The reconstruction of the churches and their subsequent protection have been regarded as a model for post-crisis collaboration between communities, a tangible example of the consensus-building later noted in 'Nara + 20': 'communities in conflict [should] agree to participate in the conservation of the heritage, even when a shared understanding of its significance is unattainable' (ICOMOS Japan 2014). Such agreement, an acknowledgement and an attempt to overcome the consequences of 'otherness', may be grudging but the application of the principle is sound if cultural diversity and individual identities are to be respected. In Kosovo the situation is particularly fraught since there are many major Orthodox monuments, including the monasteries and churches which collectively comprise a World Heritage Site, in a territory with a population which is 90 per cent Kosovar Albanian. When UNESCO embarked on the reconstruction of thirteen important sites in 2006, the organization was at pains to achieve a diplomatic balance with seven Orthodox and six Islamic buildings, but the lack of trust between communities is not conducive to long-term sustainable outcomes (The *Art Newspaper* 1 February 2006).

The political assertion of identity and an understanding of how places ought to look informed the reconstruction of the fourteenth-century House of the Blackheads in Riga, a building erected for a mercantile guild which was bombed during the Second World War, its remains destroyed and the square on which it stood enlarged during the following Soviet period. The reconstruction of the building in modern materials, reviving the spirit of independent place, was completed in 2000 in time for the celebration of the 800th anniversary of the city. This endeavour was justified in the Riga 'Charter on Authenticity and Historical Reconstruction' which acknowledged that 'replication of cultural heritage is in general a misrepresentation of evidence of the past ... but that in exceptional circumstances, reconstruction of cultural heritage, lost through disaster ... may be acceptable, when the monument concerned has outstanding artistic, symbolic or environmental ... significance for regional history and cultures' (Riga 2000). The Riga pronouncement reflected the sentiment expressed earlier in the same year in the Charter of Krakow ('Principles for Conservation and Restoration of Built Heritage') which stated that reconstruction of entire parts 'in the style of the building' should be avoided; that reconstruction of small parts with architectural significance can be acceptable, given indisputable documentation; and that reconstruction of an entire building 'destroyed by armed conflict or natural disaster' is acceptable only if there are 'exceptional social or cultural motives that are related to the identity of the entire community' (Krakow 2000: article 4).

Visual embodiment, political self-assertion and powerful beliefs in community identity were strikingly apparent in the account of Adolf Ciborowski (Chief Architect of Warsaw 1956–64) on the post-war return of the Varsovians whose 'common longing for a city which no longer existed' stimulated reconstruction as 'a spontaneous protest against the dark forces which had tried to wipe out our capital' (Ciborowski 1970: 278). This was a highly edited, politicized reconstruction in which choices were made about which periods in the long history of Warsaw carried the appropriate resonance. The razing of the city by the Nazis was an early example of urbicide – the intentional planned destruction and disintegration of an entire way of life in the city – later identified in Kosovo, Sarajevo and Dubrovnik in the 1990s as crimes against humanity. Recognizing that in the twentieth century architecture 'became, more and more, a weapon of war rather than something that gets in the way of its smooth conduct', Robert Bevan has proposed the addition of a new, specific crime of 'cultural genocide' to the 1948 United Nations Genocide Convention, 'at least in circumstances where it is intrinsically linked to mass murder' (Bevan 2006: 210). It is noteworthy that the Dayton General Framework Agreement for Peace in Bosnia and Herzegovina (1995) includes, as Annex 8, 'Agreement on Commission to Preserve National Monuments'. This is thought to be the first time in modern history that the heritage has been identified as crucial to the establishment of a sustainable peace. The reconstruction of destroyed historic monuments in Bosnia and Herzegovina is specifically allowed in the national legislation: rehabilitation includes 'the reconstruction of a national monument on the same site, in the same form, of the same dimensions and using the same or same type of materials as were used prior to its destruction, using the same building techniques wherever possible' (Law on Protection 2002: article 2).

Documentation

Although the Venice Charter ruled out reconstruction *a priori*, it allowed restoration 'based on respect for original material and authentic documents' (Venice 1964: articles 9 and 15). The importance of documentation has been emphasized in subsequent charters and advisory pronouncements, including the *Operational Guidelines for the Implementation of the World Heritage Convention* in which 'the reconstruction of ... historic buildings ... is justifiable only in exceptional circumstances ... [and] only on the basis of complete and detailed documentation and to no extent on conjecture' (UNESCO 2012a: article 86). This counsel of perfection represents a striking triumph of hope over experience and an equally remarkable belief in the absolute qualities which documentation may be thought to embody. Documentation often offers only a part of a story and it needs to be interpreted; it does not speak for itself; it is not absolute but is subject to interpretation of forms and materials and the values which inform our analyses and assessments. All conclusions drawn are ultimately the result of making the best bet (often contested) on the available evidence. This is even more the case in those circumstances such as contemporary Bosnia and Herzegovina, where although 'rehabilitation' (reconstruction) requires 'architectural, photographic and other documentation' (Law on Protection 2002: article 6), it may be permitted on the basis of very limited traditional forms of documentation which may be enhanced by the memories of the community, perhaps stimulated by their own photographs. Such pragmatism is surely allowable if the major purpose of reconstruction is to enable familiarization and the return of displaced persons – it becomes an alien place if it does not look the same as before, and believing that somewhere looks the same as before is a function of memory as much as of documentation. The 'familiar and cherished local scene' of English planning guidance is a negotiable construct dependent for its recognition and preservation on values and memory (DOE/DNH 1994: para 1.1). We have, as Adrian Forty has observed, 'an unshakeable confidence in the power of physical objects to preserve memory' (Forty 2012: 215) and, as David Lowenthal has noted, 'beleaguered by loss and change, we keep our bearings only by clinging to remnants of stability'(Lowenthal 1996: 6).

Values

Beleaguered by loss and change we seek to identify the essential attributes of those sites, buildings and activities which we would prefer to preserve, enhance or reconstruct. There is little which could be regarded as absolute about this on a collective basis, notwithstanding the certainties of individuals. The apparent consensus implicit in the notion of the 'authorised heritage discourse' (Smith 2006: 29–34) – the *de haut en bas* judgements of significance by experts – has been comprehensively undermined through the recognition of heritage as a discursive practice subject to contestation and revision, rather than an immutable set of objects to be protected (Bold 2016: 155). In such negotiable, relativist circumstances, the diktats of international charters and recommendations have become noticeably more pragmatic and inclusive. The Burra Charter, first adopted in 1979 and regularly reviewed subsequently, with major revisions in 1999 and minor adjustments in 2013, is subtitled 'The Australia ICOMOS Charter for Places of Cultural Significance', so foregrounding a notion of considerable complexity and breadth: 'Cultural significance means aesthetic, historic, scientific, social or spiritual value for past, present or future generations. Cultural significance is embodied in the place itself, its fabric, setting, use, associations, meanings, records, related places and related objects. Places may have a range of values for different individuals or groups' (Burra 2013: article 1.2). These values – aesthetic, historic, scientific and social – are not mutually exclusive; they may encompass a number of other values within each broad category; they may allow for the development of more precise categories as understanding of a place increases (Burra 2013: Guidelines 2). The values-based approach to assessment has become standard practice in some jurisdictions – English Heritage (now Historic England) for example, in *Conservation Principles Policies and Guidance* (English Heritage 2008), referred to evidential, historical, aesthetic and communal values. There are inherent difficulties here in assessment: who determines and how do we weight the significance of particular values when almost anything might have some value for somebody? The Burra Charter, perhaps optimistically anticipating rational consensus, advises against 'unwarranted emphasis on any one value at the expense of others' (Burra 2013: article 5.1).

The Charter appears to be cautious in its consideration of reconstruction – 'appropriate only where a place is incomplete through damage or alteration, and only where there is sufficient evidence to reproduce an earlier state of the fabric' – but it also allows for reconstruction 'as part of a use or practice that retains the cultural significance of the place' (Burra 2013: article 20.1). An adjoining explanatory note goes further: 'places with social or spiritual value may warrant reconstruction, even though very little may remain (… building footings or tree stumps ….). The requirement for sufficient evidence to reproduce an earlier state still applies.' There is an admirable generosity of spirit in this highly inclusive document – it is difficult to imagine how anything, given a fair wind and a good lawyer, may be disallowed. This is not a criticism but an acknowledgement that as heritage seen through the prism of values becomes ever more recognized as a function of society and ever more deeply embedded in human rights, the less it is amenable to straightforward yes or no, right or wrong answers to socially contingent questions with ramifications of increasing complexity. It is paradoxical that the electronic interactivity and immediacy conferred by the internet and social media, encouraging global access to information and a variety of points of view, both of which might stimulate profitable discourse on the heritage, its meanings and benefits, has in practice become the vehicle for moralizing anger and misplaced certainty, enabled by algorithms which ensure that our positions and attitudes are confirmed rather than challenged. In such circumstances, the Burra Charter stands as an exemplar of the application of civilized values to complex problems posed by heritage – its definitions, ownership, responsibilities, applications and desirable outcomes. All of these to varying extents present problems and all of them bear on the questions raised by the complex issue of reconstruction and the values which inform deliberations on the heritage. In assigning heritage value to an object we are arguably giving a license to historical misrepresentation and privileging present needs over past achievements. As Lowenthal has observed, 'Heritage diverges from history not in being biased but in its view of bias. Historians aim to reduce bias; heritage sanctions and strengthens it' (Lowenthal 1998: 8); elsewhere he remarked that 'the worth of heritage is … gauged not by critical tests but by current potency' (Lowenthal 1996: 127).

Consideration of values in the twenty-first century recalls the seminal contribution of Alois Riegl at the beginning of the twentieth century, in the essay which he wrote in 1903 as a preface to the legislative proposal for the protection of historic monuments in the Austro-Hungarian Empire. In questioning the meaning of monuments, he noted that 'every work of art is at once and without exception an historical monument' and 'in the strictest sense, no real equivalent can ever be substituted for it'. As Kurt Forster has suggested in his commentary on the text, he argued for the 'historical contingency of all aesthetic values', recognizing that 'contemporary concerns profoundly determine our perception of the past'. The distinction he drew between the apparently irreconcilable 'age-value' and 'historical value' is fundamental to our current concerns: 'The cult of age-value condemns not only every wilful destruction of monuments as a desecration ... but in principle also every effort at conservation .... [it] stands in ultimate opposition to the preservation of monuments.' But, 'the more faithfully a monument's original state is preserved, the greater its historical value: disfiguration and decay detract from it'. While regarding the values themselves as conflicting, Riegl allowed for the practical preservation of monuments but stopped short of total reconstruction:

> the cult of historical value, though granting full documentary significance only to the original state of a monument, is nonetheless willing to concede some values to copies if the originals are irretrievably lost. Such instances stand in irresolvable conflict with age-value only in those cases where copies are made to substitute for an original in all its historical and aesthetic aspects. (Riegl 1982: 15–37)

It is not clear whether he would have drawn a distinction between deliberate and accidental destruction. There is surely an extra moral charge to a destruction which is deliberate, shaping the contemporary concerns through which we perceive the past.

Difficulties

Reconstruction, regularly considered and reviewed in heritage theory and practice, continues to raise profound difficulties, both practically and philosophically: whether authenticity can be reproduced or renewed, whether it resides as much in the activity as in the fabric; whether reconstruction is justifiable only in exceptional circumstances or perhaps for educational or community purposes and then only on the basis of complete and detailed documentation or whether it might be allowed in order to reinstate a lost spirit of place, based perhaps at the most on a few family photographs preserved by those returning from expulsion to a devastated homeland. Justifications for actions will vary according to the infinite variety of circumstances. Numerous examples demonstrate that it is often an image as much as a building which is being pursued in reconstruction – building in a historicist style, for political and social reasons in a manner loosely related to that which has been destroyed, with the intention of creating a consolatory aesthetic and spiritual effect. If it is thought that this represents a distortion of the past and a misrepresentation of its memory, might the difficulty be resolved by clear signposting?: 'Reconstruction should be identifiable on close inspection or through additional interpretation' (Burra 2013: article 20.2). In its (draft) advisory document on 'whether or not to reconstruct heritage assets', Historic England has followed the Burra approach, noting the need for accuracy, rather than speculation, for distinguishing new from old fabric, for signposting and for involving the community (the latter being a concern also at both Nara and Krakow): 'Groups and individuals with associations with the place ... should be provided with opportunities to contribute to and participate in identifying and understanding the cultural significance of the place' (Burra 2013: article 26.3); 'Decisions on reconstruction should be taken primarily by the communities that created the heritage asset (where they still exist) and the communities that now care for the asset' (Historic England 2016). This recalls Sultan Barakat's experience of reconstruction in which 'the creativity, pragmatism and resilience' of local people has been 'of critical importance in the process of rebuilding after conflict' (Barakat 2007: 33). Rebecca Solnit has gone further. Reflecting on the aftermath of both the destruction of the World Trade Center (2001) and the devastation wrought by Hurricane Katrina (2005), she has shown that in the aftermath of disaster there can occur 'a moment of participatory democracy'. In both of these disasters there was 'elite panic' and it was the citizens themselves, rather than the authorities, who were making the major decisions – 'typical of what happens in disaster, when institutions fail and civil society succeeds'. Afterwards, the command-and-control model is reasserted, underpinned by politically slanted disaster myths, writing the citizenry out of the story to the advantage of the institutional and political elites (Solnit 2010: 126–31, 226).

It is notable in the Burra Charter that groups 'should be provided with opportunities', a formulation which presupposes an authority responsible for ensuring that provision. So movement away from the authorized heritage discourse towards a more socially inclusive approach must still be encouraged and enabled by someone in command. In its welcome encouragement of community involvement, Historic England recognizes the possibility of contestation and attempts to resolve it in a manner which potentially raises even greater difficulties and opportunities for impassioned dissent: 'If there is a conflict between the aspirations of communities that care for heritage assets and the principles set out in widely accepted international charters a solution should be sought based on respect for the legitimacy of the cultural values of all parties with a recognised interest' (Historic England 2016). When do cultural values become illegitimate? Who judges legitimacy? Is this the authorized discourse returning so soon after departure?

As Rebecca Solnit has argued elsewhere, every city contains within itself an eradication of what was there before, with resurrection or reinvention following (Solnit 2006: 18–20). This is a process which has the appearance of being subverted by attempts to reconstruct destroyed monuments as they appeared before. To reconstruct in historicist style may be read as an attempt to stop the ineluctable processes of time and decay. But the inevitable may be hastened and deliberate destruction of emblematic buildings or historic quarters in order to dominate, terrorize, divide or eradicate the population is itself a dramatic and destructive intervention in the historical continuum. To reconstruct in response to such destruction is to attempt to turn back the clock, reordering time and process, countering a physical assault upon a natural evolution with a philosophical assault on notions of time and memory, risking the distortion of both. As Denslagen notes, 'every reconstruction is a form of rebellion, a revolt against time' (Denslagen 2009: 220). To reconstruct at all, whether in modern or historicist styles, may amount to the erasing of the past. It may also be argued in the case of countries with multi-ethnicities that reconstruction in response to deliberate destruction is itself an aggressive act, manifest not only in the reconstruction in the same place of something that was there before but also in the construction of new buildings in the style of buildings which have suffered deliberate assault. History is written, and memorials erected by the victors. The embodied messages may over time be subject to shifting attitudes and changes in political circumstances. So 'whose heritage is it?' becomes a pertinent question, bearing in mind Lowenthal's contention: 'only a heritage that is clearly ours is worth having' (Lowenthal 1998: 18). The issue then becomes a matter of determining the extent of 'ours' and considering the notion enshrined in the Faro Convention of a collective responsibility for the maintenance of the heritage of all people as a shared resource: everyone has the right to benefit, and everyone has the responsibility to respect the cultural heritage of others as much as their own heritage. We are all in this together, alternately enhanced or diminished. As Lowenthal has noted, 'modern genocide and iconoclasm magnify needs for legacies to outlast ourselves ... The ruin of Mostar's bridge built to outlast the centuries ... truncates our own lives as well' (Lowenthal 1996: 7). The Croatian writer Slavenka Drakulic 'foolishly thought the bridge would be there forever', so never visited. Comparing a photograph of the destroyed bridge with that of a woman killed in the war, she questions why the former gives her more pain: 'We expect people to die. We count on our own lives to end. The destruction of a monument to civilisation is something else. The bridge, in all its beauty and grace, was built to outlive us; it was an attempt to grasp eternity ... it transcended our individual destiny.' Those who destroyed it were 'people who do not believe in the future' so do not belong to a 'civilization built on the idea of a future. Even if they rebuild the Mostar bridge and reconstruct it meticulously, they are barbarians' (Drakulic 1993). Following its destruction in 1993, the iconic significance of the sixteenth-century single-span bridge at Mostar was demonstrated by the emergence of a worldwide 'lost heritage community', 'larger and more widespread than the heritage community that the bridge had enjoyed when it still stood' (Dolff-Bonekämper 2009: 73–4). Following its reconstruction the bridge, now part of a World Heritage Site, stands as a symbol of reconciliation, international cooperation and the coexistence of communities in a city where international aid has targeted the 'iconic', leaving good but less spectacular buildings as pockmarked shells (Figure 3). Reconciliation and coexistence will not come easily or

FIGURE 3 *Mostar, Bosnia and Herzegovina: the bridge reconstructed. Source: John Bold, 2014.*

quickly: the translation from symbolic meaning to social and political reality remains a long-term dream. As Cherry has noted, questioning established heritage orthodoxies, 'a response to the loss of a cultural monument, however close to the heart of an individual's or community's sense of identity, may not be immediate … other solidarities, such as family, are more binding during periods of acute upheaval and distress. Reclaiming the connection with place as a part of the process of restoring identities appears to be a secondary stage of what is in effect a form of grieving' (Cherry 2016: 157).

Continuing initiatives

The destruction of the bridge at Mostar, together with the strategically nugatory shelling of Dubrovnik in 1991 (a crime for which military commanders have been given jail sentences by the International Criminal Tribunal for the former Yugoslavia: *The Art Newspaper* 1 November 2005), galvanized Western public opinion about the wars in the former Yugoslavia and was reflected in the UNESCO 'Declaration concerning the Intentional Destruction of Cultural Heritage' (2003) (Stanley-Price 2007: 4) in which all states were enjoined to 'take all appropriate measures to prevent, avoid, stop and suppress acts of intentional destruction of cultural heritage, wherever such heritage is located' (UNESCO 2003: article III.1). It was the destruction in Bosnia and Herzegovina which prompted the Bosnian MP Ismeta Dervoz to initiate the report to the Parliamentary Assembly of the Council of Europe which was adopted in 2015: 'Cultural heritage in crisis and post-crisis situations' (Council of Europe 2015). Noting that the deliberate destruction of buildings had become a feature of modern conflicts, the document, acknowledging the Faro Convention, affirmed the notion of the common cultural heritage and its enshrined values as key factors in sustainable reconciliation, fundamental to the well-being of communities, and argued for reconstruction 'within a socially rooted vision'. The Assembly recommended co-operation with the United Nations and other international bodies and the production of 'guidelines for the protection and reconstruction of damaged or destroyed cultural heritage as part of a broader strategy for preserving cultural identity and diversity' (Council of Europe 2015: Doc.13758, article B, 1–3). In the detailed explanatory memorandum, the body of the report, the cultural heritage was considered as a target of conflict, as a victim of the reconstruction process and as a factor for conflict resolution and reconciliation.

This would be a highly opportune moment for the international collaboration recommended by the Parliamentary Assembly since the Council of Europe initiative appears to be continuing in parallel with activities within ICOMOS which in 2013 initiated a 'debate on permissibility and standards for reconstruction of monuments and sites'. Concerned that although 'a formal professional hostility to reconstructions of all types ... has remained', there is a 'significant growth on a global scale of reconstructions of monuments and ensembles', with an 'increasing disregard of existing theoretical principles ... and a new tendency towards significant commercialisation of reconstruction activities'. Noting this development and acknowledging also that reconstructions today can be digital as well as physical, ICOMOS is considering 'whether or not a doctrinal text on reconstruction should eventually be developed': a questionnaire on conferences and other initiatives on reconstruction has been circulated to members (Jokilehto 2013). Discussions continue at the time of writing: international collaboration clearly would be desirable.

The purpose and structure of this book

This book of essays by heritage specialists is intended to serve a dual purpose. It provides a wide range of cases and discussions with a view to extrapolating general guidelines for reinstating the built fabric after war or natural disaster. It will also provide the opportunity to consider through the lens of discussions on authenticity and reconstruction the ways in which the built environment is perceived and appreciated by its users. This is not just about the buildings as bricks and mortar, but about perceptions of meaning and the social and historical values which buildings and spaces embody for diverse populations. These are not just the questions of style which often dominate debates about reconstruction, but also embrace issues of function and social purpose as well as the rather more contested and often elusive notions of community and national identity.

The essays are arranged in four sections, each of which is summarized in a short thematic introduction in which the main issues are highlighted: reconstruction of the old in traditional style and form (Germany, Poland and Kosovo); reconstruction in contemporary modern style (England, France, the Netherlands, the Balkans and Georgia); reconstruction following natural or accidental disaster, or large-scale planned change (Britain, Italy, Sweden and the USA) and political dimensions and image building (England, Macedonia and Spain). The categories are not mutually exclusive – the themes overlap since responses to reconstruction are neither tidy nor finite. In the conclusion we summarize the key findings and look forward to future possibilities and threats before returning to the question of guidelines for reconstruction of the built heritage (the existing post-natural disaster guidelines are about conservation rather than reconstruction, and the terminology for reconstruction is complex, encouraging ambiguity and confusion).

Although reconstruction is just one strategy among many following disaster, third at least in the four overlapping periods in disaster recovery identified by Haas, Kates and Bowden, following the periods of emergency recovery and immediate restoration of services and functions (Haas et al. 1977: xxvii), it is clear that there is a need for the development of broader community understanding of the issues and for institutional approaches which can offer guidance at the political and professional levels so that in a situation which tends to encourage strong feelings and expressions of great certainty, both for and against, a pragmatic, agreed set of principles and procedures may be developed in order to provide a practical starting point for those who are faced with the question of how to build anew. They are, after all, going to have to do it, and they may well want to do so in a manner inimical to current notions of good conservation and heritage management practice and contrary also to customary good architectural practice which favours building in a contemporary, rather than a historicist, style.

Reconstruction is not an isolated self-contained phenomenon of concern only to heritage professionals, devoid of wider ramifications. It is an expression of identity, fundamental to how we view ourselves, our communities and our societies and the values by which we live. As such it cannot be absolute. As we look to the future the idea that heritage is a construct serving present (and future) purposes rather than being a reflection on the past seems ever more pertinent. The Council of Europe's Faro Convention introduced the difficult concept of the 'heritage community' and this, as Jukka Jokilehto has acknowledged, is now reflected in the pronouncements of UNESCO, notably in the closing session of the fortieth anniversary of the World Heritage Convention, held in Kyoto. The conference adopted the 'Kyoto Vision' which highlights 'the importance of the role of community' in the implementation of the Convention (Jokilehto 2013): 'the concerns and aspirations of communities must be centrally involved in conservation and management efforts. Only through strengthened relationships between people and heritage, based on respect for cultural and biological diversity as a whole, integrating both tangible and intangible aspects and geared toward sustainable development, will the "future we want" become attainable' (UNESCO 2012c).

The 'Kyoto Vision' is optimistic, as visions must be. In an age which is characterized by a disturbing return to socio-political and religious certainties; by worldwide terrorism and by the continuing destructive attacks on people and sites in Afghanistan, Iraq and Syria, leading to mass migration across Europe; and by the growing threats of climate change, food shortages and impoverishment, this is more than ever the time for collaboration rather than withdrawal behind the xenophobic borders of nation states. It may be fanciful but it is also refreshing to reflect on the possibility of cultural heritage and the potential reconstruction of historic buildings not as conduits for dogma but as socially contingent subjects for civilized debate, fundamental (in the formulations of both the Council of Europe and the European Commission) to human rights, democracy and the rule of law, and, it may be added, to a future worth having. In achieving this, what we must remember, learning from Livy, is to make sure that the streets are straight.

Short notes on terminology

See also Bold and Pickard (2013) where the definitions are discussed at greater length and are directly linked to the relevant charters and conventions. It should be noted that some terms are not exclusive of others.

> Anastylosis: The reassembly of existing but dismembered parts: the use of new materials should be recognizable.

> Authenticity: The concept of authenticity now goes beyond the original, straightforward qualifying elements of form, fabric and function, to include traditions and techniques, location and setting, spirit and feeling, cultural identity and social value and other internal and external factors, raising the question of how potentially competing 'authentic' values may be understood as credible or truthful, and raising the further question, who decides?

> Conservation: Preserving from destructive influences and decay in order to maintain the significant form and appearance of the building, using wherever possible original materials and techniques for maintenance and repairs but allowing for the introduction of modern materials where needed.

Instauration: Restoration or reconstruction after decay, lapse, dilapidation or loss, or building anew in the same or another place to replicate traditional appearances.

Reconstruction: Reconstruction may refer simply to the act of rebuilding after war or disaster and may apply to services and infrastructure as well as to buildings. It may also refer to rebuilding a lost or destroyed building in the same form and with the same appearance as before – this is also referred to here as 'historicist reconstruction'. It may be distinguished from restoration by the introduction of new material which on close inspection should be distinguishable as new work: signposting and detailed records are recommended. Charters suggest that reconstruction may be appropriate when a site is incomplete following damage or alteration; where it recovers the significance of the place; where it does not constitute the majority of the fabric. It should be based on thorough documentation.

Recreation: The reconstruction of an existing building which has been deliberately removed in order to produce a modernized version with the same appearance, except the patina of age, as the original. This is a practice to be discouraged.

Relocation – dismantling and rebuilding: A practice which may be justified to safeguard a monument, particularly one of paramount importance, if protection cannot be achieved by other means. This practice has been adopted in some instances for educational and museological purposes.

Replication: The duplication of an existing building, creating an exact copy which is potentially intrinsically deceptive in intent but may be allowable for purposes of interpretation and display or education, or as a preventative measure to protect an original.

Repristination: Restoration to an original state or condition, disregarding later accretions.

Restoration: Returning the monument to its original significant form by preserving, revealing and re-establishing its aesthetic and historic value, based on respect for the original fabric and avoiding conjecture. Later accretions that detract from the cultural heritage value may be removed, although in some cases the practice would be to retain them as evidence of the evolution of the building or site.

Values and embodied meanings: These will necessarily vary from culture to culture and from community to community. There are no fixed criteria: heritage assets have to be considered in relation to their cultural context. Consideration of values and meanings will inevitably raise the question of verifiability and the value of the value: Are some values more valuable and persuasive than others? Are some embodied meanings contestable through being meaningful for some people but not for others? Who decides? In our culturally diverse world we may perforce fall back on the Faro Convention:

everyone, alone or collectively, has the right to benefit from the cultural heritage ...; everyone, alone or collectively, has the responsibility to respect the cultural heritage of others as much as their own heritage ...; exercise of the right to cultural heritage may be subject only to those restrictions which are necessary in a democratic society for the protection of the public interest and the rights and freedoms of others. (Faro 2005: article 4)

References

Barakat, S. (2007), 'Postwar Reconstruction and the Recovery of Cultural Heritage: Critical Lessons from the Last Fifteen Years', in N. Stanley-Price (ed), *Cultural Heritage in Postwar Recovery*, Rome: ICCROM, 26–39.

Barakat, S. (2010), 'Seven Pillars for Post-War Reconstruction', in S. Barakat (ed), *After the Conflict – Reconstruction and Development in the Aftermath of War*, London and New York: I. B. Tauris.

Benjamin, W. (2009), 'The Work of Art in the Age of Mechanical Reproduction', in *One-way Street and Other Writings*, London: Penguin, 228–59.

Bevan, R. (2006), *The Destruction of Memory*, London: Reaktion.

Blunt, A. (1968), *Sicilian Baroque*, London: Weidenfeld and Nicolson.

Bold, J. (2016), 'The Concept of Heritage', in J. Bold and M. Cherry (eds), *The Politics of Heritage Regeneration in South-East Europe*, Strasbourg: Council of Europe.

Bold, J. and R. Pickard (2013), 'Reconstructing Europe: The Need for Guidelines', *The Historic Environment*, 4 (2): 105–28.

Boyer, M. C. (1992), 'Cities for Sale: Merchandising History at South Sea Seaport', in Sorkin, M. (ed), *Variations on a Theme Park*, New York: The Noonday Press.

Bullock, N. (2014), 'Architecture, Rationalism and Reconstruction: The Example of France 1945–55', in A. Peckham and T. Schmiedeknecht (eds), *The Rationalist Reader*, London and New York: Routledge.

Burra (2013), *Australia ICOMOS, 'The Burra Charter (The Australia ICOMOS Charter for Places of Cultural Significance)'*, Sydney: Australia ICOMOS.

Cecil, C. (2011), '"We Shall Soon Have the Newest Ancient Heritage in the World": The Rise of the Sham Replica under Moscow Mayor Yuri Luzhkov and Its Implications for Russia's Architectural Heritage', *The Historic Environment*, 2 (1): 68–102.

Charlesworth, E. (2006), *Architects without Frontiers*, Oxford: Elsevier.

Cherry, M. (2016), Review of Walasek, H. et al. (2015), *Bosnia and the Destruction of Cultural Heritage*, Farnham: Ashgate, in *Transactions of the Ancient Monuments Society*, 60: 155–8.

Ciborowski, A. (1970), *Warsaw – A City Destroyed and Rebuilt*, Warsaw: Interpress.

Council of Europe (2013), *Action for a Changing Society*, Strasbourg: Council of Europe.

Council of Europe (2015), Parliamentary Assembly (PACE), 'Cultural Heritage in Crisis and Post-Crisis Situations' (Doc. 13758), Strasbourg: Council of Europe.

Denslagen, W. (2009), *Romantic Modernism*, Amsterdam: Amsterdam University Press.

Department of the Environment and Department of National Heritage (DOE/DNH) (1994), Planning Policy Guidance Note 15: *Planning and the Historic Environment*, London: HMSO.

Dolff-Bonekämper, G. (2009), 'The Social and Spatial Frameworks of Heritage – What is New in the Faro Convention?', in Council of Europe, *Heritage and Beyond*, Strasbourg: Council of Europe.

Drakulic, S. (1993), 'Falling Down – A Mostar Bridge Elegy', *The New Republic*, 13 December.

Dushkina, N. (2009), 'Historical Authenticity', in A. Bronovitskaya, C. Cecil and E. Harris (eds) *Moscow Heritage at Crisis Point*, Moscow: MAPS and SAVE Europe's Heritage.

English Heritage (2008), *Conservation Principles – Policies and Guidance*, London: English Heritage.

Faro (2005), *Framework Convention on the Value of Cultural Heritage for Society* (The Faro Convention), Strasbourg: Council of Europe.

Forty, A. (2012), *Words and Buildings – A Vocabulary of Modern Architecture*, London: Thames and Hudson.

Haas, J., R. Kates and M. Bowden (1977), *Reconstruction Following Disaster*, Cambridge, MA and London: MIT Press.

Hadzimuhamedovic, A. (2008), 'The Meaning of Homeland – Heritage and Uprootedness', *Forum Bosnae*, 44: 328–46.

Hadzimuhamedovic, A. (2015), 'The built heritage in the post-war reconstruction of Stolac', in H. Walasek et al. (eds), *Bosnia and the Destruction of Cultural Heritage*, Farnham: Ashgate.

Historic England (2016), *Historic England Advisory Note on the Reconstruction of Heritage Assets* (Draft), Swindon: Historic England.

ICOMOS (2004), *International Charters for Conservation and Restoration*, Paris: ICOMOS.

ICOMOS Japan (2014), '*Nara + 20: On Heritage Practices, Cultural Values, and the Concept of Authenticity*', Tokyo: ICOMOS Japan.

Inaba, N. (2009), 'Authenticity and Heritage Concepts: Tangible and Intangible – Discussions in Japan', in N. Stanley-Price and J. King (eds), *Conserving the Authentic*, Rome: ICCROM.

Jokilehto, J. (2013), 'Reconstruction in the World Heritage Context', available online: https://engagingconservationyork.files.wordpress.com (accessed 21 November 2016).

Keller, B. and E. Tsoukanas (2006), *The Alonnisos Guide*, Alonnisos.

Krakow (2000), 'The Charter of Krakow 2000 – Principles for Conservation and Restoration of Built Heritage', available online: www/smartheritage.com/wp-content/uploads/2015/03KRAKOV-CHARTER-2000.pdf (accessed 23 November 2016).

Lane Fox, R. (2006), *The Classical World*, London: Penguin.

Law on Protection (2002), 'Law on the protection of properties designated as national monuments of Bosnia and Herzegovina by decision of the Commission to Preserve National Monuments'.

Le Corbusier (1973), *The Athens Charter*, New York: Grossman.

Livy (2002), *The Early History of Rome*, London: Penguin.

Lowenthal, D. (1996), *The Heritage Crusade and the Spoils of History*, London: Viking.

Lowenthal, D. (1998), 'Fabricating Heritage', *History and Memory*, 10 (1): 5–24.

Morel, A.-F. (2013), 'Identity and Conflict: Cultural Heritage, Reconstruction and National Identity in Kosovo', *Architecture_Media_Politics_Society*, 3 (1), 1–20.

Nara (1994), ICOMOS, 'The Nara Document on Authenticity', available online: whc.unesco.org/document/9379 (accessed 23 November 2016).

Pickard, R., ed. (2002), *European Cultural Heritage (Volume 1), Intergovernmental Co-Operation: Collected Texts*, Strasbourg: Council of Europe.

Plum, G. (2011), *L'Architecture de la Reconstruction*, Paris: Nicolas Chaudun.

Riegl, A. (1982), 'The Modern Cult of Monuments: Its Character and its Origin', *Monument/Memory and the Mortality of Architecture, Oppositions*, 25: 20–51.

Riga (2000), ICCROM, 'The Riga Charter on Authenticity and Historical Reconstruction in Relationship to Cultural Heritage'.

Ruskin, J. (1988), *The Seven Lamps of Architecture*, London: Century.

Silberman, N. (2015), 'Light at the End of the Labyrinth? From Historic Preservation to Heritage Placemaking: New Approaches to the Interpretation of Historical Authenticity', available online: http://works.bepress.com (accessed 23 November 2016).

Smith, L. (2006), *Uses of Heritage*, London and New York: Routledge.

Solnit, R. (2006), 'The Ruins of Memory', in M. Klett (ed), *After the Ruins*, Berkeley: University of California Press.

Solnit, R. (2010), *A Paradise Built in Hell – The Extraordinary Communities that Arise in Disaster*, London: Penguin.

Stanley-Price, N. (2007), 'The Thread of Continuity: Cultural Heritage in Postwar Recovery', in N. Stanley-Price (ed), *Cultural Heritage in Postwar Recovery*, Rome: ICCROM.

The Art Newspaper (2005), 'Jail Sentence Upheld for Shelling of Dubrovnik', *The Art Newspaper*, 1 November.

The Art Newspaper (2006), 'UNESCO Reconstruction Plan for Kosovo', *The Art Newspaper*, 1 February.

UNESCO (2003), *UNESCO Declaration concerning the Intentional Destruction of Cultural Heritage*, available online: portal.unesco.org/en/env.php (accessed 23 November 2016).

UNESCO (2012a), *Operational Guidelines for the Implementation of the World Heritage Convention*, available online: whc.unesco.org/en/guidelines/ (accessed 23 November 2016).

UNESCO (2012b), *The Himeji Recommendations*, available online: whc.unesco. org/document/123338 (accessed 23 November 2016).

UNESCO (2012c), *The Kyoto Vision*, available online: whc.unesco.org/ document/123339 (accessed 23 November 2016).

United Nations (2011), *Second Report of the Independent Expert in the Field of Cultural Heritage*, Geneva: Human Rights Council.

Venice (1964), *International Charter for the Conservation and Restoration of Monuments and Sites*, available online: www.icomos.org/charters/venice_e.pdf (accessed 23 November 2016).

Walasek, H. et al. (2015), *Bosnia and the Destruction of Cultural Heritage*, Farnham: Ashgate.

Zetter, R. (2010), 'Land, Housing and the Reconstruction of the Built Environment' in S. Barakat (ed), *After the Conflict – Reconstruction and Development in the Aftermath of War*, London and New York: I. B. Tauris.

PART 1

Reconstruction in Traditional Style after Conflict

Introduction

Reconstruction in traditional style after conflict is considered here in examples from Germany, Poland and Kosovo, all of which in different ways demonstrate the case-specific nature of reconstruction: there is seldom a simple answer to a complex question.

In Germany, as elsewhere after the Second World War, discussions on reconstruction of destroyed towns and cities, described here by Eva von Engelberg-Dočkal and Hans-Rudolf Meier, focused on the question of whether to build in a new form for a new age or to reconstruct that which had been lost in the same style as before. In the German Democratic Republic (former East Germany), a socialist reshaping of the city initially was tempered by the use of the traditional forms and ornaments of particular regions within an overall programme of modernization and renewal. In the Federal Republic (former West Germany), reconstruction sought to strike a balance between building anew or resurrecting the image of the old centres, with modified detailing, respecting the previous scale and layout.

Since many rebuilding projects were long delayed, for financial reasons, the time lag enabled different rebuilding modes to emerge, from modernist to historicizing. The idea of the 'historical' cityscape gained ground in the 1970s as cities competed for tourism and investment and embarked upon the highly selective building of 'creative imitations' in historical styles. There has been a diversity throughout the country of forms, concepts and solutions. German approaches to reconstruction may serve as a template for the whole subject, offering all available options and responses.

In Warsaw, the reconstruction of the centre of the historic city as it had appeared before its destruction during the Second World War was regarded as a national, political and psychological necessity. Elsewhere in Poland, a more nuanced approach brought solutions which were dependent upon circumstances, with approaches varying according to relative importance, the extent of destruction and the economic situation. The reconstruction of Warsaw, however, discussed here by Ingrid Appelbom Karsten, had an extra political and moral charge: it was an assertion of identity and a demonstration that an attempt deliberately to eradicate a culture could not be allowed to succeed. But the programme was far from straightforward – precise documentation was not always available and it was not always clear which historical periods should be reflected in the rebuilt old town where buildings had evolved over time. There was also a need to accommodate new functions and to create more open spaces. The 'Historic Centre of Warsaw' was inscribed as a World Heritage Site by UNESCO in 1980 as an outstanding example of a near-total reconstruction of a span of history, with the caveat that this exceptional reconstruction should not be seen as a precedent for elsewhere.

The reconstruction of the historic bazaars in Gjakova and Peja in Kosovo, which had been deliberately targeted and destroyed in 1998–9, was an acknowledgement of their importance in the life of the cities and the identity of the people. The reconstructions, analysed here by Bujar Demjaha, have been carried out with varying degrees of fidelity and accuracy in terms of scale, materials, form and function, but ultimately they send a clear message that destruction does not equate to eradication: memory is preserved and reflected in the rebuilding. The case of Kosovo underlines the need for the compilation of documentation for management purposes and in advance of potential destruction of the cultural heritage so that if reconstruction becomes necessary, decisions on how to do it may be well informed.

Chapter 1.1

Traditional Rebuilding in Germany after the Second World War

Eva von Engelberg-Dočkal and Hans-Rudolf Meier

translated by Morgan Powell

The German-initiated Second World War left the centres of the majority of German cities largely or all but entirely destroyed. What was to be done with them? Take the destruction as an opportunity or even as manifest destiny and build new cities for new people, or rather reconstruct what had been destroyed? While the population struggled to cope with daily reality in a post-war landscape, planning commissions formed already under the Nazi regime continued working unperturbed on their concepts for rebuilding (Durth and Gutschow 1988; Düwel and Gutschow 2013). An intensive and fundamental debate was nevertheless engaged among intellectuals and planners over rebuilding, a debate very much shaped by the question of guilt and responsibility (Conrads 2003). The question of reconstruction thus developed a very pronounced moral dimension that continues to be felt today (Buttlar 2011). The debate reached its highest pitch around the question whether it was permissible to reconstruct destroyed monuments in their full importance for local identity, that is, to recreate as nearly as possible the original building. In Cologne, in the midst of the 'hunger winter' of 1946–7, well-attended public gatherings devoted themselves to lofty consideration of the fate of the Romanesque churches (Gesellschaft für Christliche Kultur 1948). In Frankfurt, Goethe's birth-house became the focus of intense discussion. While the *Hochstift* and the city council advocated reconstruction, forces generally sceptical of the idea laid out the full range of arguments against it. These same are highly representative of the debate as a whole and thus worthy of more detailed attention. In an essay *Mut zum Abschied* (courage to leave), publicist Walter Dirks insisted on the cause of the destruction:

> The destruction of the house on the *Hirschgraben* was not the result of a forgotten clothes iron or a lightning bolt or even of arson; its destruction was no accident, or to be more precise, not part of a chain of events that bore no relation to the particular significance of the house itself and thus was indifferent or exterior to its existence. Rather, this house was levelled as part of a historical event that is indeed bound up with the significance of its existence. Inner connections exist between the spirit of the house of Goethe and the destruction that became its destiny. Some of these are palpable enough: had the people of the poets and philosophers (and Europe along with it) not strayed from the path of thinkers like Goethe, from the path of reasoned moderation and the humane, it would never have unleashed the war and with it the destruction of his house ... In other words ... this house's destruction is no less an intrinsic part of German and European intellectual history than was its construction as the house of a burgher in the gothic style, no less than was its remodelling in the style of more modern times, or the blessing accorded its inhabitants two-and-a-half centuries past, or the rather thoughtless apotheosis that it underwent in the nineteenth century. We must not seek to erase the last chapter in this long history: the collapse ... its very sticking point. (Dirks 1947: 819–28)

The idea of the house's destruction as an important element of its history along with the suspicion that the erasure of the same served revisionist tendencies – 'as if nothing had happened' (Bartning 1949: 159; Steinbach 1949: 171) – is a powerful argument in a country struggling to deal with the burden of guilt for the war, where, indeed, the same burden remains today a pole of social consensus. Opponents of reconstruction further voiced the concern that a newly constructed replica of the historic building would diminish the authenticity of the objects (furniture, devices, pictures), still preserved; such heritage of the Goethe House as had been rescued would thus lose value (Bartning 1949: 161). 'The truer the copy is to the original, the less genuine the whole must inevitably seem', with the result that a reconstruction of the Goethe House faithful to the last detail would become 'an attraction for travelling collectors of curiosities' (Muschg 2003: 164). Architects in particular raised the objection that the desire for reconstruction betrayed a lack of creative imagination. Thus, as stated in one of a number of 'Fundamental Demands' laid out in an appeal signed by numerous architects, historical heritage should not be reconstructed, but instead 'only arise in new forms for new purposes' (Bartning et al. 1947: 29; Huse 1984: 198).

In the face of the plentifully flowing donations to restore the house of Goethe's birth 'as a symbol of harmony among peoples, as a symbol of peace' (Huse 1984: 202ff), along with supportive statements from writers around the world, however, these arguments proved powerless to prevent its reconstruction to the nearest possible detail. Even the idea of competition between opposing systems arising with the Cold War played a role, as Goethe's house in Weimar had already been fully restored for the 200th anniversary of his birth (1949). No debate such as the one in Frankfurt preceded in this case, since in the Soviet Occupation Zone and later GDR the new regime, as leftist antifascists, acknowledged no responsibility for the doings of the Nazis and the question of guilt thus carried no comparable weight. The reconstruction of destroyed churches and castles was likewise not among the priorities of the new state; on the contrary, numerous such monuments of superseded societies were levelled or remained in ruins. Accordingly, far fewer reconstruction projects were undertaken in the GDR (East Germany) than in the FRG (West Germany). Upon reunification in 1990, this in its turn led the East, now eager to catch up, to unleash a new wave of reconstruction activity emanating from Dresden (Meier 2009: 59–76).

Reconstruction in the GDR

The idea of new cities for new men and women was central to the construction of a new socialist society in the GDR. In addition, the transfer of land and property to state ownership enabled new planning to proceed along much more consistent lines than in the West, where the division into privately owned parcels made the realization of broadly conceived new projects very difficult and subject to lengthy delays. Thus in many places buildings that had suffered little or no damage in the war were nevertheless demolished to make way for a socialist reshaping of the city. In its initial phase of so-called 'National Tradition' (1950–55), the socialist project made use of forms and ornaments that were generated by the historical architecture of the region (e.g. baroque ornament in Dresden, stepped gables in the Hanseatic city of Rostock), as long as industrial construction methods had not taken over (Kirchner 2010). It was not until the 1970s, with the advent of so-called 'complex reconstructions' using 'adapted prefabricated construction' (angepasste Plattenbauweise), that the historical contours of the old towns were once again respected (Angermann and Hirse 2013). In the previous period of 'reconstruction' in the GDR, the term had meant above all demolition and new building; the concept of reconstruction was on the whole far more associated with modernization and renewal than with the restoration of what had been lost.

Reconstruction and urban planning in the Federal Republic

The reconstruction of entire cities or of parts of cities was exceptional in West Germany as well. There were, however, occasional cases of rebuilding plans that took their inspiration from the historical ground plan, the local building tradition or the appearance of the preceding structures. One significant example is the *Prinzipalmarkt* in Münster/Westphalen (Figure 1). The question of how to rebuild the traditional shopping street, up to 95 per cent of which was destroyed between 1940 and 1945, was under discussion even before the war ended. While city planner Heinrich Bartmann took the position that the original buildings could not rise from the ashes, 'unless it be as mummies', architect Hans Ostermann insisted that the gables of the *Prinzipalmarkt* must be restored as far as possible to their former silhouettes (Gutschow 1980: 41). What was done in the end followed the precept of the city's building conservator Edmund Scharf, who acknowledged the

FIGURE 1 *Münster (FRG)*, Prinzipalmarkt, *constructed 1947–58, photographed in 2015. Source: authors.*

architectural value of the *Prinzipalmarkt* 'without following the idea of an imitation or reconstruction. It is neither possible nor desirable to try and restore the countenance of the *Prinzipalmarkt* of yesteryear. To do so would be a self-betrayal ... The new buildings will bear the simpler exterior of our time, ... in continuing memory of that which once was' (Gutschow 1980: 43). The building alignment was preserved as well as the parcelling of the gabled façades, while behind several parcels there might in fact be a single building. The gables themselves were composed to harmonize with each other; the objective was the typical rather than the individual. Whatever seemed not to fit in – and this applied above all to the revival styles of the nineteenth century – found no representation. The same aesthetic principles were thereby applied as in the urban renewal programmes of the 1930s in Danzig, for example (Pusback 2006). Looking back from our vantage point, the results in Münster command respect: in the specialist literature, the *Prinzipalmarkt* soon figured as one of the most frequently cited examples of positively evaluated reconstruction efforts in the FRG. In its shaping of urban space above all, the *Prinzipalmarkt* reconstruction is highly successful and the gabled façades of the 1950s discreetly but effectively keep alive the 'memory of that which once was'.

For northern Germany, Münster constitutes an exception in this regard, whereas in the south other cities bear witness to distinct attempts at the reconstruction of urban spaces. Among these is Nuremberg, the city that, since the Romantic period, had stood more than any other for 'old Germany', and had served under Nazi rule as the site of the *Reichsparteitage*, the party congresses of the Third Reich. As early as spring 1947, the city held one of the first competitions in the country for plans to rebuild the old town, 90 per cent of which lay in ruins. Especially influential among the successful submissions was the design by architects Heinz Schmeißner and Wilhelm Schlegtendal, as the former was in charge of the city planning office for more than twenty years beginning in 1948 (Schieber et al. 2002).

Reconstruction or repair was undertaken for the most important partially surviving monuments, in particular the great medieval churches of St Lorenz, St Sebald and Our Lady (*Frauenkirche*). The city's ground plan was largely preserved along with the basic volumes of its structures, although in some cases significant concessions were made to accommodate motor traffic. Since the mid-1970s, an Association of the Friends of the Old Town (*Altstadtfreunde*) has served as a channel for popular advocacy and in recent years has increasingly fought for the replacement of buildings dating from the 1950s with reconstructions of what preceded. This prospect now sees some of the most notable architecture of the post-war rebuilding effort under threat, among them the Pellerhaus, for example.

Whereas the old town of Nuremberg is clearly marked by the architecture of the 1950s, in Munich today it is difficult to tell at first glance what survived the war and what has been reconstructed. Karl Meitinger, a member of the city planning council since 1938, began as early as 1945 to elaborate his 'Proposals for Rebuilding' (Meitinger 1946). This so-called 'Meitinger Plan' aimed at the 'resurrection of the old Munich'. As in Nuremberg, only the most important monuments and those with structurally significant remains were to be reconstructed. Everything else was to be newly constructed but, in keeping with the ambition to recreate the image of the old town, within a historical mould. Here, too, concessions to the needs of automobile traffic were made as a matter of course, for which purpose methods were at times applied that recalled those of Theodor Fischer or even Giovanni Giovannoni in the urban renewal programmes of the 1920s in Italy (Enss 2016a, b).

Typical of the effort is the approach that the rebuilders in Munich applied to their cathedral Our Lady, the celebrated *Frauenkirche*. The vaulting and the neo-gothic decoration had been destroyed in the bombing, so the reconstruction made no attempt to restore the latter, opting instead to maintain a plain interior. It was only with the 1970s that the decor became progressively more elaborate. In other cases, the approach was still more rigorous and attempted to repair or reconstruct only the exterior of the churches, while leaving the interior open to the realization of much more modern expression, much as Aachen's cathedral master builder Leo Hugo had done in St Foillan of Aachen in 1958 (Schild 2014: 46–65).

Reconstruction and transformation were similarly combined in the rebuilding of the city of Freudenstadt in the Black Forest. The planned late-Renaissance fortress city had been largely destroyed shortly before the end of the Second World War. In the debate over its rebuilding, representatives of the conservative *Stuttgarter Schule* carried the day over the 'Modernists', so that the basic ground plan with its very large central market square and the rows of buildings arranged around it was retained (Burkhardt et al. 1988). In keeping with their architectural heritage, the buildings bore the stamp of tradition, but as a concession to the needs in the innermost city centre at the time were erected in side-gabled rather than front-gabled orientation. New Brandenburg in the GDR, another city that had been erected according to a rigorous geometric plan and was for the most part destroyed shortly before the end of the war, exhibits a comparable tendency. There rebuilding was undertaken according to the old ground plan, but the structures were erected in block-edge development of a larger scale than previously and in a style typical of the 'National Tradition' phase of the 1950s.

Delayed rebuilding in both German states

Numerous rebuilding projects were postponed, even for decades, in many cases because of lacking finances. This is most often true of cities in the GDR, prime examples being the metropolis of Dresden, where large areas of the city centre had been cleared (Meier 2009: 59–76), but also the capital of German classicism, Weimar, where the northern market perimeter lay in ruins (Ebert and Nuethen 2013: 241–9). The inner cities of the Federal Republic also exhibited their share of neglected rebuilding projects decades after the war. The developments in architecture and urban planning of the 1970s triggered a paradigm change away from the rebuilding efforts of post-war modernism. In the wake of a renewed appreciation of history and the 'European city', historic structures once again became the touchstone, along with characteristics such as density, smaller scale, higher detail and formal diversity. At the same time, greater emphasis on harmonious integration into the existing context led to a historicizing shift in architectural style. Heritage preservation also experienced an unprecedented upswing, institutionalized in the European Architectural Heritage Year of 1975 under the motto 'A future for our past' (Meier 2005: 4–9; Falser and Lipp 2015). These developments had their effect not only on the preservation of structures of historical significance and their surroundings, but also on building ensembles and entire city centres, which now became the focus and determined the scope of rebuilding efforts.

Among the urban quarters in West Germany that were not rebuilt after their wartime destruction was the area between the cathedral (*Dom*) and the *Römerberg* in Frankfurt am Main. With the (reconstructed) landmarks of the *Dom*, the *Römer* (the old city hall), the Church of St Nicholas and the *Steinernes Haus*, along with its position on the coronation path of the kings and emperors of the Holy Roman Empire, the *Dom-Römer* quarter was of intrinsic historical significance for the now-prosperous banking and finance centre. The old town, largely destroyed and placed under a building prohibition after the war ended, was to form the point of departure for a restructuring of the city (Marek 2009: 53–98; Wagner-Kyora 2014: 105–41). This was undertaken in the forms typical of post-war modernism with minimal conformity to the historical structure and only a few selected monuments reconstructed in their exterior appearance. Within the old town itself, the Technical City Hall, completed after two competitions (1950, 1962–3), was initially the only prominent building to be erected.

In 1978, the decision was reached to reconstruct the *Schwarzer Stern* house as well as the six half-timbered façades that once formed the eastern front of the *Römerberg* square. This was part of a larger building project extending as far as the *Dom* over an area that had already lost its historical foundations and other archaeological remains through the construction of a parking garage and a subway station. The competition conducted in 1979 accorded first prize to a design submitted by a Berlin studio (Dietrich Bangert, Bernd Jansen, Stefan Scholz and Axel Schultes), which combined the buildings foreseen for reconstruction, including two annex buildings on the *Römerberg*'s eastern front to be constructed on the historical ground plan, with the art museum 'Kulturschirn' as an urban counterweight to the Technical City Hall, the Archaeological Garden, completed in 1972–3, and a row of residential buildings on the Saalgasse, extending farther south. The entire project, completed with the opening of the 'Kulturschirn' in 1986, constitutes an exception in the rebuilding efforts of the Federal Republic: the dominant structures stand in their use of contemporary architectural forms (with the exception of the historical reconstructions) and in their contextualization and integration of heterogeneous elements as one of the most successful examples of rebuilding in the post-modern mode.

The Nikolai-Quarter of East Berlin (Figure 2), planned at the same time and built from 1983 to 1987, constitutes a project in the GDR comparable to that of the *Dom-Römer* area in Frankfurt. It is likewise exceptional for East German rebuilding projects and is one of the most significant undertaken there (Urban 2007: 99–130, 2014: 444–63; Bernau 2009). The destruction of the war had left the medieval city centre of Berlin all but completely cleared of its former structures. Ideas for a reconstruction in the character of the old Berlin first arose in the 1970s (Urban 2007: 109). In anticipation of the 750th anniversary of the city's founding (1987), a competition was launched in 1978 for concepts to rebuild the vacant area, with the successful project submitted by a collective under Günter Stahn. The concept combined an inner city residential quarter with abundant shopping and leisure facilities, explicitly intended to attract (foreign) tourists. Modified for actual execution, the design was orientated on the pre-war layout, a preservation of the extant

FIGURE 2 *East Berlin, Nikolai-Quarter, constructed 1983–7, photographed in 2016. Source: authors.*

building structures and the reconstruction of residential houses around the Nikolai Church, in addition to new construction in a historicizing style with massive brick walls and *Plattenbauten* (buildings made with precast concrete slabs). In addition, a replica of the reconstructed medieval court house (*Gerichtslaube*) that had stood in the castle park of Babelsberg since 1871 was rebuilt incorporating elements of the original building.

While the overall design did not take a specific historical period as its model, the dominating impression is one of the eighteenth century. Some of the reconstructed buildings were relocated to the Nikolai-Quarter from elsewhere, following a practice that had been applied in the 1930s and was also briefly considered for the *Dom-Römer* area in Frankfurt (Bauwelt 1978: 178; Marek 2009: 71–3). The Nikolai-Quarter exhibits similarly successful contextualization through the orientation on historical scale and style in the design of new buildings, for example, in the case of the multi-storeyed residential and commercial blocks at the Marx-Engels Forum, or the two- or three-storey houses around the church. Elements such as the signage, railings, advertising pillars and cobblestones further contributed to the historicizing appearance of the whole. With its use of contextualization and the harmonious integration of the reconstructions and historicizing new construction, the Nikolai-Quarter stands apart from earlier rebuilding projects. In the words of the architect Stahn: 'The rebuilding and shaping of the urban surroundings of the Nikolai Church delivers to a great extent the character impression of the original ensemble in that the burghers' homes figure within the whole not so much as objects of individual prominence, but rather through their unity of scale and partitioning as one dominant element of the urban landscape' (Stahn 1991: 51ff). The Nikolai-Quarter has repeatedly been associated with the international movement of post-modernism, despite the resistance from GDR architects themselves, for whom such an appropriation was incompatible with socialist ideals.[1] Quite aside from the post-modern forms of the *Plattenbauten*, however, the integration of heterogeneous built elements into an integral overall design, along with the combination of surviving structures with various rebuilding modes (reconstruction, replica, historicizing new construction), exhibits a conception of rebuilding that was typical of its time.

The use of different rebuilding modes in the context of a largely original ground plan finds parallels in contemporary rebuilding projects in Poland. The quality of execution in its reconstruction of extensive areas of the city centres put the 'socialist brother-state' in a class of its own (the 'Polish Heritage School'), recognized when the Warsaw *Stare Miasto* (Old Town) was placed on the UNESCO World Heritage list in 1980. In the early 1980s,

---

[1] See Urban 2014; for post-modernism in the GDR see the dissertation project of Kirsten Angermann, 'Die ernste Postmoderne Architektur und Städtebau im letzten Jahrzehnt der DDR' (working title), Bauhaus-Universität Weimar, ongoing since 2012.

an alternative concept took shape, the practice of so-called retroversion (*retrowersja*), in the Polish city of Elbląg.[2] Decisive in this concept were the preservation of the historic street plan and division of lots along with the volumes and the arrangement of the earlier buildings, and even the integration of extant cellar structures and building fragments *in situ*. At the same time, new construction was undertaken as free variation in a clearly contemporary style, with reconstruction permitted only for single buildings of outstanding significance. Cobblestones and historicizing street lamps lent the whole an aesthetically unifying frame. The city development plan for Elbląg, elaborated from 1980 to 1983, became the basis for further rebuilding projects in Poland, including the city of Szczecin only about 150 km from Berlin, for which a competition was held in 1983, its realization coming after the fall of the Iron Curtain. The rebuilding concept for the Nikolai-Quarter was comparable in its central aspects with the Polish idea of retroversion; it was, however, less closely tied to the extant structures and previous foundation plans and conceived primarily as contemporary architecture in its own right: 'This ensemble is the product of a creative reshaping undertaken in one unified building campaign' (Stahn 1991: 58).

Simultaneously with the construction of the Nikolai-Quarter, West Berlin developed the concept of 'critical reconstruction', which sought to revivify urban structures destroyed during the war. The movement, strongly influenced by Josef Paul Kleihues, arose in anticipation of the 1987 International Building Exhibition in Berlin. Its primary objective was the new construction of residential areas in the inner city, which, guided by a modern reinterpretation of the historical ground plan (block-edge development), was to take shape in contemporary style. 'Critical reconstruction' became the standard for inner city development in the reunited Berlin beginning in 1990, which included the largely vacant areas around the former border between the occupation zones.

Characteristic of the situation in the FRG beginning in the 1970s was an increasing demand for a popular voice in questions not only of city planning but also in approval of individual building projects (Marek 2009; Maaß 2015). This was reflected both in legislation (citizens' participation in construction planning boards) and in the increased use of plebiscites. Indeed, in the case of Frankfurt's *Dom-Römer* area, the guiding idea of restoring a unified appearance to the entire square reflected the previously established wish of the population. The pressure for cities to compete for tourists and investment was generally on the rise in this period and played an increasing role in local construction planning. The objective of this new self-marketing was an unmistakably 'historical' cityscape, if necessary to be constructed anew (Marek 2009: 70–72, 82ff; Maaß 2015: 436–8) (Figure 3).

---

[2]See the publications of Maria Lubocka-Hoffmann, the former conservationist of the voivodeship: for example, Lubocka-Hoffmann 1994: 87–96.

FIGURE 3 *Berlin (FRG), rebuilding the castle, photographed in 2015. Source: authors.*

The reconstruction of the eastern front of the *Römerberg* followed from just such a desire, promulgated early on by the business community and the tourist trade as essential to local identity and thus no less essential an investment. The architecture of post-war modernism consequently came to be seen as faceless and anonymous and appeared increasingly as if in opposition to the idea of an 'historical city' and even at times as a 'second destruction' following the blanket bombardments of the Second World War (Meier 2011: 22–9).

Popular initiative and the desire for an unmistakably identifiable cityscape likewise attended the reconstruction of the market square in Hildesheim (Fischer 2010: 320ff), though in this case, unlike Frankfurt's *Dom-Römer* area or the Nikolai-Quarter in Berlin, the area had already been the object of rebuilding during the 1950s and 1960s. This moderate reconstruction of a city once celebrated for its half-timbered houses followed the historical street plan to a great extent, though in a style characteristic of post-war modernism. The new buildings were consistent with the volumes of the pre-war construction and their peaked roofs and grid-like façades alluded to the local architectural heritage (Thumm 1993: 34–6; Maybaum 2011: 76). The market square, however, formerly the showcase for the half-timbered houses representing the various craft guilds, was, in keeping with the results of a plebiscite, increased to more than double its former size. Of the historic buildings there survived alone the reconstructed city hall and the Temple House, standing in contrast to a broad row of municipal administrative buildings to the north. On the site of the famous *Knochenhaueramtshaus* (house of the butchers' guild), Dieter Oesterlen erected a hotel tower (1962–64) as the new landmark of the square. The debate over the reconstruction of the market square had begun with the war's end, leading as early as 1950 to the formation of an 'Association to Promote the Reconstruction of the *Knochenhaueramtshaus*' and, after completion of the modern construction, to the 'Society for the Reconstruction of the *Knochenhaueramtshaus*' in 1970, along with other citizens' initiatives (Rump 1995; Maybaum 2011: 78). Their various demands for a restoration of the market to its earlier dimensions and appearance finally found a place in a new concept for the inner city approved in 1977 (Maybaum 2011: 76–81). Here, too, hopes of raising the city's profile to contribute to its attractiveness in the tourism and investment market figured prominently among reasons for the turnabout. An urban planning competition was launched in 1980, and in 1983 the city council approved a measure returning the market to its former configuration. The first step undertaken was the restoration, in a form modified from the historical original, of the façade of the Wedekind House (1984–86) on the south side of the square. The adjacent Lüntzel House shows a solution that departs emphatically from the appearance of its historical predecessor, combining historicizing style elements with allusions to the typically contemporary architecture of the 1980s. The northern and southern edges of the market square were bestowed with façades more or less freely inspired by their pre-war models; only on the western edge, with the houses of the butchers' and the bakers' guilds (*Knochenhaueramtshaus, Bäckeramtshaus*, 1987–9), were reconstructions completed in fidelity to the originals (Thumm 1993: 34–50). This 'second rebuilding' of the market square, completed in 1994, thus formed a sort of conglomerate of newly erected historic buildings, reconstructions and new structures with historical façades. Similar to the buildings on the eastern front of the *Römerberg*, which lost their original shingling, here the former stucco façades with their stone imitation made way for visible half-timbering. Financing was accomplished to a great extent through donations, brought in by means of costly, nationwide advertising campaigns. Most of the subsequent reconstructive or historicizing rebuilding projects in the FRG made use of the same strategy.

Rebuilding projects after the fall of the Berlin Wall

Projects for the rebuilding of inner city areas destroyed in the war are still undertaken today and figure among the most celebrated construction projects in Germany. After 1990, reconstruction projects became especially numerous in cities of the former GDR. Dresden claimed an exceptional position in this activity, as very little of its city centre had seen rebuilding, and its major landmark, the *Frauenkirche*, having been designated a war monument in 1966, remained a ruin. Prohibited in the preceding decades by the political and economic situation, the reconstruction of Dresden's signature building became, upon the fall of the Berlin Wall, an immediate priority: a citizens' initiative in support of the reconstruction was formed as early as November 1989. The reconstruction of the church's dome, undertaken from 1994 to 2005 and the object of considerable controversy within the field, was celebrated on its completion as a symbol of reconciliation and thus also of German reunification (Marek 2009: 48; Altrock et al. 2010: 121). Moreover, the accomplishment of the task after its protracted delay over so many decades had the effect of catalysing further German reconstruction projects (the 'Dresden effect') (Marek 2009: 165ff; Meier 2009: 59–76; Altrock et al. 2010: 121).

In Dresden itself the desire arose to restore the newly resurrected *Frauenkirche* in appropriately harmonious surroundings. Plans for rebuilding the *Neumarkt* (Marek 2009: 20–4; Altrock et al. 2010: 113–46; Kulke 2015), one of the earliest settled areas of the city, had been drawn up in the 1950s and again after the area had been cleared of rubble in the 1970s. An international architectural seminar convened in 1981 demanded the reconstruction of the *Neumarkt* by means of *Leitbauten*, landmark buildings to be reconstructed as models for the rest (the *Leitbautenkonzept* of the 1970s), among them the Hotel de Saxe, which had been demolished in the nineteenth century. The plan went into execution towards the end of the 1980s. Upon the political turn and following archaeological exploration of the foundations, the scope was extended to include a larger number of reconstructions (resolution passed in 1996); the selective list nevertheless includes very few buildings from the nineteenth century. Further new construction in the area now must demonstrate harmonious integration into its site in the proportions and the design of façades. The historical city ground plan serves as the basis of this entire urban reshaping, approved in 2002 (with modification in 2006). The whole shows a number of parallels with the Polish school of reconstruction, not least among them the size of the area concerned, which is without equal in western or eastern Germany. The concept of 'retroversion' is also in evidence, although in Dresden the requisite reuse of the historic cellars was possible only in exceptional cases due to the construction of a multi-storeyed underground parking garage.

Thus the attempt to in part restore the city's architectural heritage also led to the elimination of its last remaining baroque structures.

In no small part due to the influence of Dresden's *Neumarkt*, Frankfurt's 'New Old Town' began to take shape in 2012 (Marek 2009: 53–98; Rodenstein 2009: 45–58; Dom-Römer GmbH 2014). In the wake of a debate over what to do with the much-criticized Technical City Hall (concept competition 2005), the decision was reached to demolish it and rebuild on the site of the historic old city in extension of the post-modern *Dom-Römer* ensemble. The stated objective is the restoration of the historical city ground plan with its spatial features, including reconstruction of certain buildings of the old town, for which, where available, extant fragments (*spolia*) are to be reused.[3] The role of head contractor is here filled by the Dom-Römer GmbH, as a city-owned company. As in Dresden, a variety of popular initiatives brought their influence to bear in the concept development phase with a resulting increase in the number of buildings cited for reconstruction. The fifteen selected buildings are, however, in view of the impossibility of a reconstruction true to the original, referred to by the Dom-Römer GmbH as 'creative imitations'. Designs for twenty additional buildings exhibiting elements of local architectural tradition resulted from a competition. These rely for the design of their façades on a detailed set of design regulations that derive, as in the case of the *Neumarkt* in Dresden, from a set of reconstructed *Leitbauten*. In principle any given historical style may serve as a point of reference. Unlike the post-modern rebuilding of the 1980s, these designs aim for a kind of patchwork combination of smaller elements that is nonetheless to give the feeling of a unified urban space reflecting the contemporary trend towards neo-historical architecture (Engelberg-Dočkal 2007, 2011: 30–7).[4]

Conclusion

To speak of the rebuilding effort after the destruction of the Second World War is to evoke a great diversity of forms, concepts and case-specific solutions that served to tackle the immense challenge of restoring the cities. The broad range of rebuilding methods here understood as traditionalist includes the most disparate mimetic practices: the most exact reconstructions as well as freely creative allusion to the architecture of yesteryear, or the reconstruction of single, often stand-alone landmarks as well as *Traditionsinseln* or even

---

[3]See the research of Hans-Rudolf Meier into the contemporary use of *spolias* in the subproject 'Mimetic Practices in Recent Architecture' of the DFG Research Group 'Media and Mimesis' at the Bauhaus-Universität Weimar, www.fg-mimesis.de.
[4]See the research of Eva von Engelberg-Dočkal into contemporary historicizing architecture in the subproject 'Mimetic Practices in Recent Architecture' (see note 3).

entire inner cities (*Freudenstadt*). Each rebuilding project stands as the product of diverse influencing factors peculiar to the individual case, while as a rule differing concepts of urban planning or modes of rebuilding were combined and implemented. Common tendencies do nonetheless emerge: differences between northern and southern Germany, and the change of guiding principles from post-war modernism to the idea of the 'historical city' with its creative integration of new construction. Thus neither the rebuilding concepts nor the formal solutions can be seen as separate from the architectural movements of their time. This is no less true of reconstructed buildings, which can never be reproduced in full fidelity to detail of their predecessors, but rather must be read as products of their own time. Since the 1970s a general shift can be seen in the distribution of power away from government planning commissions and in favour of economic or popular initiatives. What thereby is claimed as the 'will of the people', and more often than not conceals interest groups in favour with the local media, serves increasingly, frequently in opposition to expert opinion, as the basis for municipal decisions. This development, driven by the tourist trade and image-marketing, has resulted in an increasing tendency to historicizing rebuilding concepts based on highly selective cityscapes such as the late medieval half-timbered houses on Frankfurt's *Römerberg* or the *Neumarkt* in Dresden in its aspect around 1800. Reconstructions and historicizing new buildings alike thereby often create (through an appearance that itself lacks organically historical legitimacy) artificially harmonious inner city neighbourhoods.

References

Altrock, U., G. Bertram and H. Horni (2010), *Positionen zum Wiederaufbau verlorener Bauten und Räume*, Bonn: Bundesministerium für Verkehr, Bau und Stadtentwicklung.

Angermann, K. and T. Hirse (2013), *Altstadtplatten. Komplexe Rekonstruktion in den Innenstädten von Erfurt und Halle* (Forschungen zum baukulturellen Erbe der DDR, Vol. 2), Weimar: Verlag der Bauhaus-Universität.

Bartning, O. et al. (1947), 'Ein Aufruf: Grundsätzliche Forderungen', Bau- und Werkform 1, in N. Huse (ed), *Denkmalpflege. Deutsche Texte aus drei Jahrhunderten*, Munich: Beck.

Bartning, O. (1949), 'Entscheidung zwischen Wahrheit und Lüge', Bau- und Werkform 2, reprinted in U. Conrads (ed), *Die Städte himmeloffen. Reden und Reflexionen über den Wiederaufbau des Untergegangenen und die Wiederkehr des Neuen Bauens 1948/49* (Bauwelt Fundamente 125), Gütersloh: Bertelsmann-Fachzeitschriften.

Bauwelt (1978), Editorial discussion, 'Zur Diskussion: Was kommt zwischen Dom und Römer,' *Bauwelt*, 6, S. 187, Figure 3.

Bernau, N. (2009), *Architekturführer Nikolaiviertel*, Berlin: Stadtwandel-Verlag.

Burkhardt, H.-G., et al. (ed) (1988), *Stadtgestalt und Heimatgefühl. Der Wiederaufbau von Freudenstadt 1945–1954*, Analysen, Vergleich und Dokumente, Hamburg: Christians.

Buttlar, A.v., et al. (eds) (2011), *Denkmalpflege statt Attrappenkult. Gegen die Rekonstruktion von Baudenkmälern – eine Anthologie* (Bauwelt Fundamente 146), Gütersloh: Bauverlag.

Conrads, U. (ed) (2003), *Die Städte himmeloffen. Reden und Reflexionen über den Wiederaufbau des Untergegangenen und die Wiederkehr des Neuen Bauens 1948/49* (Bauwelt Fundamente 125), Gütersloh: Bertelsmann-Fachzeitschriften.

Dirks, W. (1947), 'Mut zum Abschied. Zur Wiederherstellung des Frankfurter Goethehauses', in Frankfurter Hefte 1, in U. Conrads (ed), *Die Städte himmeloffen. Reden und Reflexionen über den Wiederaufbau des Untergegangenen und die Wiederkehr des Neuen Bauens 1948/49* (Bauwelt Fundamente 125), Gütersloh: Bertelsmann-Fachzeitschriften.

Dom-Römer GmbH (ed) (2014), Die Stadt lebt. Willkommen in der neuen Mitte Frankfurts, text: FuP Marketing und Kommunikation, Frankfurt 2014, available online: http://www.domroemer.de/ (accessed 28 November 2016).

Durth, W. and N. Gutschow (1988), *Träume in Trümmern. Planungen zum Wiederaufbau zerstörter Städte im Westen Deutschlands 1940–1950*, Braunschweig/Wiesbaden: Viehweg.

Düwel, J. and N. Gutschow (eds) (2013), *A Blessing in Disguise: War and Town Planning in Europe 1940–45*, Berlin: DOM.

Ebert, M. and L. Nuethen (2013), 'Markt-Nordseite', in E.v. Engelberg-Dočkal and K. Vogel (eds), *Sonderfall Weimar? DDR-Architektur in der Klassikerstadt* (Forschungen zum baukulturellen Erbe der DDR, Vol. 1), Weimar: Verlag der Bauhaus-Universität.

Engelberg-Dočkal, E.v. (2007), Rekonstruktion als zeitgenössische Architektur? Das historisierende Bauen im Kontext der Denkmalpflege.

Engelberg-Dočkal, E.v. (2011), '"Historisierende Architektur" als zeitgenössischer Stil', in B. Franz and H.-R. Meier (eds), *Stadtplanung nach 1945. Zerstörung und Wiederaufbau. Denkmalpflegerische Probleme aus heutiger Sicht* (Veröffentlichung des Arbeitskreises Theorie und Lehre der Denkmalpflege Vol. 20), Holzminden: Mitzkat.

Enss, C.M. (2016a), *Münchens geplante Altstadt. Städtebau und Denkmalpflege ab 1944 für den Wiederaufbau*, Munich: Franz Schiermeier Verlag München.

Enss, C.M. (2016b), Reinventing the "Old Town" of Munich – Monuments as crystallization points for post-war reconstruction, available online: https://www.docenti.unina.it/downloadPub.do?tipoFile=md&id=550402 (accessed 15 August 2017).

Falser, M. and W. Lipp (eds) (2015), *A Future for Our Past. The 40th Anniversary of European Architectural Heritage Year (1975–2015)* (Monumenta III), Berlin: ICOMOS Austria.

Fischer, M. F. (2010), 'Knochenhaueramtshaus und Marktplatz, Hildesheim', in W. Nerdinger (ed), *Geschichte der Rekonstruktion – Konstruktion der Geschichte*, Munich: Prestel.

Gesellschaft für Christliche Kultur (ed) (1948), *Kirchen in Trümmern. Zwölf Vorträge zum Thema Was wird aus den Kölner Kirchen?*, Cologne: Pick.

Gutschow, N. (1980), 'Der Wiederaufbau des Prinzipalmarktes in Münster 1945–1961: Wiedergewinnung (Rekonstruktion) des städtischen Raumes –

Neugestaltung der Giebelarchitektur', *Deutsche Kunst und Denkmalpflege* 38: 41–9.

Huse, N. (ed) (1984), *Denkmalpflege*. Deutsche Texte aus drei Jahrhunderten, Munich: Beck.

Kirchner, J. (2010), *Architektur nationaler Tradition in der frühen DDR (1950–1955) Zwischen ideologischen Vorgaben und künstlerischer Eigenständigkeit*. PhD Dissertation, Universität Hamburg, available online: http://ediss.sub.uni-hamburg.de/volltexte/2010/4774/pdf/eDissertation.pdf (accessed 28 November 2016).

Kulke, T. (ed) (2015), *Wie bauen wir Stadt? Die Rekonstruktion des Dresdner Neumarktes und der Streit um Tradition und Moderne im Städtebau*, Petersberg: Imhof.

Lubocka-Hoffmann, M. (1994), 'Die Alstadt Elbings – eine denkmalpflegerische Herausforderung', *Mare Balticum. Kultur, Geschichte, Gegenwart*, pp. 87–96.

Maaß, P. (2015), *Die moderne Rekonstruktion. Eine Emanzipation der Bürgerschaft in Architektur und Städtebau*, PhD Dissertation, Universität Dresden, Regensburg: Schnell and Steiner.

Marek, K. (2009), *Rekonstruktion und Kulturgesellschaft. Stadtbildreparatur in Dresden, Frankfurt am Main und Berlin als Ausdruck der zeitgenössischen Suche nach Identität*, PhD Dissertation, Universität Kassel, available online: https://kobra.bibliothek.uni-kassel.de/bitstream/urn:nbn:de:heb is:34-2009101330569/7/DissertationKatjaMarek.pdf (accessed 28 November 2016).

Maybaum, G. (2011), 'Bürgerschaftliches Engagement, Chance und Herausforderung. Das Beispiel Hildesheim', in B. Franz and H.-R. Meier (eds), *Stadtplanung nach 1945. Zerstörung und Wiederaufbau. Denkmalpflegerische Probleme aus heutiger Sicht* (Veröffentlichung des Arbeitskreises Theorie und Lehre der Denkmalpflege Vol. 20), Holzminden: Mitzkat.

Meier, H.-R. (2005), 'Perspektiven für die "Zukunft unserer Vergangenheit". 30 Jahre seit dem Europäischen Jahr für Denkmalpflege und Heimatschutz', *NIKE Bulletin*, 20 (3): 5–9.

Meier, H.-R. (2009), 'Paradigma oder Büchse der Pandora? Die Frauenkirche – oder wie Dresden zum Zentrum der gegenwärtigen Rekonstruktionswelle wurde', *Die Alte Stadt*, 36 (1): 59–76.

Meier, H.-R. (2011), 'Denkmalschutz für die "zweite Zerstörung"?,' in B. Franz and H.-R. Meier (eds), *Stadtplanung nach 1945. Zerstörung und Wiederaufbau. Denkmalpflegerische Probleme aus heutiger Sicht* (Veröffentlichung des Arbeitskreises Theorie und Lehre der Denkmalpflege Vol. 20), Holzminden: Mitzkat.

Meitinger, K. (1946), *Das neue München. Vorschläge zum Wiederaufbau*, Munich: Bavarian State Office for Historic Preservation, reprinted 2014, Munich: Volk Verlag.

Muschg, W. (2003), 'Eine Sehenswürdigkeit für reisende Kuriositätensammler?', in U. Conrads (ed), *Die Städte himmeloffen. Reden und Reflexionen über den Wiederaufbau des Untergegangenen und die Wiederkehr des Neuen Bauens 1948/49* (Bauwelt Fundamente 125), Gütersloh: Bertelsmann-Fachzeitschriften.

Pusback, B. (2006), *Stadt als Heimat. Die Danziger Denkmalpflege zwischen 1933 und 1939*, Cologne/Weimar/Vienna: Böhlau.

Rodenstein, M. (2009), 'Vergessen und Erinnern der im Zweiten Weltkrieg zerstörten Frankfurter Altstadt. Ein Beitrag zur politischen Produktion eines Stadtbildes', *Die Alte Stadt*, 36 (1): 45–58.

Rump, G. (1995), *Ein immerhin merkwürdiges Haus. Eine Dokumentation zum 25jährigen Bestehen der Gesellschaft für den Wiederaufbau des Knochenhauer-Amtshauses*, Hildesheim: Gerstenberg.

Schieber, M., A. Schmidt and B. Windsheimer (2002), *Architektur Nürnberg. Bauten und Biografien*, Nuremberg: Sandberg Verlag.

Schild, I. (2014), 'Der Wiederaufbau alter Kirchen nach 1945', in C. Raabe and H. G. Horn (eds), *Leo Hugot. Der Mensch. Seine Zeit. Sein Nachlass*, Aachen/Berlin: Geymüller, Verlag für Architektur.

Stahn, G. (1991), *Das Nikolaiviertel*, Berlin: Verlag für Bauwesen.

Steinbach, R. (1949), 'Die Alte Brücke in Heidelberg und die Problematik des Wiederaufbaus', in U. Conrads, ed., *Die Städte himmeloffen. Reden und Reflexionen über den Wiederaufbau des Untergegangenen und die Wiederkehr des Neuen Bauens 1948/49* (Bauwelt Fundamente 125), Gütersloh: Bertelsmann-Fachzeitschriften.

Thumm, M. (1993), 'Zur Geschichte des Marktplatzes von Hildesheim seit seiner Zerstörung 1945', in A. Hubel (ed), *Denkmalpflege zwischen Konservieren und Rekonstruieren, Dokumentation der Jahrestagung 1989 in Hildesheim*, Bamberg: Veröffentlichung des Arbeitskreises Theorie und Lehre der Denkmalpflege Vol. 7.

Urban, F. (2007), *Berlin/DDR – neo-historisch Geschichte aus Fertigteilen*, Berlin: Gebrüder Mann.

Urban, F. (2014), 'Postmoderne als Konsens: Neo-Historischer Wiederaufbau im Ost-Berliner Nikolaiviertel 1977–1989', in G. Wagner-Kyora (ed), *Rebuilding European Cities. Reconstructions, Modernity and the Local Politics of Identity Construction since 1945* (Beiträge zur Stadtgeschichte und Urbanisierungsforschung, Bd. 15), Stuttgart: Steiner.

Wagner-Kyora, G. (2014), 'Wiederaufbaustädte der Bundesrepublik im Vergleich 1950–1990', in G. Wagner-Kyora (ed), *Rebuilding European Cities. Reconstructions, Modernity and the Local Politics of Identity Construction since 1945* (Beiträge zur Stadtgeschichte und Urbanisierungsforschung, Bd. 15), Stuttgart: Steiner.

Chapter 1.2

Reconstruction of Historic Monuments in Poland after the Second World War – the Case of Warsaw

Ingrid Appelbom Karsten

Introduction

There is a long list of towns and cities in Europe that were damaged or virtually destroyed during the Second World War. While many were destroyed more or less by accident and chance, the situation for Polish towns, especially the historic city of Warsaw, was quite different. More than 7,000 monuments were destroyed, including churches, castles, town halls, synagogues, residences and other buildings connected to the national identity. The Nazi programme was aimed at eradicating the Polish people and their culture. This chapter explores some of the issues of destruction and reconstruction, drawing on the author's interviews with key decision-makers in the early 1980s.

As a protest against the destruction of the cultural heritage, it was decided that historic objects and historic urban complexes should be reconstructed as they were regarded as an expression of Polish culture. The motivation for this decision was a national, political and psychological 'necessity'. As it was strongly felt that the decision to reconstruct should be implemented without delay, it was necessary to consider the economic and practical conditions required for reconstruction activity. Most of the building material had to be acquired from the ruins, without the use of new technology. New bricks were made of ground rubble and used for new constructions. The building technology had to be traditional, led by qualified staff and executed by skilled labour from the various long-established crafts.

As the extent and degree of destruction varied throughout the country, it was important to obtain an idea of the real problem, so the destroyed sites – the historic towns and historic cores – were classified as follows:

1   Towns that had been partly destroyed, such as Lublin, Brzeg
2   Towns with significant destruction, but where the old defence walls had been partly preserved, such as Poznan, Wroclaw, Opole, Olsztyn, Nysa
3   Towns with total destruction, such as Warsaw, the historic cores in Gdansk, Szczecin, Malbork, Chojna, Pyrzyce, Glogow, Strzegom, Koszalin, Kolobrzeg (Zachwatowicz 1965)

The reconstruction of the towns did not follow one single idea or one principle.[1] Solutions depended on circumstances, including their relative historic importance, their location in relation to the rest of the country, the artistic and architectural importance of the building structure, the extent of the destruction, the size of the town, the economic situation of the area in terms of industrialization before the war. The accuracy of reconstruction was reliant upon the availability of evidence, for instance remaining and spared fragments, satisfactory documentation and expert knowledge of historic architecture and development: these requirements were fulfilled in the historic towns and cities such as Warsaw, Poznan, Opole, Brzeg and parts of the old town cores in Wroclaw, Nysa and Gdansk. The idea behind the reconstruction process, all organized from Warsaw, was not just to take care of isolated cultural heritage, but also to consider whole urban historic complexes; it was to give new life to the historic sites, providing apartments for people, new infrastructure and so on.

Warsaw – the potential of a monument as a symbol and for identity

Warsaw as a historic site has always been connected to the River Vistula and to the old trade roads in the region. The development of trade in the tenth century gave rise to a small settlement with a small castle which then expanded to include a market place and a second castle, probably on the site where the Royal Castle subsequently was erected. Trade increased in

---

[1] From a taped interview carried out by the author in 1981 with the architect Professor J. Zachwatowicz, who was appointed General for Cultural Heritage in Poland.

the thirteenth and fourteenth centuries and grants were given for a more organized and planned building activity, based on German law, the so-called 'location *civitatis*'. Foreign settlers, principally Germans and Jews, all contributed to the acceleration of progress with regard both to the volume of production and to the quality of urban life. The town plan developed on the typical chess-board pattern, a variant of the modest earlier settlement, with a network of streets and squares. The main square in the middle became the main market place with two streets leading from each corner. The whole arrangement was surrounded by a defensive wall, dating from the fourteenth century. On the northern side of the settlement, which became known as the Old Town of Warsaw (*Stare Miasto*), a new settlement was erected in 1408, the New Town (*Nove Miasto*). The professional specialization of the inhabitants started at the very beginning of the Old and New Town development – as the architecture reveals. From 1413 Warsaw was the capital of Central-Mazovia, before the principality was conquered by the King of Poland in 1526.

The destruction of Warsaw

With the exception of the historic core (*Stare Miasto*), which the Nazis regarded as an example of German town planning), Warsaw was to be destroyed to a meticulously prepared plan. The whole of the Polish population was to be exterminated and the city replaced by a new structure. What people did not know at that time was that the Nazi town planning team in Wurzburg, Germany, had started to realize the so-called *Pabst-plan: Warschau – die neue deutsche Stadt*, named after the Nazi architect and town planner Friedrich Pabst. The project, begun in 1939, consisted of fifteen plans and photographs, based on the results of research on the historical development of Warsaw, as well as its transportation network and economic background. Plan No. 13, the most shocking of all, bore the caption *Der Abbau der Polenstadt und der Aufbau der Deutschen Stadt* (Demolition of the Polish city and Building the German city). The plan of the destruction was to reduce the number of inhabitants from the original approximately 1.3 million, down to approximately 100,000–130,000 Germans. As a complement to the new town plan (from 1939), a new plan also was prepared for the site of the Royal Castle. This was for the so-called *Weichselhalle* or *Volkshalle*, a city hall which was to be built in a monumental form with a triumphal arch and crowned with the Roman imperial Eagle. The Pabst-plan was found after the war in 1945 in Dr Hans Frank's office in the Wawel Castle in Cracow. Dr Frank was the former Minister of Justice in the Third Reich, and later was appointed Governor General of Poland (Jankowski and Ciborowski 1978).

The destruction of Warsaw was carried out in four phases. The first attack against the capital started on 1 September 1939 and was directed against the Royal Castle, the symbol of the nation, which through history had been so emotionally connected to the formation of the city. To be sure that the destruction would be achieved as quickly as possible, the Nazis drilled holes for dynamite in the castle walls. In addition to the Royal Castle, the Central Railway Station and many buildings in midtown Warsaw went up in flames. An eighth of the city's buildings were destroyed during this period. The future of the capital was determined during the very first days of Nazi occupation. Dr Frank wrote in his diary: 'The Fuhrer discussed the situation with the Governor-General, and approved his actions, particularly the demolition of the Royal Castle' (Jankowski and Ciborowski 1978).

The next attack was carried out during 1942–3. It was during this period that the Nazis undertook the final destruction of the Warsaw ghetto, where the Jewish people had been gathered together into an area of 4 km², separated from the rest of the city. Between 22 July and 3 October 1942 the ghetto was evacuated and by early 1943 the final solution and the final liquidation of the Jewish quarter were ordered by Himmler. Then the Nazis required just three weeks to trample over the heroic resistance, as the whole district was reduced to ashes and ruins. In 1943 a long and carefully prepared report was sent to Berlin with the final solution – *es gibt keinen judishen Wohnbezirk in Warsaw mehr* (there are no more living places for the Jews in Warsaw): the area was being cleared for the construction of the *neue Deutsche Stadt Warschau* (the new German city of Warsaw). In 1944 the Polish underground Resistance broke out and lasted for sixty-three days. Between 200,000 and 250,000 people were killed and those who survived were driven out of the city. A few days after the outbreak, Dr Frank again wrote in his diary: 'Almost all Warsaw is a sea of flames. Warsaw will get what it deserves – complete annihilation.'

As a reaction to the uprising, the Old Town also was bombarded and 90 per cent was destroyed. Hitler saw it as his task to remove all monuments that could be connected to the history and culture of the country. To ensure the destruction of selected objects only, special groups of experts – Nazi art historians and scientific advisers – were responsible for the operation. For three months, special so-called *Sprengkommandos* and *Vernichtungs-Kommandos* (Annihilation Detachments) were set up for the purpose, and Warsaw was divided into zones. All buildings standing in the corners of a square or a street were numbered. Specifically chosen buildings, statues, historic monuments, and so on, were labelled, and special instructions placed on the walls. These instructions included technical methods and the dates for the destruction that was to take place. Furthermore there were instructions for the destruction of trees, and instructions on how the telegraph, telephone and tram lines should be broken up, and how the sewage and water systems should be reduced. Tanks were used to tear out telegraph poles and tramway tracks. All traces were to be wiped out. The Nazis were very careful; everything in Warsaw that was connected to the Polish culture was to be removed forever. Therefore, the Krasinski Library, a former private palace, was set afire in 1944 and was almost completely destroyed, as well as the Arsenal containing an important collection of the history of Warsaw, the library Acta Nova and the National Library in November of the same year. Eighty to 100 per cent of the contents of the capital's six largest archives went up in flames. Famous palaces were burned down such as Lazienki Palace, once a summer palace for the King, where only the bare walls and colonnades remained where the Nazis had drilled hundreds of holes for explosives, as well as the Saxon Palace, designed by the Dresden architect Poppelmann. Approximately 80–85 per cent of the whole city was destroyed. Before the war, Warsaw had 957 protected historic buildings; of these 782 were completely demolished, 141 partly destroyed and the remaining thirty-four survived only because the Nazis ran out of time to set off the dynamite placed in the buildings. In December 1944 the ruins of the Royal Castle were burned, and these became a 'symbol' for freedom, tolerance and Polish Sovereignty (Lileyko 1980). As Professor Zachwatowicz summarized:

> The idea of the Nazis was to remove all monuments that could be connected to the history and culture of the Polish nation so that all traces of the people would be eradicated. The intention was to destroy their identity so that it would be easier (for the authorities) to transform places into a new system. It was therefore hugely important for them to remove all remains, evidence and symbols which had immortalized the history of Poland.[2]

Motivation for the reconstruction of Warsaw

Because of the massive scale and character of the destruction very few believed in the idea of reconstruction for the capital. The principle to reconstruct the physical parts that had disappeared was not in accordance with the principles that scholars had been discussing before the war, that is, the Resolution adopted at the First International Congress of Architects and Technicians of Historic Monuments, Athens 1931 (the Athens Charter).[3]

After the first days of occupation, in September 1939, the people of Warsaw began to live two lives, an official one, and one in the underground

---

[2]Ibid.

[3]The Congress in Athens was the first European cooperation on how to deal with and handle the cultural heritage as a common responsibility and resulted in a joint obligation to agree upon a common document. For instance, point 5 and part IV of the Athens Charter recommended that a restoration approach should be used, allowing that the use of modern techniques and materials could be used in a judicious manner, and concealed as far as possible, in order that the aspect and character of the restored monument may be preserved. The Polish scholar A. Lauterbach participated in the conference.

in defiance of the occupying forces. The administration of the city, together with Polish scholars, started 'the work of reconstruction' of the castle and the city by taking care of all authentic fragments among the ruins, especially the furnishings of the Royal Castle. Many paintings from the Royal Castle were also saved thanks to the secret action of art historian Professor Stanislaw Lorentz at the University of Warsaw, who was the leader of the operation. He rescued the twenty-six views of the city painted by Bernardo Bellotto (also known, confusingly, as Canaletto, the name of his famous uncle and teacher). After working at ducal courts in Italy, Dresden, Vienna and Munich, Bellotto arrived in Warsaw in 1767, becoming court painter to the king in the following year, remaining in the city until his death in 1780. One of the artist's main achievements, the panoramic *View of Warsaw from the suburb of Praga* (1770), was recalled by Professor Lorentz: 'How many people did not have that picture in their mind.'[4] The former vision of the city gave a 'motivational force' for the reconstruction as well as providing together with Bellotto's other *vedute* of the city, invaluable documentary evidence for its reconstruction (Rottermund 2008; Schumacher 2014).

Considering the enormous need to provide housing for people, the lack of administration, the need for official buildings and functions upon which a capital depends, a move of the capital to the former capital of Cracow was proposed; but as the Polish Union of Architects (SARP) argued: 'Warsaw in accordance to its history and geographical position must in the future and forever be the capital of the country' (Gieysztor 1989). The town of Lublin was temporarily given the function of the national capital until conditions were right to return that function to Warsaw. The need to re-establish Warsaw as the capital was an important driver in speeding up the reconstruction.

One possible solution to the question of how to reconstruct was discussed, but did not receive real support: building a new Warsaw with new architecture on top of the fragments of old foundations. The old centre of Warsaw, the heart of the city, could then be arranged like a composition of fragments, a 'documentation' of the destruction of the war, supplemented with architecture in the modern style. The principles of this kind of approach had been discussed in Athens in 1931,[5] and also debated in Dresden after the war.[6] But the idea that the oldest features of the city, the footprints and traces of the oldest buildings, the 'roots' of Warsaw and the capital of the country

---

[4]From a taped interview carried out by the author in 1981 with the art historian Professor Stanislaw Lorentz.
[5]The Resolutions of the IV International Congress for Modern Architecture 1931 (known as the Athens Charter 1931) concerned the city in its regional setting. Part E of the charter 'Legacy of History' was dedicated to historic sites. It was recommended that whole urban areas should be cared for, not only isolated monuments of exceptional value.
[6]Interview with Professor J. Zachwatowicz.

should disappear evoked patriotic emotional feelings throughout the whole nation. The struggle to assert cultural identity as a part of the Polish history was stronger than the rational solution that had been discussed in Athens. The city was a 'symbol' of elective authority and tolerance, where the first democratic European constitution, the Constitution of 3 May 1791, was adopted. The Nazi philosophy of exterminating a nation through eradication of its culture could not be allowed to succeed. Reconstruction was a way of protesting against the destruction. The discussion about cultural heritage had passed a test.

Two significant events decided the fortune of Warsaw. First, the provisional government in Lublin decided in 1945 that Warsaw should continue to be the capital of the country. Secondly, the former inhabitants of Warsaw flocked back to the city – to their 'roots'. While the structure of space in the city was lost, the *genius loci* kept them in a firm grip, confirming the correctness of the formal decision to reconstruct the city.

Reconstruction was a very clear objective which included historic responsibility and necessity. The identity of Warsaw was a product of the memories of the people who returned there. To ensure that the future generations of Warsaw would identify with the place and its history, the substance had to be reconstructed. Unless important areas of the city were reconstructed, especially the Old Town with its historic spaces and the old fortifications, memories would be repressed. 'We are a generation who has experienced the greatest tragedy in our history. If we do not reconstruct, we will most likely be criticized by the next generation' (Gieysztor 1989). The reconstruction of the historic core of Warsaw can therefore be expressed like this: there was the same motivation for destruction as there was for reconstruction by reference to the physical surroundings as an expression of the culture and identity of the people – the motive power for destruction as for reconstruction.[7] On 14 February 1945 the Office for the Reconstruction of the Capital was established.

The programme and organization of the reconstruction of Warsaw

The decision to reconstruct Warsaw demanded a programme for the building activity, which had to be worked out as soon as possible, as well as the appointment of a suitable organization which should carry out the operation. A reconstruction agency for the capital, *Biuro Odbudowy Stolicy* (BOS – Office for Reconstruction of the Capital), was established in February 1945. Before the end of the year the first ideas for a masterplan

---

[7]Ibid.

for the reconstruction of Warsaw were presented, prepared by the architects J. Zachwatowicz, P. Biegansky and M. Kuzma. The first proposition showed clearly that the *Stare Miasto*, *Nove Miasto*, the defensive walls and parts of the 'Royal Route' had to be reconstructed. The next edition of the masterplan, completed in the spring of 1946, was displayed at the exhibition 'Warsaw Lives Again' which opened in May 1946 at the Library of Congress in Washington. In the catalogue of the exhibition, Lewis Mumford, the American sociologist and town planner wrote that 'Warsaw would live again – more magnificent than ever'.

The Architecture Department of the Polytechnic University in Warsaw was transformed into a bustlingly active building department carrying out several scientific studies and generally advising all those involved in the work of reconstruction. Some students, who had continued their studies underground during the war, presented their exam papers at BOS as proposals for the reconstruction of the city. As an act of defiance many planners and architects were working with different solutions for Warsaw during the war. The war moreover had given time for new discussions to take place and new solutions to emerge, so creating a rich climate for the presentation of new propositions for reconstruction.

In 1947 the City Planning Office in Warsaw, *Biuro Urbanistyczne Warszawa* (BUW), reorganized from BOS, continued the work with the new masterplan. Foreign specialists were invited to present their opinions. The new plan included the infrastructure proposal from BOS: the important east-west route with a tunnel under the Royal Castle Square and a bridge over the Vistula River to reduce traffic in the most historically sensitive part of the city. The presentation of a proposal of that character so soon after the liberation was possible only because there had been so much discussion during the war, as a kind of continuity of pre-war discussions for '*Warszawa funkcjonalna* 1931', following the ideas of Le Corbusier relating to historic, architectural, urban, economic and social conditions (Czerner and Listowski 1981). These had been presented in London in 1934 at the International Congress for Modern Architecture (CIAM).

In 1949 the so-called six-year plan for the reconstruction of Warsaw was presented. It was a programme for the reconstruction and development of management, housing and social arrangement, distribution of green areas, graveyards, communal gardens, rebuilding of infrastructure and the modernizing of manufacturing. According to the forecast in the plan, the return of inhabitants to Warsaw would create an increase in the population from 750,000 inhabitants to one million by the end of the period in 1955 (Bierut 1951). This would result in an expansion of the city beyond its then-existing boundary. In 1951 the borders were expanded and the area increased from 140 km² to 453 km². The result was that Greater Warsaw came to include some former suburbs. The new housing areas that had to be planned consisted of *Stare Miasto, Nove Miasto, Muranow, Mlynow, Kolowest, Zoliborz, Bielano, Stodowiec* and *Praga*.

Investigations

The documentation and preservation of cultural heritage had a very special organization in Poland. As a basic operation, the work of preservation begins with scientific documentation which includes such documentary material as works of art, architectural remains and other reliable sources. All preservation work was centrally organized, more specifically and first of all, by the State enterprise *Pracownie Konserwacji Zabytków* (PKZ), 'The Atelier for Conservation of Cultural Property', which was established in 1951, initiated by the Cabinet of Art and Culture. It gathered various specialists assigned to make inventories and analyses, to carry out projects and to do the work; an organization probably unique in Europe at that time and comprising more than 8,500 employees.

Important investigations made before the war

As noted above, Bellotto's eighteenth-century townscapes rescued during the war by Professor Lorentz were of fundamental importance in reconstructing the city (Lorentz 1963). Furthermore, an important aid to the reconstruction work was the investigations of historic elements of the town that had been carried out at the Department of Architecture of the Polytechnic University in Warsaw. To give the students an understanding of Polish architectural history, they were required to make drawings of the old churches, palaces and ordinary merchant houses, including drawings of façades, sections and plans to scales of 1:50, 1:5 and 1:1. In addition to the work of surveying, the students also made a collection of photographs and iconographic descriptions of many details. The works belonged to the students and were held in many hands, so escaping the destruction of material held in libraries and other repositories. They were carefully preserved by the students during the war and were important authentic documents for the work of reconstruction.

Investigations of the building structure from the fourteenth century in the *Stare Miasto*

In connection with the work of clearing up debris in the post-war *Stare Miasto*, the BOS workers began a systematic work of recording of the basements and the ruins, including the production of photographs. They found authentic fragments and details from the middle ages, much of which was previously unknown. During the work of documentation it was possible to establish the architecture of the middle ages in great detail. The discovery gave a new picture of the oldest history in Warsaw.

The work was carried out in three phases:

1 1945–47, protection and examination of the ruins.
2 1947–50, preservation of fragments, simultaneously the
   reconstruction of the most dangerous parts was begun.
3 1950–54, a complete investigation and documentation was made
   (Zachwatowicz et al. 1956).

Apart from the monumental architecture in the *Stare Miasto,* before the war
226 buildings existed with their own numbered plots within the fourteenth-
century wall. It was found that the older houses could be differentiated
from those of 1500–1600. Based on different fragments, 139 buildings from
the fourteenth century were identified. By studying the basement and the
first level/elevation of the houses, four different types of buildings could be
identified in the area:

1 The main houses by the market square (*Rynek*) of the *Stare Miasto*
   and along the main streets. Seventy-one houses were identified, of
   which fifty-six had evidence of authentic material and form, so it
   was possible to determine both their size and their plans.
2 Smaller buildings, probably belonging to the craftsmen living on the
   outskirts.
3 Buildings with a particular design of planning and architecture,
   probably belonging to the clergy.
4 Smaller buildings for different functions.

Among the ruins there were no remains of entire fourteenth-century gothic
main walls from floor to ceiling, but fragments of walls with gothic arched
windows were found, which later on had become bricked walls, along with
a large number of doorways and niches. The bricks were of great help in
determining the age of the walls as they varied in size and design from period
to period. The largest bricks, dating from *c.*1350, were used for constructing
the defensive wall against the Vistula River. Some of the bricks were made
by hand, but bricks with special profiles later were introduced for windows
and doors.

To get a better understanding of the fourteenth-century architecture and
the typical quality of the building structure of that time, two drawings for
reconstruction were made, based on two main houses, one from about the
year 1400 and the other from around 1500. The construction of the building
types and their plastic art of decoration were most reminiscent of buildings
that had been found in the northern part of Poland within the same period.
These models were to be the prototypes when projecting and reconstructing,
particularly when the authentic fragments of the building were too small, or
when it was difficult to determine how the fragments that had been found
could be gathered together into a whole.

Investigations of the defensive wall around the *Stare Miasto*

In 1939 and 1944 the old fourteenth-century town wall, as well as buildings which formed part of the wall structure for housing the poor, had been destroyed. In the process of clearing up, the rest of these structures were removed and remnants of the old defensive wall were displayed. The investigations can be divided into three parts: the first considered the collection of historic information in literature, drawings and photographs. Comparison with similar constructions helped to identify the construction of that time. The next investigation consisted of photographic documentation, followed by detailed drawings. The third aspect consisted of a detailed investigation of the different parts of the wall. The dimensions and character of the brick were studied together with the type of bonds and the composition of the mortar. The reason for conducting this investigation was to understand the different construction periods. The technical condition of the wall was also analysed in order to understand damage caused by corrosion and mechanical attacks. To establish that there had not been a former fortification in the same place, archaeological investigations were conducted. The pre-1339 wall had to be opened up, reconstructed, and completed in places where the former building activity had existed. The new brick construction works were to be shown in the wall. By this operation, parts of the wall from different periods were to be revealed.

Reconstruction of the *Stare Miasto*

Function, programme and adaptation

The following proposals for functions were presented: as a principle *Stare Miasto* was to be reconstructed with dwellings, except for a number of services and activities, in order to create new life and attractiveness in the area. Above all, the buildings facing the main market place were given service functions such as restaurants, wine cellars and shops on the ground floor, in accordance with earlier traditions. Here the aim was to keep the disposition of the plan from the eighteenth century. At that time many monumental entrance halls dating from the middle ages and the Renaissance had disappeared and new ideas from central Europe had been introduced.

It was complicated to implement the new regulations that had been introduced after the war to improve living conditions, such as those for the provision of kitchens and sanitary installations that had to be provided for every apartment. Previously most of the houses had only one owner; the flats were rather large in size. However, in increasing the utilization of the houses, it was difficult to provide smaller apartments with smaller rooms while simultaneously maintaining the authentic and interesting room dispositions.

Compromises were necessary. If the houses proved to be without authentic fragments and the buildings were less significant, the disposition of the rooms was less strictly regulated. But if the fragments of the buildings after the investigation proved to have interiors of great architectural and artistic value, the buildings would not be used as residences if their subdivision into apartments would result in significant alterations. Instead, they would be used as cultural institutions. Alterations were generally not to be shown in the façades; it was important that the historic townscape should be kept intact. In order not to destroy the earlier roofscape, it was decided that the old chimneys should be kept for ventilation purposes, with central heating systems installed under the floors.

Preserving the typical and characteristic

The surroundings north and south of the historic area had seen significant development over the previous hundred years. Nevertheless, the urban pattern in the *Stare Miasto* had seen very little change since the fifteenth century. At that time the *Stare Miasto* was the centre of trade and the seat of the nation. During that period an architectural style had been formulated, which gave the *Stare Miasto* its character. After the fire in 1607 the buildings around the market place were given a new feature. The buildings were still narrow, mostly with three windows and, in contrast to the middle ages, were mainly four floors in height. Influences from Italy and the Netherlands were notable according to iconographical records, with descriptions of the rich decoration, gilding and painting. The portals and roofs were very characteristic. As the main interest through history had been concentrated in these central zones, being the oldest part of Warsaw and having historic value, documentation was most complete there. A precise documentation of the situation was made before the war, as is evidenced by measured plans and drawings. The reconstruction activity could therefore be carried out with an almost complete body of historical evidence.

Some changes were made to the houses in the nineteenth century, particularly in relation to detailing and decorative work. Discussions arose around the question of which period should be the fundamental one for the reconstruction of the exteriors. The following solutions were made: 'Everything must be reconstructed, into how it was before the war. The façades had at that time a light mixture of renaissance, baroque and classicism'.[8] The combination of the different elements and forms pertaining in 1939 was a part of the history of the city, and gave it a distinctive character, and should be preserved. Gothic details that had been found in combination with the investigations were to become visible in the façades. The houses that were poorly documented would not be reconstructed. It was not the time for

[8]Ibid.

fantasy. The principle was therefore not a pure style, but a style including different details from different periods, based on principles of continuity, in other words principles of restoration that had been developed before the war. An investigation of every house in the *Stare Miasto* was carried out. For the market place, drawings were made of the façades of every house as they had appeared before the war, with proposals for what they would look like after the reconstruction.

Change to the pre-war town plan in the *Stare Miasto*

Before the war the townscape of the *Stare Miasto* was rather compact. Many buildings had then been erected inside the old town wall, in order to provide more apartments. After the war, when the reconstruction work was carried out, the resultant town plan appeared to be more open and lofty. This was because the buildings immediately inside the walls, and buildings of poor quality without documentation, were not reconstructed. Instead of the rather compact historic centre, the new centre provided an improved environment, with much greenery and more open spaces for recreation, children's playgrounds and so on. And as a result of the new building regulations, the number of habitable rooms increased by 25 per cent in comparison to before the war. The programme of building activity that was formulated after the war brought in a clear social function.

It is noteworthy that the system of planning of the *Stare Miasto* from the thirteenth and fourteenth centuries, with the old market place in the centre, has been sustained over the subsequent centuries. The oldest part of Warsaw, the historic centre situated along the River Vistula, can be seen today as it was before – as a symbol of Warsaw – as Bellotto painted it (Figure 1).

Warsaw outside the old defensive wall

The former 'Royal Route', consisting of the streets *Krakowskie Przedmiescie, Nowy Swiat and Aleje Ujazdowskie*, was previously considered to be the most important axis in the city of Warsaw. The axis ran parallel to the River Vistula from the *Stare Miasto* to the summer palace of Wilanow in the south. The Royal Route had been lined with palaces, churches and fashionable dwellings from the seventeenth and eighteenth centuries. With time the axis had lost much of its attractiveness. After the war much attention was directed towards the road, *Nowy Swiat*, as the architecture of the building blocks here was held to be of little architectural value. However, the town planners understood the importance of the axis as a whole; the Royal Route was then regarded as an important urban element in relation to the *Stare Miasto*. By reconstructing the whole urban complex, and by describing and plotting out the great urban lines, coherence and continuity could be achieved. It was important to reveal all the historic stages, so presenting a city with a

FIGURE 1 *The main market place in* Stare Miasto *(the Old Town). Source: Ingrid Appelbom Karsten.*

continuing function from the middle ages until the present day. The Royal Route, varied in both architecture and character, is the axis in Warsaw which best represents this long development, showing the topographic conditions for the creation and development of Warsaw along the River Vistula. Through carrying out this operation, the emotional relationship of the people to their city was strengthened.

Motivation for the restitution of the Royal Castle

Only a very few fragments from the south façade of the Royal Castle were left after the war. As long as a historic monument consisted just of collapsed walls, a reconstruction would be in conflict with the Venice Charter of 1964. Discussions for and against a reconstruction were ongoing between the different experts up to the 1970s.[9] In discussions with Professor Lorentz about the motivation for reconstruction of the Royal Castle, he explained that:

> There are important factors not to be forgotten concerning the reconstruction and conservation of historic surroundings. In ancient towns

---

[9]Professor Zachwatowicz was a co-author of the *Venice Charter* 1964.

there are characteristic elements of importance for the understanding of 'life and times', as if they were important accents in the townscape. From the compositional point of view, the Castle acted as a pendant to the building complex of the Old Town, providing a balance. From an urban and historical point of view the Royal Castle complex belonged to the city. The castle would then be the end of the reconstruction of the historic core of Warsaw. But the most important argument is the fact that the castle through times had been fixed in the development of awareness of the nation, as a symbol of liberty and national sovereignty. These capacities were deeply rooted in the Polish people.[10]

As a symbolic and physiological reaction to the attempts by the Nazis to wipe out the memories of the castle of the nation during the war, Polish experts had secretly collected all the authentic material they could come across, while simultaneously German experts in art gave instructions concerning what should be transported to the Third Reich. As the Polish experts could not accept that the castle should disappear forever, but proclaimed that 'the castle itself had the right to determine its own destiny', they foresaw a 'reconstruction' in the future. They considered that the reuse of collected authentic fragments of walls and details would be enough to proclaim that the rebuilt castle, in physical meaning, would be authentic.[11]

On 20 January 1971 it was decided to 'restitute' the castle. Although the fragments from the walls and from the interior which were saved were 'lifted up and brought in place', it is difficult to use the term 'anastylosis' to refer to the activity which took place at the castle. Nor is it correct to use the term 'reconstruction'. Terms like 'reconstruction', 'restoration' and 'anastylosis' are not adequate terms for the process of rebuilding the castle. According to Professor Zachwatowicz, the term 'restitution' is all inclusive because its meaning embraces all that is necessary in enabling rebuilding, describing the whole working process from the stage of documentation, up to the physical work of repairing and reusing the saved authentic fragments and so on.

The reconstruction of the Old Town continued until the mid-1960s. The entire process was completed with the restitution of the Royal Castle, which had been begun in January 1971. An appeal was issued to all Poles living abroad and at home to support the project with money and the response was tremendous. The 'cultural heritage' became a great pedagogical exercise thanks to the social engagement from the whole community. The restituted Royal Castle opened to visitors in 1984 (Figure 2).

---

[10]Interview with Professor Stanislaw Lorentz.
[11]Ibid.

FIGURE 2 *Castle square with the Royal Castle and King Sigismund Column: a landmark and meeting place both today and before the war. Source: Ingrid Appelbom Karsten.*

Conclusion

Some elements in our physical environment are more influential than others. Monuments are typically linked to special situations. Ideas connected with these monuments have led to either brutal actions or the very opposite, actions of great sacrifice. The historic monument has either been a source of power and inspiration or the target of devastation. Preservation and demolition have thus continuously fought one another. After the Second World War, when the results from interventions in the physical environment were obvious, the monument as an idea came to be in focus. Eventually the connection between social and physical environment was better understood. Although most European countries today agree that historic areas are interesting and that the physical environment in these areas is of great value, the degree to which they engage in the matter differs a great deal.

The Polish ideology of preservation

When considering the Polish way of preservation many people are, perhaps, thinking of the approach advocated by Professor Jan Zachwatowicz.

However, regarding the comprehensive work of reconstruction adopted in the ruined landscape in Poland, although many commentators have looked upon it with scepticism and surprise, some have expressed enthusiasm. Some have wanted to criticize the work of reconstruction as an architectural pastiche without content and a chaos of emotional feelings; others have understood the meaning of it. One can here talk about a 'Polish School of Reconstruction' (*polskiej szkole konserwaji zabytkow*); this has both positive and negative connotations. Before going further, it is important to distinguish between the two concepts: the aim on the one side and methods on the other. The aim is here the ideology of preservation; the methods are the principles by which they are operated.

Identity: The potential of the monument as a symbol and for identity

The Polish ideology of preservation has deep historical roots. Poland was divided up no less than three times at the end of the eighteenth century, which resulted in the Polish peoples' ever-increasing need for identification in an extended sense of the word. In the identification process the historical heritage – more specifically the cultural heritage – eventually became one of the most significant issues on which the inhabitants of the nation could focus their efforts. The monuments represented a concrete reminder of freedom and independence. The physical environment thus served as a means of communication through which the agreement between the physical form and the information it was supposed to bring about came to be of the utmost importance: people in general have a need for surroundings with meaning – surroundings satisfying both the visual stimuli and socio-cultural associations and relations.

Poland at that time could therefore be a good example of how an appreciation of the surroundings – buildings, streets, squares and spaces – has been a stronger motive power than the forces which sought to efface them. A common feature of the reconstructed towns and cities has been the concern to restore the individuality of the areas around the historic cores, acknowledging the great cultural, functional and social importance of the squares and urban spaces.

The former French Minister of Culture and Communication (1978–81) Jean-Philippe Lecaut is said to have pointed out when visiting Poland that what struck him, and the French in general, was that Polish culture had always been connected with national identity. Although Poland gradually ceased to be a unified whole, Lecaut's opinion was that this was not the inhabitants' view of the cultural heritage of the country. Lecaut emphasized the fact that Poland offered an excellent example of a country's awareness of the immense impact that culture can have on the power of a nation.[12]

[12]A point made by Polish scholars in discussion with the author.

Authenticity

Reflection upon the contrasting attitudes towards restoration expressed in the mid-nineteenth century by John Ruskin and Viollet-le-Duc, the former viewing it as totally destructive (and morally offensive), the latter as an opportunity to preserve, reinstate and indeed enhance (Pevsner 1969: 38), leads to a consideration of the concept of authenticity, fundamental to restoration strategies and as capable of wide interpretation: ideas of form, substance and time must all come into play. Few objects are authentic. Few objects have been not influenced by time, although there are those which have stayed unaffected for a long time with the original parts seen as authentic. On the basis of our knowledge of 'breaking down' in nature over time, we can imagine original appearances and consequent authenticity, so with relative accuracy we can read the original nature of the object, the qualifications and influences upon it and consider the interpretations to which it has been subject. One can say here that we can talk about *authentic ideas* and *authentic substances*.

Concerning buildings, authentic form and the original substance are their most important attributes. Unfortunately, these cannot be preserved unchanged for ever – even in peacetime – since the ageing process and alterations to the functional arrangements of buildings will both impact upon the authenticity of the original object. Furthermore, in catastrophic situations – wars, earthquakes and environmental devastation – it is not only the monuments which are threatened but also the rules and guiding principles for their protection: concepts such as reconstruction, copy, originality and authenticity cease to be merely theoretical notions but guiding principles for practical applications.

It is in such circumstances that the ideology of preservation is put to the test: 'We had [in Warsaw] the intention to carry over to the next generation a tolerably authentic – if not altogether authentic – form of the monuments, because monuments to us do not only imply "documents", but also memorials in the sense of being remembered'.[13] This is essentially the Polish peoples' ideology of preservation, so deeply rooted in their history. This ideology, however, does not tell us how practical matters should be handled. No new theory has emerged out of this ideology. When asked how the realization was to be carried out, Zachwatowicz answered that people involved in the field of preservation generally agreed on the old theories developed before the war, saying that the essential feature of the monument was its characteristic authentic substance. In accordance with these theories the reconstruction was carried out by reusing the authentic parts which had been saved during the war or found among the ruins. These were then clearly distinguished from the new parts. During the reconstruction the different

---

[13]Interview with Professor J. Zachwatowicz.

building phases of the object were also taken into consideration and shown great respect. Thus, the work of several periods could appear side by side, as they had before the war, without merging into one another.

Lessons learned

The lessons learned from the example of Warsaw may now be summarized. Preservation and reconstruction was not only a national and political imperative but an emotional and ideological response to circumstances; the ambition was to rebuild the city as well as the centres of other historic towns in a form which reflected their original authenticity. This required an understanding of the genius of the place – its topographic condition, the circumstances of its development and its evolution over time. So it was not just a question of reconstructing individual monuments but one of acknowledging and reflecting the different cycles or stages of development within each historic core which could be documented, understood and reconstructed as authentically as possible. The work of preservation and reconstruction must take the existence of scholarly documentation as its starting point unless there are other overriding social imperatives. Monuments embody meanings and these should be signalled since they are expressions of the national characteristics and identity which inform society. It follows from this that heritage policies should engage society as a whole. The monument itself in its preserved or reconstructed state should not be an item in an urban museum but part of the active society to which it belongs, in use even if that new use may compromise aspects of its authenticity. Lastly it is perhaps thanks to the example of Warsaw that the preservation of a large urban area as a monument has gained ground. Although the notion of the 'ensemble' – a monument and its surroundings – had been present in French legislation since 1913, extending in 1943 to the extent of a field of vision not exceeding 500 m, it was in 1962 that the notion of *secteurs sauvegardés* was introduced to protect the urban layouts of large towns: André Malraux, Minister of Culture, referred to the Polish examples in explaining and gaining understanding for the idea.

The World Heritage Site

The *Historic Centre of Warsaw*, meaning the Old Town (*Stare Miasto*), was inscribed in UNESCO's World Heritage List in 1980 (Figure 3). The inscription describes it as 'an outstanding example of a near-total reconstruction of a span of history covering the thirteenth to the twentieth century'. Two of the selection criteria were referred to in the inscription process: Criterion II ('to exhibit an important interchange of human values, over a span of time or within a cultural area of the world, on developments in architecture or technology, monumental arts, town-planning or landscape

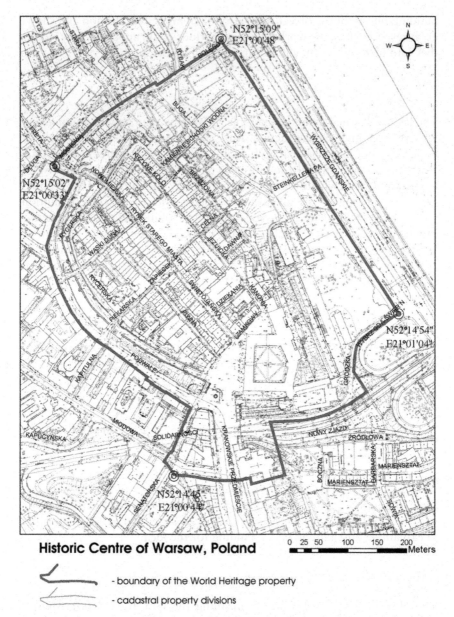

Historic Centre of Warsaw, Poland

- boundary of the World Heritage property
- cadastral property divisions

FIGURE 3 *The defined perimeter of* Stare Miasto. *Source: Permanent Delegation of the Republic of Poland to UNESCO.*

design'); and Criterion VI ('to be an outstanding example of a type of building, architectural or technological ensemble or landscape which illustrates [a] significant stage[s] in human history'). In this respect, the inscription states under Criterion II that 'the initiation of comprehensive conservation activities on the scale of the entire historic city was a unique European experience and contributed to the verification of conservation doctrines and practices', and under Criterion VI that 'the Historic Centre of Warsaw is an exceptional example of the comprehensive reconstruction of a city that had been deliberately and totally destroyed. The foundation of the material reconstruction was the inner strength and determination of the nation, which brought about the reconstruction of the heritage on a unique scale in the history of the world'.

In terms of 'Integrity' the inscription identifies the World Heritage property's boundaries as encompassing 'an entire comprehensively rebuilt portion of the city, located within the bounds of the medieval city walls and the Vistula Escarpment ... with all of the characteristic features defining its identity'. It further refers to the sense of historic and spatial continuity created in relation to the Old Town, the New Town and the Royal Route, and refers to the importance of maintaining the principles that were implemented during the process of reconstruction for underpinning the management system for the World Heritage property.

Concerning 'Authenticity', the list description identifies that the cohesive rebuilding process came to an end with the reconstruction of the Royal Castle and that, since then, the Historic Centre of Warsaw has fully retained its authenticity as a 'finished concept of post-war reconstruction'. The property includes two categories of structure comprising extant structures predating the damage of the Second World War and also reconstructed features: 'this group includes buildings recreated in accordance with pre-war records (some of the Old Town's townhouses, Sigismund's Column, churches and the Royal Castle), and those rebuilt based on historical and conservation studies pertaining to the architecture of the fourteenth to eighteenth centuries (e.g. the façade of the cathedral, and the Old Town walls with the Barbican)' (UNESCO: World Heritage Centre, undated).

It has been noted in a close analysis by Christina Cameron that the case of Warsaw prompted lengthy deliberations within ICOMOS and UNESCO on the criterion of authenticity. Warsaw was first nominated for World Heritage Site status in 1978 when it was decided that further expert study was required to see if it met the criterion. One year later, inscription was recommended by ICOMOS because the documentation was deemed excellent and the centre of the city an exceptional example of reconstruction, 'made into a symbol by the patriotic feeling of the Polish people'. But opinion remained divided and a decision was deferred pending further consideration of the notion of authenticity. It was the recognition of the association of the exceptionally successful reconstruction with 'events of considerable historical significance' which eventually tipped the balance towards acceptance and inscription in 1980, although this was not to be seen as a precedent: 'There can be no question of inscribing in the future other cultural properties that have been reconstructed.' There have, however, subsequently been further shifts towards associative values in the assessment of cultural practices and

cultural spaces. As Cameron (2008) concludes, 'one could argue that the
question [of reconstruction] remains open'.

References

Bierut, B. (1951), *The Six-Year Plan for the Reconstruction of Warsaw*, Warsaw:
    Książka i wiedza.
Cameron, C. (2008), 'From Warsaw to Mostar: The World Heritage Committee
    and Authenticity', *APT Bulletin*, 39 (2/3): 19–24.
Czerner, O. and L. Listowski (eds) (1981), *Avant-Garde Polonaise 1918–1939*,
    Paris/Warsaw: Editions du Moniteur/Interpress.
Gieysztor, A. (1989), *Warszawa jej dzieje I kultura*, Warsaw: Arkady.
Jankowski, S. and A. Ciborowski (1978), *Warsaw 1945, Today and Tomorrow*,
    Warsaw: Interpress.
Lileyko, J. (1980), *A Companion Guide to the Royal Castle in Warsaw*, Warsaw:
    Interpress.
Lorentz, S. (1963), 'Die Bedeutung der bilder Bernardo Bellottos fur den
    Wiederaufbau Warschau', in Exhibition Catalogue: *Bernardo Bellotto genannt
    Canaletto in Dresden und Warschau*, Dresden: Albertinum.
Pevsner, N. (1969), *Ruskin and Viollet-le-Duc*, London: Thames and Hudson.
Rottermund, A. (2008), *The Royal Castle in Warsaw*, Warsaw: Arx Regia.
Schumacher, A. (ed) (2014), *Canaletto – Bernardo Bellotto Paints Europe*, Munich:
    Hirmer.
UNESCO World Heritage Centre (undated), *World Heritage List: Historic Centre
    of Warsaw*, available online: http://whc.unesco.org/en/list/30 (accessed 14 June
    2016).
Zachwatowicz, J., P. Bieganski, T. Mischal, S. Zaryn and Z. Tomaszewski (1956),
    Stare Miasto w Warszawa: Odbudowa, Warsaw: Wydawnictwo Budownictwo i
    Architektura.
Zachwatowicz, J. (1965), *Protection of Historical Monuments in Poland*, Warsaw:
    Polonia.

Chapter 1.3

Post-conflict Urban Reconstruction of Bazaars in Gjakova and Peja, Kosovo

Bujar Demjaha

translated by Lumnije Ahmeti

Introduction

Kosovo is the youngest European country, originating from former Yugoslavia following armed conflict in 1999 and a declaration of independence on 17 February 2008. Located in South-East Europe, this land-locked zone of 10,908 km² borders Albania and the former Yugoslav countries, Montenegro, Serbia and Macedonia. Gjakova and Peja, the subjects of this chapter, are among the largest urban centres in Kosovo together with the capital Prishtina, Mitrovica, Prizren, Gjilan and Ferizaj. The country has been inhabited since the Palaeolithic period, more than 100,000 years ago, and evidence for the first signs of life in the territory is found in caves in Radavc and Karamakaza. The nomadic inhabitants of this early period began slowly to group in sustainable settlements, practising agriculture (Demjaha 2016: 36).

The meaning of 'Çarshia'

Life and work as two closely related categories have always been the main generators in the development of mankind. Since agriculture was more or less the only activity in rural areas, crafts and services were complementary functions serving the population. *Çarshia,* a compound of workshops and shops, is an urban entirety, a city's bazaar, a street with shops on both sides, where crafts and trade activities used to be carried out and as such was fundamental to the economic, social and political life of the city. Bazaars were meeting places where selling and exchange of goods took place, information was exchanged and crafts were developed. The old bazaars in Kosovo were public spaces for the production of goods, shopping, meeting, eating and drinking. They were inevitably transformed over time, subject to changing needs and often damaged by fire. But in 1998–9 the bazaars in Gjakova and Peja were more deliberately targeted and comprehensively destroyed in war. Their importance to the life of the city and the identity of the people was acknowledged through their reconstruction.

According to Džemal Čelić (1980) the word *çarshia* is of Persian origin and means 'four sides', conveying the message that it is a location to which people come from four sides of the world (Çerreti 2012: 8). The name reached the Balkans through the Ottoman Empire. As an urban entirety, *çarshia* (bazaar) denoted more than simply commerce and production but also had social and spiritual connotations in being at the centre of the city.

Crafts practised in the bazaar were mainly passed down within families through generations, thus jealously protecting the secrets of the trade. It is noteworthy that crafts were more or less related to national and religious backgrounds. Muslims dealt more with crafts such as watchmaking, textile production and trade, whereas Catholics dealt more with silver, the Orthodox with metal processing and the Roma with blacksmithing.

Bazaars were constructed by local master craftsmen without any prior planning. The skills of these autochthonous master craftsmen were passed down through generations, resulting in great achievements in architecture and construction engineering. The overall characteristics of vernacular architecture in Kosovo may be best identified in oriental-type houses and in bazaars. Both of these building types were maximally adapted to both natural and social environments. These buildings and ensembles were achieved through a consideration of terrain, orientation and local construction materials. The buildings responded to the needs of the users and were adapted to suit the functions to which they were dedicated. The vernacular architecture of Kosovo contains those elements of sustainable building now known as 'bio-climatic architecture' (Hadrović 2008). Moreover, these buildings were functionally flexible and easily adapted to changing requirements with the passing of time. Out of the overall number of bazaars in Kosovo, only three of them have, to a certain extent, preserved the characteristics of the old bazaars. While bazaars in Gjakova and Peja were destroyed during the armed conflict of 1999 in Kosovo, the Prizren bazaar was saved from damage. Cultural heritage is permanently endangered from numerous threats to heritage values, the largest of which come from humans themselves, whether through the ignorance of individual owners, negligence and the lack of competence of institutions, or deliberate systematic destruction during wars.

Classification of crafts

Although craftsmanship had the character of economic activity, it also had a social character. The classification of crafts has usually been carried out on the basis of religious affiliation, race, gender and geography – where the craftsmanship activity took place (village or city). But a more pertinent classification of those craft activities that had direct impact in bazaars is according to process and activity. Three groups have been classified by Statovci but, for present purposes, the discussion here is confined to the two main classifications, *production* craftsmanship and *service* craftsmanship, leaving out the less clearly divisible group, that of *production-service* craftsmanship (Statovci 1982: 132). Depending on time and resulting from the market, there were specific modalities of crafts that were later modified or ceased to exist altogether.

Production crafts

Production crafts have traditionally been of the greatest importance, not only in terms of what was produced but also because of their impact as generators of the development of the old bazaars. There was a domination of metalwork crafts such as *dyfekxhi* (the production of rifles and swords): Gjakova was well known in the region for production of the rifle *huta e Gjakoves*. There were also *dyfekxhi* in Peja and Prizren, and their products were sold throughout the territories occupied by the Ottoman Empire. Metal-working also included the crafts of *kujunxhi* (goldsmiths and silversmiths), *biçakxhi* (producers of knives) and *kazanxhi* (producers of copper dishes, trays, teakettles and plates).

While metalsmiths were of greater importance in selling their produce throughout the Ottoman Empire, textile producers had more importance at .regional level. The craft of *terzi*, (tailor) for example, sewing costumes for men and women, was developed especially in Gjakova, Prizren, Peja and Prishtina (Statovci 1982: 160). *Mutafxhi* (production of sacks and blankets for packing purposes) was a more specific craft which was dependent upon goods transportation routes for wider distribution. The craft of *qylahxhi* is of special importance for these areas for the production of white caps made of sheep's wool originally called *plis* (Statovci 1982:132), a typical hat worn by native Albanian men. In the workshops of the three main centres, Prizren, Gjakove and Peje, particular crafts were developed in order to fulfil the needs of the inhabitants of the Dukagjini Plain (the western part of Kosovo where these cities are situated) and beyond, including *jorganxhi* (duvets and pillows) and *kazaz* (silk and woollen threads, buttons and decorative braid).

Leather processing was of particular economic importance. There were *tabak* (processors of cattle skin) in both Peja (on the Lumbardh River in Peja) and Gjakova (on the river Ereniku) (Statovci 1982:160): in order to process skin the craftsmen needed a plentiful water supply.[1] An important craft related to leather processing was that of the *saraç* (craftsmen producing items made from leather: saddles, belts, weapon holsters, whips, wallets and other small items). Apart from the leatherworkers there were also craftsmen of shoes and other footwear. Other activities in the workshops of the Dukagjini Plain included the working of stone and wood (mainly related to building and civil engineering) and clay for pottery. Wood was also worked in the bazaars in the crafts of *çibukxhi* (production of tobacco pipes) and *nallanexhi* (production of wooden slippers). Other traditional production crafts included *katranxhi*[2] (processing of fat mass out of pinewood), *sapunxhi*[3] (soap producer), *mumxhi* (wax producer) and *duhanxhi* (processors of tobacco).

Service-providing crafts

Production activities are closely related to service provision in the bazaars of the Dukagjini Plain and beyond. The oldest craft, *nallban*[4] (farrier), pertains to the craft of metal processing, a category which also includes *sahatçi* (watchmaker), an activity which came into practice only after the nineteenth century since citizens had previously relied on *sahat-kulla* (public clocks on watchtowers).

Food services depended on the *kasap* (butcher) and the *mullixhi* (flour producers), the main providers since antiquity. Traditionally, bazaars also used to house such servicing crafts as *berber* (barber) and *bojaxhi* (fabric colouring) and in addition there were often mobile craftsmen such as *sharraxhi* (wood-cutting) and others who delivered or provided craft services to citizens at their homes.

It is impossible to make a rigid classification of crafts since some craftsmanship activities embrace elements of both production and service. The production category of metal processers includes the blacksmith, the group of food activity includes the baker, and the *bonbonxhi* (producer of candies). New age activities, mainly dating from the beginning of the

---

[1]The Rivers Ereniku and Lumbardh (Bistrica) are in the Rive Drini i Bardhe Basin.
[2]The person that produces *katran*, a dense liquid produced from the dry distillation of the pine tree. It served to isolate wood from moisture and also as a pharmaceutical product for animals and humans.
[3]The person that produces soap, using animal fat.
[4]The person that shoes horses, oxen and donkeys.

present century, have introduced such food crafts as *çebapçi*[5] to add to such products as *burekxhi* (traditional local pies). The craft of textile production also is wide ranging, including the production of ropes as well as shops specializing in producing traditional bridal clothes.

Crafts and bazaars

Craft production and service are crucial to the understanding of the Kosovan heritage and its role in the formation of Kosovan society. The places and periods in which crafts traditionally have been enabled and practised have a particular significance as signifiers of cultural identity. It is for this reason that the deliberate destruction and reconstruction of bazaars is so momentous, both culturally and architecturally. They have a historical resonance which goes deeper than quotidian function. They are, moreover, of considerable architectural significance. Social and economic developments in Kosovo, and more widely in South-East Europe as a whole, have been shaped by the centuries-long presence of the Ottoman Empire. A dynamic architecture was fostered, characterized by its responsiveness to the environment and to human needs, while achieving levels of sustainability which are in harmony with current thinking and trends in contemporary sustainable architecture: bazaars exemplify this.

Having in mind the cultural and historical importance of the bazaar, this chapter is focused on the evaluation and assessment of the Grand Bazaar of Gjakova and the Long Bazaar of Peja, both destroyed during the war in Kosovo in 1998–9, and both subsequently reconstructed. The chapter will address the questions of how and why they were reconstructed, by whom, how much was lost and what was gained through the destruction and subsequent reinstatement of these ensembles. While the two bazaars are comparable in function, the circumstances of the respective reconstructions are rather different, partly because of the greater size and importance of the Gjakova bazaar, and partly because of the availability of detailed documentation dating from 1979.

Historical development of Gjakova and Peja

The development of urban settlements on the Dukagjini Plain took place in four main historical periods: Byzantium, the Medieval, the Ottoman period and the years of socialism (Dukagjini 1978: 96). The significant phases

---

[5]The person that prepares *çebap*. This word originated from the Turkish *kebap* ('pieces of cut meat'): food made of grilled, ground meat, a popular food in the Balkan countries since the period of the Ottoman Empire.

of the recent past should also be added to this development: the years of
Milosevic's occupation, the break-up of Yugoslavia and the declaration of
Kosovan independence in 2008.

Gjakova and Peja, two large cities on the Dukagjini Plain,[6] together with
Prizren represent the biggest urban settlements in the western part of Kosovo.
This fertile plain, with a mild continental climate, is bounded by mountains
from which springs the river Drini i Bardhë, the basin of which has evidence
of prehistoric dwellings. Gjakova municipality lies in the western part of
the Dukagjini Region (the plain and its surrounding mountains), covering
an area of about 521 km², with a population of about 150,000, although
official data from the last census (Kosovo Statistical Office) in 2011 shows
that only 94,556 inhabitants were registered in the municipality (Demjaha
2015: 109).

Peja municipality, in the north-eastern part of the Dukagjini Region,
covers an area of approximately 603 km². According to its Municipal
Development Plan, Peja has a population of about 122,000 inhabitants
(Demjaha 2015: 98), while the census of 2011 shows that 96,450
inhabitants were registered.[7] There has been a settlement in Peja since
ancient Illyrian-Roman times when it was known as Siparantum. During
the medieval period it was variously called Pech, Peka, Pentza, Forno and
Peja, while in Latin documents (in the Medieval period) it was Pechi. When
the Turks came they brought the strong influence of spiritual and material
Ottoman culture to this area (Municipality of Peja 2014).

The Grand Bazaar of Gjakova

Gjakova was mentioned as a settlement and market place for the first
time in 1485. In 1662, the Ottoman travel writer Evlia Çelebiu wrote that
'Jakova' had 2,000 houses, two beautiful mosques, inns, one Turkish bath
and about 300 shops with about 1,000 crafts (Municipality of Gjakova
2014). Numerous rivers passing through this municipality – Krena, Ereniku
and especially the river Drini i Bardhë – make Gjakova rich with natural
resources, including the very important natural monument Kanjoni i Urës së
Fshenjtë (Canyon of the Holy Bridge).

---

[6]According to geographical, social and economic features, Kosovo is divided into two main
entireties which are defined by two plains: the Dukagjini Plain is located in the western part
and the Kosovo Plain located in the eastern part of the Republic of Kosovo.
[7]Kosovo has been faced with statistical problems for almost half a century. The century-long
conflict between autochthonous Albanians and the different governments that administered the
province made accurate and credible regular censuses impossible. In the censuses that did take
place, sometimes the Albanians abstained, many times the Serbs abstained, but there is some
suspicion that those administering the processes manipulated the results.

In the nineteenth century Gjakova had two bazaars: the Grand Bazaar, now reconstructed, and the Small Bazaar, which has almost completely disappeared. The animal and goods market (which no longer exists) was situated between the two. This was a place of exchange between shopkeepers and the villagers who brought animals and agricultural goods from the rural areas.

The bazaar

The Grand Bazaar in Gjakova, covering 34,000 m², is one of the largest of its type, not only for Kosovo but even more widely. It has been registered as a protected monument by law since 1955 (Municipality of Gjakova 2014) (No. E. K. 59/55, Ministry of Culture, Youth and Sports), with the current, updated description:

> The urban entirety of the Grand Bazaar contains 525 important buildings. It is known as the biggest bazaar in South Eastern Europe. It used to perform the function of craftsmanship, trade and central administration. Now it is a cultural-historical, touristic, craftsmanship and commercial compound. All events that are related to the city of Gjakova are related also to the development of the Grand Bazaar. An architectonic characteristic is its build; the building style is traditional, with local material: stone, wood, bricks, old roof tile, lead etc.

In the past the bazaar was central to the socio-economic and cultural development of the Gjakova region, where much craftsmanship and other service-providing activities took place. The basic unit of the bazaar is the shop, which may be of one or two storeys. Both have a public, service area at the front, often with a workshop at the back or, in the case of the two-storey buildings, upstairs. Over four centuries, the bazaar was successively developed in three directions leading from the nucleus of the site, the Mosque of Hadumi. Textile crafts were sited in the northern part, along with more delicate crafts such as watchmakers and silversmiths. In the southern part there were warehouses (wheat, salt, etc.), duvet producers, final leather processors, metalsmiths (for barrels, plates, pots and kettles), tailors and bakers. Today there are still similar shops in this part of the bazaar. To the west there were wood workshops and more warehouses.

The walls of shops were made of *çerpiq* (clay and straw bricks), reinforced by *hatulla* (wooden beams). The foundations were of stone and the roof was covered by *çeremide* (tiles). Doors and windows (frames and shutters) were of wood. Despite spontaneous (unplanned) development, the bazaar conveyed some unwritten overall principles which make this complex even more specific. The homogeneous composition with a harmony of forms and materials, together with the scale and intimate proportions, makes this urban architectonic entirety attractive for both local inhabitants and tourists. The natural materials used in the construction, obtained from nature nearby, make this compound even more embedded in both the urban and natural environment.

Transformations of the bazaar

The transformations to which the Grand Bazaar has been subjected may be considered as part of an unstoppable process. Its unplanned evolution was a process of transformation in content and size, with shops being added, renewed and adapted to changing functional requirements within the constraints of the overall, established forms. The bazaar had almost achieved its current size by the late nineteenth century when Gjakova was at the height of its development and size.

Apart from positive transformations, the Grand Bazaar has also suffered the usual endangering threats of weather, humidity, air pollution, as well as occasional fires. Road traffic has been particularly damaging – an adjacent route connects the city with settlements to the south – and heavy vehicles especially have caused damage through vibrations. The desire to accommodate such vehicles has led to the banal and architecturally damaging reduction in the overhang of roofs in order to allow them to pass.

In 1999 the Grand Bazaar of Gjakova was seriously damaged during the armed conflict (Figure 1). Together with other culturally and historically

FIGURE 1 *Grand Bazaar of Gjakova, 1999. Source: Osman Gojani, Institute for Monument Protection in Gjakova.*

significant monuments in the city it was burned to the ground. This was the greatest damage ever inflicted on this urban and architectonic entirety of great cultural and historical value. The reconstruction of the bazaar was then facilitated through the contributions of such international organizations as USAID and CORDAID (Catholic Organisation for Relief and Development Aid) from the Netherlands (Municipality of Gjakova 2016) (Figure 2).

Prior to its destruction, the Grand Bazaar had been rehabilitated in its entirety in the 1980s after a detailed technical investment document had been drawn up in 1979 by experts from the Republican Institute for Protection of Monuments in Sarajevo and the Faculty of Architecture in Sarajevo. This documentation was also to provide the basis for the later post-war reconstruction. The interventions in the 1980s were carried out by state institutions and they were generally appropriate. Following a decree in 1968, sixty-eight shops located in the southern part of the bazaar had been demolished to provide space for the construction of a new school. This action triggered the recognition of the need to take care of this compound and in 1971 the Institute for Protection of Monuments in Belgrade carried out architectural recording of most of the shops. The recording process was carried out over several years by local architects and students of architecture, mainly from Kosovo. The bazaar was also damaged when a corridor for heavy vehicles was opened to accommodate the transport of minerals from the Deva mine. At the end of the 1970s, the deep, sheltering overhangs of the roofs of the shops were cut back in order to make way for passing trucks and, later, there was a raising of some sections of the road level. In some cases this intervention reached over 60 cm and caused serious problems in the normal functioning of the shops. This steady deterioration prompted

FIGURE 2 *Grand Bazaar of Gjakova, 2016. Source: Bujar Demjaha.*

the creation of a Regulation Plan for the bazaar (Government of Kosovo 1982).[8] As well as addressing legal and ownership questions, the plan prescribed technical criteria: roofs were to be tiled in the traditional manner but old construction material could be replaced by new materials, aimed at achieving sustainability. So the identity and some of the authenticity of the Grand Bazaar of Gjakova were preserved as further destruction was prevented. An acceptable compromise was made for roads and pavements: *kalldërma* (roads paved with cobblestones) were replaced by roads paved with square blocks enabling easier movement for pedestrians and vehicles without endangering the authenticity of the bazaar. The rehabilitation was successfully achieved through keeping active a great many of the traditional crafts in the bazaar and complementing them with new service activities (TV services, boutiques, cafes and restaurants), bringing back life and so sustaining the value of the whole ensemble. The entire process of revitalizing the Grand Bazaar in this period was successful, being organized in a legal manner with the establishment of a professional committee appointed by the local government, based on the decision mentioned above. Work on the revitalization of the bazaar was in part implemented separately within the overall plan for each of the shops: owners made financial investments and employed local masters for the technical works.

The interventions of the 1980s conducted in the Grand Bazaar of Gjakova, despite the loss of authenticity in materials, managed to preserve the spirit of the bazaar. But the interventions of the first decade of the twenty-first century may be regarded as less correct, seriously diminishing the cultural and historical value of the bazaar as an urban architectonic entirety. The documentation prepared in 1979 was not used in the best possible manner in the post-war reconstruction. Serious changes were made in measure and proportion, shape and materials. In most cases shops were built taller than before, without wooden shutters, with fronts of large sheets of plate glass rather than the traditional small panes. The pavement was changed: instead of stone blocks, low-quality stones were used which do not correspond with the environment at all. Changes in use have also been damaging as traditional crafts have been replaced by new functions considered by conservation and restoration specialists to amount to a serious devastation. Viewed more positively, there may be some mitigating circumstances in the great need to enable a return to commercial activity and normal life following the devastation as soon as possible. But this encouraged interventions which perhaps were carried out too quickly and individually, without the benefit of an overall plan for the complex as a whole, as a result of which the Grand Bazaar of Gjakova has lost a large part of its traditional charm and splendour.

---

[8]Decision Fz.25/82 of the Government of Kosovo, published in the Official Gazette of KSAK (1982) on the Regulation Plan of the Grand Bazaar in Gjakova.

The Long Bazaar of Peja

Peja (and indeed the Dukagjini Plain in general) before the war in 1998–9 was distinguished by its *kullas* (fortified stone houses) of the twelfth and thirteenth centuries (many of which were targeted and destroyed in the war), *saraje* (mansions), mosques, *teqe* and *tyrbe* (mausolea), *mesxhid* (mosques without minarets), cemeteries, mills, *hane* (inns), clock towers, bridges, *shatërvan* (fountains), *çesme* (public freshwater spring) and *hamamet* (public baths). In the western suburb, the Catholic Church and the distinguished monument of the Orthodox Patriarchy of Peja are located. Numerous rivers passing through this settlement, especially the river of Lumbardh (Bistrica river) and Rugova Gorge, make Peja one of the municipalities with the richest natural resources in Kosovo.

The Long Bazaar

The Long Bazaar in Peja is one of the biggest compounds of this character in Kosovo, covering an area of around 23,000 m². Protected since 1970 (No. 02–50/70) it is described in the updated records of the Ministry of Culture, Youth and Sports as follows:

> The old bazaar of Peja as an historical and urban agglomeration began to be realized in the second half of the fifteenth century. This bazaar in its entirety was created to meet the needs of urbanism in the city with the purpose of developing crafts and trade according to the *esnaf* (association of craftsmen) principle of being localized on certain roads. This was a characteristic organization in which winding roads had the character of independent bazaars and trade. This form of division of bazaar according to certain activities is characteristic of the Ottoman-Turkish system which was spread to Albanian areas also, but which was given local elements by local masters. Peja Bazaar is composed of the grand bazaar and the long bazaar. Within each bazaar there were shops on the ground and upper floors as well as residential buildings. The bazaar of Peja was burned down several times. Lastly it was burned by Serbian forces. After the war, local institutions carried out the project for the restoration of the bazaar which is ongoing.

As in Gjakova, Peja also had two bazaars: the Long Bazaar and the Small Bazaar. This chapter deals with the Long Bazaar only. It was the economic centre and oldest part of the city. The Long Bazaar dates from the fifteenth century when the first craftsmen started providing their products. Similar to other bazaars (such as the Grand Bazaar of Gjakova) the Long Bazaar of Peja was begun at the time of the building of the Bajrakli (Bazaar) Mosque (fifteenth century). Later it was completed with other service-providing buildings such as inns, religious schools, public baths, a stone bridge, stone houses of feudal families and cemeteries. This bazaar was an authentic urban compound with original architecture that possessed valuable cultural and historical values. The basic unit of this bazaar (as in Gjakova) is the shop, both single and two-storeyed. Some of the latter had a full-size upper storey and some had only attics. In all cases the entry served for customers and the back part or upper floor for the workshop. The use of the spaces was necessarily varied according to the activity: selling, production and warehousing. It is important to note that shops on the southern side of each road were single storey to allow sunlight to reach the opposite side of the street. Similarly to the bazaar in Gjakova, certain roads were dedicated to particular crafts and activities and were often named after the crafts which dominated. As in Gjakova, the walls of shops were built in *çerpiq* (clay and straw bricks), reinforced by *hatulla* (wooden beams). Foundations were of stone and the roof of *çeremide* (tiles). The frames and shutters of doors and windows were of wood.

Transformations of the bazaar

As in other parts of the old city, the Long Bazaar has, from its Ottoman beginnings to the present day, experienced great changes. Some of these have been in response to the risk of flooding from unregulated river beds, others from the need to cater for a wider range of products and services as the city grew in size and became a commercial centre for the region (Çerreti 2012: 31). Throughout the development there was a tendency towards greater decoration in both the interior and exterior of the bazaar. Although some changes were made under an institutional umbrella, many in the later twentieth century were carried out by the shop owners themselves who wished to expand their properties by increasing ground floor areas and adding storeys above. The number of doors and windows was increased and modern, non-traditional materials used. Concrete cubes replaced cobblestones in the pavements. But, the most difficult period in the history of the bazaar was during the conflict in Kosovo in 1999 when it was looted and burned in an organized and deliberate manner (Figure 3).

The situation of this complex after the war was desperate. Local institutions, monitored by international agencies, were not able to carry out dignified interventions. There was a fragility in the relationship between the parallel administrative units, the United Nations Interim Administration Mission in Kosovo (UNMIK) and the inexperienced institutions which were understaffed and lacked expertise. There were delays in decision-making about the manner and extent of reconstruction which was required. Eventually, after several years of waiting, the complex began to be reconstructed by the owners themselves, monitored by the Regional Centre for Cultural Heritage in Peja. Unlike the situation in Gjakova there had been no comprehensive recording of the bazaar before its destruction, so the reconstruction was carried out without the benefit of proper technical documentation, except in the few cases where recording had been carried out. This was to the great

FIGURE 3 *Long Bazaar of Peja, 1999. Source: Dini Begolli, Institute for Monument Protection in Peja.*

FIGURE 4 *Long Bazaar of Peja, 2016. Source: Bujar Demjaha.*

detriment of the bazaar. In expanding the surface area and the volume of shops, owners compromised any sense of compositional unity and produced disordered and irregular façades. The absence of order in the scale, measure and proportion of the reconstructed shops has seriously damaged the urban landscape of the entire ensemble (Figure 4).

The Long Bazaar of Peja, although reconstructed at last, has lost such important elements as the fortified stone house (*kulla*) of the Gora family, as well as many characteristic details, losing the sense of intimacy and harmony of both the individual components and the whole.

A bazaar reconstructed for new generations

Kosovan cities were spontaneously created in favourable natural conditions. Bazaars were substantial components which essentially symbolized the spirit of the city. Those in Gjakova and Peja were particularly important not simply because they were located in the centre of the city but because of the sense of identity which they demonstrated; the memory and history which they embodied. The place in which they were located, the reason why and the manner in which these compounds were established were original and authentic and as such they are considered to be icons of the cities.

Both bazaars discussed in this chapter are urban-architectonic entireties that suffered great destruction during the war of 1998–9. Their hopeless situation – a gradual deterioration followed by permanent devastation – raised the question of whether it was worth reconstructing them, since any destruction takes away a considerable part of the value of the cultural heritage. But the cities of Gjakova and Peja would never be the same without their bazaars. It is not that the same value was brought back to the two cities with the reconstruction of the bazaars, but at least it has helped to bring back the memory they embody and, above all, brought back the spirit that these two urban ensembles contribute to the cities. The unplanned spontaneity of the establishment and development of these bazaars, their frequent accidental burning in the past, and their permanent transformations all inform the history and powerful memory of these places, which drives the desire for reconstruction. Although the reconstructed bazaar will never be the bazaar it used to be, it will continue to maintain the balance in the urban development, preserving the historical continuity of the development of the city, safeguarding the spirit of both old and current cities, so contributing to the city in the future. If reconstruction is not accompanied by an approach of integrated rehabilitation, then it would not fulfil the most important intentions of this action. In Gjakova and Peja, both bazaars now need an action plan giving meaning to their existence as living organisms, ensuring that the shops are fully operational, with activities that are not contrary to the character of the bazaar but complement it.

Ultimately, the reconstruction of these bazaars sends a clear message to potential destroyers in the future: that if they destroy a monument or urban entirety with cultural and historical values, they will not succeed in eradicating it from the face of the earth. The urban, architectonic and artistic complexity of these bazaars made any intervention a complex issue.

It was fortunate in the case of the Grand Bazaar of Gjakova that there was very good documentation (even though it was not used to its fullest capacity) enabling its reconstruction to be more correct and faithful than that of the Long Bazaar in Peja. The experience with the bazaar of Gjakova teaches us that the drafting of documents about the current state of selected monuments or complexes would be a valuable asset in their management today and in the process of possible reconstruction in the future. But it is almost impossible for a small and economically underdeveloped country such as Kosovo to manage to record all monuments and to keep such records up to date as situations change. But, initiating such a process, through the involvement of students and the creation of prioritized lists of monuments, would be a smart move for countries in danger of armed conflict (or natural disaster). International organizations (United Nations and European Union) should be ready to establish interim decision-making mechanisms in countries at war, in order to take care of the cultural heritage.

References

Čelić, Dž. (1980), 'Fenomen Sarajevske čaršije', *Zbornik zaštite spomenika*, 26/27: 255–9.

Çerreti, D. (2012), Pitanje zastite historijski jezgra na podrucju Kosova, Doctoral dissertation, Faculty of Architecture, University of Sarajevo.

Demjaha, B. (2015), *Role of Tourism in Rural Development in Dukagjini Region in Kosovo*, Doctoral dissertation, Vienna: Faculty of Architecture and Spatial Planning, University of Technology.

Demjaha, B. (2016), *Changing the Concept of Spatial Organization of Rural Schools in the Function of Developing the Rural Areas of Kosovo*, Doctoral dissertation, Sarajevo: Faculty of Architecture, University of Sarajevo.

Dukagjini, E. (1978), 'Posleratni razvoj urbanih naselja Dukagjina i njihove funkcije', *UDK Ljubljana*, 93–8.

Government of Kosovo (1982), Decision Fz.25/82 'Regulation Plan of Grand Bazaar in Gjakova,' *KSAK Official Gazette* (1982): 666–72.

Hadrović, A. (2008), *Bioclimatic Architecture: Searching for the Path to Haven*, North Charleston, CA: BookSurge.

Municipality of Gjakova (2014), *Vështrim i shkurtër historik për komunën e Gjakovës*.

Municipality of Peja (2014), *Qyteti dhe Historia*, available online: https://kk.rks-gov.net/peje/Municipality-(1)/Qyteti-dhe-Historia.aspx (accessed 1 July 2016).

Statovci, D. (1982), *Zhvillimi historiki zejtarisë dhe rëndësia e saj bashkëkohore ne strukturën ekonomike-shoqërore të KSA të Kosovës*, Prishtinë: Instituti Albanologjik i Prishtinës.

PART 2

Reconstruction in Contemporary Style after Conflict

Introduction

Conflict often produces damage of such scale and severity that large-scale opportunities for replanning and redesigning are offered – for example, at the scale of a region, country or countries rather than more locally, as is more often the case with other disasters such as fire. 'Opportunity' is often the word used by politicians and built environment professionals in such cases, although it is a difficult concept for those who have lost family members, friends, homes and livelihoods to accept. The wider scale does indeed provide opportunity for physical reconstruction to adopt new and contemporary forms, much less constrained by surviving cultural contexts and morphological frames than was the case in the examples discussed in the previous section.

The decision-making processes can much more closely relate to a contemporary *zeitgeist*, and this would include factors such as dominant paradigms in professional values and education, economic factors influencing property development and management, and wider cultural factors. A prominent example – but there are others – is the rise of international Modernism, large-scale industrial production and globalization in the mid-twentieth century, all of which had a profound impact on the nature of reconstruction following the Second World War; and a counter-movement, the post-industrial rise of the conservation movement, heritage industry and heritage tourism, which revalued tradition and context, and have had equal impact on both more recent post-conflict reconstruction and, over half a century later, on the fate of the physical products of mid-century reconstruction.

One problem with seeking to systematically explore approaches is the complex and sometimes contradictory nature of what takes place over significant spatial and temporal scales. There is rarely a single uniform ideological approach: the *zeitgeist* and dominant paradigms change, and do not influence every place equally. So replication of destroyed structures in one location may be accompanied, in another, by wholly contemporary construction. The examples in this section clearly demonstrate the varied nature and outcomes of decision-making processes, although it does lean more to understanding decisions to reconstruct in contemporary forms, styles and materials.

The section begins with a study of contrasting examples in England by Peter Larkham and David Adams, forming a strong link with section 1. On the whole approaches in England differed from those elsewhere across Europe. There was far less facsimile reconstruction of lost historic structures, far less evident influence of local context and traditional forms, structures and materials, and far more overt influence of Modernism in scale, form and style. This perhaps resulted from the concentration of destruction in the large industrial cities. There were deliberately targeted raids on historic towns, and here the reconstruction did show some greater historicism although, as in Exeter, this was often a generic Georgian-influenced classicism rather than genuinely local traditional vernacular. Larkham and Adams explore industrial Birmingham and Coventry, showing the range of influences in the country's 'second city' resulting in Modernism and a technocentric focus on heavy infrastructure. But Birmingham's centre had been extensively developed (or redeveloped) in the industrial era, while Coventry – although also strongly industrial – had far more late-medieval and early-modern survivors. But a radical new political elite introduced a radical young city architect, and Modernism and infrastructure also dominated here – with the additional complication in terms of authenticity that some surviving timber-framed buildings, damaged or inconveniently surviving in the city core, were demolished, stored and re-erected on another location to create almost a 'museum street'. An important specialist architect influenced this, acting against the diktats of an otherwise influential conservation body, the Society for the Protection of Ancient Buildings (SPAB). In Bath, however, the context of a much more uniform urban landscape was different, and the influence of SPAB more noticeable, although it is here, among the Georgian stone terraces, that the rare facsimile infill examples are found. Yet a facsimile challenges ideas of originality and authenticity; instead, 'character' emerges as a major issue for English planning in the post-war period.

Marieke Kuipers gives a number of examples of approaches in the Netherlands, again following the Second World War. Her examples illustrate a wider range of possible solutions considered by architects and municipalities, for example, at Sluis Town Hall ranging from retention as a ruin, demolition and contemporary replacement, or various levels of repair/ restoration. Although 'restoration to the old medieval form', including replication of lost parts, was the decision in this case, the key decision-maker Jan Kalf, a long-standing influential figure in conservation, was only too clearly aware of the dangers of a 'run into romanticism' and that future generations would have different opinions about conservation. Elsewhere, reconstructions resulted in what Kuipers refers to as 'typical compromise' decisions which may use modern materials or contemporary artwork. In Middelburg this is articulated, by Kalf, as a dual approach of conscious conservation and contemporary design. This duality is problematic, and individuals, even Kalf, might not be consistent in their views. Even he wished to see the gothic façade of Middelburg town hall 'restored to its old splendour'. And there are apparent conflicts in how these projects are seen and promoted; some in more contemporary form apparently less authentic than other replication or reconstruction projects. This dualism might, decades later, be seen as problematic.

Reconstruction in France following both world wars is covered by Danièle Voldman. The severity of damage during the First World War led to well-known examples of replication: but regionalism dominated architectural theory, and planning was scarcely a distinct profession. In 1945, though, functionalism and Modernism were much more significant, but simultaneously the Monuments Historiques department was trying to ensure 'faithful conservation'. On the whole, though, there was a move towards straightening and widening streets, 'cleaning-up' districts, and thus, especially after 1945, zoning of land uses. Many places were rationalized and a Corbusian Modernism was frequently influential (Voldman suggests that the post-1945 Ministry of Reconstruction had been 'seduced' by it). Yet old structures remained, and the problem of balancing old and new was significant in places such as Caen and Marseille. On the whole the choice of tradition or modernity was heavily influenced by the concept of *patrimoine* and the treatment of history by the administration in power, as well as professional ideology.

Moving to a more recent context, David Johnson presents an architect's perspective of reconstruction in South-East Europe and Georgia following the conflicts and socio-economic/political changes from the early 1990s, and focusing primarily on Council of Europe projects. He makes the point that heritage management systems were then, and indeed remain, in a process of development and refinement. Further, there is a problem of skills and expertise relating to heritage and reconstruction. Hence decisions may be taken for reasons of local expediency. Rural areas are facing depopulation and even abandonment, with traditional buildings undervalued, especially by a tourist economy. Hence contemporary approaches, materials and designs are often used, but at the price of eroding the character of the traditional vernacular. In urban contexts, though, more complex and explicitly politicized views often dominate, especially given the extremely problematic nature of the conflicts. In restoring Sarajevo's City Hall, for example, restoration has obliterated all traces of the conflict, 'erasing the impact from the memory of the community'. In Prizren, Kosovo, reconstruction was not 'purist' and ease of procurement and maintenance of materials clearly influenced decision-making. Overall, Johnson notes that each case of damage and reconstruction needs to be approached and understood individually. It is difficult to propose standard or generic approaches for contemporary cases, and the examples in this section show that this is even more true in looking back to the examples of previous generations. We can try to understand 'why' and 'how', but we should try to avoid value judgement such as 'right' or 'wrong'.

This section also raises problems of meaning. Kuipers, for example, makes the important point that there are distinctions between languages and ideologies, even if the same words are used in translations; the English 'reconstruction' is not always the same as the Dutch *herstel, herbouw, wederopbouw* or *reconstructive*. This issue is too easily forgotten in making international comparisons. Voldman also notes that 'reconstitution' was more commonly used than 'reconstruction' in post–First World War France and, while legislation referred to new work being 'the same', this was taken to mean similar rather than identical. Such problems of interpretation, whether in translation or implementation, mean that discussing cause, intention and even actual construction remains difficult. These chapters have illuminated, but not resolved, these difficulties.

Chapter 2.1

Originality and Authenticity in the Post-War Reconstruction of Britain

Peter J. Larkham and David Adams

Introduction

The concept of 'authenticity', however defined, seems rather at odds with almost all of the planned and built reconstruction of British towns and cities following the Second World War. There was indeed damage and destruction of traditional, 'historic', urban places ranging from individual buildings to entire streets and quarters, and this spurred much thinking about the identification of what might be regarded as worthy of preservation, and indeed its nature.

The nature of much post–Second World War rebuilding in England evidently differs from much of that elsewhere in Europe – although it is equally clear that there was little consensus, but much debate, on matters of form and style in countries such as France and East and West Germany (Nasr 1997). In particular, there was little explicit discussion of 'authenticity' and very little facsimile replication of what had been destroyed. This is despite widespread professional knowledge of post–First World War reconstruction in the professional, academic and public media and through battlefield tourism (Cammaerts 1925, Lloyd 1998). The facsimile reconstruction in post–Second World War Europe similarly made little direct impression, although the example of Warsaw was widely published.

The form of post–Second World War reconstruction in Britain was heavily influenced by a range of ideologies and issues, and this led to a dominance of urban forms, infrastructures and buildings inspired by European Modernism. The damage was widely seen by built environment professionals as an 'opportunity' (cf. Tubbs 1942). Although the reconstruction provided opportunities for refining ideas about conservation, originality and authenticity, and this is most clearly seen in approaches to bombed churches (Larkham 2010), the replication of damaged or destroyed forms was very rare. There was a limited use of fragments and architectural salvage, but radical, new and often large-scale forms dominated the new urban landscapes. This chapter uses a wide range of examples, from the smaller scale of dealing with individual bombed buildings to the largest scale of citywide visions of reconstruction to explore the origin and influence of such approaches. The Midlands cities of Birmingham and Coventry are a particular focus for attention. Heavily damaged, including historic buildings, their municipal approaches to reconstruction and the contemporary responses of citizens differed significantly; but both became icons of reconstruction – so how they dealt with the past in their visions of the future is instructive. Bath, a city of historic terraces, provides a counter-example where authenticity and replication might be expected to play a much larger role in reconstruction.

Many conventional histories of conservation (for example, Glendinning 2013) note the significant influence in English conservation theory and practice of the Society for the Protection of Ancient Buildings (SPAB). It would, therefore, be expected that its concept of 'authenticity' would be influential in the actions of the post-war reconstruction. This chapter, however, argues that other factors, such as the scale and nature of the damage, ownership and funding, and the ideas of dominant decision-makers such as city planners, were dominant especially in the earlier years of reconstruction. The Society's impact on post-bombing activities is best shown by its pamphlet *The Treatment of Ancient Buildings Damaged in War Time* (SPAB undated, c. 1941). This 'outlined the policy which *should* be adopted' (our emphasis). It focused primarily on churches and timber-frame buildings, and reiterated SPAB ideas about replication, new work not being mistaken for original, and on the focus for 'respect for the entire building as a work of art'. It also reiterates the SPAB view against confusing new work with original; something done 'in the exact manner of a past period . . . is historically misleading'.

The war damage

In this new 'total war', major attacks on English towns between 7 September 1940 and 16 May 1941 alone included 71 raids on London involving 18,291 tons of bombs, 8 on Liverpool/Birkenhead with 1,957 tons, 8 on Birmingham with 1,852 tons, down to 1 on Cardiff with 115 tons (the National Archives (hereafter TNA) AIR 41/17). By November 1945 the War Damage Commission had been notified of damage to 3,281,953 separate properties (TNA ADM 1/19037). In August 1946 the Ministry of Health estimated that, for the United Kingdom as a whole, 22,000 houses were destroyed/damaged beyond repair; 4,698,000 damaged in some way (light/ heavy) (Titmuss 1950: 329–30).

Although in some places, particularly the centre of London, there were substantial expanses of damaged and cleared sites, in many other locations the damage was quite scattered. For example, a journalist on the *Birmingham Weekly Post* noted that 'the Birmingham newspapers reported German bombing as indiscriminate ... We could never get a clear impression about the areas on which the raiders were concentrating, and so it seemed to us that the bombing was pretty general, all over the city' (H. J. Black, interviewed by Sutcliffe 1967–9: 2–3).

In many places, maps of bombs and damage survive, allowing detailed understanding of the nature and extent of the damage. However, the detail of the mapping varies from place to place, as does the categorizing of the damage. Hull, for example, uses the categories of total destruction, serious and slight damage. The City of London, in contrast, showed 'demolished', 'destroyed or partially destroyed with shell of two or more floors still standing' and 'ditto but with three floors or more standing'. Birmingham, Plymouth and others merely plotted the fall of bombs (Woolven 2005: 15). Although comparison is therefore complicated, it is possible to suggest some of the scale of damage and destruction from contemporary official statistics which include information on buildings (especially 'houses', but meaning dwellings) destroyed, and on the real extent of damage reported and the area accepted by the government for the legal purposes of reconstruction (a 'declaratory area') (Table 1).

But notwithstanding these categorizations, there is a problem with the language used about the damage, perhaps for propaganda reasons. Some overemphasized the destruction and minimized survival. A report on a lecture on London's bombed churches by Edward Yates FSA, for example, noted that some had been 'completely destroyed except for walls and in some cases steeples' (H. V. M. R. 1941: 575). That does suggest substantial survival; perhaps enough for repair/restoration in other circumstances.

Reconstruction in the industrial midlands

Bomb damage in both Birmingham and Coventry was severe (Table 1), although widely scattered for the former and closely concentrated on the city core for the latter. When in early 1941 the Cabinet Committee on the Reconstruction of Town and Country decided to review four sample heavily bombed areas, both were selected (TNA HLG 71/1570).

In Birmingham, planning was led by Herbert Manzoni, the City Surveyor and Engineer. In a forthright interview to the *Birmingham Mail* (27 February 1941) he stated clearly that 'we have not got to start replanning

TABLE 1 *Areas of damage/reconstruction.*

Town	War damage[1]	Declaratory Order applied[2]	Declaratory Order granted[2]	Number of houses destroyed[3]
Bath				1,214
Birmingham				5,065[4]
Bristol			247	2,909
Coventry			274	4,185
Exeter			75	1,700
Hull	136	300	246	4,184
Liverpool	208		46	5,487
London (all 18 boroughs)			1,312	47,314
Manchester	61		74	1,951
Plymouth			415	3,593
Portsmouth	165	507	431	4,393
Sheffield	108	198		2,906
Southampton	145	514	262	4,136

[1]Estimated figure, in acres, from TNA HLG 71/34.
[2]In acres, from TNA HLG 71/2222 and TNA HLG 71/34
[3]From TNA CAB 87/11 unless otherwise specified. 'Houses' was taken to mean most types of dwelling, including accommodation over commercial premises.
[4]12,125 destroyed according to the City Surveyor and Engineer, Manzoni.

Birmingham. All we want is the opportunity to carry out the plans we have already'. He was asked whether the bomb damage had altered those plans, and the succinct reply was 'no'. Damage was far from a 'clean sweep' and so 'any dream that a completely new city can emerge, Phoenix-like … is quite erroneous'. Manzoni asserted several times that Birmingham's redevelopment ideas predated the bombing (for example, Manzoni 1955: 90). To a great extent the city was ready because of Manzoni's contacts and influence at the national level, not solely because of the pre-war planning. He said that Birmingham was ready 'because we'd shaped the legislation for it, or at least we had been there while it was being shaped' (Sutcliffe 1967–9, Manzoni interview: 4). By 'we' Manzoni meant himself. Thus Manzoni was not in favour of an all-encompassing reconstruction plan, as many other cities were preparing at that time.

Without such a plan, city-centre reconstruction was shaped by the design for a tightly drawn inner ring road, approved via a local Act of Parliament in 1946, and by treating individual street blocks as 'precincts'. The ring road radically altered the existing pattern of streets and plots, and this included major straightening and widening of a 'cross' of streets within the ring. Although work was postponed until 1957 for reasons of national economy, this project required large-scale compulsory purchases of bombed and undamaged property, facilitated by the new legal mechanisms for planning which Manzoni had influenced (for example, including slum clearance in the war damage reconstruction provisions of the 1944 Town and Country Planning Act).

Within the ring, buildings were principally of eighteenth- and nineteenth-century date and were cleared for redevelopment with little compunction until the development of the Central Library at the end of the 'reconstruction era' in the early 1970s. This was an industrial city of relatively recent growth and very little physical fabric remaining from earlier periods. Individual buildings were replaced using new architectural styles and modern materials, although these remained rationed until the mid-1950s and progress was slow. A particular modernism, with façade bays separated by narrow projecting vertical 'fins', became dominant. Two individual structures stand out from this trend: one being an example of stone-faced late Classicism, by a Stafford-based architect (not in a major thoroughfare); the other being the first post-war office building within the city core, built on New Street in 1951–53 by a local architect/developer, Cotton, Ballard and Blow (Figures 1 and 2). Their first designs, of 1949, were plain but, although the application was approved on 26 May 1949, Manzoni asked for 'some improvement in the architectural treatment'. The result has 'rows of sawtooth projections, little pointed iron balustrades on the corner, and a *brise-soleil*. Flashy but undeniably effective' (Foster 2005: 111). This building is now Listed.

The precinct-block developments were pushed by the new City Architect, Alwyn Sheppard Fidler. He was aided by the concentration of landownership in the city core in the hands of the city council (helped by compulsory purchase) and a small number of landed estates and property companies such as the local Hortons' Estate (Hortons undated). He strongly argued in various meetings, widely reported in the professional press, against building lining main thoroughfares (including the inner ring road), and instead recommended pedestrian precincts and advocated towers within city centres (Sheppard Fidler 1959). Many of these ideas were evident in contemporary architectural publications and in other rebuilt cities, although relatively few actually found place in Birmingham. However, they were clearly evident in the Cotton/Gropius plan of 1962 for several blocks along Corporation Street and in the original proposals by the Corporation Street Estates Co. to build shops and an office block. The proposals had been 'recently modified to include a "raised shopping floor" with bridges over intervening streets. This would enable Birmingham to be the first city to carry out Mr Marples' idea of segregating pedestrians and motor traffic' (*Architect and Building*

FIGURE 1 *23–4 Bennett's Hill, Birmingham, by E. Bower Norris of Stafford, 1961. Unusually late historicism, but inauthentic. Source: P. J. Larkham.*

News 6 April 1960: 433: Marples was then Minister of Transport). The developer 'sees the scheme growing to include nearby sites not in the group's possession'. When built the segregation was achieved through underpasses (many of which have since been removed). Precincts included civic uses

FIGURE 2 *Grosvenor House, New Street, Birmingham, by Cotton, Ballard & Blow, 1951–3. Novel style which might be more authentic on a seafront. Source: P. J. Larkham.*

as well as retail/commercial, including a civic centre and law courts; and precinct designs were often rectilinear, paying little heed to street, block or plot patterns (Figure 3).

In Coventry the situation was very different. A young, modernist city architect, Donald Gibson, had been appointed just before the war. He and his equally young, radical team had prepared plans for the city core, and held a well-received public exhibition, shortly before the most destructive raid. This medieval walled city still had substantial surviving buildings and structures, but the medieval street patterns were now very congested; the plan proposed civic and retail precincts in open lawned space, and formed the basis for the adopted reconstruction plan despite some disagreements between Gibson and the long-serving city engineer, Ernest Ford (Gould and Gould 2016).

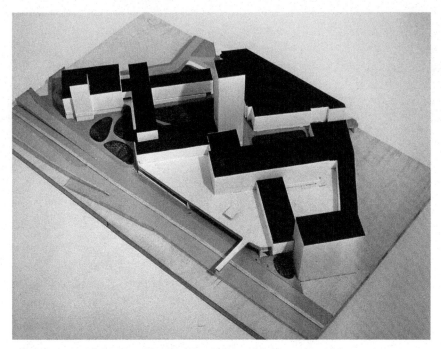

FIGURE 3 *Model of proposed Law Courts precinct, Birmingham, showing rectilinear form unrelated to road or building lines. Source: reproduced with the permission of the Library of Birmingham, BCC Acc. 1999/077 box 22/67, print dated September 1962.*

Again a ring road was designed, tightly drawn around the centre, with numerous underpasses, flyovers and roundabouts. While some of the plans suggested equally radical restructuring of the inner road pattern, in the event there was considerable survival of streets (except in the retail quarter); but historic plot patterns were again removed by the larger scale of redevelopment proposals. Many of the buildings originally proposed – and some actually built – were of a form that was later derided as toothpaste architecture: squeezed out of a tube and cut off to the desired length (Aldous 1975: 57). The retail redevelopment included a radical new form, the Precinct, which originally segregated pedestrians, vehicles and servicing. Many of the earlier reconstruction buildings were plain (partly a response to the financial situation); some virtually a 'stripped Classical', others with what has been described as 'regular "hole-in-wall" windows edged in white stone' (Gould and Gould 2016: 26) – the slightly projecting narrow stone edging became virtually a countrywide style.

A high-profile problem for the city's reconstruction was the destruction of the cathedral. The tower and outer walls remained. The Secretary of the Central Council for the Care of Churches disliked the idea of keeping the cathedral as a ruin, and favoured restoration (letter of 30 December 1940), the Mayor favoured an improved replica, Ford a new design in the style of the old and Gibson a modern design but retaining the tower (quoted by Campbell 1996: 23). SPAB argued for a 'harmonious' modern rebuilding within the retained shell (Glendinning 2013: 254–6). The cathedral Provost sought Sir Giles Gilbert Scott's advice: he suggested 'not an archaeologically accurate copy but a reinterpretation' (Campbell 1996: 23; see also Scott's papers in the British Architectural Library). Scott was invited to prepare a design, but this was disliked by the newly appointed bishop and the public (see *Coventry Evening Telegraph* 15 February 1944). Despite recasting the design neither the bishop nor the Royal Fine Art Commission approved, the latter feeling that 'as full a use as was possible should be made of the ruins' (RFAC Minutes 12 July 1946 and Memorandum 11 December 1946, TNA BP 1/9). Scott then resigned (citing age and lack of wish for a battle: Scott papers, BAL 88/1/530). The subsequent architectural competition, and Spence's winning design, are well known (Campbell 1996). Personalities, ideologies and arguments over appropriate settings for contemporary worship were key to these decisions; but treatment of the original ruins, evident by the RFAC comments and their prominence in the competition information, was significant. No competitor proposed an authentic replication, relatively few proposed rebuilding on the site, and it is suggested that many who had actually visited the site wished to retain the ruins (*The Builder* 24 September 1951).

Elsewhere in the city, some timber-framed buildings had been damaged (such as Ford's Hospital) or found themselves in the way of redevelopment proposed by the approved plan. In fact the survival of timber buildings which had survived the blitz was poor: 240 survived the war, 10 were recorded by the National Buildings Record in 1958 but only 34 remained when surveyed by the timber conservation specialist F. W. B. Charles in 1965 (Gould and Gould 2016: 76). The regimes of Gibson and his successor, Arthur Ling, were not sympathetic. This is clearly shown by the proposal by Gibson's office to remove some surviving parts of the city wall, which led the Chief Inspector of Ancient Monuments to write of Gibson that 'it is, of course, quite clear that the Coventry planner, who is a malignant, has paid no attention at all to ancient monuments because he dislikes them' (memo 4 December 1952, TNA WORK 14/1781). One bay of the *c.* 1529 Ford's Hospital was badly damaged but was repaired by local architect W. S. Hattrell in 1951–53 using salvaged timbers – although this itself seems contrary to SPAB views – but the adjoining and unscathed timber-framed building was removed. There was discussion involving Gibson about moving the hospital, but as a scheduled ancient monument and (from 1955) a Grade I listed building, it remained *in situ*. The Gibson view was expressed in the *Architect and Building News*:

An unnecessary problem, it seems, is created by Ford's Hospital. It has been bombed and for all practical purposes demolished [but see Figure 4].

FIGURE 4 *Ford's Hospital, Coventry, after bombing. Source: reproduced from Richards, 1947, original photographer unknown.*

> Part of the facade stands. It has been seriously suggested that this building should be reconstructed ... Here is a building whose sole value is historic. Is it to be allowed to stand in the way of the new plan? (*Architect and Building News* 1941: 188)

This raises a key issue in Coventry's reconstruction: the moving of buildings. Following Charles's survey and, indeed, Gibson's arguments, it was decided to dismantle a number of the timber buildings threatened by redevelopment and re-erect them in Spon Street, along with the restoration of a cluster of *in situ* survivors there. This was supported in principle by the Historic Buildings Council (this area-based approach pre-dated the conservation areas introduced by the 1967 Civic Amenities Act). This has been supported by extreme phrasing, by campaigners and others: 'as bonfires of ancient timbers blazed in Little Park Street, the *Coventry Standard* actually ran the front-page headline "Demolition recalls the days of the Blitz" ' (Gill 2004: 65).

Gill carefully charts the attitudes and decision-making processes leading to the Spon Street scheme, including its original large scale and subsequent diminution: a 1966 draft 'seems to incorporate just about every endangered timber-framed building in Coventry' (Gill 2004: 69). The 'great and the good from the HBC' later rejected any possibility of grant aid, though, as an exercise 'involving the large-scale dismantling, removal and re-erection of buildings, would be in the nature of an archaeological exercise of considerable interest and value, but quite outside the scope of [its] proper activities' (letter, HBC Secretary to City Planning Officer, August 1966: Townscape Scheme file, Coventry City Council). Nevertheless, funded by the city and by grants for the *in situ* buildings, the scheme went ahead.

F. W. B. Charles contributed much to the first part of the Spon Street scheme; he was a 'forceful character' (Gill 2004: 68) and had 'a visceral hatred of the SPAB' (AMS 2016: 47). There has been criticism of the way in which Charles prioritized timber survival and removed later work including chimneys; Ian Nairn said of another of his Coventry projects that it 'seems likely to come out more half-timbered than it has been for centuries' (Nairn 1968: 470). Charles always robustly defended his approach, for example, convincing council committees by his 'clear exposition and technical ability' (minutes of joint meeting, Planning and Development, and Estates and General Purposes Committees, 5 October 1970.) The resulting 'Townscape Scheme' is popular, but is a confection; it was always aimed at tourists, and the re-erected buildings tend to be of larger scale than those *in situ* (Figure 5).

FIGURE 5 *Spon Street, Coventry, restored by F. W. B. Charles, 1970–4. The three-storey building is relocated from Much Park Street. Source: P. J. Larkham.*

Terraces in Bath

Bath suffered a 'Baedeker raid' in 1942 (Rothnie 1992) which left extensive damage, especially in the south part of the city centre – although much was relatively minor (Bath Record Office (BRO) bomb damage map). Some sites remain unrebuilt (Figure 6), and one bombed building has been listed for that very reason (the remains were being incorporated into a new structure in 2016). The particular historic value of the city, making it both a target and a specific focus for 'authenticity' in reconstruction, was its development as a Georgian resort from *c.* 1725, and specifically its uniformity in building style, form (especially terraces) and building material. A number of individual buildings within terraces were bombed or burned out, including some in the Royal Crescent and the Circus. The recently restored Assembly Rooms (1769–71) were also gutted.

The approach to reconstructing damaged terraces posed particular problems, as even SPAB recognized. Two copies of its booklet survive in the City Council property files, and in one a key phrase has been highlighted: 'Frequently a gap is made in a terrace or crescent of an historic group; and replacement is here permissible, in order to maintain the continuity of the design' (SPAB undated: 4). It is an interesting point that SPAB felt that it had authority to 'permit' this (and, by implication, prohibit other

FIGURE 6 *Norfolk Buildings, Bath: bombite, still un-redeveloped in 2016. 'Authentic' as a recollection of the bombing, perhaps? Source: P. J. Larkham.*

responses?). In 1950 the Georgian Group wrote to the Council emphasizing 'the importance of faithfully replacing architectural details when Georgian buildings are repaired or restored' (City Planning Committee minutes, 2 May 1950, BRO).

Bath did commission a reconstruction plan, co-authored by Professor Patrick Abercrombie. The plan was very sensitive to the historic context and the damage to Georgian terraces (Abercrombie et al. 1945: chapter 8). This is hardly surprising given Abercrombie's record of conservation-related work, albeit largely rural (Dix 1981). In one of his earliest plans he explores (although not in these terms) originality and authenticity in the urban landscape of Stratford upon Avon (Abercrombie and Abercrombie 1923). But, for Bath, he was not prescriptive about authenticity or style, indeed suggesting alternative approaches for a new concert hall (Abercrombie et al. 1945: 26): he was aware that

> The amateur of antiquarian tastes is apt to ask for reproductions or adaptations of old Bath; the true archeologist [sic] will resent a fake: he is frequently a complete modernist in his sympathies for new building; another type will ask for harmony, whatever that term may mean (and it frequently covers the opposite of complete contrast); again, there is the school that proposes a classical structure, stripped of all its normal clothing. (Abercrombie et al. 1945: 22–3)

Terraces formed a particular problem for Bath, not only recognized by the SPAB leaflet but by the admiring before and after photographs of an example in Worskett's influential book on conservation: 'there is little choice but to rebuild any single unit of that design to match exactly the existing façade ... the solution will generally be to rebuild a facsimile' (Worskett 1969: 180).

The urgency of repairing damage perhaps led to some short cuts. A measured survey of c. 1948 for one damaged house in the Circus, by the local architect Beresford Smith, occupies only a standard small sheet of graph paper (Beresford Smith papers, BRO 0529/101/26). In 1946 there was a shortage of sash weights, and Mowbray Green's office suggested that it would therefore be necessary to fit casements to rear elevations (letter, 22 October 1946, BRO). Although minor details, and influenced by urgency and building material rationing, these perhaps demonstrate a concern for action and habitability over exact restoration.

The example cited by Worskett is Norfolk Crescent (begun 1792). The northern part of the terrace was gutted, but by the time of Worskett's first photograph about six bays of the façade had been lost. The façade was reinstated in 1958 by E. F. Tew and the structure converted to Council-managed flats, although the rebuilt section is deeper than the original and 'the rear does not attempt a Georgian reconstruction' (Forsyth 2003: 253) (Figure 7). The conversion of this and many other terraces followed SPAB advice by the architect Marshall Sisson and others (SPAB 1945). A

FIGURE 7 *Norfolk Crescent, Bath, reconstructed façade (bays 4–9). Source: P. J. Larkham.*

Civic Trust Award plaque commemorates the scheme. The undamaged part of the terrace was listed Grade II* in June 1950 (List description, building identification 1395745). In Queen Square the Francis Hotel's east range was badly damaged. Again, although the façade was rebuilt, by J. Hopwood in 1952–3, to match its neighbours, the new wing is deeper in section. 'As a component part of an outstanding set-piece, meticulously reconstructed in facsimile in 1955 (see inscription on front), these houses remain of great importance' and are part of the Grade 1 listing of June 1950 (i.e. even before reconstruction) (List description, building identification 1394551) (Figure 8). The two seem to have been treated similarly in terms of reconstruction authenticity, where the public façades had greater significance, yet differently for listing purposes – although Queen Square is undoubtedly a more significant architectural composition.

The Assembly Rooms saga is more complicated, particularly in its ownership and funding issues. The derelict property was purchased by the SPAB in *c.* 1931 and transferred to the National Trust. It was leased to the local authority, who had it restored by Mowbray Green, a local architect, and used it for local functions. The scale of the damage was such that the War Damage Commission had agreed, 'in the public interest', to make a cost of works payment (undated memo, 'war damage provisions', BRO, CP802 Box

FIGURE 8 *Francis Hotel, Bath, east wing reconstructed c. 1952. Source: P. J. Larkham.*

X). On SPAB advice, the eminent architect Professor Sir A. E. Richardson was involved in reconstruction designs from soon after the bombing. A SPAB and Georgian Group member, his interest in authenticity and originality led to concerns that he could expensively insist on reinstatement as original.

The Council wanted to alter the reconstructed building to make it more suitable for civic functions, especially a concert hall. Indeed it stated that 'in the considered view of this Council, building of the Assembly Rooms as an exact replica of the buildings destroyed in 1942 would serve no useful purpose nationally or locally and would in fact involve a deplorable waste of money for labour, material etc'. (Council resolution, 1 December 1953: 'destroyed' is an overstatement). The National Trust's Executive Committee felt, since the damage, 'that it was the Trust's duty to rebuild the Assembly Rooms as they were before their destruction' (letter from Rathbone, NT Secretary, 19 January 1954, BRO, CP802 Box X) and that the war damage payment 'could not be used for any other purpose except by a breach of trust, an action which could not even be considered' (letter from Lord Rosse to the Mayor, 19 December 1953, BRO, CP802 Box X). Richardson had proposed a compromise and was negotiating permissions and War Damage Commission funding (notes of meeting, 17 December 1951, BRO, CP802 Box X) but there were bad-tempered arguments between Richardson's office and that of the deceased Mowbray Green over plans. Various people involved with the Trust, SPAB and its offshoot, the Georgian Group, including Lord Esher (one-time SPAB Chairman) suggested a further compromise whereby one room could have 'major internal alterations'. The donor was identified and became involved, and was 'adamant in refusing to consider even a compromise on these lines, and was indeed somewhat upset to learn that we had even gone as far as we had . . . he would regard any compromise on this issue as a breach of trust which he would never forgive' (letter from Lord Rosse, 31 January 1954, BRO, CP802 Box X).

There was long argument, including Counsel's opinions sought in 1956, over the terms of the lease and whether the Council could extricate itself. The question of whether, when restored, the rooms can be regarded as a replica only and not as the original rooms received the response that this question is irrelevant since the new building will be subject to the old lease' (in fact the old structure remained to eaves level) (Counsel's opinion by Denys Buckley, 6 December 1956, BRO, CP802 Box X). Eventually a compromise was reached and the building restored in 1956–63, with the interiors by Oliver Messel. The building was listed Grade I in June 1950, when only temporary repairs had been made to the gutted shell (List description, building identification 1394144). Although there were debates over the restoration's authenticity, these related wholly to the interior (Cornforth, 1964 and subsequent correspondence).

Discussion

Of the examples cited, Birmingham shows absolutely no evidence of concern for authenticity in its reconstruction, even in the very rare historicist styles. The new is paramount, in style, scale and function. The dominant influence was Herbert Manzoni. He felt that the bombing presented a 'uniquely favourable opportunity' (Manzoni 1941). He also had an antipathy to conservation and old buildings. Coventry shows equal initial disregard, particularly on Gibson's part. Again, Gibson saw the bombing as an opportunity: 'in one night the site is largely cleared ready for the regeneration' (Gibson 1940: 41; although, clearly, this is an exaggeration). Battles with conservationists ensued, culminating in the project to move some timber structures to Spon Street (prefigured by Gibson's comment about Ford's Hospital). But the way in which this was done, and the personal style of F. W. B. Charles, showed a disregard for established SPAB approaches. SPAB was much more clearly influential in Bath, despite its evident focus on earlier and ecclesiastical property. Retention of two copies of its booklet in the Council property records is telling, and its influence on the Assembly Rooms case is clear, although indirect. Nevertheless funding, and the Council's wishes for interior alteration, did eventually have greater influence over this delayed restoration. The other terrace restorations were, though, inauthentic in plan, however suitable in façade.

There is, therefore, very little evidence of serious consideration of 'authenticity' *per se* in English post-war reconstruction. Plans are clearly driven by factors such as the background of plan authors (many of whom were architects, and many of these were trained at the Liverpool School of Architecture or its products, including Abercrombie, latterly at London). European Modernism was a growing influence, especially on the younger professionals. Equally, many professionals involved in replanning and reconstruction were aware of, or involved in, emerging debates about conservation, character and related issues, including polemics about urban sprawl and quality (Larkham 2003; Pendlebury 2003). Conservation is an issue in a number of reconstruction plans but the way in which it was treated, seen in a longer continuum (Larkham 2014), differs substantially from other countries' experiences.

In many places, particularly but not solely the industrial cities, damage was overemphasized. Buildings were 'destroyed' even if the walls remained sound to eaves height (the Bath Assembly Rooms, and many churches: Larkham and Nasr 2012). This legitimized plans to demolish, move (as in Coventry) or alter, structures, compromising originality and authenticity.

'Character' emerges as a factor (Pendlebury 2004). A key point is the valuing of structures or places, and the differing weights placed on concepts such as originality and authenticity, especially given the prominence afforded to 'Modernism' in contemporary UK architecture and planning. Another factor is the role of memory and commemoration, particularly relating to the reinstatement of wartime destruction. Conservation values did change significantly through the 'reconstruction era' of *c.* 1945–73.

It is also relevant to consider whether, in these cases, there is a conceptualization of authenticity that applies at the larger scales (street, district or even city). Virtually all discussion has been at the level of individual buildings or even parts of buildings, driven by SPAB's focus on architecture as art. But could the authenticity of an area's character, identity or even function be retained through a replanning that did demolish or move existing structures, whether damaged or not? Cities have always changed over the longer timescale, but we are here considering a short time frame dictated by the catastrophe of war. Yet some of the reconstruction plans explicitly concerned implementation periods of between twenty and fifty years. Many were also dominated by large-scale infrastructure projects that would, over such a period, have resulted in clearance of buildings now valued as historic. Others, though, revealed historic structures through clearance ('disencumbering' in US terms) (Larkham 2014).

Finally, the rise of concepts of conservation have necessarily involved a revaluing of structures and areas. Economic and functional obsolescence has been addressed by finding new uses. Structural obsolescence has been addressed through interventions, materials and technologies that purist SPAB members might regret; but conservation values, including the interpretation and value of 'authenticity', have plainly changed in the post-war period. The experience of the immediate post-war period, including the examples discussed here, was a key catalyst for this change.

References

Abercrombie, P., J. Owens and H. A. Mealand (1945), *A Plan for Bath*, Bath: Pitman.

Abercrombie, P. and L. Abercrombie (1923), *Stratford-upon-Avon, Report on Future Development*, Liverpool: Liverpool University Press.

Aldous, T. (1975), *Goodbye, Britain?*, London: Sidgwick and Jackson.

Ancient Monuments Society (AMS) (2016), 'Review of Gould and Gould (2016)', *AMS Newsletter*, Summer 2016: 47.

Architect and Building News (1941), 'Coventry: A Plan for the City Centre', *Architect and Building News*, 21 March: 188–95.

Cammaerts, E. (1925), 'The Reconstruction of Belgian Towns', *Journal of the Royal Society of Arts*, 73 (3779): 538–48.

Campbell, L. (1996), *Coventry Cathedral: Art and Architecture in Post-War Britain*, Oxford: Oxford University Press.

Cornforth, J. (1964), 'The Bath Assembly Rooms Restored', *Country Life*, 9 January: 56–8.

Dix, G. (1981), 'Patrick Abercrombie', in G. E. Cherry (ed), *Pioneers in British Town Planning*, London: Architectural Press.

Forsyth, M. (2003), *Bath*, Pevsner Architectural Guides, New Haven, CT, and London: Yale University Press.

Foster, A. (2005), *Birmingham*, Pevsner Architectural Guides, New Haven, CT, and London: Yale University Press.

Gibson, D. (1940), Lecture given at the Royal Society of Arts, London, reported in *The Times*, 4 and 7 December.

Gill, R. (2004), 'From the Black Prince to the Silver Prince: Relocating Mediaeval Coventry', *Twentieth Century Architecture*, 7: 61–86.

Glendinning, M. (2013), *The Conservation Movement: A History of Architectural Preservation*, London: Routledge.

Gould, J. and C. Gould (2016), *Coventry: The Rebuilding of a Modern City 1939–73*, London: Historic England.

Hortons' Estate (undated), *A History of Hortons' Estate 1892 – Present Day*, Available online: http://www.hortons.co.uk/images/hortons_agmbook.pdf (accessed 14 June 2016).

H. V. M. R. (1941), 'War Damage to City Churches', *The Builder*, 6 June: 575.

Larkham, P. J. (2003), 'The Place of Urban Conservation in the UK Reconstruction Plans of 1942-1952', *Planning Perspectives*, 18: 295–324.

Larkham, P. J. (2010), 'Developing Concepts of Conservation: The Fate of Bombed Churches After the Second World War', *Transactions of the Ancient Monuments Society*, 54: 7–34.

Larkham, P. J. (2014), 'Changing Ideas of Urban Conservation in Mid-Twentieth-Century England', *Change Over Time*, 4 (1): 92–113.

Larkham, P. J. and J. L. Nasr (2012), 'Decision-Making Under Duress: The Treatment of Churches in the City of London During and After World War II', *Urban History*, 39 (2): 285–309.

Lloyd, D. W. (1998), *Battlefield Tourism: Pilgrimage and the Commemoration of the Great War in Britain, Australia and Canada, 1919–1939*, London: Berg/Bloomsbury.

Manzoni, H. J. (1941), *Central City Planning: Preliminary Report*, confidential report typescript, 16 October 1941 (copy bound with the Birmingham Library's copy of Public Works Committee Minutes of 23 October 1941).

Manzoni, H. J. (1955), 'Redevelopment of Blighted Areas in Birmingham', *Journal of the Town Planning Institute*, March: 90–102.

Nairn, I. (1968), Comment on Spon Street scheme, *Architectural Review*, 144 (862): 470.

Nasr, J. L. (1997), 'Reconstructing or Constructing Cities? Stability and Change in Urban Form in Post-World War II France and Germany', PhD thesis, University of Pennsylvania, Philadelphia.

Pendlebury, J. (2003), 'Planning the Historic City: Reconstruction Plans in the United Kingdom in the 1940s', *Town Planning Review*, 74 (4): 371–93.

Pendlebury, J. (2004), 'Reconciling History with Modernity: 1940s Plans for Durham and Warwick', *Environment and Planning B: Planning and Design*, 31: 331–48.

Richards, J.M. (1947), *The Bombed Buildings of Britain*, second edition, London: Architectural Press.

Rothnie, N. (1992), *The Baedeker Blitz*, Shepperton, Ian Allen.

Sheppard Fidler, A. G. (1959), 'The Redevelopment of Urban Centres', paper presented at the conference of the Royal Society of Health, London.

Society for the Protection of Ancient Buildings (SPAB) (undated, *c*.1941), *The Treatment of Ancient Buildings Damaged in War Time*, London: SPAB.

Society for the Protection of Ancient Buildings (SPAB) (1945), *The Preservation of Terraced Houses in Bath by Adaptation to Meet Present-day Requirements*, London: SPAB.

Sutcliffe, A. R. (1967–9), *Transcripts of Interviews with Prominent Birmingham People 1967–9*, copy in the Birmingham Library, LF71.

Titmuss, R. M. (1950), *Problems of Social Policy*, London: HMSO.

Tubbs, R. (1942), *Living in Cities*, Harmondsworth: Penguin.

Woolven, R. (2005), 'Introduction', in A. Saunders (ed), *The London County Council Bomb Damage Maps 1939–1945*, London: London Topographical Society with London Metropolitan Archives.

Worskett, R. (1969), *The Character of Towns: An Approach to Conservation*, London: Architectural Press.

Chapter 2.2

Dutch Reconstructed Monuments in Review

Marieke Kuipers

Built heritage has had a peculiar position in the Netherlands in comparison to other European countries. Until 1961 a legal framework for statutory protection was lacking but, from 1918, a State Committee and a State Office has been actively working for the inventory and conservation of the Dutch historic buildings (*monumenten*). The key figure was Jan Kalf, who had not only been the main author of the 'Principles for the Conservation of Ancient Buildings', published in 1917 on behalf of the Netherlands Archaeological Association (Nederlandsche Oudheidkundige Bond, NOB), but also the bureau's director (1918–39), the committee's secretary (1924–46) and State 'Inspector for the Protection of Treasures of Art and Science against Risks of War' (1939–47) (Kalf and NOB 1917; Kuipers 2016).[1] Despite the Dutch policy of international neutrality, the Netherlands were brutally invaded by German troops, and the old towns of Rotterdam and Middelburg were particularly heavily bombed in May 1940. The bombardments led first to the military capitulation and next to a complicated administrative situation, while the Dutch Queen Wilhelmina was governing with her ministers in exile in London. After D-Day, the liberation efforts by the Allied forces caused immense destruction throughout the country.

Both population and heritage had suffered so greatly that Kalf sighed in 1946: 'The question now is if all those ravaged monuments should be repaired, or even, if they are totally destroyed, be rebuilt, … if also the economically not indispensable buildings need to be maintained and if the

---

[1]All quotes are translations from the Dutch texts by the author, unless otherwise stated.

others need to be repaired or rebuilt either in the old form or in a modern spirit' (Kalf 1946: 557). He considered initially maintaining the wrecked Town Hall at Sluis only as a ruin or letting it make way for a new building, but in the end he heeded the local pleas to restore it to the old medieval form, which meant a full reconstruction of the lost belfry. Hinting at the traditionalist regeneration practices in Middelburg, Kalf was similarly critical about 'the rebuilding of devastated areas of an old town to old forms, instead of complying with the requirements of the new era and giving the floor to modern architecture'; as for the provincial capital of Groningen, he declared that the losses of the Great Market ensemble were not to be answered by a 'run into a romanticism' which he could only see as a sign of weakness (Kalf 1946: 558–9). By then, he was no longer in a position to forbid a full, or even a partial, reinstatement of lost monuments as 'lies against history', but he rightfully foresaw that a later post-war generation would have a different opinion about conservation, renewal, use and adaptation.

This chapter will further investigate what happened with these sites of wartime destruction and post-war reconstruction, while bearing in mind that the English term 'reconstruction' does not always comply with Dutch equivalents: *herstel* (repair or restoration), *herbouw* (rebuilding), *wederopbouw* (reconstruction or regeneration) and *reconstructie* (reinstatement or renewal). This imaginary journey will go from Sluis in Zeeuws Flanders via Middelburg to Groningen after a short sketch of the general background.

Background

Unlike many other European countries, the Netherlands had not been directly involved in the armed conflicts of the Great War and had not suffered the war-related destruction of cherished monuments. In 1938 Kalf published timely advice for 'art protection' against the possible 'risks of war', when it became evident that the Third Reich was becoming increasingly aggressive and expansionist (Kalf 1938). Soon afterwards he started to develop technical precautions for the preventive protection of 108 conscientiously selected monuments of major national significance (Berends 1995: 65). Five years earlier, the national Provisional List of the Monuments of History and Art had been completed. The series of twelve volumes included no less than 12,000 immovable objects, including the most important religious and public buildings and many private houses pre-dating 1850. Yet this listing was only intended as a preliminary basis for the envisaged scholarly research for the Inventory, and not for legal protection. Nobody had presumed in those days that this Provisional List would become a pivotal instrument of formal protection during the Second World War, with two Decrees on the Reconstruction by the Dutch commander-in-chief, General Henri Winkelman, dated 21 and 25 May 1940. Winkelman, entrusted (together with the highest civil servants of the ministries) with the main civic power, had been responsible for the capitulation of the Dutch military forces, except for the navy, in two stages after the successive bombardments of Rotterdam and Middelburg (Bosma and Wagenaar 1995; Polano and Kuipers 1995).

Winkelman's military orders for a civil cause implied that Kalf remained a crucial actor for art protection and architectural conservation throughout the period of hostile occupation with two different regimes. The Austrian (honorary) SS officer Arthur Seyss-Inquart was installed as *Reichskommissar* on 29 May 1940, charged with directing the civil administration which remained, basically, with the Dutch. Just before this, Winkelman had appointed the civil engineer Jan Ringers as General Deputy of all Reconstruction Works in the Netherlands, reaching from the distribution of building materials to the rebuilding of destroyed bridges and towns and, surprisingly, the restoration of provisionally listed monuments.[2] The Dutch State Commission's permission was required for any demolition or alteration, even if the monuments were in ruins, like the Town Hall, Abbey ensemble and nearby St Jorisdoelen in Middelburg, or the Belfry at Sluis.

Sluis and its unique belfry

The small fortified town of Sluis, once a competitor of Bruges and later also a magnet for tourists, became unexpectedly a victim of the liberation battle for the mouth of the Scheldt (and Antwerp) in October 1944. Of all ruined buildings, the loss of the medieval Town Hall and its belfry, for the Netherlands unique, was most regretted. The ruin was consolidated as far as was technically possible, because the local authorities hoped ultimately to rebuild their beloved landmark, both for sentimental and touristic-economic reasons. Thoughtfully, old bricks were kept for the awaited reuse, while a new town planning scheme was drafted by the regional architect Frans Klokke. He proposed to revive the historic street pattern to an adapted width, and to enhance the hoped-for views to the belfry which was to be reconstructed (Roosmalen 1994: 33–8). As a result of frequent changes and the lack of finance, it would take until September 1960 before the reinstated Town Hall could be inaugurated to its former function and glory (Figure 1).[3] The event was preceded by a three-day-long festivity for the local community, partly in Brueghelian style. About 800 families had collectively donated the twenty-four bells for the carillon in the resurrected belfry and they were happy to see the sculptured wooden bell-riser 'Jan with the Hammer' (which had survived the bombing) reinstalled.[4]

---

[2]Yet, in 1943, Ringers was detained and brought to the hostages' camp St. Michielsgestel, where he could still be consulted; see Siraa 1989: 11–14, 24–31.
[3]*De Tijd/De Maasbode*, 10 September 1960.
[4]*Gereformeerd Gezinsblad*, 16 August 1960.

FIGURE 1 *The restored Town Hall of Sluis with its reconstructed belfry. Source: photographed by G. T. Delamarre from the Market Square in 1961. Reproduced by courtesy of the RCE (Netherlands Agency for Cultural Heritage), Amersfoort.*

The restoration works were led by Elias Canneman, who since 1933 had been an architect with the State Office and its post-war successor the Netherlands Department for Conservation, with local assistance. As Canneman stated in his almost apologetic essay about the unusual assignment (as he saw it), various sources were available and used for a historically reliable reconstruction: old drawings, photographs, measuring documents and plaster casts.[5] He was well aware of his ambivalent position, not only for the infringement of the NOB principle of conservation prior to renewal, but also towards the previous restoration of 1894–1904 under the supervision of the great master Pierre Cuypers and the Middelburg-based architect Jan Frederiks. In this restoration Canneman observed some 'mistakes' in the forms of the windows, entrance stair and other elements which were, in his opinion, historically incorrect. So he emphasized that no 'fantasies' were applied. If the historic forms (pre-Cuypers) were not known, Canneman preferred a simple, though aesthetically fitting, form, like the new extension on the foundations of the *schepenhuis* that had been removed under Napoleonic rule. The main intention was to restore the exterior and basement close to the form that the Town Hall had at the end of the fourteenth century, as far as possible based on historical evidence, directly or indirectly, and not to aim at a stylistically pure result. For the rebuilding of the belfry similar or reused materials were used – partly original bricks and partly from dismantled houses in Bruges, and natural stone. Where Canneman was not certain about the forms of the belfry windows, he did not reconstruct Cuypers' details, although he respected some elsewhere if he had the impression that they were historically correct. The former *poortershuis* extension at the north side was not rebuilt. This was not in accordance with the NOB principle of respecting successive historical layers, but was motivated in part by the need for daylight in the main hall.

Apart from history-based considerations, functional requirements had to be met. The local authorities had stipulated that the Town Hall would be reused in full. The civil hall was located on the *piano nobile* and administration on the upper floor. This distribution allowed the architect to 'maintain' the windows as they were, with shutters below. The furnishing was chosen to create a harmonious atmosphere in a well-considered combination of contemporary art works and historical originals from elsewhere, like the Baroque *Vierschaar* gate from Middelburg and a painting by Pieter Brueghel. As a typical compromise of the post-war reconstruction, the upper rooms were provided with clearly visible wooden beams and bridging joists as 'historical' constructions, though embellished with sculptures in stone and wood that were partly copies of original ornaments (remade from the plaster casts) and partly newly designed by regional artists in line with the historical tradition.[6] The mayor's room was decorated with golden leather wall hangings on the new partition wall, a simple chimney and other historicist elements to establish the character of a state room. This luxury seemed

---

[5]Canneman, though made an 'honorary citizen of Sluis' for his work on the belfry, was anxious about the justification of the reconstruction because the annual NOB meeting would take place in Sluis in 1964; see Canneman 1964: 144.
[6]See the anonymous Belfort visitors guide, *Het Belfort van Sluis* (c. 2014) for further details: available online: www.belfortsluis.nl (accessed 23 August 2016).

not to have been disputed by the local population or by the conservation authorities. On the contrary, the completely reconstructed Town Hall and integrated *Vierschaar* was inscribed on the national monuments register for legal protection, after the national Historic Buildings and Monuments Act was approved; the in-built tower was explicitly mentioned as delivering 'a characteristic image of a Flemish belfry'.[7] Because the surrounding houses were all post-war buildings (mainly in traditional style), the urban core was not designated as a 'protected townscape', in contrast to Middelburg.

Middelburg: Towards an exemplary 'Monuments City'

The capital of the Zeeland archipelago Middelburg, centrally located on the island of Walcheren, was traditionally a town of great importance for administration, port and trade activities. Both historic beauty and regional power were symbolized in the richly ornamented flamboyant gothic Town Hall, and the Abbey ensemble, secularized since 1574. Both were included in Kalf's protective list of 108 monuments (Kalf 1938: 69). However, not all scheduled precautions had been completed when Zeeland became the battlefield for German and French troops on 17 May 1940 (Black Friday). Middelburg's inner city and its admired city jewels were devastated, posing the immediate question of how to rebuild.

The mayor invited Jan de Ranitz, the regional Inspector of Public Health and Social Housing and co-author of the regional planning survey, to draft a vision for the rebuilding of their home town and to quickly consult the national Dutch stakeholders at the Hague.[8] De Ranitz suggested not making a 'copy of what Middelburg once was' but coming to 'a new architecture grafted onto the old scenic beauty of the city, on the foundations and principles of the ancient architecture'; in other words, Middelburg should remain 'the intimate provincial town, though more beautiful and sunnier' than before.[9] This view was shared by Jan Kalf after his inspection visit shortly after the disaster, and he gladly noted that orders had already been given to shore the remaining walls of the Town Hall, Abbey and other historic buildings, in anticipation of future restorations.[10] Nonetheless, the organization, decision-making and execution of the whole process of what would later be known as 'integrated planning' of both conservation

---

[7]Monument number 33890; available online: www.rijksmonumentenregister.nl (accessed 23 August 2016).
[8]De Ranitz's Regional Survey for Walcheren (co-authored with Dirk Roosenburg) dated from 1937; see Bosma 1988: 31.
[9]*De Courant Het Nieuws van de Dag*, 10 and 15 June 1940.
[10]*De Maasbode*, 26 July 1940.

and development proved very complex and sometimes controversial. Since the reconstruction of the inner city and its medieval monuments was such a prestigious affair and was also influenced by the divided ownership of the properties, serious difficulties arose about responsibilities, expertise, ideologies and finance, not only among local and national stakeholders but also with the German occupants – who saw a possible reconstruction of the Town Hall and Abbey ensemble in the context of a 'Great-German' cultural revival and tried to intervene in the restoration projects (Verschoor 1988, Sijnke and van Drunen 2006).

To orchestrate the rebuilding of the inner city, the Foundation for the Reconstruction of Middelburg was set up by the local government by the end of 1940 with architect-urbanist Pieter Verhagen as its director.[11] He opted for the reconstruction of the inner city in an adapted version of the pre-war situation with slightly broader streets and the reinstatement of the Town Hall and Abbey, so aiming to revive the characteristic Middelburg 'atmosphere' (Bosma 1988, 1990). When his advice was sought about these key monuments, Kalf had proposed a dual approach of conscious conservation and contemporary design. The first team, for the Town Hall, was formed by Hendrik van Heeswijk (a member of the State's Committee for Monuments Care and respected restorer of St Jan's Cathedral at s'Hertogenbosch) and Ad van der Steur (municipal architect of Rotterdam and son of the State Committee's chairman). The recommendation of Van Heeswijk may seem remarkable because he openly favoured a stylistic reconstruction in line with the old-school ideas of his master Cuypers (restorer of the Town Hall of Middelburg) instead of the modern approach, but apparently even Kalf wished to see the gothic façade restored to its old splendour (Verschoor and Bosma 1988, Sijnke 2009).[12] This mattered all the more because the reconstructed Town Hall was intended to become the dominant freestanding structure overlooking the rearranged market square. The second team, for the revival of the Abbey ensemble, consisted of Henri de Lussanet de la Sablonière (since 1934 affiliated with the Department of Government Buildings at The Hague) and, from 1941, the traditionalist architect Jo Berghoef.

Alongside the philosophical issues related to the NOB principles, politically driven attempts were made by the pro-German *Kultuurraad* in 1941–44 to intervene in the rebuilding of the lost parts of the Town Hall and the Abbey ensemble, proposing a more archaic design; but, thanks to the other Dutch authorities, this was in vain (Bosma 1988). Meanwhile, the two projects met serious practical problems, such as the scarcity of similar building materials since the Belgian quarries were closed.

---

[11] *Nieuwsblad van het Noorden*, 21 November 1940.
[12] See also Meischke 1995 for a general background of other restorations.

The reconstruction of the Town Hall

In autumn 1941 Van Heeswijk began the restoration of the façades and tower of the Town Hall, but little progress was made and he died soon after the war (Verschoor and Bosma 1988: 48).[13] He was succeeded by the local architect M. J. J. van Beveren, who tried to conserve as much as possible of the surviving fabric and elsewhere to use natural stone in a similar colour, while wondering 'what to do with the more or less successful restorations of the previous century' (i.e. those made by Cuypers). His response was to 'try to "help" those parts of which the design was good' while replacing the heavily damaged parts with totally new elements (Beveren 1948: 34). He also restored the interior of the Meat Hall in the basement, which was to be reused as the Zeeland War Museum. Meanwhile, van der Steur elaborated his designs for the interior of the old part by creating a 'gothic sphere', by which he meant a liberal translation of the gothic which reconstructed without imitating a gothic style, and as far as possible enhanced the gothic remains (Steur 1948: 34). The result was a distant echo of the Golden Age mixed with modest or hidden modern comfort: 'historic' wooden beams, copper chandeliers, specially acquired old mantelpieces, tapestries and doors; a replica of the city arms combined with newly designed furniture by the architect, and a concealed heating system. Some of the movable objects were special gifts. The official reopening of the Town Hall, on 18 August 1950, by the new Dutch Queen Juliana and her husband Prince Bernhard, was a majestic event.[14]

Similar considerations had guided the design of the new additions, which were arranged around a new inner court and had a frame of steel and concrete clad with brick and, though only on the street side, with natural stone (Figure 2). The architect hoped that the 'gothic end gable of the Civic Hall in all its whiteness would form a splendid culmination of this court' and that 'the total complex would bear the stamp of an entire urban and architectural element of the restored city' (van Beveren 1948: 35).

The revival of the Abbey ensemble

The reconstruction of the Abbey ensemble was equally, if not more, ambitious. Here the higher levels of provincial and state administration were urgently in need of adequate accommodation. The Abbey dated from the twelfth century and, over time, a picturesque group of buildings of various periods

---

[13]Kalf himself made a study of the construction history of the Town Hall based on bills of the historic craftsmen, and the municipal archivist Dr W. S. Unger had published a survey of the local monuments in 1941 based on his personal knowledge, which was helpful for the reconstruction. Many original documents were lost in the city fire of Black Friday; see Sijnke et al. 2010.

[14]For the furnishing a special advisory and acquisition committee had been established (Steur 1950: 670); the reconstruction of all twenty-five sculptures on the main façade was executed by the local sculptors Philip ten Klooster, Peter de Jong and Hansje den Hollander (Sijnke 2009: 20).

FIGURE 2 *The revived Town Hall of Middelburg with its post-war additions as seen from Lange Noordstraat. Source: photographed by G. J. Dukker in 1982; reproduced by courtesy of the RCE (Netherlands Agency for Cultural Heritage), Amersfoort.*

and functions had evolved around an irregular inner court accessed by three gate buildings. The private plots (including a hotel) could be expropriated for rebuilding by the municipality, but the two related churches could not. Kalf introduced Jan de Meijer from Amsterdam for the redesign of the *Lange Jan* church tower, while the experienced architects Herman van der Kloot Meyburg and Arend Rothuizen were commissioned to restore the two related churches (Verschoor 1988, Sijnke and van Drunen 2006).

During the strenuous years of occupation, de Lussanet stayed at his post in Middelburg, measuring the remaining walls of the Abbey, and drawing and safeguarding the piles of historic building materials for the restoration. The work suffered not only from shortages of materials but also from interference from various parties. Kalf, for instance, had demanded the use of reinforced concrete for the new floors, assuming that this would be a safer precaution against fire than wood. As de Lussanet explained, little data were available as a historically reliable base for the restoration, including drawings and publications on the previous restoration by Jan Frederiks and the *Bauforschung* studies by C. C. Labouchère and Th. Haakma Wagenaar, who were engaged by the pro-German *Kultuurraad* (de Lussanet 1980: 7,

Verschoor 1988, van der Peet 1995: 106, Sijnke and van Drunen 2006). Although Middelburg was liberated in November 1944, effective restoration works could begin only after the total liberation of the Netherlands in May 1945. Obtaining essential building materials was difficult, and there were problems of funding and concerning the infill of the vacated plot that was transferred to the municipality. Finally, it was determined that the provincial administration would receive new accommodation in extensions at the northern and eastern sides of the Abbey court, while the restored buildings on the north-western side would house the newly established Zeeuws Museum with its precious collection of historic tapestries and other special items of regional or national value. Exactly twenty years after Black Friday, the provincial premises by Berghoef were officially inaugurated in 1960, but the completion of the authentic reconstruction of the rest of the Abbey ensemble would require another decade during a period of radical change in society and culture. The rebuilding of the Abbey ensemble was as important for the townscape of Middelburg as its counterpart, the Town Hall. Looking back, de Lussanet observed that it was 'a great piece of luck that the surrounding parts of the town had sustained the old character in colour and scale, by which a unity has been preserved' (Figure 3) (de Lussanet 1980: 27).

FIGURE 3 *The restored Abbey ensemble at Middelburg as seen from the* Lange Jan *church tower by W. Riemens towards the north; at the right the new post-war Provincial administration building. Source: reproduced by courtesy of the RCE (Netherlands Agency for Cultural Heritage), Amersfoort.*

The partial replication of the *Sint Jorisdoelen*

Successive mayors of Middelburg had aimed for a coherence of urban fabric and major and minor monuments, in order to promote the provincial capital as an attractive place for residents and tourists, a living city of monuments. The designation of the reconstructed city centre as a nationally protected townscape with about 1,100 legally protected buildings fitted well with these ambitions, which were supported by private initiatives. As a culmination of the joint programmes of urban rehabilitation and architectural conservation, Middelburg was selected as one of the three exemplary towns of the Netherlands for European Architectural Heritage Year in 1975 (Klarenbeek 1975, Kuipers 2015: 240–4).

It was at the request of the municipal authorities that de Lussanet had been involved in the partial re-construction of the *Sint Jorisdoelen* (originally a club for the citizen forces, an armed volunteer militia) as the state's regional office for employment and cantonal court (1965–70). The U-shaped building, constructed with concrete floors, received a broad and bright façade in natural stone with a central gable towards Balans square, crowned by a sculpture of the patron Saint George, and another replicated façade in natural stone at the rear. The two side aisles were designed in a distinctive traditionalist style in brick. The ornamental anchor plates of the original construction year, 1582, were attentively remade and replaced, just as the 'Renaissance' entrance gate, windows and shutters were copied from historic drawings and photographs. The small lettering 'RENOVATA 1970' in the tympanum indicates that the façade is a replica. Whereas an extraordinary cinematic registration of the wartime destruction is available, made by the owner (a hotel director) at the time, hardly anything is published about the adaptive reconstruction.[15] Presumably, the building of two replicated façades of historic form but without historic fabric is regarded as less authentic than the Middelburg Town Hall and Abbey or the partially reconstructed and refurbished Renaissance jewel in the centre of Groningen.

The *Goudkantoor* on the Great Market at Groningen

In April 1945, when liberated Middelburg was already under reconstruction, the heart of Groningen was severely damaged by the Allies in their destruction of German munitions transport in the old market area. The mutilation of

---

[15]*Trugkieke* (Omroep Zeeland); available online: www.youtube.com/watch?v= UW5EqFOi3Sg&feature =youtu.be (accessed 23 August 2016); the rebuilt monument of the *Sint Jorisdoelen* is explicitly mentioned in the description of the protected townscape.

the Great Market was considered a sacrifice for the liberation, while it was called a miracle that both the Martini tower and the *Goudkantoor* (Gold office) had survived (Tellegen 1949a: 4, Pinkster 1996: 15). Yet both belonged to the 108 specially protected historic buildings, so the local firemen, equipped with lists of protected buildings, had made enormous efforts to safeguard these landmarks in the burning city.[16] The neoclassical Town Hall also survived, but it was less appreciated for either its style or functionality. Standing amidst the ruins, this provisionally listed monument was rather a problematic *pièce de résistance* for the post-war reconstruction of the Market square and its immediate surroundings. The building was obviously too small to accommodate the post-war city administration and its greatly expanded staff. The alternatives for the Town Hall of extension or total replacement after demolition, as well as a possible transfer of the *Goudkantoor* to another location, caused fierce debates both locally and nationally. In June 1945, the grand old Professor Marinus Jan Granpré Molière was engaged to draft an urban plan for the inner city of Groningen and to solve the 'Town Hall problem'. The State Committee and State Office on Monuments Care did not approve any demolition proposal for the two administrative monuments on the Market square; some stakeholders had wished to obtain more space for modernization, just like the rebuilding of Rotterdam, and had supported further clearance of ruins (Tellegen 1949b, Tuin 2009, 2010). The traditionalist plans met so many objections that Granpré withdrew. His former academic assistant Jo Vegter was commissioned to design the 'New Town Hall' as a separate extension to the historic monument together with a thorough restoration of the *Goudkantoor* and the old Town Hall (Emck et al. 1947, Tellegen 1949b, Wagenaar 1991, Fischer and Kuipers 2013: 38–9). Vegter, based as a private architect at Leeuwarden, was experienced in both restoration and new building, as he demonstrated in badly damaged Arnhem. There he restored the medieval town gate *Sabelspoort* and connected it via a glazed overhead bridge with his new 'House of the Province Gelderland'.[17] In Groningen Vegter also created a transparent overhead corridor, between the old Town Hall and the new city office building, in Corbusian style, extending it with a grand staircase in front of the formerly blind southern face of the *Goudkantoor*. The staircase was intended as an urban democratic gesture in the newly created public space (Figure 4). From the corridor a small secondary access was provided to the upper floor of the restored *Goudkantoor*. Underneath, a transparent extension in glass and steel was added, marked by a neon 'Information' sign: the ground floors of these two contrasting volumes had to serve as 'representative accommodation' for the tourist office.[18]

---

[16]*Groningen in vuur en puin*, 1945.
[17]Vegter was appointed part-time State Government Architect (*Rijksbouwmeester*) in 1958.
[18]B(raber), H(endrik), in Schuitema Meijer 1964: 13.

FIGURE 4 *The 'new Town Hall' extension with staircase and glazed corridor as connection with the restored* Goudkantoor *by J. J. M. Vegter on the Great Market Square of Groningen. Source: photographed by A. J. van der Wal in 1967; reproduced by courtesy of the RCE (Netherlands Agency for Cultural Heritage), Amersfoort.*

The *Goudkantoor*, with its typical shell ornaments and coats of arms, was originally built as the provincial tax collection house in 1635. The symbolic decorations of the north and east façades expressed the desire of the provincial authorities to demonstrate their importance in the city. After the French occupation (1795–1813) and the transfer to the municipality, the spaces were rented out for various purposes, including the state warrantee office for gold and silver. The nickname 'Gold office' lasted even after the office had moved and the building reused as two museums, for which it was restored in 1928–31 to the design of regional architect Siebe Jan Bouma. He replaced the large nineteenth-century windows by quasi-eighteenth-century sash windows, although he had no historical source to justify this intervention (Schuitema Meijer 1964: 9). After the war, the surviving monument served again as the Northern Navigation Museum until 1961, when grants and funds became available for partial integration with the new Town Hall corridor and a stylistic restoration combined with reuse. All the façades were given windows with small stained glass panes and shutters in Renaissance mode, but the old vanished portico and balustrade were not reconstructed. The south façade received a similar treatment at the upper level, meticulously replicating the lost Panser house at the Market; the lower part was simply decorated by *spekbanden* strips of natural stone.

The interior was adapted to new uses while being restyled with wooden beams and sculpted consoles to create a historic atmosphere. In the cellar and upper floors 3,500 antique tiles, that the architect had specially bought for this reuse, were applied.[19] Such mixed practice of partial reconstruction, modernization and stylish add-ons was not uncommon in the architectural conservation of the 1960s and certainly not for Vegter, who also incorporated historic fragments in his post-war students' club Mutua Fides, and the Amsterdam Bank, on the north and east sides of the Market square, respectively (Fischer and Kuipers 2013: 14–15, 28–9).

Just as with the Town Halls of Sluis and Middelburg, the *Goudkantoor* at Groningen was legally protected as a historic monument after its partial reconstruction.[20] Moreover, the historic inner city and its partially rebuilt heart was designated as a protected townscape later in the 1970s.

Aftermath

Fifty years after the Second World War ended in the Netherlands, drastic changes were evident in society, culture, commemoration, politics and preservation. On the one hand, a fresh interest arose in the recent heritage of the Reconstruction period (1940–65), followed by very selective assignments for legal protection (Kuipers 2011). On the other hand, the practice of architectural conservation has become deeply affected by two opposing trends: replication of vanished monuments and historic interiors versus ostentatious adaptation to new use by means of contrasting architectural interventions. Many museums have embraced the 'experience economy' to generate a substantial income for their activities. In this context, replication has become an important tool to provide the public at large with a particular experience of the past, not only in such instances as the Rembrandt house, Amsterdam, but also, remarkably, in such 'burdened' sites of wartime cruelties as Kamp Vught: buildings which were demolished after the war for a fresh post-conflict era have now been reconstructed both for educational and commemorative purposes, aiming at reconciliation in the present day (Halbertsma and Kuipers 2014: 92–4, 152–4).

It would require another study to dig further into the current justifications of full replication – varying from 'ancient' watchtowers of the Roman period to sheds, watchtowers and other elements related to the Second World War and decolonization – but here I mention just one telling example. This is the partial reconstruction of the southern abutment of the railroad bridge over the river Waal at Nijmegen that originally had two

---

[19]*Friese Koerier*, 5 February 1964.
[20]Final registration in 1971 with an explicit reference to the added Panser top; monument number 18467; available online: www.rijksmonumentenregister.nl (accessed 23 August 2016).

gate buildings designed by Cuypers. The controversial rehabilitation of the 'scalped' monument was justified by the polemical argument that 'the entire rebuilt city heart of Nijmegen forms, after all, a memento to this period' of wartime destruction; the addition was meant to 'recall the lost image' and 'to make the monument readable again to enhance the quality of the site' (Peterse 2006: 9, 11).

Reinstating a historic image versus conserving authentic material is an old opposition in a new context with new consequences. There has been a shift from Monuments Care to heritage care in which historic buildings and sites are considered as adaptable resources for the future, underpinned and justified by malleable stories of the past in a culture of profit instead of protection; increasing knowledge and development in technologies have enabled replications based on historical research. In addition, the role of the national government has been drastically decreased under the influence of neoliberalism and the decentralization of powers in the enactment of national legislation. At local level, some hundreds of municipalities have been forced to merge and to focus on efficiency and energy saving. As a consequence, the original functions of many historic Town Halls have been abandoned in favour of civic and wedding ceremonies, concerts and presentations, alternating with private parties arranged on a commercial basis to generate an income for the conservation of the monument.

Sluis

The old town of Sluis lost its administrative independence in 1995 then began in 2003 after another revision, an adaptive reuse of the Town Hall. A much larger intervention for a multiple public-private reuse followed in 2011–13. The cellar was made suitable for temporary exhibitions of contemporary art while the medieval prison compartment was enhanced for evocative presentation, specifically for children. The council chamber maintained the museified interior of the post-war reconstruction but received contemporary furnishing and technical installations. The upper floor now houses a permanent exhibition on the history of the town in which the mayor's room is incorporated in its 1960s manifestation to explain the recent history of destruction and reconstruction of the Town Hall and the revival of Sluis as a magnet for tourists. The restrained arrangement also allows visitors to experience the 'authentic' atmosphere of the post-war reconstructed stateroom, be they interested in the history or received as special guests for a festivity. The attic is totally devoted to the work of the famous teacher, archivist and maker of the Dutch dictionary, Johan Hendrik van Dale.[21]

---

[21]Belfort visitors guide, see Note 6.

Most conspicuous, however, is the new external addition, built on the former site of the *schepenhuis* next to the Market as a tourist information centre. The glass-box extension is wilfully designed in clearly distinctive forms and materials with the claim that the main views on the old Belfort would not be disturbed and that better access could be established for the public (including disabled persons).[22] Even the European Union has contributed to the recent project, matching national, local and private funding. The fact that the belfry is a full post-war reconstruction was hardly an issue in the deliberations; it demonstrates that the tower is now considered an integral part of the monument and the city's collective memory.

Public access has become extremely important in justifying the large investments in the architectural conservation and adaptive reuse of state-protected monuments. The case of the Sluis Town Hall is no exception, as the comparable treatment of the gothic Town Hall of Gouda illustrates. Notwithstanding restorations, this building became redundant in 2012 after the city administration had moved to a new office building opposite the railway station. It is now adaptively reused as 'the Old Stadhuys' for wedding ceremonies, conferences, private and commercial events and guided tours for tourists.[23]

Middelburg

The reconstructed Town Hall of Middelburg underwent almost the same kind of transitions. The local administration left the former pride of the town for a new office near the railway station in 2004. The vacated monumental building kept its partial use as an exhibition hall for contemporary art in the former Meat Hall, but the remainder was adapted for a new user. The city had searched for a worthy occupant of the 'second most beautiful building in the country' and so the decision was made to host an internationally oriented academic institution – named after Eleanor and Franklin Delano Roosevelt, whose family roots were historically tied with Zeeland – because this would give a new boost to the intellectual and cultural life of the provincial capital (Sijnke 2009).[24] The University College Roosevelt is located in the van der Steur premises and the related Roosevelt Conference Centre occupies the reconstructed spaces of the 'gothic' volume, with few changes.

---

[22]RDH Architects is the successor of Arend Rothuizen's firm: Rothuizen, van Doorne, 't Hooft; Vries, G. de, 'Zeeuws Museum eindelijk weer open', NRC Handelblad 1 June 2007, available online: http://vorige.nrc.nl//kunst/article1802804.ece/Zeeuws_Museum_ eindelijk_weer_open; www.rdh.nl/rdhmain/nieuws/nieuwsbrief/vierkantpaars3.pdf (accessed 23 August 2016).

[23]See http://stadhuysgouda.nl (accessed 23 August 2016).

[24]Two new busts of Eleanor and Franklin Roosevelt are now placed in the semi-public court.

The Town Hall is now an exclusive location for congresses, events, weddings, receptions, workshops and alike for various organizations. Virtual tours can be made on the internet with guided tours from April to November. From a societal point of view that favours access for all in all seasons, the current relatively limited physical accessibility could possibly be criticized; but, seen in a larger historical perspective, the new situation is close to that of the pre-war period and the mid-twentieth-century perception of the Town Hall as a dignified place of civilization.

The same spirit of dignity, study, education, art, culture and meeting is cautiously continued in the mixed Abbey ensemble. In the late 1980s a new post-war generation called for new adaptations and commissioned Cees Dam to redesign, internally, the Provincial Deputies Hall for more clarity and, externally, the pavement of the square. About twenty years later, the new director of the Zeeuws Museum strove even harder for more openness in the northern parts of the Abbey ensemble which were not individually protected. The proposed transparent extension was designed by the same architectural firm, RDH, that had been engaged for the new access to the Belfort museum at Sluis, but this glass-box proposal of 2007 was significantly larger and therefore evoked much criticism; the extension was only approved after reduction.[25] Outside this enclosure, the adjacent Balans square underwent, more smoothly, an important revision, reflecting a radical review of Dutch and local history. In front of the reused *Sint Jorisdoelen* the old neglected fountain was replaced in 2005 by a new one and a non-figurative art work in black and white (Figure 5). This new memorial was designed for this location by the regional artist Hedi Bogaers to commemorate the controversial past of the slave trade, which had made Middelburg a wealthy city. Her idea was to create here, close to the former trade buildings, a public meeting place for consolation and reflection for today's multi-cultural population.[26]

Meanwhile, seventy years after Black Friday, new efforts were made to inform the Dutch people outside Middelburg about the almost 'forgotten bombardment' of the inner city, lost to national memory since the post-war reconstruction had been so harmoniously designed to maintain the local 'atmosphere' (Sijnke et al. 2010).

Groningen

A harmonious 'atmosphere' was more difficult to find in the rebuilt zone around the Groningen Great Market square. The post-war modernist buildings, which sharply contrasted with the few surviving historic buildings, were not really appreciated by the local community. When, in

---

[25]http://vorige.nrc.nl//kunst/article1802804.ece/Zeeuws_Museum_eindelijk_weer_open; www.rdh.nl/rdhmain/nieuws/nieuwsbrief/vierkantpaars3.pdf (accessed 23 August 2016).
[26]See www.stichtingmonumentmiddelburg.nl (accessed 23 August 2016).

FIGURE 5 *The new slavery memorial by Hedi Bogaers in front of the reconstruct-ed* Sint Jorisdoelen *on the Balans square at Middelburg. Source: Marieke Kuipers (2016).*

1985, some cladding stones of the New Town Hall suddenly fell onto the street, the first step was set for a total makeover, a second post-war reconstruction of the city heart. After a local referendum, the contested post-modern design of the Italian architect Adolfo Natalini was selected in 1992 for the Waagstraat project (Pinkster 1996). This implied the demolition of Vegter's post-war city office to make way for four blocks of shops, office spaces and apartments. The *Goudkantoor*, now reused as a café-restaurant, received a huge steel-framed window in the southern façade. As another modern element, a separate arcade in steel and glass between the historic building and the new Natalini block was made to allow views onto the square, with an ambivalent effect.[27]

At the time of writing all of the post-war buildings at the east side of the square and others behind it have been demolished for the realization of the New Market square and the new Groninger Forum project, partly projected on the pre-war building line and partly negating all historic street patterns. This new building for cultural activities could be regarded as a late echo of Granpré's propositions for the rebuilding of the city heart, but the spectacular high-rise building by NL Architects is controversial in size, form and cost. It is truly ironic that a new centre for debate will be part of the new Forum building while the radical renewal of the post-war city centre is still a matter for debate among the citizens.[28]

Conclusion

The 1917 NOB Principles for Architectural Conservation showed an ambivalent character towards conservation and renewal, reflected in the results of the post-conflict reconstructions of Dutch monuments discussed previously. When the explicit distinction was made between *conservation* of historic fabric and *renewal* by means of contemporary additions in a harmonious manner, nobody in the Netherlands had foreseen the scale and extent of wartime destruction and subsequent reconstruction of historic monuments and townscapes. For the challenge of restoring heavily damaged monuments during and after the Second World War, Kalf drew an analogy with similar situations of sudden loss by fire in peacetime, like the rebuilding of the church tower at IJsselstein, and he admitted in 1946 *à propos* the belfry at Sluis that the eventual reconstruction of the vanished parts of old forms was not in all cases unacceptable as untruthful (Kalf 1946: 558–9).

---

[27]The project architect was Cor Kalfsbeek; details available online: http://www.staatingroningen. nl/55/waagstraatcomplex (accessed 23 August 2016).

[28]'De nieuwe Markt – concept plan maart 2016'; available online: https://gemeente.groningen. nl/sites/default/files/concept-ontwerp-nieuwe-markt-maart-2016.pdf (accessed 23 August 2016).

In his wartime advice on how to deal with the Town Hall and the Abbey ensemble at Middelburg he held more or less the same position as in 1929 for the burnt Town Hall of Leyden and its surviving Renaissance façade by proposing two teams for the two different tasks (Ommen 1999: 132). With hindsight, it may be seen that this dualism led unintentionally to a further division of knowledge and experience among Dutch architects in the restoration and reuse of historic buildings, a division which would become more evident from the 1970s when radical renewal began to make the immense impact on the urban fabric which has continued to the present day.

Obviously, the advocates of the distinctive approach were not aware that they were, in their zealous striving for historical truth in form and fabric in conservation, at the beginning of the façadism that would become a trend in the later post-war decades as a pragmatic compromise under the pressure of property developers. This delivered even greater contrasts between the old façade and the new volumes behind than had been demonstrated in the first attempts at post-conflict reconstruction, which had been sincerely based on profound historical research, with the incorporation of old fabric. What one can also learn from the recent developments is that sharp contrasts made by modern architects are often less appreciated by the general public than by the experts. As was already raised as a critical issue during the debates on the reconstruction of the Great Market at Groningen, all decision-makers and designers need to take into account that their work is meant for the public domain and that the preferences of the local community may differ from the professional standards of aesthetics and authenticity. These standards are still, often implicitly, influenced by the ideas of the Modern Movement on the relation between form and function as well as on transparency and architectural truth, which is reflected in the recent 'glass-box' additions to the rebuilt monuments. All in all, the recent trends of re-architecture and reconstruction call not only for a critical reflection on the current guidelines for architectural conservation in relation to authenticity and 'sphere', but also on architectural practice in general in relation to context and integrity.

References

Berends, G. (1995), 'De bescherming van monumenten tegen oorlogsgevaren', in A. G. Schulte et al. (eds), *Monumenten en oorlogstijd. Jaarboek Monumentenzorg*, Zwolle/Zeist: Waanders Publishers/Rijksdienst voor de Monumentenzorg.

Beveren, M. J. J. van (1948), 'Vijf eeuwen later: de restauratie van het stadhuis te Middelburg', *Bouw* 3: 33–5.

Bosma, J. E. (1990), 'Planning the Impossible – The Fundament of the Future. The Reconstruction of Middelburg 1940–4', in J. M. Diefendorf (ed), *Rebuilding Europe's Bombed Cities*, Basingstoke: Macmillan.

Bosma, K. (ed) (1988), *Architectuur en stedebouw in oorlogstijd. De wederopbouw van Middelburg 1940–1948*, Rotterdam: De Hef.

Bosma, K. and C. Wagenaar (1995), *Een geruisloze doorbraak. De geschiedenis van architectuur en stedebouw tijdens de bezetting en de wederopbouw van Nederland*, Rotterdam: NAi.

Canneman, E. A. (1964), 'De restauratie van het stadhuis te Sluis', *Bulletin van de Koninklijke Nederlandse Oudheidkundige Bond (KNOB)*, 6 (17): 145–58.

Emck, J. H. et al. (eds) (1947), *Bouwend Groningen. Een wandeling door de eeuwen en eenblik in de toekomst*, Groningen: Vereeniging tot bevordering der Bouwkunst Groningen.

Fischer, S. and M. C. Kuipers (2013), *Ir. J. J. M. Vegter (1906–1982) Architect Rijksbouwmeester (1958–1971) Stedenbouwkundige*, Leeuwarden: Tresoar Fries Historisch en Letterkundig Centrum.

Halbertsma, M. E. and M. C. Kuipers (2014), *Het Erfgoeduniversum. Een inleiding in de theorie en praktijk van cultureel erfgoed*, Bussum: Coutinho.

Kalf, J. and NOB (1917), *Grondbeginselen en voorschriften voor het behoud, de herstelling en de uitbreiding van oude bouwwerken*, Leiden: Théonville.

Kalf, J. (1938), *Bescherming van kunstwerken tegen oorlogsgevaren*, The Hague: Algemene Landsdrukkerij.

Kalf, J. (1946), 'Behoud en vernieuwing beide. Herstel en herbouw van door oorlogsgeweld getroffen monumenten', *Bouw* 1: 557–59, 562.

Klarenbeek, H. (1975), *Middelburg binnenstad. Monumentenjaar 1975*, Middelburg: Gemeente Middelburg.

Kuipers, M. C. (2011), 'Postwar Reconstruction and Preservation in the Netherlands', in B. Franz and H.-R. Meier (eds), *Stadtplanung nach 1945. Zerstörung und Wiederaufbau. Denkmalpflegerische Probleme aus heutiger Sicht*, Holzminden: Arbeitskreis für Theorie der Denkmalpflege (Vol. 20).

Kuipers, M. C. (2015), 'Dutch Conversions in Conservation. The European Architectural Heritage Year and Its Aftermath in the Netherlands', in M. Falser and W. Lipp (eds), *Eine Zukunft für unsere Vergangenheit. Zum 40. Jubiläum des Europäischen Denkmalschutzjahres (1975–2015). A Future for Our Past. The 40th Anniversary of European Architectural Heritage Year (1975–2015). Un Avenir pour Notre Passé. 40e Anniversaire de l'Année Européenne du Patrimoine Architectural (1975–2015)*, Berlin: hendrik Bäßler Verlag (Monumenta III).

Kuipers, M. C. (2016), 'Art Protection and Architectural Preservation in the Netherlands, 1938–45', in M. Bushart, A. Gasior and A. Janatkova (eds), *Kunstgeschichte in den besetzten Gebieten 1939–1945. (Kunst und Kunstgeschichte im Nationalsozialismus: Brüche und Kontinuitäten)*, Cologne: Böhlau.

Lussanet de la Sablonière, H. de (1980), *Verslag van de restauratie en herbouw van de Rijks- en Provinciale gebouwen behorende tot het Abdijcomplex te Middelburg. Uitgevoerd door de Rijksgebouwendienst gedurende de periode 1940–1971*. The Hague: Ministerie van Volkshuisvesting en Ruimtelijke Ordening.

Meischke, R. (1995), 'Het stille einde van een bruisende restauratieperiode', in A. G. Schulte et al. (eds), *Monumenten en oorlogstijd. Jaarboek Monumentenzorg*, Zwolle/Zeist: Waanders Publishers/Rijksdienst voor de Monumentenzorg.

Ommen, K. van (1999), 'Als de Phoenix uit de assche herrezen. De prijsvraag en de herbouwplannen voor het raadhuis van Leiden, 1929–1933', *Bulletin van de Koninklijke Nederlandse Oudheidkundige Bond (KNOB)*, 98: 116–33.

Peet, C. J. van der (1995) ''s-Rijks monumenten en ir. H. de Lussanet de la Sablonière', in A. G. Schulte et al. (eds), *Monumenten en oorlogstijd. Jaarboek Monumentenzorg*, Zwolle/Zeist: Waanders Publishers/Rijksdienst voor de Monumentenzorg.

Peterse, H. (2006), *Stadspoorten revisited. Spoorbrug bij Nijmegen, reconstructie zuidelijk landhoofd*, Nijmegen: Municipality Nijmegen, available online: www2. nijmegen.nl/mmbase/attachments/371863/b061219.pdf (accessed 23 August 2016).

Pinkster, N. (ed) (1996), *De Waagstraat, het stadshart van Groningen terug naar nu*, Groningen: Municipality Groningen.

Polano, M. K. and M. C. Kuipers (1995), 'Monumenten in nood: het ontstaan van de monumentenwetgeving in 1940–1950', in A. G. Schulte, et al. (eds), *Monumenten en oorlogstijd. Jaarboek Monumentenzorg*, Zwolle/Zeist: Waanders Publishers/Rijksdienst voor de Monumentenzorg.

Roosmalen, P. K. M. (1994), *Andermaal herrezen. Aspecten van de wederopbouw van West Zeeuwsch-Vlaanderen*, Sluis: Stichting Raadskelder.

Schuitema Meijer, A. T. (1964), *Het Goudkantoor te Groningen*, Groningen: Bureau Vreemdelingenverkeer Groningen.

Sijnke, P. (2009), *Het Stadhuis van Middelburg: 'Een bijzonder fraai raadhuis met een prachtige toren'*, Vlissingen: Den Boer/De Ruiter.

Sijnke, P. et al. (eds) (2010), *Middelburg 17 Mei 1940: Het Vergeten Bombardement*, Vlissingen: Den Boer/De Ruiter.

Sijnke, P. and A. van Drunen (2006), 'Verwoesting en wederopbouw', in J. Dekker (ed), *De Abdij van Middelburg*, Utrecht: Matrijs.

Siraa, H. T. (1989), *Eén miljoen woningen. De rol van de rijksoverheid bij wederopbouw, volkshuisvesting, bouwnijverheid en ruimtelijke ordening (1940–1963)*, The Hague: Sdu uitgeverij.

Steur, A. van der (1948), 'De verzorging van het interieur', *Bouw* 3: 34–5.

Steur, A. van der (1950), 'Middelburgs Stadhuis. Herstel van het interieur', *Bouw* 5: 668–71.

Tellegen, B. D. H. (1949a), *De Markt te Groningen. Een beschouwing over de grote markt te groningen in haar oorspronkelijke staat en de daaruit te putten richtlijnen voor de wederopbouw*, Groningen: NV Erven B. van der Kamp.

Tellegen, B. D. H. (1949b), *De Markt te Groningen. Zal zij haar Gronings karakter behouden?*, Groningen: NV Erven B. van der Kamp.

Tuin, B. (2009), 'De ruïnes op de Grote Markt. Een Geschiedenis van Goed en Kwaad. Deel 1', in R. H. Alma et al. (eds), *Hervonden Stad 2009. 14e Jaarboek voor archeologie, bouwhistorie en restauratie in de gemeente Groningen*, Groningen: Stichting Monument & Materiaal en de Dienst RO/EZ van de Gemeente Groningen.

Tuin, B. (2010), 'De ruïnes op de Grote Markt. Een Geschiedenis van Goed en Kwaad. Deel 2', in R. H. Alma et al. (eds), *Hervonden Stad 2010. 15e Jaarboek voor archeologie, bouwhistorie en restauratie in de gemeente Groningen*, Groningen: Stichting Monument & Materiaal en de Dienst RO/EZ van de Gemeente Groningen.

Verschoor, K. (1988), 'De herbouw van de Abdij', in J. E. Bosma (ed), *Architectuur en stedebouw in oorlogstijd. De wederopbouw van Middelburg 1940–1948*, Rotterdam: De Hef.

Verschoor, K. and K. Bosma (1988), 'De herbouw van het Raadhuis', in J. E. Bosma (ed), *Architectuur en stedebouw in oorlogstijd. De wederopbouw van Middelburg 1940–1948*, Rotterdam: De Hef.

Wagenaar, C. (1991), *Tussen grandezza en schavot: De ontwerpen van Granpré Molière voor de wederopbouw van Groningen*, Groningen: Noordhoff.

Chapter 2.3

The Reconstruction of France in the Twentieth Century Following Two World Wars: A Political or Technical Challenge?

Danièle Voldman

translated by Sarah Cartwright

Twice in the twentieth century, in 1914–18 and 1939–45, France was laid waste by the military operations that took place across its territory on land and in the air. Once peace was restored each time, twenty years apart, the restoration of the ruins constituted one of the key objectives of state institutions. What action would they take to erase all trace of the war, to rehouse the dispossessed and reconstruct public buildings and historic monuments razed or disfigured by the bombs and shells? In the past the country had suffered other destructive conflicts: notably during the 1870 Franco-Prussian War and the Paris Commune, when the capital's Municipal Hall, which dated from the Renaissance, had been completely destroyed by fire. However, throughout the course of the two world wars, unparalleled destruction affected rural areas and urban contexts alike. Even before the end of the conflicts those in professional and political circles were reflecting on how to tackle reconstruction. Would the task of restoration be abandoned to individual initiative on a piecemeal basis in the absence of an overarching plan, or would the state implement a coherent and coordinated policy for reconstruction? Which theories of urban planning and architectural doctrine were to be adopted for this purpose?

How would such building projects be financed? Over and above these debates and the options to which they led, the question posed is whether these reconstruction initiatives were conceived as a collection of technical challenges left to the judgement of experts, architects and engineers or whether they were envisaged rather as a political issue which engaged the responsibility of government. Moreover, would the experience of the first post-war period, in which these issues had given rise to intense debate, prove relevant the second time round?

Dissimilar post-war periods

As far as the reconstruction of this war damage is concerned, everything seems at first sight to set apart the two post-war eras. In the aftermath of the two quite distinct victories, neither the tally of loss and destruction nor, even less so, the role of professionals and the state in the construction process had many characteristics in common (Voldman 2011: 60–71).

The majority of French citizens throughout the course of the 1914–18 war had not seriously questioned the justification for the conflict in which they were caught up. Their leaders accordingly benefited from the 'sacred union' proclaimed at the outset of hostilities. This unanimity was strengthened by the military successes in the autumn of 1918. In 1945, however, the situation was totally different. First and foremost, victory belonged to the Allies rather than to liberated France, even if the Gaullists could rightly lay claim to their political and military presence alongside their Allies. Above all, in the wake of the collapse of the Vichy regime, the provisional government of the French Republic was tasked with restoring democracy and repairing the fissure which had led the country to the brink of civil war.

The political consensus of the 1920s was certainly facilitated by the traumatic experience of a country which was grieving for the death of 1,300,000 soldiers and had to learn to live with almost as many war-wounded, disabled servicemen and thousands of others suffering from psychological damage. The loss of life in the Second World War was half as much. Furthermore, because of the official armistice in June 1940, these losses were both civilian and military, in about equal numbers. In contrast, the devastation was incomparable. During the first conflict, those thirteen departments overrun in the north-east of France endured the whole weight of destruction alone. For the most part rural in character, this territory stretched across the battle front where the artillery battles took place. The agricultural land had been ruined by troop movements and, in particular, was devastated by the tunnels and trenches dug from 1915 onwards. Some villages, caught in the middle of the combat zone, had disappeared. A few were not to be rebuilt; instead just a simple plaque was placed to indicate their former location. Some towns and cities had undergone repeated assaults, such as Amiens which was retaken and lost more than once, and Rheims, bombed for the first time on 4 September 1914, then without let-up until the end of the war. At the time of the 1940 campaign, destruction had been considerable, especially in the north and the east and across the region of the Loire. Then, after the defeat in June, Maréchal Pétain's petition for an armistice and the establishment of the Vichy regime largely sheltered France from combat for a while. Yet, although the country had no stable battle front on its land mass, it was affected by German air raids and those of the Allies from 1940 to spring 1945. The entirety of the country was targeted – rural areas as well as urban zones. By the end of the conflict, eighty departments had been bombed: some cities such as Saint-Lô, Le Havre and Caen were judged to be razed to the ground. Elsewhere the destruction of urban districts covered several hectares, as in Marseille or Saint-Nazaire.

In addition, the evolution of building professions between 1920 and 1940 must be considered. In the 1920s constructors were not organized either legally or professionally. Although some technical training and some university pathways existed for these different trades, the titles of engineer, architect and land surveyor were not regulated and anyone could adopt such a status. Entrepreneurs, draughtsmen or quantity surveyors could call themselves architects, engineers or geometers to gain credibility on building sites. Furthermore, while at the level of architectural theory, regionalism dominated the field of construction, urban planners – whether they were tempted by modernism or supporters of neoclassicism or regionalism – were only just beginning to see themselves as a true profession. Few in number, they were nearly all engineers or architects. Convinced that they were the harbingers of future modernization, they demanded a place in state bodies concerned with urban planning. Throughout the 1920s and 1930s, firstly buoyed up by the reconstruction sites in the north and east, then spurred on by the economic crisis, they wanted to tackle a situation which made themselves vulnerable to competition. The title of chartered engineer was protected in 1934, that of architect in 1940 and that of land surveyor in 1945. Under threats of legal action for illegal practice, from then onwards they had to obtain a diploma awarded by colleges recognized by the state before they could award themselves such status and use these titles in their professional activity.

Thus, in 1945, the situation had radically changed: the construction occupations were better differentiated and better recognized. Ideas on town planning and functional cities had taken hold – at least in the confined circles of modern architecture and social reform, whereas the powerful administration of the Monuments Historiques department was trying to ensure the faithful conservation of ancient buildings. Understanding of the role of the state had developed greatly, above all outside the strictly political arena. During the First World War, in France as in other combatant countries, the imperatives of the war effort had led governments to intervene in the name of the state in areas such as the conduct of the economy and social structures which were not their traditional territory. This first experience of state interventionism did not last beyond the war. On the contrary, from 1918, suspicion with regard to state intervention had spread widely across all sectors of society, as a desire to return to the liberalism of the *Belle Époque* became manifest. In 1945, 'the interventionist drive born in war stretched beyond the duration of hostilities' (Kuisel 1981: 457). The intervention of the state in all sectors of the economy seemed thereafter essential in order to ensure the rescue of the country as well as the protection of individuals. The legitimacy of a welfare state was expanded to include urban problems and town planning.

Institutions charged with reconstruction

In the 1920s, the milieu of architecture and that of city planning, hoping for decisive action from the state in the organizing of reconstruction in devastated regions, was swept away by the liberal wing which was dominant from then on in government institutions and Parliament. Several organizations and bodies shared responsibility for the restoration of ruins and were often in competition with each other. Communes were left to judge planning options, as in the case of consolidating small units of land. For the enormous challenge of land consolidation in the countryside and towns did not constitute an obligation. A number of commune authorities refused to comply. This partly explains the criticism a quarter of a century later which focused on three key areas: the compensation for war damage, the notion of like-for-like reconstruction and the role of the state and national and local bodies in the organization of construction sites.

The legislation of 17 April 1919 on the repair of damage caused by war, which had been drawn up and promulgated at a time when France was still relying on German reparations to finance its own reconstruction, was magnanimous and generous. All property damaged as a result of the war qualified for compensation, and the state took on responsibility for all repair work which was declared war damage by property owners. The sincere motivation of legislators was explained by their hope for a return to the pre-war situation. As it was impossible to bring back the dead or to repair the physical and psychological suffering of citizens, the principle of national solidarity was extended as broadly as possible to material losses. This is also the reason why the term 'reconstitution' was used more frequently than 'reconstruction'. It was a question of attempting to erase all trace of four years of suffering and destruction. The law stipulated that as far as 'civic and religious buildings were concerned, compensation amounted to the sum required to rebuild a structure of the same character, of the same proportions, the same usage and guaranteeing the same qualities as the destroyed edifice'. In reality the notion of the 'same' referred to what was similar rather than identical, according to other clauses in the text of the law. For, while the deputies wanted to enshrine the word 'identical' in the future law, the Senate, in the name of individual liberty, managed to insist on the possibility of the compensation being redirected to ends other than identical restoration. The three options open to the dispossessed (use of the grant for reconstructing a similar or identical structure, or the decision not to spend but reinvest this financial compensation for other ends) were, in the eyes of the most liberal representatives of the nation, a means to reconcile national interest with respect for individual freedom and the right to property. Accordingly, victims of war damage – individuals as well as communities – had the chance to sell or to redeem their credits. They could, therefore, use their compensation grant for something other than the restoration of the damaged property to its former state. Furthermore, the sum received could be invested elsewhere than on the site of destruction. Finally, with justification of the benefit of the change envisaged (e.g. modernization of a factory, improvement of a block of flats), the compensation could be spent to construct a building with a design and function far removed from the original purpose (Voldman 2000: 146–63).

The 1919 law made the interest of individuals paramount. As the parliamentary commission tasked with working out the detail of the proposal had stated, it was good that the state had the right to keep a check on the reality of how war damage compensation was spent, but that was not intended to imply 'interference in the damage industry'.[1]

Haunted by the defeat in 1940, for which the so-called individualism of the period between the two wars was deemed responsible, the legislators of the second post-war era had their eyes trained on the 1919 text. Not only did they strive to eradicate its liberal character, but with the non-payment of German reparations very much in mind, they made a link between the affirmation of the supremacy of the general interest and the limited resources of the state's coffers. With the law of 28 October 1946 on war damage, they made the award of compensation dependant on proof that it would serve the common good. In its principles, the law only concerned reconstruction work of public utility or that where private utility chimed with general interest. The increasing numbers of studies of cases of these two war reconstructions demonstrate clearly that, in reality, the difference between the two periods was not so fundamental. In 1918, although the damage victims could more or less conduct the repair work themselves, they depended on the calculation of indemnity and had to compromise with general regulations on the selection of new urban and industrial sites. In 1945, despite tight state control which required the war damage victims to group together in

---

[1]Rapport général de la commission d'examen du projet de loi de la commission parlementaire sur les conditions d'exercice du droit à la réparation des dommages de guerre, 1915.

reconstruction associations, the central administration had to come to terms with local council preferences and the right of property owners to legal redress in order to effect changes in contradiction of ministerial decrees, which often had a successful outcome.

In 1918, architects, urban planners and engineers had not succeeded in imposing an autonomous body which would have required communes to comply with central directives. Nonetheless, in debates of the period there was no absence of reflection on the capacity of the state to accomplish the restoration of bomb damaged ruins in a coherent fashion. In 1917 the creation of a Ministry of Liberated Regions bore witness to the desire of public authorities to implement an overall policy in the damaged departments. All the same, the proliferation of administrative responses and decision-making in similar circumstances detracted from its efficiency. For, from 1919 onwards, no less than three bodies were tasked with reconstruction alongside this ministry: the Office of Agricultural Regeneration created in August 1917, the Department of Civil Engineering which took over from the Department of Urgent Works and the Department for Industrial Regeneration. That led to overlaps in responsibility, notably in prefects' administrations, local government and the external services of the Ministry for Liberated Regions, which was a factor in waste and hold-ups. What is more, the communes and individuals managed the repair work alone once finance had been secured.

The grouping of all reconstruction administrations into a single body was the major demand made by professionals from the beginning of the 1940s. Strengthened by the Vichy regime's authoritarianism and by the absence of democratic checks, they made their opinions triumph without difficulty. Pleased to have been recruited by the new state as experts in urban planning issues, during the war they had experienced centralized institutions which were expected to override local agendas and their parochialism. Evoking the organizational flaws of the 1918 reconstruction was, for them, a way of giving legitimacy to their current behaviour, to demonstrate the soundness of their proposals and their actions within the administrative structures Vichy had created. In November 1944 when, for the most part, they had been confirmed in their previous posts by the provisional government, they hailed the setting up of a Ministry for Reconstruction and Urban Planning (MRU) as their victory. While ensuring continuity with what had been done during the war, particularly in the drawing up of plans for destroyed cities, this initiative confirmed the dominance achieved by architects and engineers in the management of reconstruction. But that did not weaken the position of the Monuments Historiques which came under the department of Beaux-Arts in the Ministry of National Education. Moreover, the development of the Modern Movement in architecture from the 1940s onwards coincided with a weakening of support for the doctrine of regionalism after 1945.

Which architectural and planning options?

The originality of reconstruction in the second post-war period stems from the eminent position of central bodies in making city planning decisions. Indeed, urban planners did not secure building sites unless they had been certified by such bodies. The criteria behind this process of recognition were political (no history of compromise with the occupying Nazis), technical (possession of a business capable of managing a large site) and theoretical (making the most of the destruction to modernize cities by transforming the structure they had inherited first from neoclassicism and then from industrialization in the nineteenth century). In agreement with government authorities, they wanted to remove narrow winding streets lined with slums and to clean up districts where small workshops, polluting factories and working class accommodation were packed tightly together, constituting a source of disease and insalubrity. That is why, according to the directives of the MRU, all plans for reconstruction were to be drafted in line with the principle of separating the main urban functions, known as zoning. Bomb-damaged companies were required to rebuild their premises on the edge of cities. The space freed up by these relocations was reserved for the construction of more spacious and less densely packed housing. Commercial and administrative offices were regrouped in single function centres, which were an important innovation in the 1950s.

To achieve this opening up of space, the MRU undertook to piece together small units of land. These had a long urban history and were fragmented into a large number of narrow interlinking strips. This process of land consolidation was long and complex because it was necessary to obtain the permission of proprietors and to calculate the equivalences of surface area, location and orientation. Could a shopkeeper from the town centre who was a property owner in a thriving commercial district readily agree to being rehoused several hundred metres away from his former shop, with the risk that clients might be less frequent? Tough negotiations were required until solutions acceptable to both the authorities and the bomb victims were reached. This search for amicable solutions, the only outcomes acceptable in the context of a return to democracy, caused the results of land consolidation to be less radical than urban planners had hoped for. Nonetheless, as after 1918 in the countryside, the piecing together of strips of land, even if it allowed for an expansion and general regularization of land parcels, more or less respected the pre-destruction spirit.

Urban planners likewise wanted to rationalize the highways, another subject for debate with the inhabitants who stood to lose precious square metres for the sake of a common good, which was not always discernible by citizens still deeply shocked by the war, the Occupation and the loss of their property. There were consequently some large-scale innovations such as the wide avenues stretching from the railway stations to the town centres in

Caen and Saint-Nazaire. However, as with land consolidation, the planners had not succeeded in imposing major upheaval everywhere, and the new roads, despite the ample space available for straightening, ran along the traces of former highways.

The MRU demonstrated pragmatism in design choices. Reconstruction projects were assigned equally to proponents of the Modern Movement as to the followers of tradition as taught in the École des Beaux-Arts. That explains why the reconstruction overall was neither totally modernist nor totally like-for-like. One can dub the reconstruction 'moderate', aimed at not breaking too brutally with history. The design of new buildings tried to fit into the ancient landscape. Some communities nonetheless were singled out for their symbolic power. Thus, in Oradour-sur-Glane, a village in the Limousin which had been burned to the ground during the German retreat in June 1944, the ruins were preserved in memory of the martyrdom of its inhabitants and a new village was built a few hundred metres away from the original site. This conservation of ruins to bear witness to the horror of war was, however, the exception. Those reconstructing France preferred to look to the future and erase all ruins.

The majority, in agreement with the majority of victims, pledged their support for like-for-like reconstruction. In Saint-Dié, this was the outcome of the inhabitants' opposition to Le Corbusier's modernist project. In Gien, Saint-Malo and Blois, local communities' attachment to the old designs was expressed through the economic case made by those highlighting the touristic attraction of their town. Conversely, apologists of modern architecture drew satisfaction from Le Havre which had been handed over to Auguste Perret, from the town of Royan which had lost a number of its late nineteenth-century rococo buildings when the seaside resort was redeveloped, and from Sotteville-les-Rouen reconstructed by Marcel Lods (Figure 1). Alongside these reconstructions according to modern architectural taste, experts of the art world were forced to sew back together the web of urban devastation and ensure a smooth transition between the repaired old buildings and completely reconstructed districts. Marseille and Caen, where ancient abbeys and churches were rebuilt stone by stone, are examples of balanced reconstruction bridging the pre- and post-destruction eras.

Even if the debates between architects and planners to reach these solutions were fierce, they barely took into account the preferences of the victims. These people found that the directives from Paris, both those from the MRU and those from practitioners who for the most part came from the capital, did not take into consideration the wishes of the bombing victims or their specific situation. From this point of view the story of the reconstruction can be read as a narrative of the relationship of conflict between the central power which established the general rules and the municipalities who were more attuned to the desires of the victims. The inhabitants of the bombed towns were hardly *au fait* with debates between different schools

FIGURE 1 *Reconstruction in Le Havre. Source: Robert Pickard.*

of architecture. The tall blocks of flats favoured by the Modern Movement architects were seen as an 'American' import which was alien to the French traditions with which they were comfortable. Moreover, the tenets of urban planning developed from the beginning of the century promoted the destruction of slums, the widening of streets and the displacement of small industries from residential areas, none of which reflected the daily life of the war victims in any respect. They did not appreciate the concrete and the roof terraces, a mindset which Le Corbusier and his friend Eugène Claudius-Petit deplored. On several occasions this Minister of Reconstruction regretted the choices made by the French who were reluctant to embrace modern forms.

Indeed this type of architecture was preferred by the Ministry of Reconstruction which had been seduced by the Corbusians' slogan, 'air, sun, light', implying the destruction of low-rise flats and the end of roadside housing in favour of perpendicular blocks built in green spaces. The Ministry viewed reconstruction as a single project to which the same answers applied. The municipalities, however, knew their own individual circumstances. In Lorient for example, the first plan for reconstruction envisaged a broad green expanse which would have cut off the arsenal from the rest of the city, a solution which went against the preference of the local council. Extensive negotiations were necessary for a consensus to be reached. This was likewise the case for Marseille. No less than three large-scale projects were designed before the buildings lining the ancient port were reconstructed without any tower blocks alongside the old quays. In Dunkirk, the issue of land consolidation set the victims' associations against the chief urban planner.

In the same way the Ministry's idea of reconstructing Dugny, which had been severely damaged by bombing raids aiming for Le Bourget airport, was swept aside by the townsfolk who refused outright such a radical solution.

The reconstruction of churches provides a good illustration of the range of these debates and choices. No fewer than 5,800 places of worship were destroyed, for the most part simple rural chapels or buildings without recognized historic interest. Only 370, cathedrals and monastery or convent churches, were classified as historic monuments. Among them, Notre Dame de Royan (Charente maritime) and Sainte Jeanne d'Arc de Gien (Loiret), both cited in histories of French architecture as major achievements of the post-war years, are like-for-like reconstructions. They bear witness to the architectural debate which was born in the early years of the first post-war period and shook the department of Monuments Historiques from 1920 onwards. This debate contrasted two concepts of conservation: the one moderate, the other a sharp break. For if the great majority of the architects of the Monuments Historiques refused to contemplate imitation, rejecting buildings in 'neo' of any style, partisans of the Beaux-Arts tradition, who were keen to preserve the original spirit of buildings by using traditional techniques while avoiding any pastiche, refused to fall in with their colleagues who were resolutely committed to contemporary architecture. Discussion focused on large structures such as Rheims cathedral which, as an exception, had been rebuilt as it was in former times, whereas beside part of the preserved choir of the church of Saint Pierre à Roye (Somme), for instance, the architects Charles Duval and Emmanuel Gonse had erected a 64-metre bell tower in reinforced concrete which was similar in form to Notre-Dame du Raincy (Seine-Saint-Denis) built in 1923 by Auguste Perret as a statement of modern architecture (Gonse 1936: 76–81). The major difference between the two conceptions lay in the choice of material (brick or stone as opposed to concrete), in the silhouette (pitched roof rather than a terraced roof) and in the floor plan (a church with side aisles rather than a single space with a sloping floor, allowing the faithful to follow the Mass more easily).

In 1945, Sainte Jeanne d'Arc de Gien, an example of modern reconstruction merged with the traditional style of the region, is often referred to as one of the principal achievements of religious French architecture of the post-war period (Figure 2). Its uniqueness is also derived from the fact that Gien, first destroyed in combat in 1940 before being bombarded again in 1943 and 1944, was selected by the Vichy government to be the showcase of its own reconstruction efforts. Work began on the project during the Occupation. It was, above all, a matter of reconstructing the town's two churches: Saint Pierre and Saint Louis. Unlike the political struggles which gripped a number of French municipalities between 1939 and 1945, the various transfers of municipal powers took place quietly (Voldman 1997: 93–107). Due to a lack of funds, it was decided to rebuild only one church from the ruins of that which had best resisted collapse.

FIGURE 2 *The reconstructed church of Sainte Jeanne d'Arc de Gien. Source: Jack-ogamer (Wikimedia Commons).*

The plan was entrusted to Paul Gélis, the most senior architect in the Monuments Historiques who had been in post since 1943 and enjoyed the confidence of the local council, notwithstanding the political changes during the war and post-war period. The architect strove to preserve the essence of the bell tower by drawing inspiration from the forms of the primitive church, in the simplicity of the Norman tradition but employing a modern vocabulary. Stone was retained for only the foundation, the pillars and the altar. Everywhere else pink brick was dominant, the local material which had been used across the town since the fifteenth century. The wide nave, completely made of pink brick decorated with patterns picked out in black and yellow brick, was separated from the side aisles by slender round pillars topped with capitals in terracotta. The ceiling vault was pierced by windows where yellow and red tones dominated, the work of the master glassmaker Max Ingrand, who was responsible for the stained glass in many churches in France and abroad and in the chapels of several of the Loire châteaux.[2] The warm golden light they diffused was in harmony with the colour of the brick whose patterning drew some decorative effects from the sober Norman style. The new building was consecrated to St Joan of Arc, in memory of her visit to the town when she was en route to free Orléans. In a fusion of symbolic meanings, Joan of Arc, who had been honoured by Vichy as the icon of resistance to the English, became with the Liberation in 1945 the symbol of resistance to all invaders.

Unlike Gien which had been chosen by the authorities to be reconstructed exactly as it was by local firms and artisans, Royan was marked out for modernism (Ragot 2003). In tune with the covered market and the waterfront portico, the reconstruction of its church, Notre Dame, was a technical feat in reinforced concrete (Figure 3). It incarnated the rebirth of the town following the deadly English bombing raid in January 1945. Notre Dame displayed a distinct architectural vocabulary developed through a highly technical use of concrete. Its architect, Guillaume Gillet, employed two inventions with industrial application by the engineer Bernard Lafaille: the V-shaped beam of pre-stressed concrete for the building's skeleton and the thin veil of reinforced concrete for the cover. Made entirely of bare grey concrete, roughly set, the building rose 40 m high above the earth, a vault less than 10 cm thick in the shape of a saddle. It was supported by twenty-four posts arranged as an ellipsis and separated by windows forming the façade. At its prow, another monumental V shape 56 m in height constituted the spire which was topped by an arrow. Its total height of nearly 90 m, visible from afar, expressed a celebration of the power of spirituality as well as the renaissance of the city. On the design level, Gillet took inspiration from organ music. In this way he reconnected with the Gothic tradition of the spiritual quest for light achieved by reducing the volume of the building's frame. This effect was increased by constructing the church on sloping ground. The monumental porch, which was situated at the west end at the highest point of the site, respected the traditional orientation. Thus the entrance to the building dominated the unique nave which was surrounded by a pathway round the edge which the faithful reached by steps.

---

[2]Médiathèque de l'architecture et du patrimoine, 0081/045/0021–0097, *Le Figaro*, 28 and 29 March 1954.

FIGURE 3 *The reconstructed church of Notre Dame de Royan. Source: Wolfgang Pehlemann (Wikimedia Commons).*

Conclusion

At the outset of the twenty-first century when the long-unloved architecture of reconstruction was beginning to emerge from purgatory, the two buildings which had been in opposition at the time of their construction were finally recognized as structures equally worthy of interest. Following the classification as a historic monument of Notre Dame de Royan and a campaign for its restoration came heritage status for Gélis' building, fully classified in the supplementary inventory of 2001. The various stages in the reconstruction of these two churches, representative of all the buildings destroyed in the two wars, demonstrate the extent to which choices of design and technique were dependent on both architectural theory and the conception of *patrimoine* as well as the treatment of history by public authorities. If the choices of reconstruction of an authoritarian regime such as that of Vichy, which turned its face towards tradition and the conservation of the past, are compared with the modernizing drive of the Fourth Republic, it is evident how far technical issues and political motivations merge. The architects who conceived the reconstruction of the country between 1940 and 1944 could not ignore the advantages of innovations of their time such as prefabrication and the use of concrete, despite their love for ancient architecture and regionalism. They were, indeed, encouraged in this direction by the authorities in a search for rapid methods by which to raise the ruins. As for the architects and modernist urban planners favoured by the Fourth Republic, they were not free to make a radical clean start which would have removed forever all traces of a thousand years of building from which nations are constructed.

The razing of all traces of war allowed people to find peace again, but could they to the same extent forget what was irreparably lost – the dead, the homes, the landscapes, all the memory of a nation? That was what was at stake in the rebuilding of a country which had just been torn apart by five years of war and foreign occupation.

References

Gonse, E. (1936), 'L'église Saint Pierre de Roye', *L'Art sacré*, 9 (March): 76–91.

Kuisel, R. F. (1981), *Le capitalisme et l'État en France. Modernisation et dirigisme au XXᵉ siècle*, Paris: Gallimard.

Ragot, G. (ed) (2003), *L'invention d'une ville. Royan années 50*, Monum: Éditions du patrimoine.

Voldman, D. (1997), *La reconstruction des villes françaises de 1940 à 1954. Histoire d'une politique*, Paris: L'Harmattan.

Voldman, D. (2000), 'Comment réparer les dommages de la guerre?', *Les Cahiers pour la paix*, 7: 146–63.

Voldman, D. (2011), 'La France d'un modèle de reconstruction à l'autre, 1918–1945', in N. Bullock and L. Verpoest (eds), *Living with History, 1914–1964. Rebuilding Europe after the First and the Second World Wars and the role of Heritage Preservation*, Leuven: Leuven University Press.

Chapter 2.4

Reconstruction in South-East Europe and Georgia: An Architect's Perspective – Scale, Materials and Appearances

David Johnson

Introduction

Under the ICOMOS Charter for the Conservation of Places of Cultural Significance (the Burra Charter, 2013), 'reconstruction' involves returning a place to a known earlier state and is distinguished from restoration by the introduction of new materials into the fabric. The process of reconstruction from an architectural practitioner's viewpoint almost always embraces all of the processes of conservation: consolidation, repair, restoration and, importantly, rehabilitation, in which it is not just individual buildings which may be reconstructed, but entire communities.

This chapter explores recent approaches to the reconstruction of buildings and sites in South-East Europe and Georgia which have taken place following the conflicts and the socio-economic and political changes in the regions, particularly since the early 1990s. It is based on fieldwork carried out on a number of projects implemented by the Council of Europe since 2003 (Council of Europe 2014, Bold and Cherry 2016). The approaches may be explored in three main areas: in rural settlements where depopulation and changes in traditional industries have seen large-scale abandonment of buildings and communities; in urban sites which have often experienced large-scale population increases, with a consequent impact on the built environment accompanied by political and economic change; and in areas where large numbers of people have been displaced from their homes and communities as a result of direct conflict.

Heritage management systems in the new market economies which have prevailed in the two regions under consideration since the major social, economic and political realignments of 1989–90 are in a process of ongoing development and refinement, a fluid situation exacerbated by shortages of staff and funding (Rikalović and Mikić 2014). Whereas in Western Europe there has been over many years a great increase in the number of heritage professionals including architects, surveyors, engineers, project managers, access consultants, educational and activity planners and business planners, together with a resurgence in trades and craft skills, supported by a growing number of specialist contractors in such disciplines as masonry, joinery, glass and iron work, there has been no such rapid growth in South-East Europe and the Caucasus. It has been one of the aims of the Council of Europe and the European Commission in recent heritage projects to stimulate an expansion in skills and training for young professionals as well as to stimulate investment and recognition of the built heritage as an economic asset (Bartlett et al. 2015), going beyond mere restoration towards identifying beneficial, sustainable new functions, thereby encouraging a positive attitude from the public towards the conservation and reuse of historic buildings and sites.

The beginning of a process of re-education in craft and other specialist skills has included the introduction of methodologies for identification and assessment of historic buildings and sites through the creation of building inventories, followed by the technical assessment of historic buildings and sites in both rural and urban situations (Council of Europe 2005). The Heritage Survey, building on the documentation standards established by the Council of Europe (Council of Europe 2001), has aimed to create a methodology to carry out a basic, quickly produced survey of (initially) vernacular heritage. This has been completed as a pilot study in Croatia and Macedonia and has created a tool to help with the management of often large numbers of otherwise unrecorded buildings and to draw to the attention of the responsible authorities and the wider community the problems being faced by these sites. These initiatives have in many cases been adopted by the countries involved and are being used in the continuing process of rehabilitation and reconstruction.

Reconstruction, depopulation and abandonment of traditional skills and industry

In rural areas, depopulation and the abandonment of settlements inevitably lead to a deterioration of the buildings and the environment. Changes in the local economy and the movement of the population to urban centres prompt a gradual decline in the services provided to these rural communities, with a consequent effect on the control of the subsequent reconstruction and reuse of the buildings. The move towards abandonment of the settlements is often slow but progressive and the impacts of the lack of ongoing maintenance and care of the infrastructure and the buildings themselves often go largely unnoticed: but these can ultimately and quite rapidly reach a point where the reconstruction and rehabilitation of the sites can be difficult if not impossible.

The examples of the Island of Cres in Croatia and the region of Debar and Reka in Macedonia illustrate the social and economic problems affecting numerous sites across many rural areas in the region. There has been a gradual depopulation on Cres since the later part of the twentieth century, following the decline of the traditional industries of agriculture and fishing which has resulted in the progressive deterioration and decay of village settlements. The infrastructure is relatively poor: car-ferry services with the mainland stop during the night, public transport is poorly developed and the northern part of the island has no public water supply. Around 800 buildings are considered to be of importance to the heritage. Of these, the majority are stone-built dwellings, and there are also religious, public, fortified and industrial or agricultural buildings. Many are in a state of collapse and either beyond economic repair or requiring immediate and long-term maintenance if they are to be saved. Of those buildings that remain in use, many have experienced a loss or change of function and local, uncontrolled alteration. Inexpert repairs and restoration techniques have been carried out which has led to a loss of authenticity and the gradual erosion of the heritage and sense of place. These types of change are mostly confined to vernacular building which has not generally been recognized as of major significance to the heritage. Resources tend to be focussed on the more obviously monumental public or religious buildings which have a positive effect on tourism and community value but often limited functional value, making only a minor contribution to the wider appreciation of the heritage. To date, notwithstanding economic decline, extreme examples of complete alterations to the vernacular buildings of Cres are limited (76 buildings are registered as having been largely rebuilt, 365 are partially altered and 355 are authentic).

The rural region of Debar and Reka in Macedonia presents similar problems. Almost all elements of the traditional agricultural economy are in decline, which is reflected in the partial or complete abandonment of many villages. Only two villages in this region – Zhirovnica and Vrbjani – are densely populated and indeed in this type of village there are many examples of traditional buildings being demolished or modified using contemporary techniques which significantly alter the architectural and traditional typology of the place. There is little tourism but the reconstruction in whole or part of individual buildings follows similar patterns to the changes occurring in Cres.

Accompanying depopulation and the decline in traditional industries there have been the major demands placed on the built heritage through the development of tourism. Often seen as a panacea for the treatment of economic ills as it replaces the traditional economies in many of these regions, offering employment and the opportunity to invest in the infrastructure, tourism also brings a shift in attitude and approach to building rehabilitation and reconstruction. The older traditional buildings are regarded as leaky, poorly insulated and expensive to maintain but many tourists demand high levels of servicing, en-suite accommodation, air conditioning and a high level of accessibility. Without careful management this can lead to large-scale changes to the ambience of the heritage both in terms of landscape setting, where car movement and parking can dominate the streetscape and environment, and on the appearance of often vulnerable and sensitive buildings. Such changes can naturally lead to a loss of historical layering, and an unalterable change to the ambience and cultural significance of the place. Small rural communities are often overcome by vast increases in population during the summer months. In Cres tourism has replaced the traditional industries and during the summer the island receives around 10,000–12,000 visitors, up to four times the indigenous population: the island covers an area of around 405 km² and currently has a population of around 3,200 inhabitants, of whom around 2,200 live in the main town of Cres. The expectation of tourists here is changing, with a growing demand for highly serviced accommodation, including air conditioning, putting pressure on electrical and water supplies and drainage. The adaptations required to fulfil these new demands often come at the price of the erosion of the fabric of these modest but important buildings. For planning authorities the challenge is to encourage sensitive, sustainable tourism while protecting against the widespread damage consequent upon uncontrolled development. The Croatian Ministry of Culture has recognized the vulnerability of the heritage in Cres and has completed a heritage survey which identifies the extent of risk and loss. It is working to encourage a local collaborative and interdisciplinary approach to manage these issues, stimulating owners, developers and the local population to recognize the potential of the built heritage in economic regeneration.

The changes in both these regions in Croatia and Macedonia are characterized by a gradual move to the use of modern (often unsustainable) technologies and building methods and materials including the widespread use of prefabricated panels and concrete block work as facing materials, and the use of unplasticized polyvinyl chloride (upvc) in place of timber for windows and doors. The loss of skills in traditional building and repair techniques contributes further to these changes. Such skills are often labour intensive, may require learning through apprenticeship and therefore become costlier to employ. There is currently little support from local authorities towards addressing the needs or consequences of these changes.

The skills shortage, which is apparent in works on small-scale vernacular buildings, has also affected the availability of local skills on buildings of national and international importance, leading to the employment of specialist contractors from other parts of the region. Besac Fortress, overlooking Skadar Lake, is situated in one of the five national parks in Montenegro. Built in 1478 by the Turks, on a hill rising above the town of Virpazar, it was abandoned after the Second World War and by 2008 was in a ruinous condition with only parts of the original masonry walling of fortress and barracks remaining: the Ministry of Culture drew up proposals for its rehabilitation (Johnson 2016: 127–9). As a building of international importance it was imperative that the works were completed to meet appropriate standards of repair and reconstruction and contractors were brought in from Italy and Serbia to carry out the first phase of the project. A highly restorative approach has been adopted, the majority of the external walling rebuilt including that of the former barracks building which will be used as a visitor centre. While the standard of the work is considered good, there are questions over the appropriateness of some of the materials used and the rather heavy-handed approach which has removed much of the patina and quality of place of the buildings, giving them a heavily cleaned and rather sanitized appearance. But it is important to recognize that the buildings and site have been saved from ongoing deterioration and if managed properly will become an important part of the local tourist offer.

The Jusuf Maskovic Han in Vrana, Croatia, has recently been reconstructed (Johnson 2016: 120–1). This long-abandoned and badly damaged building has been given a new life through careful management and design and a major grant from the European Union's Pre-Accession Fund. The construction of this caravanserai was begun in 1644 but it was left uncompleted upon the untimely death of its patron. Since the building was incomplete, some elements of the restoration had no design precedent. For example, the chimneys to each of the fireplaces in the accommodation wings had not been constructed but, as prominent elements of the design, they have assumed an important function providing ventilation to each of the spaces. Their design is modelled on Ottoman precedents but has been completed in a simple render over masonry (Figure 1). An important collaboration with experts from Bosnia and Herzegovina and Macedonia, familiar with Ottoman architectural and decorative characteristics, helped in the design process. A number of other new facilities have been constructed, including a block of new toilets and a fully equipped kitchen to serve the spacious restaurant. These have been completed using simple, functional forms that respect the ambience of the location and its context. The approach adopted here has saved the building and promises to be successful so long as its future management promotes a compatible use and the site continues to be popular. Some of the techniques adopted might, from a contemporary, purist point of view

FIGURE 1 *Jusuf Maskovic Han in Vrana, Croatia. Note the reconstructed chimneys and other elements of the construction designed without clear knowledge of the original design intention and modelled instead on Ottoman precedents. Source: Kvarantan.*

be challenged; the reconstruction is complete but in its recreation of parts of the building for which there are no records and its creation of other parts which did not previously exist, there is a lack of clarity in terms of historical progression since the new sections cannot be read as modern interventions. The accepted conservation approach might have been carefully to restore those parts of the building which remained, but to reconstruct the lost or unfinished elements in a modern idiom, introducing a new style, recovering the old but clearly defining the new. Such a style-based debate may inform future interventions in historic buildings as the countries develop their own philosophy about the reconstruction process. The main point here, however, is that the site has been saved and if properly interpreted represents an important stepping stone in the process of rehabilitation.

Preservation, consolidation, repair, restoration and reconstruction in an urban environment

The City Hall in Sarajevo is an example of a high-profile major building which has been restored to its original design, involving wide public involvement and engagement in the development process (Bartlett et al. 2015: 34–5, Johnson 2016: 114–6). One of Bosnia and Herzegovina's most significant cultural monuments, the City Hall was built in 1892–96 to the designs of Alexander Vittek in a pseudo-Moorish style. After serving various municipal functions it became the National and University Library in 1948. In August 1992 the City Hall was hit by heavy artillery fire, resulting in major structural damage. The outstanding library holdings were destroyed by fire. The reconstruction of the building has become a symbol of the city's recovery from the impact of the shelling. Its rehabilitation has involved a wide section of the local community, as well as regional and international experts, in drawing up proposals for the implementation of a project which has brought a new understanding of the values and significance of the building and a consideration of options for its reconstruction, future use and management. The quality of work is generally of a high standard and has been largely carried out with local resources. But following the highly restorative approach, there is now little evidence of the evolution of the building in terms of its historic layering, particularly relating to the damage sustained during the war in 1992: this was severe, the fire destroying virtually all of the roof construction, much of the interior and exterior walling and associated finishes. The extent of the reconstruction suggests a desire to obliterate almost all signs of the damage inflicted on the building, erasing the impact from the memory of the community, although a plaque outside records the circumstances (Figure 2).

The extent of damage to the City Hall can be compared with that sustained by the mid-nineteenth-century Neues Museum in Berlin during the Second World War, and during Soviet occupation after the war when the ruin was left to decay for a long period of time. Some reconstruction work was carried out by the East German Government in the late 1980s, but was halted after the fall of the Berlin Wall and German reunification. The work resumed in 1997 and the building reopened in 2009. The architects referred to the restoration as following 'a principle of conservation rather than reconstruction', maintaining much of the historical layering of the site as found, designing each of the individual spaces around what remained and applying a carefully researched discipline to the conservation and reconstruction of original features (*dezeen magazine* 2009).

Reconstruction in urban areas shows some of the same characteristics as in rural areas, but the factors involved are often more complex. It is in the nature of urban development that the building stock is often under pressure to adapt and change, in response to changes in population, to commercial and economic demands and to shifts in people's attitudes towards their environment, as well as to evolution in architectural taste. As a result there is often a continuous or cyclical modification through demolition and alteration of the buildings to adapt to new demands. This is perhaps most obvious in Western Europe where the economic performance of buildings is carefully monitored. Planners and architects then face new challenges in managing the process of change, developing an awareness of what should be preserved and how, determining how we can adapt and find new uses for buildings of architectural significance without diminishing their place and value in the built environment, and how we should prioritize change and

FIGURE 2 *Sarajevo City Hall, Bosnia and Herzegovina. Work in progress showing the completeness of the reconstructions and removal of almost all traces of the historical patina of the building. Source: Mirzah Foco.*

make decisions about what can be lost or modified. From an architectural perspective, the preferred approach should be to conserve buildings and sites in a way which preserves and enhances the historical, social or economic contributions they have made but which also provides sustainable solutions to the demands of development upon the urban fabric, so enhancing the environment and the quality of life.

The challenges of such an approach in South-East Europe are numerous but a key issue remains the lack of adequate planning control and protective legislation. Buildings are often exploited for commercial interest or simply left to deteriorate through lack of investment in maintenance and repair, a problem compounded by questions of ownership (often absentee) and responsibility in a situation in which the benefits of restoration or sympathetic reconstruction, and their positive contribution to civic well-being, are ill-defined and imperfectly understood. The reconstruction process in such situations can be damaging. The absence of sensitive controls and political interference has resulted in the loss or change in character of many urban centres. Looking beyond South-East Europe, the Old Town of Tbilisi, Georgia, has seen large swaths of significant, historically important buildings demolished and replaced with either poor imitations of traditional styles or simply inappropriate and poor quality modern building (Council of Europe 2002) (Figure 3). As a result there is great confusion about what is old and new and the ambience and characteristics of the heritage are lost.

FIGURE 3 *Residential infill building, Old Town, Tbilisi, Georgia. Recent recon-struction of dwellings demonstrating poor quality design integration and inappropri-ate detailing. Source: David Johnson.*

Appropriateness of technique and material selection in reconstruction

Reconstruction following social conflict and deliberate vandalism may be illustrated by the example of the episcopal Church of St George, the adjacent Runovic Chapel and the Bishop's Palace in Prizren, Kosovo, which were among thirty-five sites which were severely damaged in riots in spring 2004. The roof of the church was completely destroyed, the central bell tower collapsed into the nave and the walls and all finishes were badly disfigured by fire; the interior and wall paintings of the chapel were damaged by explosion and fire; and the nineteenth-century residence gutted, with only its perimeter walls remaining. Following rapid technical assessments, recording the condition of each building and making proposals for its immediate protection, a detailed reconstruction project was negotiated and a team headed by the Council of Europe began work. This brought together a number of different interests and agencies in the 'Reconstruction Implementation Commission' and was successfully completed in 2009 (Council of Europe 2004).

The reconstruction was not purist: modern building standards were met, using materials which were easy to procure and maintain (marble flooring rather than stone slabs) and such features as underfloor heating were installed. The case for reconstructing and funding iconic buildings which have limited functions remains controversial, but in this case the project had a very significant impact beyond mere restoration in bringing together a wide range of interest groups and agencies drawn from Kosovo, Serbia and the international community: this collaboration was central to the success of the project and its legacy.

While compromises were made in the approach to the reconstruction of the Church of St George, the reconstruction of the site of Holy Archangels Monastery in the Bristica Gorge just outside Prizren (also badly damaged during the riots) was completed by the Orthodox Church without reference to outside agencies or influences. The design of new buildings on parts of the site, particularly the gatehouse, has been controversial. The buildings have been constructed in timber and have adopted a 'chalet style' which has no obvious precedent on this site and accordingly disregards the status of the site as one of international importance (Subotić 1998: 220–32). But such issues have to be seen in context: this was a community where homes had been destroyed and people were living in shipping containers. This was an occupied zone and international efforts had perhaps not been focussed closely enough on providing the detailed level of investment that this particularly historically significant site required. In the absence of control or of any meaningful dialogue between the users of the site and the heritage agencies, new buildings now provide shelter and meet essential community needs but detract from the architectural quality of the site and its significance.

Senjski Rudnik, Serbia's oldest coal mine, lies at the centre of a small urban settlement for which European Commission funding was obtained for the reconstruction of a number of buildings with the long-term aim of rehabilitating the town, enabling economic growth and social cohesion. The first phase of the works was completed in 2012, under the direction of a university team from Belgrade, although the buildings themselves (a museum and events centre) have yet to be fitted out. Senjski Rudnik holds a key place in Serbia's industrial and social history, but it had gradually deteriorated as the mining industry declined, buildings fell into disrepair, and much of the original production processes and ephemera of the mine had been lost, particularly during the 1980s, when a desire to obscure and remove the harsh industrial history and landscape of the place held sway.

The architects' vision was to see the project not just as a museum but as an environmental experience, in which visitors could engage with the history of the town in a way which reflected as much of the surroundings, the buildings and the industrialization of the place as could be presented through a three-dimensional design process; at the same time contributing to the social and economic well-being of the town and its inhabitants, many of whom having left when jobs were lost, would be expected to return. In the interiors of the museum building the architects aimed to leave as much 'authentic' space as possible retaining the industrial aesthetic. The highly advanced historical use of concrete in the detailing of the original museum was carefully repaired and exposed and has proved particularly successful in the re-presentation of the existing staircase and mezzanine floor structures. The simple application of black paint to the new steel elements inside the building clearly identifies the new structure (Figure 4).

FIGURE 4 *Mining and Local History Museum, Senjski Rudnik, Serbia. Sensitively restored and extended museum interior – note the simple but effective differentiation of new structural elements in contrasting tones. Source: David Johnson.*

In the former smithy and machine workshop a key design decision was to close the roof construction in part of the building to improve thermal performance. This has had a fundamental impact on the appearance of the interior, significantly altering the industrial aesthetic. The interiors now present a clean, almost gallery-like quality and it will be interesting to see how the artefacts that are due to be placed in them invoke the spirit of place that the architects have been keen to adopt in other areas of the project. A further modification to improve the thermal performance of the buildings has been to apply insulation to the workshop's façades, masking the industrial quality of the exterior.

Reconstruction following conflict in a rural environment

The reconstruction of communities following conflict and displacement represents perhaps the most extreme challenge in satisfying the need for immediate humanitarian aid and the creation of new homes, requiring the mobilization and coordination of many agencies for successful implementation (Zetter 2010). The need for temporary or permanent accommodation is often not predictable: the number of people involved may be large, speed is essential and funding often a problem. These restrictions can create serious technical problems in respect of the available construction techniques and skills. The selection of new sites may often be based on existing infrastructure or access which may in the longer term be inappropriate. It is often difficult to create temporary accommodation which meets social needs; community fragmentation may follow.

Following the Georgian–Russian conflict in 2008 around 22,000 people were displaced: the Georgian government took immediate measures to resolve the resettlement problem and set about building new 'cottage' settlements for many internally displaced persons (IDPs) in the Mtskheta-Mtianeti and Shida Kartli regions in the post-buffer zone villages north of Gori in a period of just four months following the conflict. In early 2016 this accommodation still provides a temporary shelter for nearly 1,400 families (13,800 IDPs). The design and construction of the settlements was conducted at an unprecedented speed which may have contributed towards a number of technical and socio-economic issues which have arisen. The funding for the works came from the state, supplemented by international loans and grants. Although not absolutely clear, it appears that the settlements were built as permanent, rather than temporary, accommodation, it being clear that the IDPs would be unable to return to their own homes in the foreseeable future.

Three main criteria were adopted in the choice of site, the first being to respond to the fact that the majority of the IDPs came from an agricultural background: a key decision was taken to locate and design the settlements in an agricultural area, offering the people the opportunity to redevelop their traditional way of life. Secondly, flat sites were chosen to simplify planning, construction and cost; and thirdly, where possible, they were sited close to existing services and infrastructure. Initially the settlements were constructed to provide residential accommodation only, with public buildings to follow: these are still to be completed. Schools and nursery spaces are available in nearby villages. The speed of the work and lack of a comprehensive and technically complete strategy prevented proper consideration and attention to building techniques. As a result, serious problems arose very soon after construction with high levels of humidity, damp ingress and the lack of suitable thermal insulation, problems which have yet to be fully addressed and which have had a negative impact on the health and quality of life of the people and their consequent satisfaction with their new homes.

The settlements have been planned as a series of single-storey dwellings, standing in parallel lines, broken by streets at right angles, resulting in a series of rectangular sectors. The layout has not provided for the private, garden space to which the people had been accustomed. There is no storage space for tools or for crops. Generally the living areas are considered by the residents to be functionally and aesthetically inferior to the houses they left behind. As a result of this dissatisfaction, they have resorted to modifying the dwellings, constructing extensions to improve their social space, to give more protection against the weather and to provide storage for tools and equipment. Setting aside the visual and physical implications that these unplanned changes are having, there is also an uncertainty on the part of the residents about future ownership and how this might affect the investment they are making in their new homes. This has been a major and recurrent problem in the countries of the former Soviet bloc: the post-1989 privatization of formerly state-owned buildings has often not encouraged maintenance and restoration since a situation once reversed may be reversed again, so effort and expenditure may have been to no personally beneficial purpose.

The problems which these new Georgian settlements face seem to revolve around the method and more specifically the time available for planning and constructing settlements on such a large scale. A comparison can be made with the reconstruction of Nahr el-Bared in Lebanon where the homes of 27,000 Palestinians were replaced following the destruction of their refugee camp, built in 1948, during the 2007 conflict between the Lebanese armed forces and the extremist group Fatah Al-Islam. Here the refugees were immediately housed in a temporary refuge at another nearby camp. This gave the United Nations Relief and Works Agency working alongside the community based Nahr el-Bared Reconstruction Commission a breathing space in which to develop a masterplan for 5,000 houses, 1,500 shops and 6 school complexes to be built on the site. Like the Georgian project the reconstruction included the replacement of all the infrastructure for the camp including water, sewage and electricity networks. The first families began returning to their homes in 2011, four years after the conflict (*dezeen magazine* 2013). This compares with the four months it took to complete the first houses in Georgia.

Conclusion

The depopulation of rural communities following the decline of the traditional industries of agriculture and fishing is a common problem across South-East Europe. As well as leading to the large-scale abandonment of these communities, there has also been a breakdown of the traditional skills and crafts which previously helped to maintain the visual characteristics of the region and the features that have contributed to the heritage. The growth of tourism has in many ways exacerbated this situation through the development of a museum-based investment in the heritage and indeed where tourism has impacted on the traditional dwellings it has often been detrimental to the way in which buildings and communities have been reconstructed. The work of the Council of Europe and others has started to shift the focus towards a greater local and institutional understanding and respect for the heritage which it is hoped will develop in time to save many of these places from further deterioration.

Urban redevelopment and reconstruction are natural processes with both positive and negative impacts. That the heritage needs to be brought into the redevelopment process is clear. This has been taking place in much of Europe for many years and the lessons that have been learned need to be extended into those countries which have undergone recent political or economic change to ensure that the continuity and richness of their urban centres is maintained.

The manner of reconstruction of buildings and sites following conflict is often rightly influenced by the communities which have experienced it. The cases of Kosovo and Sarajevo clearly illustrate how these influences can shape the way in which the built heritage is reconstructed. The lesson here is that architects need to work closely alongside community groups as the reconstruction process evolves, gathering information and discussing options, while at the same time promoting an understanding of the importance of the heritage and the need to respect its evolution; understanding and recording the historical, social and environmental factors that have influenced the style and typology of the buildings and bringing this knowledge to bear in the reconstruction process.

Through recent political change and conflict South-East Europe has lost many of the traditions and skills of maintenance and care for its heritage both at management and craft levels. At the same time building techniques have evolved and traditional methods of construction have been threatened through skills shortages and economic pressures. These traditional skills need to be re-established at both local and regional levels much as they have been in Western Europe and elsewhere, encouraged by the intervention of national and international organizations.

Clearly there are many complex and diverse issues which bear on the reconstruction of buildings and our appreciation of how scale and appearance, and the appropriateness of materials used affect our enjoyment of them. The case studies examined demonstrate how it is difficult to generalize or propose standard or generic approaches to reconstruction or to measure the relative importance and choice of technique of preservation, consolidation, repair or restoration in the process. Perhaps the key lesson is the importance of approaching each case on an individual basis using a simple methodology of survey and assessment to understand the problem, working with the means available in terms of skills, funding and timescale: generic solutions are to be avoided since individual cases demand creativity and flexibility in order to arrive at the individual, specific treatment which circumstances demand. Approaches should be transparent, the limitations or constraints of the site discussed and proposed solutions explained. This will involve the establishment of heritage education and training at community level so that practical approaches may be better understood and accepted. In an improved climate of understanding, disaster recovery and reconstruction may become less generic, more closely related to the specific site, more flexible and responsive to circumstances and more comprehensible to the community. A collaborative approach in which architects, planners, heritage specialists and other experts work with those who have been directly involved in the disaster on a case-specific basis may help us to move away from off-the-shelf solutions and fixed academic methodologies.

Acknowledgement

Information on the resettlement project in Georgia was received through personal communication with Nano Zazanashvili, January 2016. See also his essay 'Dwelling Adaptation in the Settlements of Internally Displaced Persons' in Gutbrod, H. ed. (2015), *From Private to Public – Transformation of Social Spaces in the South Caucasus,* Tbilisi: South Caucasus Regional Office of the Heinrich Boell Foundation.

References

Bartlett, W. et al. (2015), *The Wider Benefits of Investment in Cultural Heritage,* Strasbourg: Council of Europe.

Bold, J. and M. Cherry (eds) (2016), *The Politics of Heritage Regeneration in South-East Europe,* Strasbourg: Council of Europe.

Council of Europe (2001), *Guidance on Inventory and Documentation of the Cultural Heritage*, Strasbourg: Council of Europe.

Council of Europe (2002), *Urban Rehabilitation Policy in Tbilisi (Georgia)*, Strasbourg: Council of Europe.

Council of Europe (2004), 'Preliminary Technical Assessment Report on the Religious Buildings/Ensembles and Cultural Sites Damaged in March 2004 in Kosovo', May 2004 (AT04 171 rev); and subsequent reports July (AT04 245 rev) and August 2004 (AT04 245 bis), Strasbourg: Council of Europe.

Council of Europe (2005), *Guidance on Heritage Assessment*, Strasbourg: Council of Europe.

Council of Europe (2014), 'Kyiv Initiative: Pilot Project on the Rehabilitation of Cultural Heritage in Historic Towns', available online: www.coe.int/t/dg4/cultureheritage/cooperation/kyiv/urbanrehab (accessed 21 August 2016).

dezeen magazine (2009), 'Neues Museum by David Chipperfield Architects and Julian Harrap Architects', 4 March 2009, available online: www.dezeen.com (accessed 21 August 2016).

dezeen magazine (2013), 'Reconstruction of Nahr el-Bared Refugee Camp', 2 May 2013, available online: www.dezeen.com (accessed 21 August 2016).

Johnson, D. (2016), 'From Saving to Conservation', in J. Bold and M. Cherry (eds), *The Politics of Heritage Regeneration in South-East Europe*, Strasbourg: Council of Europe.

Rikalović, G. and H. Mikić (eds) (2014), *Heritage for Development in South-East Europe*, Strasbourg: Council of Europe.

Subotić, G. (1998), *Art of Kosovo*, New York: Monacelli.

Zetter, R. (2010), 'Land, Housing and the Reconstruction of the Built Environment', in S. Barakat (ed), *After the Conflict*, London and New York: I. B. Tauris.

PART 3

Reconstruction after Natural or Accidental Disaster

Introduction

There are many different forms of natural disaster which can have a detrimental impact on cultural heritage, particularly on buildings and settlements of recognized heritage value: earthquakes, volcanic activity, hurricanes, cyclones, tornadoes and other wind-forces, tsunami, flooding, avalanches, landslides and mudflows, storms, fires, other environmental problems and long-term climate effects. The number of disasters around the world is increasing every year, often with serious consequences for heritage resources, as has been reported through the United Nations Office for Disaster Risk Reduction, the International Scientific Committee of ICOMOS for Risk Preparedness (ICORP) and the European and Mediterranean Major Hazards Agreement co-operation platform (EUR-OPA).

In dealing with this issue, much attention has been placed on risk preparedness and disaster planning. At the European level, a key starting point in this discussion was the 1989 Council of Europe Colloquy on

Regulatory Measures Concerning the Protection of the Architectural Heritage against Natural Disasters in Europe, the proceedings of which, published in 1992, concluded on the need for action in this sphere. Following this the Committee of Ministers of the Council of Europe adopted a recommendation on this subject, recommending to the Governments of the Member States to adopt 'all legislative, administrative, financial, educational and other appropriate measures' for conserving the architectural heritage, making reference to risk assessment, disaster prevention and disaster plans, as well as mitigation strategies (Council of Europe 1993). The technical appendices highlighted the need for local and regional authorities to supervise salvage and recording operations and to be involved in any decisions on demolition and/or in the control of emergency repairs and making safe or good. However, the recommendation made only brief references to the need for preparing and implementing plans and priorities for restoration projects after disaster; the term 'reconstruction' was not mentioned. This was despite the fact that the conclusions of the European Colloquy had stressed the need for education of architects and other professionals engaged in reconstruction of damaged areas.

Indeed, there have been many instructive documents since this recommendation which have reiterated the need for risk preparedness, disaster planning or protecting cultural heritage from natural disasters including advanced planning for site-specific preparedness and documentation on the current state of properties sufficient in order to enable reconstruction. However, they are less coherent on what happens next, preferring to highlight the need for 'conservation principles' to be followed according to recognized standards, or that the recovery phase should be led by heritage-conservation experts in assessing damage for particular types of disaster, or emphasize the need for training among heritage professionals to deal with such natural disaster as climate change impacts on cultural heritage (see, for example, Herb Stovel's report *Risk Preparedness: A Management Manual for World Cultural Heritage* published by ICCROM in 1998; the *Kyoto Declaration 2005 on Protection of Cultural Properties, Historic Areas and their Settings from Disaster*, adopted at the ICOMOS Kyoto International Symposium of 2005; the European Parliament report *Protecting the Cultural Heritage from Natural Disasters* of 2007; and UNESCO's *Strategy for Risk Reduction at World Heritage Properties* 2007). They are not clear on dealing with 'what is done afterwards', an issue referred to in a 2014 report to the Parliamentary Assembly of the Council of Europe on *Europe's Endangered Heritage*, which highlighted the absolute priority to save lives, recognizing that the adequate protection of historic buildings is an inordinately expensive task, but that rebuilding of places supports the rebuilding of broken communities. More significantly, it has been argued that, despite the cultural and social significance, 'restoration or recovery of damaged heritage is often neglected in post-disaster reconstruction plans and in the development of disaster mitigation strategies' (MacKee 2013).

Some key documents make a number of salient points. The World Bank publication *Safer Homes, Stronger Communities: A Handbook for Reconstructing after Natural Disasters* (2010) highlights the fact that cultural heritage conservation helps communities to both protect economically valuable physical assets and preserve its 'practices, history and identity, and a sense of continuity and identity'. It highlights the need to avoid systematic destruction of vernacular buildings, the need for guidelines and codes compatible with vernacular practices and emphasizes the importance of minimizing impact on heritage value, authenticity or the integrity of a building and its surroundings, as well as using local skills. The UNESCO Resource Manual on *Managing Disaster Risks for World Heritage* (2010) specifically addresses the question 'How do you recover and rehabilitate your property after a disaster?', providing a number of examples of approaches to restoration, reconstruction and rehabilitation of the property following disaster and how they link to issues such as identity and the utilization of the property.

The following chapters in this part concentrate more specifically on the question of reconstruction and the issue of authenticity following disaster.

Gail Sansbury's chapter reviews the role of authenticity for historic preservation policies and practices in the context of post-disaster reconstruction in the United States. It considers restoration and reconstruction approaches following earthquake damage in California and the impact of Hurricane Katrina and the damaging effects of the consequent flooding in the city of New Orleans, as well as the terrorist attack which destroyed the World Trade Center in New York. The issue of authenticity is considered in relation to attitudes of preservation professionals, displacement and community participation in decisions, as well as in relation to tourism and visitor experiences.

Robert Pickard's chapter considers the impact of fire on historic buildings and places, including international and national reports in Scandinavian countries and the United Kingdom, centring on the different options that may be taken following fire damage including contemporary redesign, equivalent reconstruction and authentic approaches. A number of examples are referred to including where action has been completed, as well as projects which are in progress (at the time of writing), including the reconstruction of the Charles Rennie Mackintosh-design library in the Glasgow School of Art, which was destroyed by fire in 2014.

The damage incurred through the earthquake in the Italian region of Abruzzo in 2009 is examined by Alberto Lemme, including the path from emergency to reconstruction in relation to the regional capital of L'Aquila. The methods of action for the whole process of reconstruction in the historic centre is viewed through regulations, plans, policies, procedures and different types of repair and reconstruction works, including the quality certification of those works. Particular reference is made to the Palazzo

Ardinghelli as an example of repairing seismic damage, reconstruction works and seismic improvements.

The unusual story of the mining town of Kiruna, a heritage site of national interest located in the north of Sweden, is explored through the chapter by Jennie Sjöholm. The issue here centres on the proposal to relocate the town as the continued working of an underground mine is causing subsidence, which will gradually affect the whole town. The proposed town relocation is examined from the viewpoint of Kiruna being wholly dependent on iron-ore mining, employing a significant number of people within the region, but also raising questions concerning how the relocation of the town is likely to affect the authenticity of the heritage site.

References

Council of Europe (1993), *Recommendation No. R (93)9 of the Committee of Ministers to Member States on the Protection of the Architectural Heritage Against Natural Disasters* (adopted by the Committee of Ministers on 23 November 1993 at the 503rd meeting of the Ministers' Deputies).

MacKee, J. (2013), 'Reconceptualising Cultural Heritage: The Adaptive Cycle as a Means of Rebranding the Risk and Vulnerabilities of Cultural Built Heritage in the Face of Natural Disasters'. Proceedings of the International Conference on Building Resilience, Ahungalla, Sri Lanka 17–19 September 2013. Available online: http://www.buildresiliencore.org/2013/proceedings/files/papers/364.pdf (accessed 17 November 2016).

Chapter 3.1

Post-Disaster Reconstruction in the United States: A Review of the Role of 'Authenticity' in Historic Preservation Policies and Practices

Gail Sansbury

A review of the role of 'authenticity' as a key term in historic preservation practices in post-disaster reconstruction in the United States suggests that, while international charters and conventions influence policy and guidelines, the term has not been widely adopted in these circumstances or critiqued extensively by participants in the field. Nevertheless, more general debates about historic preservation seem to mirror those among international heritage professionals. In the United States, preservation scholars and practitioners have increasingly called for a move from a material-based focus on the integrity and significance of monuments and sites to a consideration of the broader cultural landscape and a more nuanced 'values-based' approach.

This has prompted key questions, particularly for reconstruction after a disaster, including: Whose history is at stake? Whose values must be considered? Who makes decisions? How can local stakeholders participate in a democratic process of decision-making? Can reconstruction restore and promote historical memory as an aid to recovery? Can this complex process be managed in an equitable, economically viable, and environmentally sustainable manner? The history of disasters in the United States, as elsewhere, suggests that post-disaster reconstruction is always contentious, reflecting many – but rarely all – voices.

In this chapter, I review historic preservation legislation and guidelines in the United States, the responses of preservation professionals to the 1994 Nara Document on Authenticity, and then explore the preservation practices relating to the reconstruction of the World Trade Center after the 11 September 2001 terrorist attacks, the evolving preservation practices in the state of California, and in New Orleans after Hurricane Katrina and the floods.

US historic preservation laws and guidelines at the national, state and local levels

Preservation of historic sites predates government-regulated preservation policies: one of the most cited examples of early preservation efforts is the pre–Civil War organization of the Mount Vernon Ladies' Association which saved President George Washington's home and plantation in Virginia. Under their auspices, the property was saved from possible damage during the Civil War, and is one among many stories of historic preservation led by wealthy elites. Government responses at the federal level include the 1906 Antiquities Act, the 1935 Historic Sites Act, the Historic American Building Survey during the Great Depression of the 1930s and the founding of the National Trust for Historic Preservation in 1949. The passage of the 1966 National Historic Preservation Act and its subsequent updates represents the formal legislative framework which coordinates preservation practices at the national level with the states and local jurisdictions.

The historic preservation movement, however, has been shaped not just by legislation but by the social movements of the 1960s and 1970s (Page and Mason 2004: 6–9). In the fifty years since the Historic Preservation Act, preservation professionals have debated many of the policies and their requirements in light of new scholarship and a movement for broader participation in preservation decisions, especially in terms of the eligibility criteria for listing as a historic property or site. Without listing or eligibility for listing, a historic structure or landscape might be at risk of destruction after a disaster, and access to federal emergency funding would not be assured.

The concept of authenticity, particularly just before and after the Nara Document of 1994, prompted debates about the categories of significance and the meaning of integrity as it related to the listing of historic properties and cultural landscapes. A central theme of these discussions concerns the relationship between the tangible and intangible. Efforts to move away from an emphasis on the built form, particularly architectural style and form, and shift towards giving equal weight to history itself, were significant, not least in the United States (Longstreth 2008: 12).

The discourse of historic preservation professionals does not always adequately address the dilemmas of post-disaster reconstruction. In this specific circumstance, the preservation professional must work with a variety of stakeholders in a charged atmosphere. Perhaps the most important aspect of US historic preservation legislation is Section 106 of the Historic Preservation Act, which provides protection in an emergency for properties listed on the National Register of Historic Places. In addition, state and local preservation and landmark commissions provide protection for historic buildings and districts. Listing, or documented eligibility for listing, on the National Register can be critical after a disaster when it may be necessary to protect a structure or site. The US Federal Emergency Management Agency (FEMA), and other federal agencies, must consult with the Advisory Council on Historic Preservation on any actions, such as demolition, that might be taken with regard to a listed property or site. Meeting the requirements for listing as an historic resource is not just essential for protection, but also for funding, whether for restoration or reconstruction.

This selective and necessarily brief review illustrates several key concerns about issues that frequently influence post-disaster reconstruction – displacement of the most vulnerable residents after Hurricane Katrina, the politics of redevelopment at the World Trade Center and the under-reported stories of local groups as a force for both recovery and reconstruction.

Post-disaster reconstruction and historic preservation policies and practice intersect at the federal, state and local levels, involving multiple agencies and programmes. While emergency funds for the preservation of historic resources may be supplied by federal agencies, at the local level, private and non-profit organizations also play a key role, and ideally actions taken towards reconstruction of a listed historic property or landscape would involve local stakeholders and preservation professionals. The federal guidelines define reconstruction as follows:

> the act or process of depicting, by means of new construction, the form, features, and detailing of a non-surviving site, landscape, building, structure, or object for the purpose of replicating its appearance at a specific period of time and in its historic location. (Weeks and Grimmer 1995)

As will be discussed below in more detail, while the standards for reconstruction might be negotiated to meet local needs and circumstances, reconstruction itself is rare. By definition, the non-surviving historic structure must be deemed significant, and its reconstruction is required to be 'essential to the public understanding' of a particular time and place. The standards for reconstruction require extensive research of form, materials and setting; when completed, the reconstructed structure or landscape must be identified as a 'contemporary re-creation' (Weeks and Grimmer 1995, Jokilehto 2013: 11).

Significance and integrity are key determinants for listing historic properties and sites. The National Register of Historic Places and the National Historic Landmarks are overseen by the US Department of the Interior, which also includes sites operated by the National Park Service. Determining significance, however, can be arbitrary when the prescribed categories of significance do not always mesh with the 'values' of a particular structure or site as they are experienced by local residents. In addition, the requirement to identify one historical period may go against community understanding and experiences of the evolution of a particular building or place (Avrami et al. 2000, Mason 2004). Further, to be listed on the Historic Register, a historic resource must demonstrate historic integrity, defined as the 'unimpaired ability of a property to convey its historical significance'. Michael wrote that '[i]n particular we need to consider how integrity is determined; how the period of significance is defined; and how the Secretary of the Interior's Standards are applied' (Michael 2014: 5). He identified three problems with 'integrity':

> The first is the word itself, which was adopted when we created the National Register of Historic Places in 1966, largely because the international word 'authenticity' seemed too problematic. In fact, it is the opposite. In international practice, the process of preservation defines authenticity in a culturally specific way, allowing a broader analysis of significance beyond simply the visual and architectural. 'Integrity' is a legacy of the visual, formal, and architectural focus of the preservation movement over time. (Michael 2014: 6)

The second problem concerns the binary aspect of integrity. No historic resource can have 'some' integrity for there is no scale of integrity. A resource either has the ability to convey its significance or it does not. A third problem is that integrity is defined solely in architectural terms, which diminishes historic resources which are not directly represented by architectural form. Longstreth commented that

> Just as the concept of cultural landscape can mitigate polarized views of nature versus artifice, so it can bridge divisive opinions on the relative importance of 'architecture' versus 'history' .... This bifurcation can wreak great mischief, for it reduces 'history' to intangibles – associations with persons, events, and the like – robbing it of any physical dimension. (Longstreth 2008: 12)

This critique of significance, integrity and historic preservation standards runs parallel with the impact of social history beginning in the 1970s, prompting calls for a more inclusive preservation practice which promotes accurate representations of women, minority groups, working people and LGBT communities in US history (Hayden 1995, Sandercock 1998, Kenney

2001, Dubrow and Goodman 2003, Page and Mason 2004). At the same time, cultural landscape studies challenged the scope of historic preservation practices to include everyday spaces (Wilson and Groth 2003).

Preservation professionals respond to the 1994 Nara Document on Authenticity

In the mid-2000s, US-based historic preservation conferences and journals featured presentations and papers on the concept of 'authenticity' and the 1994 Nara Document on Authenticity. For example, Stovel recounted the meetings and debates that led to the Nara Document as well as later responses to it, and found ongoing challenges. These included problems for those preparing nominations, which 'demonstrate the difficulty of transmitting the nuances of an expert debate to the operational level in meaningful ways'. Other challenges concerned authenticity as it related to 'tourism-driven transformations that trivialize this experience' (Stovel 2008: 15) and the need to address authenticity in terms of cultural landscapes (Jokilehto 2006; Mitchell 2008).

Cameron (2008) and Thomson (2008) discussed post-disaster preservation efforts, both referring to the reconstruction of the bridge in Mostar. Cameron questioned

> Is meticulous conservation necessary, or are reconstructions acceptable, sometimes or in all circumstances? Should these two examples of Warsaw and Mostar be considered as special cases, given the deliberate destruction of cultural resources through war and the deep-seated desire to resurrect identity? What does this mean for the practice of conservation and preservation technology? Does this give a blank check for reconstruction? At this time, one could argue that the question remains open. (Cameron 2008: 23)

Thomson discussed three cases of post-disaster reconstruction: Stari Most in Mostar; the World Trade Center in New York City; and Kaiser Wilhelm Gedächtniskirche, Berlin, to discuss a complete reconstruction, the absence of reconstruction, and partial reconstruction, respectively. His discussion of the World Trade Center, though only a few years after the attack on the twin towers, provided a good summary of the preservation dilemmas, and he concluded that 'the use of "absence" to satisfy a historic authenticity requirement – even in a newly constructed memorial – underscores the variability in authenticity determinations at post-conflict reconstruction sites' (Thomson 2008: 74). The subterranean footprints of the twin towers, the evidence of their destruction, recall Solnit's essay about the 1906 San Francisco earthquake, 'The ruins of memory', and her quote from the landscape historian J. B. Jackson, 'the negative image of history' (Solnit 2006: 18). Are our memories of the past more 'authentic' with a material prompt?

Based on his discussion of the three cases, Thomson suggested three new categories of authenticity to assist historic preservation professionals in post-conflict settings: 'the authenticity of connections, the authenticity of renewal, and the authenticity of experience'. Using the reconstruction of Stari Most as an example of the 'authenticity of connection', Thomson wrote that the 'faithfully and precisely' reconstructed bridge restored both its traditional use and a link to the pre-conflict period, but the relationship with the actual period of its destruction may be diminished. The reconstruction of the World Trade Center site with new high-rise office buildings, a transportation hub and new underground infrastructure, and the memorial 'Reflecting Absence', express for Thomson the concept of the 'authenticity of renewal', but the absence of material authenticity creates the risk of 'conveying a mixed message'. The preservation of the Kaiser Wilhelm Gedächtniskirche illustrates Thomson's 'authenticity of experience' category. Eiermann's design of the new church buildings alongside the damaged tower responded to the concerns of Berlin residents, and represented both the destruction of the church in 1943 and the subsequent recovery of this section of Berlin. Use of these categories, Thomson writes, created wider approaches to authentic reconstruction, yet they still required preservation professionals to facilitate discussions and inform local communities and decision-makers (Thomson 2008: 77–8).

Lowenthal (2008) asked questions about authenticity itself: why is authenticity important or desired, what guidelines can be used to determine authenticity? Ranging across region, culture and time, he explored multiple facets of the authentic, including concerns about the fake, romanticism, simulation, memory and our presentist sense of the past. The epigraph for his essay was from the author Michael Crichton: 'Authenticity will be the buzzword of the 21st century …' (Lowenthal 2008: 6). The buzzing stays with the reader although, at the very end, we are left with the idea of accepting a level of uncertainty and a humble working approach to all the debates about this difficult term, authenticity. 'Let us relish rather than regret being aware, unlike our self-confident forerunners, that what we do is in some ways wrong, in most ways imperfect, and in all ways ephemeral' (Lowenthal 2008: 16).

This is particularly relevant for post-disaster preservation efforts, which necessarily involve many actors and affect prominent monuments and sites which are listed as historic resources, but post-disaster preservation and reconstruction must not be limited to these alone. The structures and spaces of everyday life – homes, neighbourhoods, workspaces, parks and open spaces – must also be considered. Historic preservation professionals must develop the less-confident temper advocated by Lowenthal as they consider and consult with multiple stakeholders on the meaning of 'authentic' reconstruction.

'Ground Zero': Historic preservation at the World Trade Center

Since the attacks on the World Trade Center on 11 September 2001, the complex process of rebuilding the 16-acre site has involved multiple stakeholders. As an act of international terrorism, the entire nation has had a stake in this process, especially the development of a memorial at the site. Residents of the New York City metropolitan area, and the politicians and government agencies who represent and serve them at the national, state and local levels, played key roles. These stakeholders included the owners of the land, the Port Authority of New York and New Jersey, and the site leaseholder, real estate developer Larry Silverstein. In addition, a host of architects, planners, preservationists, real estate developers and other professionals participated in competitions, boards and commissions such as the Lower Manhattan Development Corporation (LMDC). Other stakeholders included the Council of 9/11 Families, as well as the police, fire fighters and emergency workers who were among the 'first responders'. The overall project involved competitions for a masterplan, a memorial, cultural facilities (which later became a museum), along with the development of a new office tower and the construction of a transit hub and retail space.

This complicated narrative included the initial struggles over the master plan for the site, for which Beyer Blinder Bell was selected in May 2002. The firm presented its plans in a 'Listening to the City' event, but they were rejected by most of the large crowd who attended the meeting and the LMDC initiated a new competition for an 'innovative design study'. Michael Sorkin participated in this process, and documented his experience and his critical viewpoint from the time of the terrorist attack to 2003. He attended public meetings, submitted his own design study and skewered the press and others in essays about the process (Sorkin 2003).

As a participant/observer of the planning process, he found little public participation, and described the 'listening' meeting as 'thinking inside the box'. When a facilitator of this large meeting claimed it as an example of democracy because attendees were given a chance to speak, Sorkin felt forced to point out her error by jumping up and saying, 'Democracy means the people have the power to choose!' (Sorkin 2003: 58). He and his studio worked up their own submission for the 'innovative design study' competition, which received more than 400 proposals, many of which featured commercial office towers. His submission is included in the Architectural Record book by Suzanne Stephens, along with many other plans for the high-rise towers (Stephens 2004). In the end, the Studio Daniel Libeskind plan, *Memory Foundations,* was selected in 2003. In the last essay in his book, Sorkin reviewed the various iterations of his design plan and came to the conclusion that 'nothing need be built here' (Sorkin 2003: 136). Perhaps if Larry Silverstein, the WTC leaseholder, had not been required to replace the high-rise office buildings, a green space might have been proposed and selected.

The initial collaboration of Daniel Libeskind and David Childs of Skidmore, Owings and Merrill was supposed to strengthen the design concept of Libeskind's 1,776-foot Freedom Tower with Childs's high-rise design experience, a concern of Silverstein. After conflicts between Libeskind and Childs, the new office building (now called 1 World Trade Center), was designed by Childs alone. The competition for the design of the 9/11 Memorial was won by the architect Michael Arad in 2004, although he was asked to work with noted landscape architect Peter Walker. Their collaboration seems to have worked well.

In this same period, Section 106 of the Historic Preservation Act was invoked to protect historic artefacts at the site, ranging from the very small to the large slurry wall on the west side of the site. Although the site was not listed on the National Register of Historic Places prior to the terrorist attack, and would not have been eligible because it was less than fifty years old, the site was ultimately deemed eligible because of its 'exceptional importance' in US history. This initiated a review to identify and preserve historic resources, a long process followed very closely by the Council of 9/11 Families which argued against any decisions that might jeopardize or obscure the site's historic integrity. Sagalyn's account of the Section 106 review process emphasized the complicated interactions between agencies and groups like the 9/11 Families. The review caused significant delays, but the efforts of the Federal Transit Administration and the Port Authority were recognized by preservation groups and agencies, including the National Trust for Historic Preservation, for their careful review. The artefacts that were identified, some only after pressure from the 9/11 Families, would become key elements in the Memorial Museum (Sagalyn 2016: 494–502, 674–82). In 2006, revisions to the original memorial design were made in response to the first responders and 9/11 families. In 2011, the memorial plaza was completed in time for the tenth anniversary of the terrorist attacks.

The cultural facilities originally planned for the site were opposed on the grounds that the arts and cultural organizations were not directly related to 9/11. They were replaced by the 9/11 National Memorial Museum designed by Snøhetta. This, opened in 2014, was located between the twin tower footprints and incorporated many of the elements of the original towers, among them the shards of the façade, the stairway that victims used to escape, and many artefacts from the site (Blais and Rasic 2014, Sagalyn 2016: 674–82).

In September 2016, the Westfield Shopping Center opened to the public in the dramatic space designed by Santiago Calatrava for the PATH Transportation Hub. A reporter for The New York Times described the mall, and reminded readers that in the immediate post-attack period, Mayor Rudy Giuliani told residents of New York City to go about their normal lives, to 'go shopping'. Perhaps this accurately recalled an authentic experience as well as a new example of preservation, memorialization, tourism and commercial development. The World Trade Center is still 'sacred ground' to many Americans, despite these often conflicting requirements (Kelleher 2004, Dunlap 2016).

California preservation policy and practices for post-disaster reconstruction

Although natural disasters of all sorts have occurred across the nation, California is known for its devastating earthquakes. Secrest and Secrest (2006) identified more than 250 'major disasters' in the nineteenth century; between 1812 and 1899, they documented earthquakes, epidemics, explosions, fire, shipwreck and storms. Many are familiar with the major California earthquakes of the twentieth century, such as the 1906 San Francisco earthquake, the 1989 Loma Prieta earthquake which impacted a region from Santa Barbara to San Francisco and the 1994 Northridge earthquake in Los Angeles. California has a complicated network of national, state and local preservation policies and practices to address the protection of historic and cultural resources, but grass-roots pressure and advocacy have been critical to the preservation of many historic sites.

The National Historic Preservation Act established the state preservation commissions and tribal preservation offices. Programmes under the auspices of the State Office of Historic Preservation included the California Register of Historical Resources, preservation tax incentives, protections under the California Environmental Quality Act, the California Main Street Program, Tribal Historic Preservation Programs and state and local building codes for historic structures. In the case of reconstruction of a historic structure, the guidelines and standards of the US Secretary of the Interior apply. To be eligible for listing in the California Register of Historic Resources, the criterion of 'significance' must be met. Local jurisdictions are empowered to create Historic Preservation Commissions and programmes that meet the standards of the California State Office of Historic Preservation.

Non-profit organizations, such as local historical societies and architectural preservation groups, also play a key role – as advocates for preservation as well as participating in educational programmes on cultural heritage and historic sites. For example, the California Preservation Foundation, a statewide non-profit organization founded in 1977, developed *20 Tools That Protect Historic Resources After an Earthquake: Lessons Learned from the Northridge Earthquake*' (Eichenfield 1996) after the 1994 earthquake in Los Angeles. Cultural organizations have played a key role in the preservation of structures and landscapes representing the history of the state's diverse population, advocating when necessary for a much wider interpretation of what is historically 'significant'.

Adobe is a natural earthen building material which requires continuous maintenance. Even with the greatest care, however, adobe structures can easily fail in an earthquake. As a result, many missions, as well as other adobe structures from the Spanish colonial era, such as the colonial *presidios* and *pueblos* (forts and towns), have been reconstructed. In the nineteenth century, the level of maintenance and reconstruction of the missions was uneven, affected by political changes. After Mexican independence from Spain, the missions were secularized and mission land divided and absorbed by the *ranchos* of the *Californios* (as the ranches and residents were called under Mexican rule). In 1848, after the Mexican–American War, the territory of California was ceded to the United States by treaty. By the time California became a state in 1850, adobe was no longer a dominant building material (Craigo 2009: 80–1).

The Mission La Purísima Concepcíon, founded in 1787 in what is now Santa Barbara County, was destroyed by an earthquake in 1812, and the mission was moved to a new location nearby. Now a state historic park and a national landmark, the mission was restored and reconstructed during the Great Depression by the Civilian Conservation Corps (CCC) under the supervision of the National Park Service. The construction methods for rebuilding the adobe structures were based on archaeological and historical research. Orchards, gardens and paddocks for livestock were 'recreated'. Streatfield describes this ensemble of mission buildings, gardens and farm structures: it 'evokes the larger visual landscape of a feudal mission more powerfully than any other remaining mission in California' (Streatfield 2005: 112–13). Not only does this reconstruction inform visitors about the mission era, but it also tells a story about one of the important Roosevelt public works programmes of the 1930s: the Native American builders are linked with the CCC workers through the reconstruction process, creating a layered and more complicated narrative of California's past.

Although Manzanar, in the eastern desert of California, is not a historic site which has suffered natural disaster, it is a reconstruction which is worth noting here as a 'site of conscience'. This was one of ten internment camps across the nation where 110,000 Japanese-Americans were held against their will during the Second World War, after the Japanese attack on Pearl Harbor. Manzanar was the first camp to be constructed. Like the other internment camps, it was located in a remote location and provided the bare minimum of shelter. 10,000 men, women and children crowded into row after row of barracks. Page describes Manzanar as a 'site of conscience', a place of 'pain and shame in American history', in an article that also describes historic sites associated with slavery and the massacre of Native Americans. The efforts to preserve these 'sites of conscience' had been led by grass-roots groups (Page 2015).

After years of advocacy for its preservation by the Japanese-American community, including former internees and their descendants, Manzanar was designated a California Historic Landmark in 1972. Twenty years later, after the US government formally apologized for the internment in 1988, Manzanar became a National Historic Site run by the National Park Service. An interpretive centre was opened in 2004, but very little physical evidence of the 1940s camp remained. The reconstruction of the two barracks, completed in 2015, was based on oral history interviews and personal accounts of internees, along with historic photographs, including those taken by Dorothea Lange. One barrack represents the crude living structures provided when the camp opened in 1942; the other recreates the conditions of a barrack after 'people settled in and created homes within the prison'. Archaeological research has revealed twenty of the more than one hundred gardens that internees created. The barracks and gardens at Manzanar are examples of reconstruction which are 'essential to the public understanding', and are clearly identified as a 'contemporary re-creation'. Although Page writes that the voices of the former internees are powerful, the reconstructed barracks and gardens provide a visual narrative about a period of racist fear and incarceration in the United States (Page 2015, 2016: 151–6; US Department of the Interior, National Park Service: Manzanar National Historic Site n.d.).

Page (2016) has written about Manzanar and other 'difficult places', often the result of disasters caused by conflict. Inspired by a photograph taken by the Italian artist Mimmo Jodice which shows a damaged bust with a reconstruction of the missing portion of the face, both held together by a hand, Page has reflected on the importance of preservation as a means towards understanding the past:

> We cannot erase the injuries of the past. But it seems to me a central duty of historic preservation to lead today's citizens of the world to historic buildings and landscapes that represent humankind's worst histories, or capture our most fundamental disagreements, and, like the hand in Jodice's image, hold us there with creativity and compassion, and make us think again about who we are. (Page 2016: 160–1)

Hurricane Katrina: Displacement, democratic participation and tourism

The story of Hurricane Katrina and the catastrophic floods of September 2005 is by now well known. The lack of an integrated response across federal, state and local government agencies was reported and televised in real time, and the challenges of the devastating impacts on the residents of this historically rich and culturally diverse city set in an environmentally sensitive landscape not only highlighted New Orleans's underlying political and economic vulnerabilities, but raised awareness of the racial and class divides in the region, and across the nation. Reactions to the failed disaster response, both immediate rescue and recovery and reconstruction, galvanized volunteers and drew many from outside the city to the most affected areas of New Orleans. The displacement of so many residents, the efforts of non-profit organizations to foster participation in rebuilding decisions and debates about the importance of the tourism sector are just three aspects of this complicated process of rebuilding and reconstruction.

New Orleans is an exceptional city, its quality acknowledged by Boyer, whose account provides a useful starting point for an understanding of the impact of Katrina:

> One American city, above all others, holds a central place in the invention of American traditions and in the development of cultural tourism that the nostalgic art of historic preservation has spurred. This is the city of New Orleans. We might argue that the preservation of the Vieux Carré, as the original center of New Orleans is called, began the moment when Jefferson annexed Louisiana, the moment the French Territory became American. But this 'Carré', this Cartesian square carved out of the wilderness of the New World, has captured the fascination of travelers since the early eighteenth century. (Boyer 1996: 322)

The Vieux Carré, the French Quarter, was not flooded after the levees broke. The oldest settlement in the city, it is located on one of the 'natural levees' of the Mississippi, the higher ground developed naturally along the turns of the river over centuries; the levees that failed were those constructed by engineers in other sections of the city. Nevertheless, as the most important tourist attraction and a key economic centre of the city, the devastation of the hurricane and the floods threatened the Vieux Carré as well.

It was first designated an historic district by a city ordinance passed in 1925, which created the Vieux Carré Commission (VCC). The Commission had only advisory powers however, so to address this, an amendment to the Louisiana Constitution, describing the intention to preserve the historic area in New Orleans, was passed in 1936. A citywide referendum, passed in 1937, then created regulatory powers for the Commission, described in the City Code (Vieux Carré Commission Foundation 2015: 1–2). The VCC oversees preservation of this district, including the popular tourist destination of Bourbon Street. The district was designated a National Historic Landmark in 1965. As historic photographs and postcards show, the buildings, the streets and public spaces all contribute to the signature images of New Orleans (Campanella and Campanella 2005).

The evolution of New Orleans as a city and its growing vulnerability to storm surges are described in detail by Lewis (2005). While the city's fame as being located below sea level is well known, the importance of the surrounding wetlands would be highlighted after Hurricane Katrina. Lewis recounts the shift over time in the region's economic base, its diverse and growing population, and the fluctuations of shipping and the oil industry and their negative impact on the delta wetlands. Tourism became even more central to the economy of New Orleans after oil prices fell in the 1980s. Though tourists in the 1970s were numbered in the thousands, by 2000 the New Orleans Metropolitan Convention Visitors Bureau estimated that between eight and eleven million tourists visited in a year, spending $4.78 billion, and providing employment, though often low paid, in the burgeoning hospitality sector (Lewis 2005: 156).

On the evening of Sunday 28 August 2005, Hurricane Katrina became a Category 5 storm, and it was clear that it would make landfall in Louisiana and Mississippi. Evacuation orders were issued, but many did not or could not leave, and either stayed in their homes or went to shelters such as the Superdome. Although the winds of Hurricane Katrina had passed by Monday morning, the resulting storm surge had raised the waters and the man-made levees in three areas of the city were breached. Eighty per cent of New Orleans was under water, with 200,000 homes destroyed. Across the five-state region, more than 1,300 people died. The Superdome, the shelter of last resort in New Orleans, was itself surrounded by water. The US Coast Guard, FEMA and the National Guard led rescue efforts, but residents were still being rescued from the roofs of their homes one week after the hurricane. Around the world, television news showed residents rescuing their neighbours, and famously, in an emergency that left few with access to food, media reports described white people 'searching' for food and diapers, and people of colour in the same predicament as 'looters' (Ralli 2005). In the immediate rescue and recovery stage, access to basic safety and services revealed the racial and economic differences among residents of the city.

Communication between Mayor Ray Nagin and Louisiana Governor Kathleen Blanco complicated the critical rescue mission, and the federal response was understood as drastically unprepared. By 13 September, Michael Brown, the Director of FEMA, resigned. Two days later, US President George W. Bush gave a speech in Jackson Square, in the heart of the Vieux Carré, aided by temporary lighting. City leaders began to discuss large-scale post-disaster plans, including proposals for a moratorium on rebuilding in the Ninth Ward, which includes a large section of the city east and north of the Vieux Carré. The Lower Ninth Ward, which had a high concentration of African American homeowners and a population of 14,000 in 2000, suffered the most devastating flooding when the storm surge breached the flood walls along the Industrial Canal. The flooding reached as high as 12 feet in some places, and the neighbourhood was the last to receive water and power services (Brinkley 2006: 255–9, Allen 2015).

By the end of September, an advisory group on rebuilding the city was formed. Some residents were allowed to return to their homes, but more than 40,000 were forced to live in shelters until temporary housing or the famously toxic FEMA trailers were made available. The devastation was such that many officials believed that all homes in the Lower Ninth Ward should be demolished, but in early 2006 residents were able to prevent the demolition with a restraining order. Nevertheless, in 2015, only 37 per cent of the former homeowners had returned. Rebuilding was difficult, in part because the original home values, on which federal rebuilding funds were based, were low (Allen 2015).

Katrina: Resident displacement

By the end of 2005, less than half of the former residents had returned to New Orleans. Many wanted to return, but lack of available housing, other than FEMA trailers, made it impossible. Fears that the disaster would become the vehicle for 'slum clearance', blatant mismanagement of emergency funding and racist statements by public officials also discouraged many. For example, US Congressman Richard Baker, a Republican from Baton Rouge, told *The Wall Street Journal*: 'We finally cleaned up public housing in New Orleans ... We couldn't do it, but God did' (Babington 2005).

Baker's comments prompted strong responses. The New Orleans chapter of INCITE! Women of Color Against Violence was organized specifically to address the role of race, class and gender in the recovery and rebuilding process. Bierria et al. describe the importance of recovery narratives that acknowledge sexual and domestic violence, under-reported or prosecuted at the time, and they cite the lack of affordable housing as a key contributor to issues of safety. The city demolished 4,500 public housing units, the former homes of mostly low-income women of colour and their children. The alternative was a new housing voucher system, which frequently created a barrier for many wishing to return. Former residents of 'The Bricks', the four large public housing developments, could not understand why these sturdy brick buildings, which they believed could have been renovated, were demolished. Members of INCITE! called this process the 'whitening' of New Orleans (Bierria et al. 2007: 38–42).

Former residents of public housing called it a 'forced migration and displacement'. A 2006 study by the Institute for Women's Policy Research (IWPR) found that 'more women than men left the region after the storm' and many were not able to return (Bierria et al. 2007: 39). In 2015, a follow-up study by the IWPR explored the longer-term impacts of lack of access to housing for low-income women, in light of the fact that only 700 new affordable units were built as part of mixed-use developments (Henrici et al. 2015).

Vale has compared post-disaster rebuilding after Katrina with the Great Fire in Chicago in 1871 and the San Francisco earthquake and fire in 1906, noting in particular the impacts of building regulations and resettlement on working class and non-white residents. In Chicago, advocates for fireproof building 'ignored the disconnection between increased regulation and decreased affordability' (Vale 2006: 151) and in New Orleans, proposed flood-elevation regulations had the greatest impact on low-income residents. In San Francisco, after residents of Chinatown were relocated to a temporary camp, there was considerable uncertainty whether they would be able to return to their original location. The decision was not made by the Chinese community; it was decided by the major landowner who wanted to continue collecting rents and promote tourism by constructing exoticized versions of Chinese architecture (Vale 2006: 155). Vale's comparison of Chicago and San Francisco disasters with Katrina underscores his claim that, in the rebuilding process, urban elites normally, although not invariably, tell the story (see also Sandercock 1998).

In New Orleans, Mayor Nagin's rebuilding organization was called Bring New Orleans Back (BNOB), but whose city would be 'brought back?' And whose homes would be renovated or reconstructed? In early 2006, a subcommittee of BNOB developed a plan for a smaller 'footprint' for the reconstructed city. For public safety reasons, it was determined that building permits would not be issued for such areas as the Lower Ninth Ward and eastern New Orleans that had been severely flooded. But as in the aftermath of so many other disasters, some property owners were already beginning to rebuild their homes in these areas. At a meeting with planners prior to the public discussion of this so-called 'footprint plan', a Vietnamese woman who was told she could not get a permit to rebuild said: ' "Now they tell me I can't live there? No way they can tell me that." Her pastor, Father Vien, put it this way, and there was no answering him: "We cannot leave this area; we have buried our dead here" ' (Horne 2006: 317).

Horne recounts the public presentation of the 'footprint plan' to more than 500 residents. Developed by the Urban Land Institute on a *pro bono* basis with the national planning firm of Wallace Roberts & Todd, the slide presentation showed residential neighbourhoods which had experienced the most severe flooding as designated for green space, rather than residential development. In addition, the plan included a proposal for an expensive new light rail line, and the replacement of the public housing projects with large-scale mixed-use developments inspired by New Urbanist guidelines. The response was not positive, and marked the 'effective collapse of the months-long BNOB planning process at what was supposed to be the moment of its consummation' (Horne 2006: 315).

In the end, the city did not impose the smaller footprint, and homeowners who had the financial resources were able to rebuild in the Lower Ninth Ward or east New Orleans. While some geographers and engineers worried about the threat of future hurricanes and floods, residents claimed that if the levees were repaired along with other mitigations, safety and sustainability were not immediate concerns (Campanella 2015).

Katrina: Grass-roots responses

A number of already existing locally based community groups played important roles in the immediate recovery as well as the rebuilding process. Others were founded in direct response to the disaster, such as the health clinics developed by INCITE! New Orleans, or Safe Streets/Strong Communities. In the immediate recovery period, Malik Rahim, a former Black Panther and activist, called white activists across the country to come to New Orleans and act as a buffer in conflicts between black communities and white militias. Thousands of volunteers came in response to Rahim's call, and Common Ground Relief, which included a distribution centre and a health clinic, was founded. Growing out of the health clinic, the Latino Health Outreach Project was developed (Flaherty 2007, Hilderbrand et al. 2007, Solnit 2009). A white activist/volunteer who had been living in New Orleans for several years prior to the hurricane described the recovery and reconstruction in the first year, remarking on the solidarity of these community-based efforts. This spirit extended to everyday interactions and the many neighbourhood meetings, but also in cultural expressions, including the exuberant New Orleans tradition of the 'second line', that is, those who follow the 'first line' of a marching brass band or a particular social club as they parade through city streets:

> Every time I see a family moving back, I am inspired by this small act of resistance and courage, this dedication to community. Every day, I see little acts of resistance, in second lines and other cultural expressions. I see people going to what seems like the thousandth neighborhood planning meeting. I see people demonstrating in the streets, I see people being kind and generous in the face of the cruelty of the city's elite who tried to keep them out. I see people giving their neighbors places to stay and food and always being ready with a friendly greeting. (Flaherty 2007: 118–19)

This resilience, described here as resistance as well as generosity and hope, reflects the responses to other disasters as described by Solnit (2009). Her exploration of the immediate post-disaster period reveals empathy, generosity and cooperation, virtues that we associate with utopian communities. Based on historical research and personal interviews, including with Malik Rahim in New Orleans, Solnit writes that those who experience disasters find themselves using skills they did not know they had, including what might be called a 'radical openness' to others. In the immediate period after a disaster, distribution of food and efforts to shelter people is frequently organized by everyday citizens. Volunteers organize methods for locating missing friends and relatives. They provide support for emergency responders, and they create community space for fellow citizens to express their grief, including spontaneous memorials. This 'odd mix of heaven and hell', when so much good comes out of horror, sadness and loss, is often displaced over time by the weariness of the rebuilding and reconstruction period. In New Orleans, this would include long neighbourhood meetings, fighting against elite planning proposals and demolition, or learning about corruption and mismanagement of relief funds. For example, the Red Cross, which received $1.3 billion in donations to assist the recovery and rebuilding, was one of the key international organizations, though it was later criticized for its housing programme, Means to Recovery, as well as the management of its overall response (Brinkley 2006, Dewan and Strom 2007).

Another national organization, ACORN (Association of Community Organizations for Reform Now), founded in 1970 and active as a grass-roots neighbourhood organization with a special focus on affordable housing, was already operating in New Orleans before Katrina. The organization had 9,000 member families, according to a document outlining their planning principles in 2006. Shortly after Katrina, ACORN assembled a team of architects and planners from leading graduate schools across the country and developed a series of planning workshops. Although offering a wide range of community services including voter registration, one of ACORN's 2006 goals for their work in New Orleans was not only to construct 1,000 new homes, but to work in partnership with the Preservation Resource Center (PRC) in New Orleans to renovate historic buildings (ACORN 2006: 10).

Unfortunately, in the fall of 2009, the national organization was the subject of a 'sting' by a conservative political activist. At the same time, internal financial irregularities also became a problem, and by the end of 2010, the entire national organization was closed, and presumably its efforts in New Orleans were either absorbed by other groups or terminated.

The PRC had been founded in 1974 by the Junior League, an elite young women's social and service organization, to promote the preservation of New Orleans architecture. The PRC mission broadened over the years with their Operation Comeback programme for the renovation of homes for first-time homebuyers. In the wake of Katrina, PRC teamed with the National Trust for Historic Preservation, the federal non-profit organization which developed the Main Street Program to assist the preservation and revitalization of commercial districts. At the same time, Operation Comeback was expanded to additional neighbourhoods. A partnership between PRC and Rebuilding Together New Orleans provided construction services for renovation or reconstruction of homes by using volunteer labour and staff from the AmeriCorps, a federally funded volunteer programme (Figure 1A and 1B). Between 2005 and 2011, the PRC saved over 5,000 homes, and it has brought 100 low-income families back to their homes (Benfield 2011). PRC ran educational workshops to assist residents, and because demolition of badly damaged historic buildings continued, the organization developed the Preservation Salvage Store to recycle architectural elements and hardware.

FIGURE 1, A and B *This small shotgun house was flooded by Hurricane Katrina, and sat vacant (1A). It had been stripped of some of its original historic material when it was donated to PRC's 'Rebuilding Together' programme. The revitalization was managed by PRC's Operation Comeback programme (1B). Source: reproduced by courtesy of the Preservation Resource Center of New Orleans.*

Katrina: Authenticity and tourism

In 2014, the PRC and the Tulane School of Architecture co-sponsored a symposium to celebrate PRC's fortieth anniversary on the theme of 'The Economics of Authenticity: how US cities are reversing decline through historic preservation programs'. This event addressed historic preservation and economics from several perspectives, including landscape preservation, planning practice and real estate development. In his notes for the symposium, Campanella summarized the discussions:

> Because historic preservation imbues a sense of 'authenticity' which in turn stimulates economic activity, it returns investment dollars at positive ratios – not marginally but five, ten, a hundred, sometimes 250 times over costs, and that's not including the social, cultural, and environmental benefits. (Campanella 2015: 1)

The economic argument for preservation is often presented in this way, though in many cases the result is displacement. But a walking tour for conference attendees provided the opportunity for reflection on PRC's history and preservation efforts in general. Campanella listed some of the key observations in his chronicle of the symposium, including: improvements in the downtown area since Katrina; the importance of tax credits and other financial incentive programmes for revitalizing neighbourhoods and the observation that gentrification has spread into new areas of the city. The likelihood that Charity Hospital would not be reopened and instead would be located in a part of Ward 3 which would destroy 263 historic buildings is described as the greatest defeat for preservation (Campanella 2015: 2).

Not every speaker at the symposium embraced the term 'authenticity' in their presentations. One keynote speaker, Charles Birnbaum of the Cultural Landscape Foundation, offered a subtitle in jesting manner: 'Authenticity and you'. According to Campanella's notes, Birnbaum referred to 'authenticity' as a buzzword or a 'marketing brand for this era', perhaps echoing Lowenthal. Lowenthal focused instead on the experience of place:

> smells, soundscapes, foliage, scale and granularity, spatial integrity, landscape, a recognition of carrying capacity and when it has been exceeded – in addition to individual historic structures, which he termed 'fabric-based preservation'. (Campanella 2014: 3)

Preservationists should move beyond fabric-based preservation, towards an 'authentic' experience of the landscape. As evidence of the value of this approach, Birnbaum cited a 2004 study by the Smithsonian Institution which found that 60 per cent of the visitors surveyed said that their 'most satisfying experience' was seeing the 'real thing'. In terms of cultural heritage tourism, what visitors think is most important is their experience of a place, and if they get to experience the 'real thing', this will be a boon to tourism (Campanella 2014: 3).

Historic districts such as the Vieux Carré in New Orleans do provide a sense of the 'real thing'. A term frequently used in preservation documents in the city is *tout ensemble*, the entirety of a historic district, and its surrounding context. The term appears in the state law authorizing the downtown historic district and the Vieux Carré Commission includes this term in the VCC guideline glossary and as defined by city code:

> *Tout Ensemble* – The historic character and ambience, characterized by quaint, historic or distinctive architectural styles; landscaped patios, courtyards, public alleys and squares; interesting and diverse retail shopping stores and shops; pleasing and proportionally scaled streetscapes; buildings attractive to and compatible with pedestrian activity; use and presence of indigenous building materials and flora; and diverse peoples, cultural attractions and facilities. (Vieux Carré Commission Foundation 2015)

While the official code is general, the guidelines developed by the Vieux Carré Commission state that the notion of the *tout ensemble* covers not just geographical territory, but the entire history of the French Quarter from its original settlement to its use today by diverse residents and visitors, an evolving concept that includes 'commercial activity, residents, musicians, artists, festivals and second lines'. The second lines, defined above by a neighbourhood activist as an act of resistance and cultural expression, happen all over the city, but in the Vieux Carré, local ordinances also allow street musicians and performers to use city streets, creating a sense of perpetual entertainment. These spontaneous (usually) activations of public space suggest that with all of the many challenges still to be addressed in New Orleans, there are forms of authentic experience that bode well for urban resilience. Yet despite the work of preservationists and grass-roots activists, displacement, economic and racial divisions, and the fragile environment of the Mississippi Delta still threaten this exceptional city.

Learning from disaster: Authenticity, resilience and sustainability

How can people celebrate, remember and learn from past disasters? How can preservation practices, both formal and informal, encourage sustainable and broadly authentic reconstruction and help prevent disaster in the future? Page, among others, makes the argument that reconstructions of historic properties and landscapes are more sustainable than new construction because they capture the value of previous investment and energy. Gentrification, as in New Orleans and elsewhere, is often a consequence of renovated historic buildings (Page 2016: 103–28). A standard approach of sustainable planning is to consider impacts on the environment and economic factors, as well as equity, but how well does this fit with historic preservation practices? A community programme associated with the 2006 centenary celebration of the 1906 San Francisco Earthquake and Fire provides an example of the variety of ways in which authentic reconstruction can be understood.

The 2006 centenary was the occasion for a citywide celebration with a variety of public events. The kick-off followed the long tradition of meeting at Lotta's Fountain, a meeting place for survivors after the earthquake, on Market Street at 5:12 am on 18 April (Found SF n.d.). 2006 was different: there was a formal programme, a parade, and a very large crowd stood in the dark morning hours to hear speeches from politicians, sing songs and listen to a group of survivors. One woman was not technically a survivor, since she was just 99 years old. 'I'm the best of the earthquake … I was conceived and born in a tent in Golden Gate Park', she said. Life goes on, that's the message of survivors (Nolte and Yollin 2006).

The centenary-related programmes continued for days. The eighth US National Conference on Earthquake Engineering met in San Francisco with the theme 'Managing risk in earthquake country'. Historians promoted their latest books about the 1906 disaster, museums hosted exhibits, new documentary films were presented and the city director of public safety, echoing the earthquake engineers, called for everyone to prepare for the next quake. The photographer Mark Klett's exhibition at the Fine Arts Museums paired 1906 with his 2006 images of the city, and the accompanying exhibit publication included essays by Fradkin and Solnit (Klett and Lundgren 2006). Events were scheduled across the city, even in Bernal Heights, a small working class neighbourhood with small homes on small lots located just south of the Mission District. It was not greatly affected by the 1906 earthquake and fire because of its location on a rocky hill, but it contained hidden reminders of the recovery in 1906 and 1907.

After the earthquake, temporary tent housing for the homeless was built all over the city, including Golden Gate Park, but by the autumn of 1906, tents were not warm enough. Out-of-work carpenters were hired to build rough temporary shelters made of California redwood. Arrays of tightly grouped temporary wooden housing, like the tents they replaced, appeared in parks and open space across the city, including at Precita Park on the north side of Bernal Hill (Figure 2). By 1907, however, many began to find permanent housing, and the remaining residents were given first chance to purchase the wooden 'earthquake shacks', as they were called, and move

FIGURE 2 *Earthquake shacks in Bernal Heights, San Francisco: Camp 23, Precita Park, 1906. Source: San Francisco History Center, San Francisco Public Library.*

them to a new site. These small buildings then became permanent homes, or parts of permanent homes (Bernal History Project 2006).

Members of Bernal Heights Preservation (now Bernal History Project) began surveying their neighbourhood, and with the assistance of a local expert they authenticated a number of earthquake shacks by the pitch of their roofs, the colour of the original paint used by the carpenters and the still strong redwood that had often been obscured by subsequent changes. A walking tour was developed by Terry Milne, and on a sunny day in April 2006, a brigade of several tour groups began their trek around the neighbourhood. Some shacks were simply an addition to a larger house, but sometimes two shacks were combined. After the tours, there was no rush of earthquake shack owners to list their small houses or attached wings as historic resources; that was not the intention of the walking tour. Part of the name change from Bernal Heights Preservation to Bernal History Project was a reflection of a general distrust of historic preservation practices and professionals who were often perceived as elitist. Putting their trust in their own research, the Bernal History Project was a grass-roots group interested in sharing the history of their neighbourhood. Few knew the story of the earthquake shacks, and the tour made visible these remnants of resilience (Figure 3).

FIGURE 3 *Earthquake Shack, 48 Cortland Avenue, San Francisco, 2009. Source: Wade Grubbs, Bernal History Project.*

The 'authenticity' of the earthquake shacks had been determined, though not to standard historic preservation criteria for integrity or significance. Yet no one doubted that they were the 'real thing' and this provided a tangible connection to the survivors of the 1906 earthquake and fire. Historical narratives about each house, as well as for pre-1906 buildings on the main commercial street in the neighbourhood, added another layer of meaning to the everyday landscape. The tours drew a larger crowd that the organizers expected, demonstrating that people really do want to see the 'real thing' (Bernal History Project 2006).

The earthquake shacks are hardly examples of Solnit's 'paradise built in hell' since their construction and reuse did not happen in the immediate period following the disaster of the earthquake and fire. But the shacks contribute to San Francisco's narrative of resilience and serve as examples of sustainable use of energy and resources. A walking tour around a sunny neighbourhood was just one of many events during the centenary celebration, each memorializing the events of 1906 and those who survived the disaster. These stories and landscapes are also important for reminding San Franciscans that there will be another earthquake; resilience against this particular form of natural disaster depends on preparation.

But the identification of these interesting earthquake 'relics' challenges the definition of historic resources in terms of the current standards for integrity and significance, and ideas about reconstruction and authenticity. Local historians and activists researched and authenticated the shacks in Bernal Heights, not preservation specialists or architectural historians. No one thought that a renovated shack was less valuable because it had been modified; the purpose of the shacks was to provide shelter and that particular use continued in 2006. There was no particular plan for the location of the shacks, nor were there guidelines for their use or preservation. Perhaps the relative poverty of the neighbourhood prior to the recent technology boom in the Bay Area helped preserve them. The only negative aspect of the tour is the affordability of the shacks today. In 2006 the earthquake shack homes in Bernal Heights were probably affordable, but now, with gentrification and the interest in very small homes, they can easily be priced at over a million dollars. Preservationists should celebrate these local treasures, expand their ideas about authenticity, integrity and significance, and help neighbourhoods like Bernal Heights address the threat of another earthquake and the pressures of gentrification.

References

ACORN (Association of Community Organizations for Reform Now) (2006), *Rebuilding After Hurricane Katrina: ACORN Planning Principles*, New Orleans: ACORN Housing.

Allen, G. (2015), 'Ghosts of Katrina Still Haunt New Orleans' Shattered Lower Ninth Ward', *National Public Radio* transcript, 3 August 2015. Available online: http://www.npr.org/2015/08/03/427844717/ghosts-of-katrina-still-haunt-new-orleans-shattered-lower-ninth-ward (accessed 15 November 2016).

Avrami, E., R. Mason, and M. de la Torre (2000), *Values and Heritage Conservation: Research Report*, Los Angeles, CA: The Getty Conservation Institute.

Babington, C. (2005), 'Some GOP Legislators Hit Jarring Notes in Addressing Katrina', *The Washington Post*, 10 September: A4.

Benfield, K. (2011), 'Sustainable New Orleans: How Katrina Made a City Greener', *The Atlantic*, 13 May. Available online: http://prcno.org/news/sustainable-new-orleans-how-katrina-made-a-city-greener/ (accessed 24 September 2016).

Bernal History Project (2006), *Earthquake Shacks*. Available online: http://www.bernalhistoryproject.org/index.php (accessed 18 November 2016).

Bierria, A., M. Liebenthal, and Incite! Women of Color against Violence (2007), 'To Render Ourselves Visible: Women of Color Organizing and Hurricane Katrina', in South End Press Collective (eds), *What Lies Beneath: Katrina, Race, and the State of the Nation*, 31–47, Cambridge, MA: South End Press.

Blais, A. and L. Rasic (2014), *A Place of Remembrance: The Official Book of the National September 11 Memorial*, Updated Edition, Washington, DC: National Geographic Society.

Boyer, M. C. (1996), *The City of Collective Memory: Its Historical Imagery and Architectural Entertainments*, Cambridge, MA: MIT Press.

Brinkley, D. (2006), *The Great Deluge: Hurricane Katrina, New Orleans, and the Mississippi Gulf Coast*, New York: HarperCollins.

Cameron, C. (2008), 'From Warsaw to Mostar: The World Heritage Committee and Authenticity', *APT Bulletin*, 39 (2/3): 19–24.

Campanella, R. (2014), 'Chronicle of the 2014 Preservation Matters III Symposium: The Economics of Authenticity, co-sponsored by the Preservation Resource Center of New Orleans and Tulane School of Architecture Preservation Studies Program.' Available online: http://richcampanella.com/assets/pdf/Chronicle%20of%20the%202014%20Preservation%20Matters%20 Symposium.pdf (accessed 27 September 2016).

Campanella, R. (2015), 'The great Katrina Footprint Debate 10 Years Later, in the Series "Hurricane Katrina: 10 Years Later" ', *Times-Picayune*, 29 May 2015. Available online: http://www.nola.com/katrina/index.ssf/2015/05/footprint_gentrification_katri.html (accessed 17 November 2016).

Campanella, R. and M. Campanella (2005), *New Orleans: Then and Now*. Gretna, LA: Pelican Publishing Co.

Craigo, S. (2009), '"To Do No Harm": Conserving, Preserving and Maintaining Historic Adobe Structures', in M. Hardy, C. Cancino and G. Ostergram (eds), *Proceedings of the Getty Seismic Adobe Project 2006 Colloquium*, 80–9, Los Angeles, CA: Getty Conservation Institute.

Dewan, S and S. Strom (2007), 'Red Cross Faces Criticism Over Aid Program for Hurricane Victims', *The New York Times*, 10 August: A10.

Dubrow, G. and J. Goodman (eds) (2003), *Restoring Women's History through Historic Preservation*, Baltimore, MD: Johns Hopkins University Press.

Dunlap, D. (2016), 'At Ground Zero, a Mall Uninformed by its Sacred Land', *New York Times*, 6 September: A19.

Eichenfield, J. (2006), *20 Tools That protect Historic Resources After an earthquake; Lessons learned from the Northridge*, Oakland, CA: California Preservation Foundation.

Flaherty, J. (2007), 'Corporate Reconstruction and Grassroots Resistance', in South End Press Collective (eds), *What Lies Beneath: Katrina, Race and the State of the Nation*, 100–19, Cambridge, MA: South End Press.

Found SF (n.d.), 'Lotta's Fountain', San Francisco: Shaping San Francisco's Digital Archive. Available online: http://www.foundsf.org/index.php?title=Lotta's_Fountain (accessed 18 November 2016).

Hayden, D. (1995), *The Power of Place*, New Haven, CT: Yale University Press.

Henrici, J., C. Childers and E. Shaw (2015), *Get to the Bricks: The Experiences of Black Women from New Orleans Public Housing after Hurricane Katrina*. Washington, DC: Institute for Women's Policy Research.

Hilderbrand, S., S. Crow and L. Fithian (2007), 'Common Ground Relief', in South End Press Collective (eds), *What Lies Beneath: Katrina, Race and the State of the Nation*, 80–98, Cambridge, MA: South End Press.

Horne, J. (2006), *Breach of Faith: Hurricane Katrina and the Near Death of a Great American City*, New York: Random House.

Jokilehto, J. (2006), 'Considerations on Authenticity and Integrity in the World Heritage context', *City & Time*, 2 (1): 1–16.

Jokilehto, J. (2013), *Reconstruction in the World Heritage Context*, Rome: European Association for Architectural Education.

Kelleher, M. (2004), 'Images of the Past: Historical Authenticity and Inauthenticity from Disney to Times Square', *CRM: The Journal of Heritage Stewardship*, 1(2): 6–19.

Kenney, M. (2001), *Mapping Gay L.A.: The Intersection of Place and Politics*, Philadelphia, PA: Temple University Press.

Klett, M. and M. Lundgren (2006), *After the Ruins: 1906 and 2006, Rephotographing the San Francisco Earthquake and Fire*, Berkeley: University of California Press.

Lewis, P. (2005), *New Orleans: The Making of an Urban Landscape*, Second Edition, Santa Fe, NM: Center for American Places.

Longstreth, R. (ed) (2008), *Cultural Landscapes: Balancing Nature and Heritage in Preservation Practice*, Minneapolis: University of Minnesota Press.

Lowenthal, D. (2008), 'Authenticities Past and Present', *CRM: The Journal of Heritage Stewardship*, 5(1): 6–17.

Mason, R. (2004), 'Fixing Historic Preservation: A Constructive Critique of "Significance" ', *Places*, 16(1): 64–71.

Michael, V. (2014), 'Diversity in Preservation: Rethinking Standards and Practices', *Forum Journal, National Trust for Historic Preservation*, 28(3): 5–12.

Nara (1994), ICOMOS, 'The Nara Document on Authenticity.' Available online: whc.unesco.org/document/9379 (accessed 23 November 2016).

Nolte, C. and P. Yollin (2006), 'The Great Quake: 1906–2006: Thousands Celebrate Centennial of Disaster', *San Francisco Chronicle*, 18 April.

Page, M. (2015), 'Sites of Conscience: Shockoe Bottom, Manzanar, and Mountain Meadows', *Preservation Magazine* Fall. Available online: https://savingplaces. org/stories/sites-of-conscience (accessed 18 November 2016).

Page, M. (2016), *Why Preservation Matters*, New Haven, CT: Yale University Press.

Page, M. and R. Mason (eds) (2004), *Giving Preservation a History: Histories of Historic Preservation in the United States*, New York: Routledge.

Ralli, T. (2005), 'Who's a Looter? In Storm's Aftermath, Pictures Kick Up a Different Kind of Tempest', *The New York Times*, 5 September.

Sagalyn, L. (2016), *Power at Ground Zero: Politics, Money, and the Remaking of Lower Manhattan*, New York: Oxford University Press.

Sandercock, L. (1998), *Making the Invisible Visible: A Multicultural Planning History*, Berkeley: University of California Press.

Secrest, W. B. Jr. and W. B. Secrest, Sr. (2006), *California Disasters, 1800–1900*, Sanger, CA: Word Dancer Press.

Solnit, R. (2006), 'The Ruins of Memory', in M. Klett and M. Lundgren (eds), *After the Ruins: 1906 and 2006, Rephotographing the San Francisco Earthquake and Fire*, 18–31, Berkeley: University of California Press.

Solnit, R. (2009), *A Paradise Built in Hell: The Extraordinary Communities that Arise in Disasters*, New York: Penguin.

Sorkin, M. (2003), *Starting from Zero: Reconstructing Downtown New York*, New York: Routledge.

Stephens, S. (2004), *Imagining Ground Zero: Official and Unofficial Proposals for the World Trade Center Site*, New York: Rizzoli.

Stovel, H. (2008), 'Origins and Influence of the Nara Document on Authenticity', *APT Bulletin*, 39 (2/3): 9–17.

Streatfield, D. (2005), ' "Californio" Culture and Landscapes, 1894–1942: Entwining Myth and Romance with Preservation', in C. Birnbaum and M. Hughes (eds), *Design with Culture: Claiming America's Landscape Heritage*, 103–35, Charlottesville: University of Virginia Press.

Thomson, R. G. (2008), 'Authenticity and the Post-Conflict Reconstruction of Historic Sites', *CRM: The Journal of Heritage Stewardship*, 5(1): 64–80.

US Department of the Interior, National Park Service (n.d.), 'Manzanar National Historic Site: Japanese Americans at Manzanar.' Available online: https://www.nps.gov/manz/learn/historyculture/japanese-americans-at-manzanar.htm (accessed 18 November 2016).

Vale, L. (2006), 'Restoring Urban Viability', in E. Birch and S. Wachter (eds), *Rebuilding Urban Places After Disaster: Lessons from Hurricane Katrina*, 149–67, Philadelphia: University of Pennsylvania Press.

Vieux Carré Commission Foundation (2015), Introduction and Appendix A: Glossary, *Vieux Carré Commission Design Guidelines*, New Orleans, LA: Vieux Carré Commission Foundation.

Weeks, K. and A. Grimmer (1995), *The Secretary of the Interior's Standards for the Treatment of Historic Properties: with Guidelines for Preserving, Rehabilitating, Restoring & Reconstructing Historic Buildings*, 36 CFR Part 68, 12 July 1995 Federal Register, 60 (133). Available online: https://www.nps.gov/tps/standards/four-treatments/treatment-guidelines.pdf (accessed 29 September 2016).

Wilson, C. and P. Groth (eds) (2003), *Everyday America: Cultural Landscape Studies after J.B. Jackson*. Berkeley: University of California Press.

Chapter 3.2

Reconstruction after Fire

Robert Pickard

Natural disasters represent a major threat to cultural heritage. There are many different types of natural disaster that can cause significant damage to cultural heritage. This chapter concentrates on the issue of fire and whether damage to cultural heritage assets can be remedied through restoration and reconstruction action.

Causes of fire damage to cultural heritage

An EU study on protecting cultural heritage from natural disasters has highlighted the risk of fire damage due to climate change, with long dry periods increasing the danger of fires – particularly forest fires (Dimitrakopoulos et al. 2002), and that fires can be started by lightning, short circuits due to faulty electrical wiring, human error caused by carelessness, smoking and the improper use and storage of combustible materials (Drdacky et al. 2007).

The vulnerability of historic buildings to fire hazards can be affected by a number of factors including the presence of combustible building or exhibition materials, the use of supplementary premises such as stores and workshops and defective services, appliances and installations. It can be caused by failures to follow fire safety rules, such as through the use of cooking facilities for food services. There may be a high risk when repair or restoration work is in progress including from welding and cutting materials (Fielden 1994, Karlsen undated, Laurila 2004, Delev 2007).

There is also the issue of deliberate damage to historic buildings through arson. For example, many historic buildings were deliberately torched during the Balkan wars of the 1990s, including traditional *kullas*, Orthodox churches, mosques and other historic buildings in Kosovo[1] and Bosnia and Herzegovina (Morel 2003, UNESCO 2004, Hoxha 2012, PACE 2015). Other deliberate acts can be highlighted, such as the burning and destruction of a twelfth-century wooden stave church at Fantoft in 1992 by Satanists, and of other wooden churches in Norway (Grønvold 2010, Williams 2012, Anderson 2014: 99–140).

Fire loss to historic buildings: Measures to counter the disastrous effects of fire

In 1993 the Council of Europe adopted a recommendation directed to governments of its member states which reflected the need for legislative, administrative, financial, educational and other appropriate measures to protect the built heritage from fire and other natural disasters. It emphasized the need to find a balance between technological and management solutions to counter the disastrous effects of fire (Council of Europe 1993). Indeed, appendix II to the recommendation identified some 'fire organisation measures' to reduce the risk of fire by undertaking systematic fire prevention measures and associated 'practical and technical measures', including the provision of fire detection and alarm systems, firefighting facilities, and indicated actions that should be taken following a fire:

- making safe in order to allow inventory-taking, salvage and rescue work;
- recording of valuable artefacts and fittings *in situ* and then carefully removed, under the supervision of conservation specialists, to a safe place for urgent conservation measures;
- emergency inventory-taking by appropriate means;
- temporary covering of damaged roofs and securing the property against unauthorized personnel and theft;
- removal of residual water by mechanical and physical methods and drying by the maintenance and improvement of ventilation and the use of dehumidifiers;
- investigation, by non-destructive techniques, of hidden structure and fabric;
- reinstatement of alarm systems and firefighting equipment;
- structural works, including proposals for restoration and repair, or for demolition, after full consultation with, and the approval of, the authorities for the architectural heritage.

---

[1]See the reference to the Grand Bazaar of Gjakova, Kosovo in the chapter by Bujar Demjaha in this book.

Building on this, the intergovernmental framework for European Cooperation in the field of Scientific and Technical Research (COST) identified, through its draft Memorandum of Understanding for the implementation of a concerted European research action designated as COST Action C17 'Built Heritage: Fire Loss to Historic Buildings' (COST 2001), an intention to develop a four-year research project in Europe, following the recognition that historic buildings are a finite resource and that the need to address their loss to fire is an issue transcending national boundaries.

After an extensive research project to facilitate the co-ordination of nationally funded research at the European level involving nineteen countries, the main outcome of the resultant evaluation report (COST 2006) was an improvement in understanding of practices and techniques to limit the devastating impact of fire on heritage buildings. Moreover, an important impact of the action is that it has helped to influence, at the European level, the need for fire protection awareness to safeguard many symbolic national icons of cultural heritage for the future. Similar and connected studies have also built on this work (see, for example, Kidd 2005, Maxwell 2008, CFPA-Europe 2013).

Despite this, little has been said on the issue of rebuilding/reconstruction after fire damage. Moreover, the Council of Europe recommendation used the term 'restoration' only for works after disaster, although this reference is likely to have been used in a broad sense and a more recent report on *Europe's Endangered Heritage* by the Parliamentary Assembly of the Council of Europe (PACE) has emphasized that the best course of action after natural disaster is to seek the 'rebuilding' of places (PACE 2014), although it was not specific on the meaning of this term.

One aspect that has been considered is the importance of damage limitation. The Historic Scotland Technical Advice Note on *Fire Safety Management in Heritage Buildings* (Kidd 2005: 43–56) refers to experience gained from a number of major fire disasters in the United Kingdom where significant restoration or reconstruction activity has taken place, indicating that there are major advantages in planning to deal with the impact of a fire on the fabric and contents of historic buildings. It refers to 'principles of damage limitation', originally known as 'salvage', including:

- reducing loss by relocating vital or significant items of the contents of a building to a safe place;

- minimizing the impact of a fire by restricting the spread of smoke and heat and by reducing the collateral damage caused by water;

- recovering important records or other key documents and maintaining architectural records of places;

- protecting damaged buildings against weather and intrusion to prevent further loss or damage.

However, while relocation of items, minimizing impact and potential post-fire damage, and maintaining records are important considerations in terms of what to do once a fire breaks out and after it has been extinguished, few studies look at the issue of reconstruction in depth.

Reports referring to the reconstruction of historic buildings after fire

UNESCO

The UNESCO World Heritage Resource Manual on *Managing Disaster Risks for World Heritage* cites the UNESCO World Heritage Site of Bryggen (the historic harbour district of the city of Bergen) as an example of the different approaches that may have to be considered in terms of restoration, reconstruction and rehabilitation following fire and how it links to issues such as identity and use of the property (UNESCO et al. 2010: 51–2). Many fires had, over the centuries, damaged Bryggen's characteristic wooden houses. Their rebuilding has followed traditional patterns and methods, although not to the exact dimensions of earlier warehouses; but it has remained a good example of the wooden urban structures once common in Northern Europe (Grønvold 2010). However, the fire in 1955 destroyed half of the then preserved buildings, which had mainly been in residential use, requiring a decision to be made regarding what had been lost. There was a parallel discussion concerning the remaining buildings, which were in a poor state of repair, but the decision to preserve them was finally taken in 1963. Debate on the options for reconstruction of the vacant part of the harbour area was reopened some twenty years after the fire (1976–7) following a thirteen-year archaeological excavation carried on without a break to 1968 (the investigations were not fully finished until 1979).

The reconstruction debate opened up five possibilities for the vacant area formerly covered by timber houses (Myklebust 1987):

- *Total reconstruction of the original wooden buildings*: Bearing in mind proposals to regenerate the area (including shopping malls and an hotel), the exact replication of previous buildings would have limited the floor space possibilities and the proposed new function would have required extensive fire precautions and, therefore, this option was not considered viable.

- *New development taking no account of surrounding buildings*: This would have had a destructive effect on the harbour district.

- *New development designed to fit in with adjacent old buildings, but in modern design*: This raised issues concerning the materials (brick or wood) and the dimensions of the new buildings, and the possible impact on the appearance of existing preserved buildings.

- *Pastiche architecture, i.e. new architecture designed to appear old*: Either designed in imitation of existing buildings or reconstructions of actual buildings, but not using solid timber logs.

- *Various combinations of the above*: This was the chosen option which included a two-part solution to create a hotel with a modern building in brick to the rear of the site and a reconstruction of buildings that had existed before the 1955 fire at the waterfront location, but in concrete with wooden walls and roof.

The result had many critics, but also many supporters as was evidenced by the award of a Europa Nostra award for good architecture in 1984. However, the significant issue was that there was a thorough analysis of various options, and the possible results of the different options were evaluated before the final decision was made.

Some national heritage bodies in Europe have also scrutinized the issue of reconstruction of historic buildings following fire.

Nordic countries

By reference to another Scandinavian example, a report made by the national heritage bodies in Finland, Norway and Sweden, where the risk of fire is a serious concern due to the majority of historic buildings being constructed of wood, asked the question: Can we learn from the heritage lost in a fire? It also identified the need for philosophical evaluation and discussion on 'what to do after the fire', as well as a need for associated practical instructions (Laurila 2004).

The report highlighted a number of case studies from each of the three countries, including a mansion, farmhouse, logging hut, five churches and two blocks of buildings in cities. There was a range of outcomes from the fire damage, from partial damage to total devastation, and a variety of approaches in terms of subsequent action ranging from deciding not to rebuild, partial reconstruction with modern services, part restoration and reconstruction, reconstructing different parts to different past time periods, reconstruction to an 'original plan', reconstruction as a modern interpretation and total reconstruction. The outcomes in each case were determined by a variety of factors including the importance of the building in terms of historic values and place/landscape, importance to the local community (especially in the case of churches), documentation and knowledge including whether an archaeological investigation was carried out and to what extent, the availability of know-how/craftsmanship/specialist advice and traditional materials, the level of insurance cover and other economic considerations, and the desire to maintain a function (especially social/communal/religious).

Moreover, the final part of the report centred on the question: *Conservation, Rebuilding or What?*:

> One way to approach the question is to analyse the values of the lost building. If the value was age (or authenticity), it is something that cannot be reconstructed. If the value is in its use, the building should be rebuilt but in this case, a contemporary design might be a good solution. If the value of the building was in its art, it might be possible to reconstruct it after a thorough investigation and analysis. These were just examples of values that might be related to buildings. (Laurila 2004: 60)

It further identified that there are usually three main alternative actions which could be considered for a historic building damaged by fire:

- *Rebuilding* – frequently the first reaction is a desire to reconstruct, but there is often insufficient documentation or knowledge and, even if it would be possible, the patina of age is lost forever, although there are opportunities for learning and training in traditional techniques and materials.

- *Nearly Rebuilding* – this is based on the idea of building something reminiscent, but more simple, with contemporary techniques. The report identifies that this solution is often chosen in Nordic countries although the end product 'can be a disappointment as it does not sufficiently resemble the lost building but it is not really a new one either'. So the approach is criticized but without the level of criticism that is often applied to works of stylistic reconstruction.

- *Contemporary Design* – building something new heralds a new beginning and provides the opportunity to improve the functionality, but if the new design is not considered to be successful it can lead to a greater sense of loss.

Perhaps the most interesting aspect of the report's observations is regarding the attitudes to authenticity and reconstruction in each of the three countries, which have largely followed the approach of the Venice Charter (Laurila 2004: 61–2).

Until the 1980s, reconstruction was not regarded as being an acceptable approach in Finland, being a falsification of the past based on the strict interpretation of the principles enshrined in the ICOMOS *Venice Charter*. The question of 'authenticity' was related to the use of authentic materials. More recently attitudes have changed with reconstruction being regarded as a skills learning opportunity, in certain circumstances, particularly where only part of a building is lost to fire, i.e. when it may be considered as a recovery or repair; it is not normally acceptable when there is total loss. The Venice Charter is followed in the sense that the reconstructed part must be distinguishable from the original, usually with simpler detailing.

A similar approach is followed in Norway. Reconstruction is generally not acceptable in cases of total loss, but where there is partial loss reconstruction may be allowable to save the authenticity of the remaining parts. Reconstruction may be also pursued for structural reasons, to better understand or present a monument. Traces of authentic material are the starting point for reconstruction action which is followed through the use of traditional techniques and methods.

The report identified that there has been no clear policy or established practice on how to handle the issue of protected buildings lost in fire in Sweden, but the Venice Charter has been important in influencing the approach, i.e. with caution towards reconstruction. Each case is examined on its merits, but special consideration is given in the case of churches, as is the case in Norway, particularly with regard to the views of the local congregation/community; and for other protected buildings where dialogue between the owner and cultural heritage authorities is pursued to ensure that a decision is both 'historically credible and democratically acceptable'. In same cases an acceptable solution has been to reconstruct the exterior elements using traditional materials and techniques, while allowing a more pragmatic solution for interiors.

However, the Nordic Countries report, while referring to the Venice Charter, makes no reference to the Australia ICOMOS Burra Charter, which is now widely accepted in terms of the definitions of 'restoration' and 'reconstruction'.

United Kingdom

In the United Kingdom, English Heritage produced a report in 2003 to provide a framework to re-evaluate the situation following fire damage to historic buildings following fires affecting a number of historic palaces, mansion houses and churches (for example, York Minster, 1984; Hampton Court, 1986; Uppark, 1989; Prior Park, 1991; and Windsor Castle, 1992) and Brighton's timber West Pier (2003). The report aimed to set down philosophical approaches with a view to tackling the central question of authenticity in relation to where reconstruction had taken place following fire damage (Morrice 2003).

This report set out the development of philosophical approaches to historic building work at the time, contrasting the normally accepted view in England developed from principles set down by John Ruskin and William Morris – based on *conservative repair*, with the historic building fabric being the key to cultural value – to the approach of Viollet-le-Duc, in which design was given pride of place. Reference was made to emergence of the unifying concept of *cultural significance* derived from the Australia ICOMOS Burra Charter (further elaborated by the *Riga Charter on Authenticity and Historical Reconstruction in Relationship to Cultural*

Heritage),[2] citing commentary on the actions at Uppark and Windsor Castle in terms of the appropriateness of restoration and reconstruction[3] action if it returns the *cultural significance of the place* (Pickard 1996). However, Morrice (2003: 7) indicates that the decisions taken in the cases of fire damage studied in the report had not been informed by the notion of *cultural significance*, but rather by conservative repair; *authenticity of fabric* was the first concern following the disasters, with their homogeneity as works of architecture being judged to be of greater significance than their state of alteration, as can be seen in the following examples.

At York Minster, the roof destroyed by fire in 1984 was essentially eighteenth century in date. There was much consultation and debate about the design of the new roof and vault, and the materials to be used in the reconstruction. The Dean and Chapter (effectively the estate manager for the cathedral) decided that the new roof should match the original design (with small differences), in order to keep architectural unity within the Minster. After much deliberation it was decided that seasoned Oak should be used. However, the boards which originally covered the web of the vault, and which had contributed to the spreading flames, were replaced by a metal mesh covered on both sides with fire-retardant plaster (York Minster 2013).

The Grace and Favour Apartments[4] at the Royal Palace of Hampton Court were largely burnt out in the 1986 fire, resulting in the roof collapsing and destroying other elements below. After an intensive rescue and salvage operation carried out in the period 1986–88, it was decided that the palace should be restored using traditional materials and techniques. Reusable remains were stored for reinstatement and 60 per cent of the salvaged

---

[2]The Riga Charter, agreed in Riga, Latvia 23–4 October 2000, identified that 'in exceptional circumstances, reconstruction of cultural heritage, lost through disaster, whether of natural or human origin, may be acceptable, when the monument concerned has outstanding artistic, symbolic or environmental (whether urban or rural) significance for regional history and cultures' (point 4 of the *Riga Charter*). This is on the basis of three tests being fulfilled: (i) that appropriate survey and historical documentation are available (including iconographic, archival or material evidence); (ii) the reconstruction does not falsify the overall urban or landscape context and (iii) existing significant historic fabric will not be damaged; and 'providing always that the need for reconstruction has been established through full and open consultations among national and local authorities and the community concerned'.

[3]Morrice defines the term 'Reconstruction' as meaning 'returning a place to a known earlier state and is distinguished from restoration by the introduction of new material into the fabric'. This is the definition that was adopted in the Australia ICOMOS Burra Charter 1999 but, in the 2013 version, the words 'into the fabric' have been removed from the definition. (The Burra Charter states that '*Restoration* means returning a *place* to a known earlier state by removing accretions or by reassembling existing elements without the introduction of new material'.)

[4]A 'Grace and Favour' home is a residential property owned by the UK Monarch by virtue of her position as Head of State and is provided, often rent-free, to persons in the Sovereign's employment or in gratitude for past services rendered.

material was found to be suitable for reuse. Over 900 contract drawings were prepared for the reconstruction process, mainly developed from a comprehensive survey and archaeological analysis of the 'as existing structure' carried out by English Heritage. Wherever possible, a 'like-for-like' philosophy was adopted in the design process for the scheme of reconstruction. The roof was reconstructed to the original form (apart from the addition of forty-seven smoke hatches and other fire safety measures), based on knowledge of Sir Christopher Wren's roof gained from other sections which survived, including the reuse of suitable trusses, replacement timber trusses in Oak and Douglas Fir manufactured on site, and the reuse of the majority of Wren's original wrought iron straps and hangers (Kindred 1992, Thorneycroft 1992).

Uppark, a grade I listed[5] mansion house (c. 1690), which had been donated to the National Trust in 1954, suffered extensive fire damage in 1989. While the roof had completely collapsed and the ceilings were destroyed, the walls and much of the decorative woodwork and plaster work remained. After the fire an extensive investigation and recording exercise was commenced, facilitated by a management plan, with each room being separated into grid squares in order to record the location of remains. However, there were many different viewpoints as to what form of action to take (Rowell and Robinson 1996). The Society for the Protection of Ancient Buildings (SPAB) urged that 'no attempt should be made to create a lifeless replica of the eighteenth century rooms', arguing that the shell should be consolidated, a roof added and the internal spaces reconstructed as a museum for National Trust contents (Venning 1989). A local MP suggested that the remains should be demolished to improve the landscape, while others argued for either authentic reconstruction or rebuilding in a modern idiom, or a mixture of the two (Rowell 1995: 41).

Despite SPAB's standpoint, the National Trust embarked on a meticulous reinstatement based on a 'like-for-like' philosophy. While an attempt was made to satisfy the qualms of those favouring the 'repair' approach, rather than reconstruction, by sending some of the site managers on the SPAB conservative repair course, the pressure of costs arising from an obligation to seek competitive tenders meant that pure repair work had to be compromised to satisfy the insurance cover (Spring 1991). Indeed the National Trust's insurance was designed to cover reinstatement. It was

---

[5]In England and Wales buildings of special architectural or historic interest are statutorily protected by their inclusion on the list of buildings compiled under the Planning (Listed Buildings and Conservation Areas) Act 1990. Buildings can be listed in three categories: Grade I buildings are of exceptional interest, with only 2.5 per cent of listed buildings in this category; Grade II* buildings are particularly important buildings of more than special interest, with 5.5 per cent of listed buildings in this category; and Grade II buildings are of special interest, with 92 per cent of all listed buildings in this category.

FIGURE 1 *Uppark, as reconstructed after the fire, reopened to the public in 1995. Source: Robert Pickard, 2016.*

decided to 'reconstruct' the building as it was before the fire (Figure 1). The use of detailed photographic and photogrammetric records and computer-aided design (CAD) to produce measured elevations had enabled this work to be carried out with speed and a degree of accuracy never before attainable (Rowell and Robinson 1996: 42–3). Wherever possible, original material was reinstated following the analysis of debris which had been collected and deposited into 3,860 labelled dustbins marked with the grid references, each representing a grid square of the house, and otherwise replacement work was carried out.

The particular example of Windsor Castle – equivalent reconstruction

The disastrous fire at Windsor Castle in 1992 brought further issues concerning whether it is better to restore, reconstruct or repair and provide new sympathetic replacement designs to replace lost features (Pickard 1996). Fire damage occurred to the State Apartments including the Grand Reception Room, St George's Hall, the Private Chapel and drawing rooms. The extensive destruction of St George's Hall, particularly the roof and ornate plaster ceiling comprising 624 shields of arms of the 'Order of the Garter', provided an opportunity to make a 'new' building within.

SPAB argued that, because Sir Jeffry Wyatville had remodelled the hall in the early nineteenth century in a theatrical medieval style, disguising his predecessors' work in a way which did not deceive anyone, it would be incorrect to go beyond this work as little evidence remained of what he obliterated. Certainly English Heritage did not favour a conjectural restoration. Thus the opportunity was presented to maintain the evocative castellated outline of the castle, yet replace what had been destroyed in a way in which new work would be clearly identifiable (Darley 1992).

The need for a replacement roof to prevent further damage to the interior was an urgent requirement. In 1993 the external elements of the roof of St. George's Hall were restored to the same profile as existed before the fire. The decision was made to allow time for discussion on the approach to be taken on the interior with the possibility of creating new designs for both the hall and adjoining private chapel. Furthermore, a meticulous archaeological investigation commenced immediately after the fire (Thorneycroft 1993, Kerr 1994) so that significant parts of the interior could be, in English Heritage's view, 'accurately repaired' (English Heritage/RICS 1994).

Senior members of the Royal Institute of British Architects were not in favour of returning the interior to an authentic design 'since one doesn't exist' and argued for an architectural competition (Nicholson 1997). The leading architectural historian Mark Girouard published a book with a selection of possible schemes and Giles Worsley, the architectural editor of *Country Life*, the 'quintessential' English magazine, organized a competition (Girouard 1993, Thurley 2016).

There was much debate concerning whether 'to restore or not to restore, to be authentic in the restoration or to use equivalent means to produce the same effect' (Nicholson 1997: 72), although as Morrice (2003: 10 and 18) points out, the term 'restoration' in this context really means 'reconstruction' according to the *Burra Charter* definitions.[6] However, this was a living building, not a museum; a national symbol as well as a home of the Royal family of the United Kingdom. Indeed both the Duke of Edinburgh (Chair of Advisory Committee for the Windsor Castle works) and the Prince of Wales (Chair of sub-committee with responsibility for those parts of the castle that might be subject to new designs) took an active part in the decision-making process. The situation was very different to Uppark, as for Windsor Castle there was no insurance. These factors led to the examination of different options, through an Options Report, which provided for *Authentic Restoration* (meaning 'authentic reconstruction'), *Equivalent Restoration* (meaning 'equivalent reconstruction') and *Contemporary*

---

[6]The Burra Charter was not widely referenced in the United Kingdom at the time of the Windsor Castle Fire, which may explain the reference to 'restoration', as used in the Venice Charter, rather than 'reconstruction'. Morrice implied this when changing the term restoration to reconstruction by stating that 'current thinking' was based on the Burra Charter definitions of restoration and reconstruction.

Redesign. This has similarities to the approach recommended in the Nordic Countries report (which used the terms *Rebuilding, Nearly Rebuilding* and *Contemporary Design*).

Thus a compromise solution was devised by allowing the outcome of the archaeological investigation of the fire debris and existing documentary and photographic evidence to determine the approach to be followed. Therefore, as the State Dining Room and the Octagonal Dining Room had been completely consumed by fire, an equivalent reconstruction was adopted (there was virtually no physical evidence – only photographic evidence). The Surveyor of the Queen's Works of Art had argued against contemporary redesign on the basis that the area that Wyatville had remodelled was 'a superb and unrivalled sequence of rooms … widely regarded as the finest and most complete expression of Georgian taste' using different styles which had been carefully organized to 'emphasize the function of different rooms and to harmonize with the furniture chosen or designed for them'. Indeed, all the furniture for the State Dining Room was intact (Nicholson 1997: 74). Moreover, as the interiors had been designed as a fitting setting for furniture and to provide a background for state occasions, the integrity of the architectural design was regarded as being at least as important as the authenticity of the fabric (Morrice 2003: 10).

However, no furniture was directly associated with the Chapel, there had been problems of movement between this area and St George's Hall, and the staff rooms had been regarded as a 'rabbit warren'. It was argued that this presented an opportunity for contemporary redesign. Thus the staff bedrooms were replanned and the Private Chapel and St. George's Hall were 'to a greater or lesser extent' redesigned (Nicholson 1997: 76–82, Morrice 2003: 12).

Recent fires in the United Kingdom

Battersea Arts Centre

A severe fire at Battersea Arts Centre, London (formerly Battersea[7] Town Hall and a grade II* listed building) on 13 March 2015 destroyed much of the upper parts of its Grand Hall and caused considerable damage to low-level fabric, finishes and fittings. Some other elements in the building were damaged by smoke, such as the Octagonal Hall and Grand Hall Bar, and other areas suffered water damage following firefighting action. A feasibility study was undertaken to examine the options for rebuilding in May 2015 bearing in mind that the Centre was fully insured against damage by fire and the insurer would meet the cost of rebuilding the Grand Hall and internal

---

[7]Battersea is an inner city district of south London in the London Borough of Wandsworth.

components. The rebuilding will use up to 10,000 of the bricks from the original building following a salvage operation.

The architectural assessment was carried out on the basis of rebuilding the external envelope to match the original, with minor modifications. Regarding the interior, it was decided that the elements of the Grand Hall that had survived the fire would be retained and, where necessary, improved or stabilized including a new timber lattice ceiling, demountable side galleries and a technical gallery at high level to replace lost elements. The Lower Hall level, which had been refurbished before the fire, will also be returned to its pre-fire condition.

The proposals for reconstruction and refurbishment works were given planning permission on 10 May 2016. The works combine different types of action and therefore follow an equivalent reconstruction approach with the particular aim of making improvements to allow for a wider range of events in the centre (Haworth Tompkins 2016).

Clandon Park

A significant amount of the grade I listed Clandon Park, a Palladian mansion house dating to 1720 designed by the Venetian architect Giacomo Leoni located in south-east England, was destroyed by fire in April 2015. The house had been in the family of the Earls of Onslow until 1956, when, after struggling to maintain the house, it was given to the National Trust with an endowment of £40,000 GBP. The National Trust subsequently spent over £200,000 GBP in restoring it (Chamberlin 1979).

The fire in 2015 destroyed 95 per cent of the house with only one of the original eighty rooms (the Speakers' Parlour) remaining in something approaching its original state (Morrison 2015) as well as the external walls. However, following an archaeological investigation, thousands of objects were recovered such as fireplaces, panelling and decorative plasterwork, including the marble chimney pieces and overmantels in the 'Marble Hall'. A number of options for the house were considered over a nine-month period.

Despite the many surviving features, the National Trust decided against recreating the rooms as they were the day before the fire, as had happened at Uppark. Instead, it was decided to bring back the most architecturally important rooms of the ground floor to their original eighteenth-century plan, removing later alterations and additions, to make what Dame Helen Ghosh, the Director-General of the National Trust, described as a 'a purer, more faithful version of Clandon as it was when it was first built' (National Trust 2016). With the first and second floors having collapsed, and been completely destroyed, and the fact that these rooms were less architecturally significant having been much altered over time, it was decided that a different approach should be taken here, despite the fact that they could be restored from visual records. It is intended that the upper floors will have a 'modern' treatment by transforming them into flexible spaces which could be used for exhibitions, events and performances through an architectural competition.[8]

These proposals caused some debate. The 8th Earl of Onslow, whose ancestral home was the subject of the proposals, indicated that 'This hybrid scheme is the worst choice for me' and was very critical of the National Trust's creative ideas, arguing that the insurance money would be better spent on other buildings in need. Marcus Binney, the Executive President of the campaigning body SAVE Britain's Heritage, compared the proposals to the rebuilding of St. Mark's Campanile in Venice after its collapse in 1902. However, in terms of reconstruction it was clear that the National Trust was less concerned about authenticity, with the Director for London and South-East England commenting that Clandon would be 'rebuilt in some shape or form'. However, Dame Helen Ghosh clarified that many different options were scrutinized 'from leaving it as a ruin to a complete rebuild'. The Master Carvers Association welcomed the opportunity for present-day carvers to 'match the skills of their forebears and continue the tradition' (Morrison 2015, 2016, National Trust 2016).

Glasgow School of Art – Mackintosh Library

Glasgow School of Art (GSA), designed by Charles Rennie Mackintosh and recognized internationally as being of architectural significance, suffered fire damage in May 2014. Most of the Library was completely destroyed, which led to a debate about whether it should be rebuilt *in situ* or whether a newly designed landmark library building should be created for the students to use. There was an intense debate including an international symposium at the Venice Biennale and discussions at the Royal Institute of British Architects in London, as well as at the GSA.[9]

Some thought that it should be rebuilt as a replica showroom in another location. Writing in *The Architectural Review*, William Curtis expressed the view that Mackintosh's Library was really 'a shrine of universal values', the loss of which was 'immeasurable', and while it should probably be reconstructed it 'will always be a simulacrum without the spirit of the initial creation and its accretions of age' (Curtis 2014) (Figure 2). There was an overriding feeling in the City of Glasgow that the destroyed Library should be reinstated, and the Chair of the Board of Governors of GSA, Muriel Gray, and the Director of the GSA, Professor

---

[8]The National Trust announced in January 2017 that the competition would be organised by Malcolm Reading Consultants, going live on 9 March, with the winner likely to be chosen in September 2017.
[9]The different project teams working on Battersea Arts Centre, Clandon Park and the Glasgow School of Art have created a dialogue to exchange information and discuss approaches.

FIGURE 2 *Glasgow School of Art Mackintosh Library before the fire (2004).*
Source: © Historic Environment Scotland.

Tom Inns, were of the view that it should be rebuilt as closely as possible
to Mackintosh's design (Weldon 2016). Professor Alan Dunlop, a leading
Scottish architect, was critical of the decision arguing that Mackintosh
himself sought new forms in architecture and was 'never a copyist'
(BBC Arts 2015). However, support came from Michael Davis of the
Architectural Heritage Society of Scotland, who argued that restitution of
the original Mackintosh scheme would be the only credible approach for
the world-famous Library:

Charles Rennie Mackintosh's GSA represents architecture of real appeal and significance, and the Library at its core was one of the world's great interiors. By reconstructing it, people – students and visitors – will again be in that room, experience its spatial effects and see and feel exactly what its architect intended. The Library can be rebuilt with integrity and conviction. The original which Mackintosh saw is gone forever. But the Library is possibly Scotland's most documented room. We know exactly what it looked like. (BBC Arts 2015)

Another key argument in favour of the Library's reconstruction is that the fire damage in total affected only 17 per cent of the whole of the GSA.

Page\Park Architects were appointed to lead a team to restore and reconstruct the GSA in March 2015. The Project Managers explained the approach to be adopted in the project,[10] which is expected to cost £35 million GBP, and be completed by 2018/19 with the aim of bringing it back into use for students in academic year 2019/20. Page\Park Architects have much experience of working on historic buildings, including the GSA, over the last twenty years, and therefore know the building and its materials. Page\Park had been the architects for the building elements of a major Mackintosh Conservation and Access Project[11] carried out over a three-year period 2007–09 and funded by the United Kingdom's Heritage Lottery Fund and Historic Scotland. This aspect had resulted in a Conservation Plan 2010–11 which addressed issues of change and recorded change as far as it was possible to determine from the original GSA drawings.

The starting point for the reconstruction project was to determine what is known about the Library. An extensive archaeological investigation was carried out of the debris (Figure 3), and with other evidence such as archival evidence, photographs of the GSA (in particular, the Library from 1910 through to very recently), personal memories and the Conservation Plan. The investigation was carried out over a four- to five-month period, including three months on site and a writing-up period. The Library was gridded off, as in traditional archaeology, into 130 squares so that the exact location of everything found was recorded.

From this it has been determined that there is approximately 95 per cent knowledge of what existed before the fire. This will enable what the Project Managers described as an 'authentic' approach to the reconstruction in terms of bringing back Mackintosh's original design. In other words, with the extent of this knowledge, the work to reconstruct will not be speculative. The aim is for the end result to be what Mackintosh drew on plan, and using the same source of materials (including extensive use of Poplar timber from

---

[10]Information about the project was provided by Liz Davidson, Senior Project Manager, Mackintosh Restoration, Glasgow School of Art and Brian Park, Head of Architecture, Page\Park Architects in an interview held at the Glasgow School of Art on 17 March 2016.
[11]The other elements of this project were the archive and the collections (distinguished from the archive as it included Mackintosh-designed furniture).

FIGURE 3 *Forensic archaeologists begin work on the fire-damaged Mackintosh Library. Source: © Jeff J. Mitchell/Getty Images.*

the east coast of the United States), achieving structural integrity but with someone else building it; the view being that the Library will add its own patina very quickly, particularly as it is intended to bring it into everyday use by students again.

Over the years the Library had ceased to function as the main Library; rather, it was used as a special collections Library opening only by special appointment and, due to the preciousness of information stored, had been closed off to students for approximately fifteen years before the fire. However, the intention is for the reconstructed Library to be returned as part of the working school for all disciplines, as was the case with Mackintosh's design brief. Consideration will be given to the needs of the modern laptop using student for ergonomically designed furniture in other parts of the GSA including the need for modern power servicing.

The project has since developed a process of looking at the building as a whole, much broader than the Conservation Plan 2010–11, by creating a three-part Conservation 'Atlas' for the whole of the GSA.[12] This looks at three aspects:

- *Building as a whole*: This constitutes the formal introduction and executive summary of the Conservation Atlas. It is the first port of call for understanding the history, significance and context of the

---

[12]Glasgow School of Art Conservation Atlas – the title had not been finalised by March 2016.

project, the guiding principles for the approach to be taken and
the principles for future communication and access. It refers to
various international charters and documents including the Venice
Charter and the Burra Charter (2013) and provides a glossary
of terms including adaptation, conservation, intangible heritage,
reconstruction, repair, restoration and tangible heritage.

- *Room by Room*: This will look at every room in the building
  and will act as the key navigational tool of the atlas. It will be
  the reference point to find the area or detail to be examined,
  based on a variety of indicators including level, historic use and
  room number. It will be the starting point for gaining a deeper
  understanding of specific parts of the building, defining the
  relative significance of each space, examining issues relating to the
  external fabric and circulation and forty-two defined areas within
  the building. It will consider the tangible and intangible aspects
  for conservation, record the process of decision-making and
  work undertaken, and provide an in-depth justification for each
  component of work to be carried out.

- *Piece by Piece*: It will provide a tool to analyse elements that are
  common across the whole building, categorized by floor and area, in
  the same system as the area reports and form the building blocks of
  the coherent design including in relation to doors, timber windows,
  floors, panelling, skirtings, screens, ducting, metal windows, fixings,
  stained glass, tiles and mosaics. It will act as a repository of all
  information including a huge amount of research carried out over
  time.

The atlas provides a document of all information found or researched
in one place and is an ongoing project of logging information, including
anecdotal evidence. Another document is being formulated to set out
'Principles' for driving the decision-making process, with the issue of
functionality for the twenty-first century being all-important, reflected by
the fact that the GSA is a working art school.

Furniture and fittings are also part of the reconstruction process.
Archived information and the results of the archaeological investigation
and salvage operation have been stored. The variety of materials and
fragments ranges from brass numerals, stained glass, clocks, lamps and
furniture, and for each category of item a special project group will be set up
and will involve timber conservators, furniture makers and other specialist
services. Detailed photographs and fragments of Mackintosh-designed
chairs and the 'iconic' periodical table will enable the commissioning of
work to remake them to Mackintosh's design with the aim of returning the
key pieces of furniture to the Library.

The archaeologists[13] engaged in the investigation spent a significant amount of time investigating the Mackintosh-designed clocks and a lot of the original materials relating to light fittings for three types of lamps used in the original design scheme including 632 pieces, ranging from fragments to almost intact elements. There was one surviving complete lamp, which had been loaned out at the time of the fire, and about 60 per cent of the lamps survived in parts sufficient to be put back together with enough fragments to conclude what the new pieces should look like. These will be made up to exact dimensions, fitting, weight/gauge and materials (including analysis of the coatings and glazing of the surviving lamp by Glasgow University Technical Art History Group with electron-microscopy assistance from the Rijksmuseum, Amsterdam, to obtain the exact composition of brass fittings).

The analysis work on light fittings will be used to the benefit of teaching and architectural skills training at the GSA in the future. The GSA also intends to develop other traditional skills (masonry, fine arts and crafts, metal working, etc.) from the reconstruction project. Indeed, it is seen as a huge opportunity for students to work with the contractors and design team and for continuing education over the two- to three-year period of the project.

The intention to bring back Mackintosh's design will mean that the Library will be returned to its original concept and, therefore, be more 'original' than it has been for decades through the reversal of changes that had been made over time (but destroyed by the fire). The various discussions, debates and commentaries have been about listening to the different sides and finding all the arguments. The Board of Governors of the GSA came to the considered decision that reconstruction is the right approach for the building and it is believed there is sufficient evidence and craftsmanship available to complete the task. How the reconstruction will be explained in the future is still to be determined but the aim will be to document the process and make it available. Public access to the building has been by organized tours in recent years, and part of future tours will include revealing what was done and the decisions made.

Conclusions

Reconstruction after fire inevitably brings a significant amount of debate as to whether this is the right approach to take. An authentic approach is more likely to be viable when only part of a building has been destroyed.

---

[13]Kirkdale Archaeology, a private archaeological consultancy, and the AOC Archaeology Group, a conservation consultancy organization, both based in Edinburgh.

The decision to reconstruct is also partly dependent on the views of the community, funding (often the type of insurance cover), the extent of knowledge and recovered/useable fragments, and the opportunity for developing traditional skills using traditional materials.

The case of Bryggen shows a pattern of rebuilding over time following the destruction by fire of wooden buildings and their replacement as being important for local identity, maintaining a sense of place. Indeed the Nordic countries' report emphasizes that the approach taken after fire can be dependent on the position of the building(s) in the place or landscape and the importance to the local community, which is also represented by the Glasgow School of Art and Battersea Arts Centre.

Although the Bryggen example presented five options, there seem to be three main alternatives for historic buildings damaged by fire: Contemporary Redesign, Authentic Reconstruction or Equivalent Reconstruction or a combination of these. Contemporary redesign means designing something new to replace what has been lost and provides the opportunity to improve functionality for modern use, although if the new design is not considered to be successful it can lead to a greater sense of loss. Reconstruction according to the Burra and Riga Charters requires that there is sufficient evidence of the former fabric to be able to return to an earlier state based on an appropriate level of survey and historical documentation, that the overall context is not falsified, that existing significant historic fabric will not be damaged and that the course of action is pursued only if there have been full and open consultations among relevant authorities and other interested parties. While the patina of age may have been lost, the reconstruction on a like-for-like basis will allow opportunities for learning about traditional materials and providing training in techniques. Equivalent reconstruction is the approach which may be adopted if there is insufficient evidence of the former state and is based on the idea of building something reminiscent, but more simple, with contemporary techniques. It is, therefore, more likely to be considered where the 'significance' lies, not in the materials and techniques, but the overall effect. It can be a pragmatic solution, but it can also be subject to criticism, although not at the level of criticism that is often applied to works of 'stylistic reconstruction'. The evidence of examples also shows that the pragmatic solution may be to combine these approaches, depending on the circumstances.

A like-for-like – authentic approach to reconstruction – was taken at York Minster and Hampton Court Palace (with minor modifications for fire resistance or protection in both cases), and at Uppark. The decision not to go for authentic repair/reconstruction at Windsor Castle was pragmatic. For example, the authentic reconstruction of St George's Hall was estimated at £4.5 million GBP, less £800,000 for equivalent reconstruction, but the room had been regarded as 'too long, too boxy and too flat', hence the decision to redesign. Moreover, unlike Uppark, where the building had insurance cover for total reinstatement, Windsor Castle was not insured[14] and the Royal Household and Government Department of National Heritage did not like the idea of millions of pounds of public money being spent on historical authenticity (Nicholson 1997: 80–2).

The decision to reconstruct at Uppark was controversial because of the extent of damage. The Burra Charter definition of reconstruction as returning a place to a known earlier state was severely tested in this case. However, extensive archaeological investigation and recording enabled a significant amount of original material to be reinstated. The importance of archaeological investigation and careful recovery of fragments is very relevant to the issue of authenticity, as is also revealed in the cases of Hampton Court Palace, Battersea Arts Centre, Clandon Park and Glasgow School of Art.

The definition of reconstruction is less tested in the case of Glasgow School of Art, particularly as fire damage affected only 17 per cent of the building and with the existing archive resources, conservation plan and the new atlas, and comprehensive salvage, the opportunity taken to return the Library and some other aspects to a known earlier state, removing past alterations made over time, while also factoring the continued modern use needs of students, provides a very effective exemplar of authentic reconstruction.

At Clandon Park, returning to the eighteenth-century 'plan' on the ground floor, and removing later alterations and additions, is less convincing, although the extensive archaeological work will play an important role here. The decision to redevelop the extensively damaged upper floors brings a new beginning and will improve the functionality of the place as a visitor attraction, as it is now, rather than a family home.

The approach at Battersea Arts Centre provides an example of authentic reconstruction of the exterior (with minor modifications) and equivalent reconstruction mixed with contemporary design to the Grand Hall. Here the decision was to make manifest the changes caused by the fire by replacing lost elements with contemporary material rather than replicas. This solution was also determined by the needs of functionality in line with an existing long transformation project for the building, balancing the preservation of the listed fabric of the old town hall with the twenty-first-century creative

---

[14]The UK Government's long-standing policy on insurance for Crown Buildings (including Palaces owned by the United Kingdom Monarch 'in right of Crown', i.e. held in Trust for the next Monarch) was explained through 'written answers' to questions raised in Parliament (House of Commons) in 1995. Across Government as a whole, the cost of paying premiums could be expected to exceed the value of claims met by insurance companies. Therefore, use of commercial insurance, including buildings or contents insurance cover, is confined to a very small number of cases and the cost of insuring Windsor Castle would be too high, and, therefore, not one of those cases. See Hansard: HC Deb 23 January 1995 vol. 253 cc18-9W.

activity that it aims to accommodate in order to serve the local community as an events venue.

It is clear that authentic reconstruction provides opportunities for learning and training in the use of traditional techniques and materials or improving existing skills as is indicated by the Master Carvers Association in relation to Clandon Park. The work started at the Glasgow School of Art will have many benefits in terms of skills development, not only for students, but also for practitioners through short courses.

There are many different approaches to the issue of reconstruction after fire, depending on the particular circumstances. While the Venice Charter identifies that reconstruction should be distinguishable from the original, the Australian Burra Charter provides more scope and the Riga Charter provides some important tests. It is, nevertheless, important to inform and explain the actions taken. In this respect, the extensive exhibitions and publications linked to Uppark and Windsor help explain the extent of change to a wider audience. Another method for informing people is through guided tours, as is proposed at the Glasgow School of Art.

References

Anderson, R. C. (2014), *Authenticity and Architecture: Representation and Reconstruction in Context*, Tilburg: Tilburg University.

BBC Arts (2015), 'Mackintosh Library to be Restored: A Lost Opportunity?' Available online: http://www.bbc.co.uk/programmes/articles/4tR37dg3bZtcWl tqPRD8cfZ/mackintosh-library-to-be-restored-a-lost-opportunity (accessed 25 June 2016).

Chamberlin, E. R. (1979), *Preserving the Past*, London: Dent.

Confederation of Fire Protection Association Europe (CFPA-Europe) (2013), Managing Fire Protection of Historic Buildings, European Guideline No. 30, Helsinki. 2013. Available online: http://cfpa-e.eu/wp-content/uploads/files/ guidelines/CFPA_E_Guideline_No_30_2013_F.pdf (accessed 23 May 2016).

Council of Europe (1993), *Recommendation No R(93)9 on the Protection of the Architectural Heritage Against Natural Disasters*, adopted by the Committee of Ministers on 23 November 1993. Available online: https://search.coe.int/ cm/Pages/result_details.aspx?ObjectID=09000016804fd763 (accessed 18 May 2016).

Curtis, W. J. R. (2014), 'Burning Questions: Reconstructing the Fire Scene at Mackintosh's Glasgow School of Art', *The Architectural Review*, 10 July. Available online: http://www.architectural-review.com/rethink/burning- questions-reconstructing-the-fire-scene-at-mackintoshs-glasgow-school-of- art/8665000.article (accessed 25 June 2016).

Darley, G. (1992), 'A Time when History Should Not Repeat Itself', *The Observer*, 29 November: 59.

Delev, K. (2007), 'Bulgarian Experience & Approach', in M. Drdacky, L. Binda, I. Herle, L. G. Lanza, I. Maxwell and S. Pospišil (eds), *Protecting the Cultural Heritage from Natural Disasters*, Annex 3, European Parliament Directorate

General Internal Policies of the Union, Policy Department Structural and Cohesion Policies. Available online: http://www.europarl.europa.eu/RegData/etudes/etudes/join/2007/369029/IPOL-CULT_ET(2007)369029_EN.pdf (accessed 6 May 2016).

Dimitrakopoulos, A. P., D. Mitrakos and V. Christoforou (2002), 'Concepts of Wildland Fire Protection of Cultural Monuments and National Parks in Greece. Case Study: Digital Telemetry Networks at the Forest of Ancient Olympia', *Fire Technology*, 38: 363–72.

Drdacky, M., L. Binda, I. Herle, L. Lanza, I. Maxwell and S. Pospišil (eds) (2007), *Protecting the Cultural Heritage from Natural Disasters*, European Parliament Directorate General Internal Policies of the Union, Policy Department Structural and Cohesion Policies. Available online: http://www.europarl.europa.eu/RegData/etudes/etudes/join/2007/369029/IPOL-CULT_ET(2007)369029_EN.pdf (accessed 6 May 2016).

English Heritage/Royal Institution of Chartered Surveyors (RICS) (1994), *Insuring Your Historic Buildings: Houses and Commercial Buildings*, A joint statement by English Heritage and the Royal Institution of Chartered Surveyors, London: English Heritage.

European Cooperation in the field of Scientific and Technical Research (COST) (2001), *COST Action 17: Memorandum of Understanding*, COST 327/01, Brussels 21 December 2001. Available online: http://virtual.vtt.fi/virtual/proj6/cost/c17mou.pdf (accessed 13 May 2016).

European Cooperation in the field of Scientific and Technical Research (COST) (2006), *COST Action 17: Built Heritage: Fire loss to Historic Buildings, External Evaluation Report*, 18 December 2006. Available online: http://w3.cost.eu/fileadmin/domain_files/TUD/Action_C17/evaluation_report/evaluation_report-C17.pdf (accessed 23 May 2016).

Fielden, B. M. (1994), *Conservation of Historic Buildings*, Oxford: Butterworth.

Girouard, M. (1993), *Windsor: The Most Romantic Castle*, London: Hodder and Stoughton.

Grønvold, U. (2010), *Bryggen in Bergen and Fantoft Stave Church*, Article in the catalogue for the exhibition *Geschichte der Rekonstruktion: Konstruktion der Geschichte*, 15.07.2010 – 31.10.2010, *Architekturmuseum der TU München, Pinakothek der Moderne*. Available online: http://omarkitektur.blogspot.co.uk/2010/05/bryggen-in-bergen-and-fantoft-stave.html (accessed 26 May 2016).

Haworth Tompkins (2016), *Planning Permission Granted for Reconstruction and Refurbishment of the Grand Hall at Battersea Arts Centre*, Press Release: 10 May 2016. Available online: https://www.bac.org.uk/resources/0000/2461/Battersea_Arts_Centre_News__Planning_Permission_Granted_for_Grand_Hall_Rebuild.pdf (accessed 20 June 2016).

Hoxha, G. (2012), 'The Impact of Conflict on Cultural Heritage in Kosovo', in S. Lambert and C. Rockwell (eds), *Protecting Cultural Heritage in Times of Conflict: Contributions from the participants of the International course on First Aid to Cultural Heritage in Times of Conflict*, Tome: ICCROM. Available online: http://www.iccrom.org/ifrcdn/pdf/ICCROM_18_ProtectingHeritageConflict_en.pdf (accessed 12 May 2016).

Karlsen, E. (undated), *Fire Protection of Norwegian Cultural Heritage*. Available online: http://www.arcchip.cz/w04/w04_karlsen.pdf (accessed 11 May 2016).

Kerr, B. (1994), 'The Windsor Castle Fire: Learning Lessons from the Ashes', *Conservation Bulletin*, 24: 12–14.

Kidd, S. (2005), *Fire Safety Management in Heritage Buildings*, Technical Advice Note 28, Edinburgh: Historic Scotland.

Kindred, B. (ed) (1992), 'Case Study (3) – Palace Restored', *Context*, 36 (December): 34–5.

Laurila, A. (ed) (2004), *Can we Learn from the Heritage Lost in a Fire? Experiences and Practises on the Fire Protection of Historic Buildings in Finland, Norway and Sweden*, publication No. 26, Helsinki: National Board of Antiquities, Department of Monuments and Sites.

Maxwell, I. (ed) (2008), *COST Action C17: Built Heritage: Fire Loss to Historic Buildings: Action C17 Publications*, Edinburgh: Historic Scotland Technical Conservation, Research and Education Group. Available online: http://www. fireriskheritage.net/wp-content/uploads/CDbooklet.pdf (accessed 24 May 2016).

Morel, A.-F. (2003), 'Identity and Conflict: Cultural Heritage, Reconstruction and National Identity in Kosovo', *Architecture_Media_Politics_Society*, 3 (1): 1–20. Available online: http://architecturemps.com/wp-content/uploads/2012/07/amps-vol-3-no-1-full-paper-identity-and-conflict_-cultural-heritage-reconstruction-and-national-identity-in-kosovo-docx.pdf (accessed 12 May 2016).

Morrison, J. (2015), 'Let Fire-Ravaged Ancestral Home Run to Ruin, Says Earl', *The Times*, 28 November: 5.

Morrison, J. (2016), 'Trust Plans to Salvage Earl's Family Home', *The Times*, 19 January: 9.

Morrice, R. (2003), *A Report into Recent Practice Following Catastrophic Damage at Historic Places, with Particular Reference to Brighton's West Pier*, London: English Heritage. Available online: https://historicengland.org.uk/images-books/publications/catastrophic-damage-at-historic-places/ (accessed 13 May 2016).

Myklebust, D. (1987), *Bryggen: A Problem in Infill Architecture*, ICOMOS Bulletin 7: Norway / Norvège: 241–9. Available online: http://www.icomos.org/publications/bulletin1987/bulletin1987-22.pdf (accessed 1 June 2016).

National Trust (2016), *A New Life for Clandon*. Available online: http://www. nationaltrust.org.uk/news/a-new-life-for-clandon (accessed 22 June 2016).

Nicholson, A. (1997), *Restoration: The Rebuilding of Windsor Castle*, London: Michael Joseph Ltd. in association with The Royal Collection/Penguin Group.

Parliamentary Assembly of the Council of Europe (PACE) (2014), *Europe's Endangered Heritage*, Doc. 13428, 18 February 2014, Report of the Committee on Culture, Science, Education and Media. Rapporteur: Ms Vesna MARJANOVIĆ, Serbia. Available online: http://assembly.coe.int/nw/xml/XRef/Xref-DocDetails-EN.asp?FileID=20524&lang=EN (accessed 20 May 2016).

Parliamentary Assembly of the Council of Europe (PACE) (2015), *Cultural Heritage in Crisis and Post-Crisis Situations*, Doc. 13758, 18 April 2015, Report of the Committee on Culture, Science, Education and Media. Rapporteur: Ms Ismeta DERVOZ, Bosnia and Herzegovina. Available online: http://assembly. coe.int/nw/xml/XRef/Xref-DocDetails-en.asp?FileID=20030&lang=en (accessed 12 May 2016).

Pickard, R. D. (ed) (1996) *Conservation in the Built Environment*, Harlow: Longman.

Rowell, C. (1995, reprinted 2014), 'The Fire and Rescue of Uppark', in *Uppark*, London: National Trust.

Rowell, C. and J. M. Robinson (1996), *Uppark Restored*, London: National Trust.

Spring, M. (1991), 'The Caretakers', *Building*, 27 September: 42–6.

Thorneycroft, J. (1992), 'Death and Transfiguration: Research and Reconstruction at Hampton Court', *Conservation Bulletin*, 18 October: 12–4.

Thorneycroft, J. (1993), 'Windsor Castle Fire', *Conservation Bulletin*, 19 March: 32.

Thurley, S. (2016), 'From the Great Flames, Great Homes Rise Again', *The Times*, 23 January: 24.

Venning, P. (1989), 'Uppark: Accept No Facsimile', *SPAB News*, 10: 10–11.

Weldon, V. (2016), 'Scots Author Muriel Gray Responds to Criticism of Glasgow School of Art', *The Herald*, 26 May. Available online: http://www.heraldscotland.com/news/14474161.Scots_author_Muriel_Gray_responds_to_criticism_of_Glasgow_School_of_Art/ (accessed 23 June 2016).

Williams, T. J. T. (2012), 'A Blaze in the Northern Sky: Black Metal and Crimes Against Culture', *Public Archaeology*, 11 (2): 59–72.

UNESCO (2004), *Protection and Conservation of a Multi-Ethnic Heritage in Danger*, Mission Report 26–30 April 2004, Cultural Heritage in South-East Europe Series N° 2, Venice: UNESCO Office in Venice (Roste) Culture Section. Available online: http://portal.unesco.org/en/files/23707/11011375003Kosovo_Mission_Report_2.pdf/Kosovo+Mission+Report+2.pdf (accessed 12 May 2016).

UNESCO, ICCROM, ICOMOS, IUCN (2010), *Managing Disaster Risks for World Heritage*, World Heritage Resource Manual, Paris: UNESCO.

York Minster Learning Team (2013), 'The 1984 Fire', Factsheet 12, The Chapter of York. Available online: https://yorkminster.org/geisha/assets/files/The%20 1984%20Fire.pdf (accessed 1 June 2016).

Chapter 3.3

The Path of Reconstruction of the City of L'Aquila after the Earthquake of 2009

Alberto Lemme

From emergency to reconstruction

On the path from emergency to reconstruction following natural disaster there is a well-established sequence of activities to be carried out on the way to normality and socio-economic recovery.

The phases of the process begin before the disaster has occurred:

- *Prevention* – the protection of natural resources and the existing buildings; risk reduction for natural and anthropogenic disasters;
- *Managing the emergency* – this starts immediately after the event and lasts for the first few days with immediate relief to the population, the first interventions to allow safe access to rescuers and a quick assessment of damage and fitness for use; and
- *Post-emergency* – various levels of intervention and management will be required in preparation for the return to normal conditions and rebuilding. These include surveying damage and vulnerability, making buildings safe and the detailed planning and selection of operations to be performed subsequently.

The 2009 earthquake in Abruzzo

The seismic sequence that had been affecting Abruzzo since early 2009 reached its peak on April 6 of that year, with an earthquake of the magnitude of 6.3 on the Richter scale, and a depth of 8.8 km. The event was felt in much of Central Italy and caused extensive damage to public and private structures and to the cultural heritage of the city of L'Aquila, capital of the Abruzzo region. Many small towns, including Onna, Villa Sant'Angelo and Tempera, were devastated. There were 308 deaths, more than 1,500 injured and almost 70,000 displaced persons. The cost of damage has been estimated at more than 10 billion euros; 124 municipalities were affected, of which 57 were located within the epicentre. A State of Emergency was declared by a Decree of the President of the Council of Ministers (DPCM), and the Head of the National Civil Protection Department was appointed as Special Commissioner for the emergency. Subsequently the responsibilities were passed on to the President of the Abruzzo region and after the period of emergency they were passed on to the different municipalities.

Early relief and assistance was guaranteed to the population and in the first forty-eight hours nearly 28,000 people were rescued by the National Civil Protection Department. Over 50,000 inspections were carried out during the first sixty days to verify the safety of buildings and their fitness for use. Altogether more than 70,000 inspections, to verify the accessibility of buildings, were made with the assistance of about 5,000 volunteer technicians from all over Italy.

The assessment of accessibility (Table 1) in post-seismic emergency situations is a temporary evaluation formulated on the basis of an expert judgement in limited time through a simple visual analysis and by the collection of easily accessible information to determine, in the event of a seismic crisis, whether the buildings affected by the earthquake can continue to be used without

TABLE 1 *Accessibility outcome (ITC-CNR 2010)*

Accessibility outcome	Private buildings (%)	Public buildings (%)	Heritage buildings (%)
Accessible (A)	52	53.6	24.1
Partially or temporarily not accessible (B,C), Temporarily not accessible to review (D)	15.9	25.2	22.2
Not accessible (E) or not accessible due to external risk (F)	32.1	21.2	53.7
Final outcomes of accessibility	71,302	2,219	1,800

threat to human life. Temporary structures were built for housing displaced persons (the C.A.S.E. Project – nineteen areas) and to provide temporary school facilities (the M.U.S.P. project).

There were two principal types of intervention, as well as the restoration of basic services and public works:

- *Fast and light reconstruction* – performed in the early months, for buildings not seriously damaged located outside the historic centres; and
- *Heavy reconstruction* – which took longer, for buildings severely damaged and unusable located within historic centres.

Reconstruction after the 2009 earthquake and the path indicated by the regulations

In the case of the city of L'Aquila, this was the first time that a regional capital in Italy had been hit by such a severe earthquake, and the entire old town was declared unfit for use, which meant abandoning homes and productive activities. To be able to give homes back to citizens in a relatively short time, villages were planned on the outskirts, which had a questionable socio-economic and environmental impact, even though technologically they solved the problem in an advanced and adequate way. A distinction must be made between the reconstruction of the area outside the historic centre, where newly designed buildings were foreseen together with some scope to reduce urbanization, and of the old town. In the old town, where many buildings that were seriously damaged, had collapsed or were incongruous with the urban fabric, the problem was to determine 'what and how to rebuild' and what techniques and procedures should be followed.

Some aspects that characterized the reconstruction of L'Aquila and accompanied the cultural and social debate were the opportunity to achieve a high level of seismic safety combined with work in keeping with local building tradition guaranteeing high energy efficiency and restoring a wired city in a historical context stretching back for centuries. The enormous impact of a work site covering the entire city created enormous difficulties related to logistics and the organization of work in a ghost town (made safe during the post-emergency phase). This was a veritable open-air museum of the earthquake which could be visited only for a limited time. The difficulties of socio-economic recovery, making the most of a situation that had been neglected for many years, and building temporary housing for citizens whose homes had been damaged or destroyed were major challenges in the post-disaster recovery programme.

The possibility of achieving a high level of seismic safety with interventions that are in keeping with local tradition is important in the restoration and consolidation with seismic structural improvement of buildings of heritage value: testing the earthquake resistance of the buildings strengthened revealed the limitations of some very common techniques. Over the last seventy years, seismic improvement work has been carried out using techniques making extensive use of rigid materials, such as coating the walls with concrete grout and electro-welded steel mesh, and roofing with reinforced concrete. The seismic testing of this work has shown its limitations. In particular, after the earthquake of 1997–8, which struck the Umbria and Marche regions, in some municipalities of Val Nerina (Sellano and Cerreto di Spoleto in the province of Perugia, rebuilt after a previous earthquake in 1982), there was serious damage to buildings that had been reinforced using such techniques. This led to reconsideration by the scientific community and a search for work that would enable seismic improvement to be made in compliance with local building technologies, using conservative restoration techniques and rediscovering local seismic cultures with an analysis of safeguards to counteract seismic action.

The seismic regulations and directives of the Ministry of Cultural Heritage (DPCM 2011) provided useful indications for the choice of actions and the analysis methods also made it possible to improve the checking and evaluation of such work. Examples include: the widespread use of devices such as chains, cleaning of masonry with traditional techniques, the use of natural lime mortar and avoiding work that involves the use of reinforced concrete and epoxy resin materials.

The guiding principles of the actions are, in addition to repairing the damage, the restoration of the resistant structure and the improvement of the behaviour of the structural elements by means of reinforcement and consolidation, while at the same time safeguarding and restoring elements of the architectural and artistic heritage.

In this context, repair work performed on vertical structures can be summarized as involving the repair of damage by regularization and remediation of the wall facings (mending the damage, like-for-like replacement, keying and deep plastering) including the regulation of the masonry and the reinforcement of the openings and consolidation of the masonry with mortar injections compatible with the walls, and cross connections or confinement with reinforced plaster. For horizontal structures, the works that cannot be postponed are connections between storeys with chains and steel profiles, and the consolidation of the ceilings, the wooden and steel floors, and any rebuilding. On the roof it includes the making of connecting curbs and eliminating thrusts.

The rebuilding of the suburbs, carried out prior to work on the old town, was based on a choice of action linked to fitness for use and, in many cases the solution was radical action, sometimes resulting in the replacement of buildings. This approach influenced the expectations of the citizens and the choices of the designers; in fact, for the next phase of activities in the old town there was a strong social push for the replacement even of buildings of heritage value, although this was limited to ones that had collapsed or were incongruous.

Some reflections should also be made about the phases of the emergency and post-emergency. In the historical centre of L'Aquila, as has been the case in previous seismic events, interventions involving shoring components in steel and/or wood were carried out at high cost. The regulation of such interventions could reduce the extent of works and the expense by applying the principle that every intervention, provisional or definitive, must be justified in a balanced relationship between effectiveness and cost.

In addition, the execution of temporary works during the emergency phase can also be extended to making public buildings fit for use so that they can be reopened as soon as possible, using techniques that insert technological and modern solutions into the old building and preserve the memory of the earthquake (Collemaggio Basilica and the Chiesa delle Anime Sante all'Aquila – Church of the Holy Souls).

As well as the technical aspects, making a city safe raises social issues. During the emergency phase the old town of L'Aquila was open only to the workers and the Fire Brigade, while during the post-emergency and reconstruction phase the public areas were open to the citizens. For some months, the propped-up city was visited by students and scholars to observe the temporary works and damage to buildings as if it were an open-air earthquake museum, unique and only available for a limited period of time, which could be repeated with virtual reality. The city slowly changed from a town secured with temporary works to a rebuilding site that, day by day, returned restored pieces of the historic built environment.

The economic recovery of such an environment is difficult and needs assistance. The production activities relocated outside the old town have gradually returned to their original locations, but inevitably there will be empty buildings because the amount of available accommodation has greatly increased due to the existence of many buildings built in the outlying areas during the transitional period.

Temporary housing for citizens, whose homes had been damaged or destroyed, was provided by creating small urban neighbourhoods located on the outskirts of the city, which, in many cases, transformed the landscape and the territory. Temporary villages were built using traditional prefabricated solutions or by building on reinforced concrete or steel platforms with seismic isolation at the base. This inevitably led to strong social dispersion in the absence of the meeting places in a city hitherto strongly characterized by historical centrality, being one of the most populated old towns in Italy. The result was a sprawling city, typical of the suburbs of metropolises or of North American cities, far removed from the local culture.

The Historic Centre of L'Aquila

The old town of L'Aquila has preserved its original urban design based on squares, with streets and alleys, and settlements with walled gardens and courtyard houses, organized around the monumental presence of grander buildings and churches. It has retained the stylistic elements and the original materials and legibility of the medieval village offering, also because of the particular topography of the area, striking views that can be seen both from the urban areas (alleys, slopes, hillsides, squares) inside the centre and from the foot of the hill on which it stands. It also has a particular historic-traditional and scenic value due to the presence of buildings of considerable architectural interest. These buildings and their appurtenances taken as a whole constitute an architectural complex of great historic and monumental importance, defining the impressive urban scene of L'Aquila.

This area is served by two road links. The first one is curved to follow the original topography of the site, traceable to the first settlements, which most characterizes the south-eastern sector. The other orthogonal one is attributable to the *Angevin* town and defines the north-eastern sector.

Natural disasters and alternating political and economic supremacies have changed the city's image many times by repositioning values and reference points. The current appearance of the historic centre is due both to the monuments and to the urban fabric as a whole. The layout of the buildings and their aggregation, their relationship, through the connective tissue of the public spaces, streets, squares, plazas, with numerous architectural features, the variety of construction types and volume, both private and public, together with all the evidence of commercial, social and residential life, define the shape and identity of the city. The buildings are often aggregated, architecturally and structurally in the ancient fabric, forming complex entities that fit in with the scenery. The value of the historic centre lies in the architectural quality of the buildings and the presence of many monuments including churches, the Spanish Fort, the Fountain of 99 Spouts and many palaces. The churches include the 'Holy Souls', the basilicas of San Bernardino and Collemaggio and the Cathedral.

Features of the Building Stock

The stock of buildings in the historic centre is mainly privately owned (96 per cent), with 63 per cent being primary residences. It is composed mainly of interconnected buildings (72.66 per cent) of which about 64 per cent were built before 1945. The majority of buildings are of masonry construction (about 95 per cent), with 13 per cent listed as monuments and subject to heritage protection and many other buildings of heritage value and worthy of preservation.

A major feature of the city is the high concentration of public tertiary sector offices, the presence of the university and residences for a significant number of students (about 6,000). This has resulted in many businesses (about 900), including the weekly market in the Piazza Duomo (operating since 1303), many banks and professional activities, and a significant cultural life, thanks to the presence of the municipal theatre, an innovation theatre ('the Egg' theatre company) and the Conservatory.

The reconstruction after the 1703 earthquake and the city before 2009

A long list of earthquakes has marked the history of the city of L'Aquila: the seismic activity in January and February 1703 caused widespread damage and generalized collapse of all the buildings. In particular, the churches, most of which were of a Latin-cross plan, were badly affected because of insufficiently firm surfaces or horizontal elements between floors with the exception of the roof. All the churches of the city underwent reconstruction and repair work in baroque style including strengthening of piers and sometimes a reduction in height.

Reconstruction to reshape a city with eighteenth-century styles took dozens of years. Building activity was still being carried out at the beginning of the nineteenth century, both in the marginal part near the city walls and on the inside, redesigning the *Decumano Massimo* (high street). The city before 1703 is represented now by only a few buildings (including the Palazzo Cappa-Camponeschi, Casa Jacopo Notar Nanni and Palazzo Carli) and by stylistic elements such as main doors with pointed arches or multifoil windows in reconstructed buildings. Even in the 1930s some important work was constructed in rationalist architecture, in particular along the Decumano Massimo. From 1950 until about 1980 reinforced concrete buildings, both residential and public, were built in the historic setting, out of context and repeating the high-rise buildings that negatively characterize the suburbs.

Most of the buildings along the 'Central Axis' underwent renovations or were actually rebuilt between the eighteenth and nineteenth centuries, sometimes with additional storeys. This can be seen in the orderly architecture of the smaller buildings but even in the most famous buildings (for example, the Palazzo Ciolina). This constructive vivacity is undoubtedly a sign of a particular economic vitality of the bourgeois and merchant classes.

Another moment of particular importance for the mark that it left on the city's architecture was the period of rationalist architecture when nearly the whole high street was redesigned from the square of the Fontana Luminosa, with the twin buildings that form the entrance from the north, continuing with the buildings on the Via San Bernardino and Via Federico II and ending up at the buildings around the Massimo Cinema. These works, on an urban scale, were in keeping with the historic architecture (Portici San Bernardino Arcade, Massimo Cinema, etc.). In particular, the style of the complete replacement of a city block at the intersection of the two main roads of the old town, the Corso Federico II and Via San Bernardino, shows that although it clearly belongs to the historic period when it was designed, it was still planned to achieve continuity with the nineteenth-century building on the opposite side and aligned with it, maintaining the street line, the alignment of the height of the eaves, the string course lines and recreating the arcade front of the same height as the nineteenth-century frontage. In work undertaken between the 1950s and the end of the 1970s such references to the scale of the building, block, or urban structure are not apparent and both public and residential buildings were constructed in reinforced concrete and masonry.

After the earthquake of 2009, particular attention was paid to the 'incongruous' buildings and/or elements that alter the visual impact through the planimetric/volumetric dimensions and the types and sizes of the buildings. The space inside the city walls, as mentioned, was not completely saturated, at least until the end of the nineteenth century when building started in the free and large empty urban spaces, often pertaining to convents or palaces and historically used for vegetable gardens, gardens and even planted with vines. More recently (1970–90) nearly all the spaces were filled, bringing into the old town the 'high-rise' type of building without the mediation of the disciplines of architecture and art history, clashing sharply with the existing structures both in formal aspects and in the treatment and composition of the façades.

Incongruous buildings that do not 'converse' with their surroundings in terms of planimetric/volumetric size, typological characteristics, dimensional characteristics of the structures, finishes, etc. were identified, distinguishing buildings as a whole from the incongruous elements of minor importance, so that the typical features of the urban context could be preserved and safeguarded. Particular attention was paid to the Via Sallustio, one of the roads into the city which, conceived as a new access road, has profoundly altered the urban fabric. The opening of the Via Sallustio, which leads to the Decumano Massimo, allowed the connection between the city centre and the Via XX Settembre. New buildings were started here in 1940, as well as the conversion of historic buildings such as the convent of Beata Antonia and the former convent of Santa Chiara. The post-earthquake reconstruction, given the serious damage to many of these buildings, was an opportunity for urban upgrading, and the rebuilding regulations provide for replacement of buildings deemed incongruous, so as to express architectural quality at the local level (Cialone et al. 2015).

Methods of action

The whole process of reconstruction in the historic centre was regulated by the '8-Reconstruction Plan-PDR-2012' (Città Dell'Aquila 2012a) which, along the lines of the *Piano Regolatore Generale* (PRG) (Overall

Development Plan), defined the strategic lines of action and combined the various financial-economic actions and town planning and building activities for the reconstruction of the city's old town.

Returning people to homes affected by the earthquake was the main strategic line of reconstruction encouraging, wherever possible, the recovery and renovation of damaged buildings. The Municipality of Aquila (the Municipality) activated direct participation by citizens collectively and commenced action by developing a 'Design Protocol' to guide technicians in the formulation of proposals and projects, which made it possible to define the framework of knowledge, the manner and the timing of works and to estimate the costs of action. The proposals for action, presented in 2010 to the Municipality highlighted the existing construction types and consequently the methods of action and the economic needs have been defined by the PDR and the 'Parametric Model' (USRA 2014).

After approval of the PDR the executive design phase was commenced according to the maximum financial contribution that could be granted by the drafting of the first part of the projects. Subsequently, depending on available funds and municipal planning, the preparation of the second part of the executive projects was authorized leading to the commencement of works.

The historic centre has been divided into three main areas:

- Zone A coincides with the old town, where mainly restorations in accordance with the PRG have been foreseen.
- Zones B and C, on the outskirts of the old town, where unitary urban rebuilding projects are also foreseen.

In 2011 reconstruction started in the outskirts and continued inside the old town, first with the listed buildings (2012) and then with the other buildings (2013), starting from the Axis Central and from this to the inner areas.

The City implemented the reconstruction plan in different phases according to the building and urban planning controls and by functional phases related to the reconstruction of buildings in accordance with the existing PRG and through both public and private works.

The construction types and activities in the historic centre of L'Aquila

Different construction types can be found among the buildings located in the historic centre, including ordinary masonry buildings, masonry buildings with architectural and/or historical and artistic value, including listed buildings, and those built in reinforced concrete. The main types of assistance provided for these buildings were:

- repair of the damage and seismic strengthening of masonry buildings with remedial maintenance and/or restoration and conservative renovation in accordance with local building technologies (this work concerns more than 70 per cent);
- reconstruction of the masonry or reinforced concrete buildings collapsed and/or seriously damaged;
- reconstruction preserving the volumetric and external features of the building with the possibility of rebuilding the structures with different technologies (reinforced concrete, masonry, steel). This mode of action has been planned and applied for the replacement construction of buildings collapsed or seriously damaged, not of value, or incongruous. In this case there is the problem of how and what to build as part of the landscape of the old town.

Private sector work on buildings was divided into direct construction projects to be implemented in accordance with the PRG (about 70 per cent of the total) and unitary operations variant to the PRG (about 15 per cent of the total) mainly to be carried out outside the old town. Reconstruction was also strongly characterized by the redevelopment of the public building portfolio such as the numerous places of worship and religious buildings (monasteries), school buildings, the buildings connected to specific public and social functions such as the Prefecture, the headquarters of the Regional Government, the City Hall and other public institutions that provide for the participation of several public and/or private parties (University, Cultural and Administrative centres) in strategic actions in compliance with or variant to the PRG.

The demolition and subsequent reconstruction of the existing buildings were deemed possible: for collapsed buildings or ones demolished by orders of the Mayor; for masonry buildings with partial collapse of load-bearing walls, floors and roofs; for reinforced concrete buildings with relative displacements of the floors caused by the earthquake of 2009 and the low resistance of the concrete; and for buildings damaged by the earthquake that are considered incongruous. The first three conditions are linked to the level of damage caused by the earthquake and the seismic vulnerability and the fourth condition is aimed at upgrading the building stock.

The parametric method: A virtuous example for determining the actions and estimating the costs (USRA 2013, Vitis et al. 2013, USRA 2014)

The works will be paid for by a contribution paid entirely by the state, fixed objectively taking into account the damage and vulnerability and the construction characteristics of the buildings. In general, four levels of unitary contribution have been fixed and the maximum cost coincides with the maximum contribution identified for facilitated housing reconstruction. For the evaluation of the damage, reference was made to the European Macro-seismic Scale which has five levels of damage, while for the determination of the seismic vulnerability the approach followed took into account the structural weaknesses of the buildings.

The principal methods of action were *light* and *heavy* reconstruction. The lightest and fastest reconstruction was performed for slightly damaged buildings and the work was carried out within one or two years of the earthquake. The work consisted mainly of repair of the damage and localized work such as floor links, eliminating thrusts outside the level of the masonry walls and reinforcement of the structural elements that can trigger the most frequent collapse mechanisms. All these actions made it possible to raise the level of seismic safety of buildings, in an authentic manner, without significantly altering the stiffness, strength and/or ductility of those construction elements. Light reconstruction also involves the partial restoration of finishes and structures.

The heavy reconstruction of severely damaged buildings commonly involves all the work referred to above (remediation, regulation and consolidation) and the complete renovation of the finishes and structures at a higher cost. In many cases, experience has shown that it is possible to extend light reconstruction to a greater number of buildings damaged to a medium-serious extent, regardless of the fitness for use result, which does not give a full picture of the damage, providing for numerous local strengthening actions. This intervention strategy, if applied in the short term (one or two years), makes it possible to limit the deterioration that would result from waiting until such time as full-scale action can be taken after, say, seven or eight years, and reduce the overall costs. In the historic centre of L'Aquila, in all the buildings including protected buildings, heavy reconstruction with improved energy efficiency, wire networks and seismic strengthening was mainly performed in an authentic manner.

Quality and protection of the building heritage and territory

The procedures for reconstruction include actions for the preservation, in an authentic manner, of the historical and artistic heritage, as agreed between the Municipality and the Ministry for Cultural Heritage, for the buildings in the old town (Città Dell'Aquila 2012b, DPCM 2013). To benefit from a higher level of financial contribution in relation to the reconstruction of buildings of merit, actions should provide for the conservation and recovery of original materials, the preservation of the building types and structural functioning, possibly with the support of new materials resulting from technological innovation, to be selected according to the criteria of compatibility and durability. Moreover, non-reversible invasive interventions that fail to respect the original techniques and concept of the structure, or which are rigid with respect to seismic response, have also been identified and banned. The increases also take into account the time of construction (before 1703, between 1704 and 1799, from 1800 to 1942, between 1943 and 2009).

The indicators identified by the agreement for quantifying for the increased contribution were:

- *the importance relative to the perceptual aspects*: façades, plasters (to be recovered or replenished), fine outer walls, painted decorations, embossed elements in wood/stone/iron;
- the position with respect to public space;
- decorative and/or monumental elements (stone doorframes, stone balconies with corbels and/or railings in stone/iron/cast-iron, cornices in stucco/wood/brick and original windows and doors in wood/ iron, traditional flooring and/or furnishing elements;
- *the decorations of artistic historical interest* (frescoes, paintings, stuccowork, etc.);
- interaction with public space (courtyard opening onto public space, arcades and/or galleries, monumental staircases and hallways, roofing in antique tiles, characteristic morphological configuration of urban space);
- *relevance with regard to the traditional material culture* as regards type and construction techniques with original materials; and
- *relevance in relation to the time of construction*.

The parameters identified to determine the increased contributions were graduated according to the period of construction and were determined on the basis of an estimate of the costs of the operations related to the recovery of those elements.

The increased contribution was foreseen in the awareness that the restoration/reconstruction of the historical and artistic features and consolidation of the structures must be designed so as to ensure the preservation of architecture in all its forms, taking into consideration any possible interference with the decorations so that they integrate with the existing structure without radically transforming it, respecting the original concept and techniques of the structure and any significant changes that occurred during the history of the building. The challenge is not to rebuild and reach a level of security at any cost (a trivial result that is often achieved by destroying or modifying the behaviour of the housing stock and using improper materials and techniques), but to respect the local construction techniques.

The choice of actions is also connected to tampering works over the years, such as in relation to openings, the addition of projecting elements and additional storeys in non-original materials. In such a context, the masonry has lost its original composition and this situation has been found mainly in buildings that are not listed but have special architectural value, particularly in the inner walls. Many other tampering actions are recent and were done with reinforced concrete (for example, in roofs) or hollow bricks used to build extensions and new walls. All these works were seriously damaged by the 2009 earthquake.

Generally speaking, even the heavy reconstruction increased the structural authenticity of the buildings, restoring firmness to the masonry such as by the use of reinforced angle irons in floor connections with walls and wall toothing, in the knowledge that the structure, as a whole, is a heritage asset and as such should be protected by avoiding excessive and unjustified interventions. In this context, the designer must not be left alone in the choice of operations and the scientific community must provide effective support with local codes of practice accompanied by appropriate training and regulations that require their application, like the aforementioned agreement between the Municipality of L'Aquila and the Ministry of Cultural Heritage.

Palazzo Ardinghelli: An example of repairing seismic damage, reconstruction works and seismic improvements

Located in the historic centre of L'Aquila between the Via Garibaldi and Piazza S. Maria Paganica, the palace was built between 1732 and 1743 for the Florentine family of Ardinghelli. It was substantially damaged by the 2009 earthquake (Figure 1).

Artistic-historic architectural restoration and reconstruction work with seismic improvements were undertaken (Figure 2); fragments were recovered and classified by type, restored and integrated using innovative techniques and replaced in the structure with a view to improving the seismic response of the building. The methodological approach involved classification of artistic elements according to the different types of material, and checks were made for reduction of the seismic risk of the heritage protected. The masonry work involved like-for-like replacement of walls where serious damage had occurred as well as sealing minor damage, improvement of masonry textures including reinforcing joints with composite material in basalt lime, improvement of the connections between the linings and the wall tissue, closing and reducing voids, replacement jambs and flat arches, and some reinforcement work. Some strengthening work was carried out in steel including the insertion of cross connections, tie rods and intermediate

FIGURE 1 *Palazzo Ardinghelli (L'Aquila) after the earthquake of 2009. Source: Alberto Lemme, 2009.*

FIGURE 2 *Palazzo Ardinghelli (L'Aquila) after restoration and reconstruction works. Source: Alberto Lemme, 2016.*

chains and the insertion of elements aimed at reducing minor deflections in the walls of the main floor.

The most significant piece of work was the authentic reconstruction of the loggia set in an inner courtyard, semicircular in shape. The loggia, on two levels, is characterized by pillars connected by arches joined to the walls of the Palace with transverse gable arches and cross vaults. All of the stone elements recovered from the collapse were examined using ultrasound equipment to check the integrity of the various stone material portions, whether whole or in fragments. Cleaning and biocide treatment was undertaken and the elements used to replace and reintegrate the stone parts that had collapsed were reinforced, ensuring the readability of the context, the work and the seismic damage. Before reconstructing the pillars, the assembly of the stone elements of the pillars and of the arches following collapse was carried out on site (on an adequate horizontal surface), dry to assess the gaps and their reintegration. When the pillars of the collapsed loggia were recovered they were remounted on the spot, dry, using steel pins, placed between one ashlar stone and another, and by the insertion of steel strips. After the reconstruction work on the pillars was finished, work was carried on to remake the arches and reconstruct the cross vault in bricks, reinforced with basalt mesh and cement-free lime mortar (De Vitis et al. 2013, Lemme et al. 2015) (Figure 3).

FIGURE 3 *The Loggia of Palazzo Ardinghelli after reconstruction works. Source: Alberto Lemme, 2016.*

Examples of reconstruction in the historic centre

After the earthquake of 2009, many works of reconstruction and building replacement of badly damaged and/or incongruous collapsed buildings were carried out. These works were compliant with the PRG, repeating the dimensional and volumetric characteristics in continuity with the historic buildings, and their scenic integration was assessed by the Municipality with the assistance of the Ministry for Cultural Heritage. One example of this can be indicated in relation to building work to replace a reinforced concrete building constructed after 1942 in the Piazza Santa Maria Paganica alongside Palazzo Ardinghelli (Giancola 2015).

Beyond the reconstruction

The analysis carried out for 'Reconstruction Aquilana' after the earthquake of 2009 offers the opportunity for a reflection. This mainly involves two aspects that can be developed in the context of a greater efficacy of the planned actions: the formulation of an organic law for the national and/or European management of the subsequent phases of a natural disaster and the actions necessary to transform a calamitous event into an opportunity for protection and enhancement.

After each seismic event, including that of 2009 in Abruzzo, measures and defined local procedures for the management of the different stages of the reconstruction were adopted, but there was no complete and definitive vision of the necessary actions. Following the earthquake, the first phase was adjusted by measures for the recognition of practicability, while the second phase, focussed on historic centres, has followed a procedure governed by the Parametric Model already used in previous events (Umbria-Marche in 1997 and Molise in 2002).

It would be useful to define procedures applicable after every natural or man-made disaster for events that have similar problems to seismic events. The procedures used for the programming and the determination of the costs, and the Agreement between the Municipality of L'Aquila and the Ministry responsible for the protection of buildings of heritage value, were good practices that can be expanded and included in the framework of legislation at the national level. The effective and relatively quick reconstruction and restoration experience in L'Aquila, with acceptable costs, made a significant contribution in this regard.

The encoding of these interventions in the perspective of a quality certification for building works is a goal that was reached in the historic centre of L'Aquila. In fact, the design protocols and reconstruction formalities established by Decrees have provided, in addition to the repair of the damage and to seismic improvements, energy efficiency improvements, and allowed the updating of networks, technological plant and finishes. The digital recording of reconstruction projects and the creation of a dossier for maintenance, management and valorization of the territory are relevant in this context.

The formulation of appropriate policies for this purpose is of great importance for the prevention/mitigation of natural and man-made risks since natural disasters have grown in intensity and extent in recent years and more areas have become exposed to seismic risk. The seismic upgrading of existing buildings with the support of public funding and the involvement of insurance also becomes the occasion for the redevelopment of the urban fabric. A further aspect concerns the economic recovery of the areas affected by anthropic and natural disasters. Reconstruction after a natural disaster can become an opportunity for the development of the territory and, in the case of recent earthquakes in Italy, has led to the commitment of substantial public funds for reconstruction, without modifying or substantially improving the socio-economic fabric of the areas affected.

Earthquakes often affect mountainous regions characterized by weak economies. The reconstruction has always been based on the principle of repairing the damage and provision of seismic improvements and is strongly connected to the return of the populations. The financial contributions are issued to individual citizens or to municipalities for the execution of public works and to entrepreneurs for supporting economic activities. This approach has allowed the reconstruction of buildings, but they are often not fully reoccupied, as is apparent following other similar events that have hit Italy in recent years (Abruzzo-Molise-Lazio 1984, Umbria and Marche 1997, Molise 2002, Abruzzo 2009).

The economic recovery and the valorization of the territory could be improved by introducing incentive mechanisms and co-financing by private individuals and the dedicated public funds for reconstruction, in particular for marginal areas, enabling projects of enhancement that involve economic operators for the execution of the works of reconstruction and the possible management of economic activities that are envisaged.

References

Cialone, G., A. Petracca and G. Petrucci (2015), 'Initial Evaluations of Works and Incongruous Buildings in an Urban Context Damaged by the Earthquake: the Case of the City of L'Aquila,' paper presented at Anidis (Italian National Association of Earthquake Engineering) 2015 – 16th Conference, Polo Ingegneria Roio (Facoltà di Ingegneria), L'Aquila.

Città Dell'Aquila (2012a), *Il Piano di Ricostruzione* (Reconstruction Plan of L'Aquila): *la delibera n. 23* (city council decision no. 23). Available online: http://www.comune.laquila.gov.it/pagina199_il-piano-di-ricostruzione.html (accessed 12 July 2016).

Città Dell'Aquila (2012b), 'Ricostruzione, presentata l'intesa di Interesse paesaggistico tra la Soprintendenza e il Comune' ('Reconstruction, Presentation of the Understanding of Landscape Interest between the City and the

Soprintendenza'), Press release, 10 December. Available online: http://www. comune.laquila.gov.it/index.php?id_oggetto=3&id_cat=0&id_doc=1393&id_ sez_ori=5&template_ori=3&&gtp=1 (accessed 13 July 2016).

Decreto del Presidente del Consiglio dei Ministri (Decree of the President of the Council of Ministers) (DPCM) (2011), *Valutazione e riduzione del rischio sismico del patrimonio culturale con riferimento alle norme tecniche per le costruzioni di cui al decreto ministeriale 14 gennaio 2008 (Guidelines for the assessment and mitigation of seismic risk of cultural heritage, in line with the New Technical Standards for construction 14 January 2008)*, DPCM 9–2–2011, Official Gazette No. 47 – Ordinary Supplement No. 54, Rome: Italian Republic.

DPCM (2013), *Adempimenti per la ricostruzione – Ricostruzione (Formalities for the Reconstruction – Reconstruction)*, DPCM 4–2–2013, Official Gazette No. 54, Rome: Italian Republic.

Giancola, F. (2015), *Edificio Santa Maria Paganica (New Reconstruction in Piazza Santa Maria Paganica, L'Aquila)*. Available online: http://www.2studio.eu/ edificio-santa-maria-paganica-5/ (accessed 13 July 2016).

Institute for Construction Technologies and National Research Council (ITC-CNR) (2010), National Civil Protection: Data Analysis of the Usability Inspections, *L'Istituto per le Tecnologie della Costruzione* and *Consiglio Nazionale delle Ricerche*, published in L'Aquila Reconstruction Plan Strategic Guidelines. Available online: http://www.comune.laquila.gov.it/pagina200_le-linee-di-indirizzo-strategico.html (accessed 13 July 2016).

Lemme, A., A. Mignemi, F. De Vitis and C. Miozzi (2015), 'Historical, Artistic and Seismic Improvement: The Innovative Approach to Critical Reconstruction of Collapsed Buildings, the Case of the Palace Ardinghelli,' paper presented at Anidis (Italian National Association of Earthquake Engineering) 2015 – 16th Conference, Polo Ingegneria Roio (Facoltà di Ingegneria), L'Aquila.

Ufficio Speciale per la Ricostruzione dell'Aquila (Special Office for the Reconstruction of L'Aquila) (USRA) (2013), *Discipilna per la progettazione e la realizzazione degli interventi sugli edifici privati, ubicati nei centri storici del comune dell'Aquila danneggiati dal sisma del 2009 (Discipline for the Design and Implementation of Interventions on Private Buildings, Located in the Historical Centre of the City of L'Aquila Damaged by the earthquake of 2009)*, Decree no. 1/2013: L'Aquila: USRA.

USRA (2014), *Sisma Abruzzo 2009:Il Modello Parametrico: Manuale Istruzioni della Scheda di Accompagnamento ai Progetti di Ricostruzione del Comune dell'Aquila – V02 (Abuzzo Earthquake 2009: The Parametric Model: Design Protocol: Instruction Manual for Reconstruction Projects in L'Aquila – Version 2)*, Decreto del Presidente del Consiglio dei Ministri (Decree of the President of the Council of Ministers) DPCM 4–2–2014 and USRA Decrees No. 1 and No. 3/2013, L'Aquila: Ufficio Speciale per la Ricostruzione dell'Aquila (Special Office for the reconstruction of L'Aquila). Available online: http://www.usra.it/wp-content/ uploads/2014/05/ManualeIstruzioniParte2-V02.pdf (accessed 13 July 2016).

Vitis, F. de, B. M. Colasacco, A. Mignemi, A. Lemme, C. Cicolani, C. Canullo, M. Liris and G. Olivieri (2013), *Progettazione esecutiva ed esecuzione dei lavori di Restauro e Consolidamento con miglioramento sismico di Palazzo Ardinghelli in Piazza Santa Maria Paganica (Executive Project for the Restoration and Consolidation of Palazzo Ardinghelli in Piazza Santa Maria Paganica)*, approved by Soprintendenza of L'Aquila in 2013. Available online: http://docplayer. it/13723952-Cantieri-della-ricostruzione.html (accessed 13th July 2016).

Chapter 3.4

The Town Reassembled: Authenticity and Transformation in Kiruna, Sweden

Jennie Sjöholm

Introduction

It is technically possible to move buildings, for example, as a means of conservation, although the process raises important issues of authenticity and originality. But is it equally possible to move a town? That is the focus of this chapter. Sweden has a long tradition of moving buildings. During agricultural land reforms in the eighteenth and nineteenth centuries, villages were split up and the houses, typically wooden, were relocated to allow more large-scale farms. The transformation by industrialization and urbanization of agricultural built environments was perceived by some as a threat. This led to the establishment of open air museums, collecting historic buildings, at the end of the nineteenth century (Rentzhog 2007). In the early twentieth century, these museums also began to collect buildings from urban areas, as demolitions occurred in many towns when early nineteenth-century small-scale built environments were replaced with what were, in comparison, large-scale stone and brick buildings (Schönbeck 1994). These urban developments and proposed demolitions of older buildings spurred protests in many towns, and numerous local heritage societies were established to preserve specific buildings. This was sometimes successful, and buildings were either preserved *in situ* or relocated within the town (Schönbeck 1994). There is also a tradition of moving settlements; towns such as Luleå and Piteå on the Swedish northern coast were relocated in the seventeenth century following post-glacial land

rise. In the northern part of Sweden, there are also many long-established
settlements that have developed around natural resources and industries
(Book and Bergman 2008). Towns such as Kiruna, Malmberget and Laver
were based around mining, whereas others including Porjus, Messaure and
Harsprånget were based around hydro-power projects along the Luleå River.
Laver, Messaure and Harsprånget were flourishing settlements for a few
decades in the twentieth century, but when the ore was no longer profitable
to mine and when the hydro-power stations had been built, people moved
on and the settlements were dismantled as buildings were moved elsewhere,
leaving only traces of street patterns and overgrown public spaces.

This chapter will explore the example of Kiruna, a mining town, which is
about to undertake a large-scale transformation in response to the demands
from the mining industry. It is said that the town will be moved; the question
is how this will affect the town's built heritage and authenticity related to
the site.

Kiruna is located in the northernmost part of Sweden, approximately
140 km north of the Arctic Circle. Today, the town has about 18,000
inhabitants, and is located in an area of low population between the iron-
ore mountains of Luossavaara and Kiirunavaara. The town was founded
in 1900 by the mining company Luossavaara Kiirunavaara AB (LKAB) to
enable the area's rich iron-ore deposits to be exploited. Historically, single
companies built company towns to provide housing for their workers,
often to utilize natural resources in scarcely populated areas (Garner 1992).
Company towns were designed and organized in different ways, depending
on the degree of planning and how permanent they were expected to be
(Ahnlund and Brunnström 1987). Kiruna was originally divided into three
main areas: a model company town managed by LKAB; a service and supply
town which developed into a civil municipality; and a railway area designed
by Kungliga Järnvägsstyrelsen (the Royal Railway Board). The three areas
merged in 1948 as Kiruna was granted the legal status of a town by the state.

During the 1980s, conservation became a growing concern in urban
planning in Sweden and more widely. The entire town, including the iron-ore
mountains, was designated as an area of national interest for the purposes
of conservation of the cultural environment. This was motivated by Kiruna
being an 'urban environment and industrial landscape that shows a unique
settlement from the twentieth century, where planning ideals at the time
were realized on underutilized lands' (National Heritage Board 2010; all
text translations are by the author).

The local authority adopted a conservation plan in 1984, which identified
a number of significant historic environments and individual historic
buildings that should be protected (Kiruna Council 1984). Many of these
historic buildings have gradually gained protection in detailed development
plans adopted by the local authority (Kiruna Council 2008). Some buildings,
for example the Town Hall (Figure 1), the railway station (Figure 2) and
the residence of LKAB's first manager, Hjalmar Lundbohmsgården, were

FIGURE 1 *The Town Hall, built between 1959 and 1962 and designed by Artur von Schmalensee. The clock tower was designed by Bror Marklund. The building was listed in 2001 by the Heritage Conservation Act, and then delisted in 2014 following a court decision. Source: Daryoush Tahmasebi © Norrbottens museum.*

FIGURE 2 *The railway station, built in 1915 after the first station burned down, and designed by Folke Zettervall. The building was listed in 1986 but had the protection repealed in 2011 by request of the Kiruna Council and LKAB, and it will be demolished. Source: Jennie Sjöholm.*

FIGURE 3 *The Kiruna Church, inaugurated in 1912 and designed by Gustaf Wickman. Source: Daryoush Tahmasebi © Norrbottens museum.*

FIGURE 4 Bläckhorn *workers' housing, located in the company area and built in the early 1900s, designed by Wickman. Today, forty-four of the fifty-six original* Bläckhorn *buildings remain. Up to twelve of these buildings will be relocated according to the 2011 agreement between LKAB and the local authority. Source: Jennie Sjöholm.*

protected by the Heritage Conservation Act in 2001–03. The designated built heritage comprises some of the town's oldest parts. Most of the historic buildings are small-scale and wooden, built in the early twentieth century and designed by some of Sweden's most renowned architects. The architecture often has distinct features, for instance in joinery and colouring. This includes the church (Figure 3), which was voted Sweden's most popular building in 2001 (Bergström 2002), and buildings such as Bolagshotellet (the company hotel), and the *Bläckhorn* workers' housing in the company area (Figure 4).

The Kiruna town move

In 2004, the local authority issued a press release saying that the town was to be moved in order to enable mining to continue (Kiruna Council 2004). This is because LKAB's main iron-ore deposit reaches beneath the settlement; the company operates an underground mine, causing subsidence which will gradually affect the town (Figure 5). The proposed town relocation must be seen in the context of Kiruna being wholly dependent on the iron-ore mining, and LKAB being the largest private employer within the county with about 3,700 employees. At the beginning of the twenty-first century the

FIGURE 5 *LKAB's prognosis for subsidence, from December 2014, caused by mining at the current sub-level in the Kiirunavaara mine. Source: LKAB.*

increased market price of iron ore was an incentive; the state-owned mining company's share dividend peaked at around €550 million (5.5 billion SEK) in 2014 (LKAB 2014).

The announcement about relocating the town was followed by a number of planning processes: the local authority initiated detailed comprehensive planning investigation of how to handle the urban transformation, followed by detailed development planning; Banverket (the Swedish National Rail Administration) planned for a new railway route passing Kiruna; and Vägverket (the Swedish Road Administration) for new routes for public roads. The Kiruna Council decided in 2011 that a new town centre would be established north-east of today's settlement, and that the town would gradually develop in that direction. The winners of an urban design competition for the new town centre were announced in 2013, which was followed by development planning for the new areas. The winners of an architectural competition for a new town hall were also announced. Areas affected by the subsidence will gradually be evacuated, buildings moved or demolished, and the areas turned into a park before, eventually, the ground becomes unsafe and the sites are closed. This so-called Mine Town Park is intended to form a buffer zone between the town and the mining area, to avoid housing next to the fenced subsidence areas. Over time, new areas will become part of the park as the subsidence proceeds.

At the time of writing, in 2016, the transformation has started to show. New sewage and electricity supply systems came into use in 2009. The Mine Town Park was established in 2011, and a new railway route opened in 2012. A new sub-level for mining was opened in the Kiirunavaara mine 1,365 m underground in 2013 and, as a consequence, part of lake Luossajärvi was emptied and a new dam was built to prevent water leaking into the mine. The construction of the new town hall has begun: it is the first building to be built in the new town centre. The town hall is planned to be open for use in 2018, and buildings around the adjacent new main square are expected to be completed in the following year. In 2015, the first residential buildings were demolished, after thorough documentation, in the area that will be the first to be affected by subsidence. These were 1960s apartment buildings; after the demolition, artists were engaged to compose an artwork 'to preserve the memories from the neighbourhood' as the area was incorporated in the Mine Town Park (Forsberg 2015: 26–7). Building materials from the demolished buildings were used to build patterns that reflected the shapes of the original building foundations, an event one of the artists described as 'we think the material in itself has a value and carries memories and history … This can be a place where you come and remember your history. Here, you will always know where the building was, even when there is a fence' (Dahlström 2015: 21).

The town reassembled

It is unclear what 'moving a town' means in the Kiruna context, and ideas of how to manage the built environment and the built heritage have changed over time since the announcement of the project, and between the main stakeholders LKAB, the Kiruna Council and the County Administrative Board. The local authority's 2004 press release stated that 'we will move a town', but it also raised a number of questions, revealing some uncertainty about the situation:

> Should we build something completely new somewhere else and really start over, free from the shackles of tradition? Should we preserve all the old but at a new location? Should we mix the best of the old with building anew those things that did not completely succeed last time? How far away from the mine must we build to prevent us from having to do this again? ... Could LKAB use other techniques so that the mountain does not crack? Might the new calculations and measurements be wrong, so that the centre of Kiruna does not need to be moved at all? (Kiruna Council 2004: 2)

The local authority's detailed comprehensive planning process that followed indicated that historic buildings would, to a large extent, be moved. The plan, which was approved in 2006, stated that 'as many buildings as possible' would be moved to new locations as the mine expanded, and the document also concluded that 'it is technically possible to move almost all types of buildings. That means it is fully possible to move larger buildings such as the Town Hall, the church, Bolagshotellet and Hjalmar Lundbohmsgården' (Kiruna Council 2006: 157).

During a stakeholder consultation as part of the detailed comprehensive plan-making process, LKAB presented a spectacular vision of 'New Kiruna'. The proposed plan for the town's built heritage was that

> The church and cultural buildings from the Company Area are moved as an entire environment, not as individual buildings. They are placed in a visible and, for the town, strategic location with the Kebnekaisemassif in the background. Other valuable cultural buildings fit well in the suggested block pattern. (LKAB, ÅF-Infraplan and Wilhelmson arkitekter 2006: 3)

Around 2010, in the process of adopting a new detailed development plan for the first part of the Mine Town Park, attitudes towards the town's built heritage clearly shifted. In the draft consultation version of the detailed development plan, the local authority proposed to relocate all of the more than twenty protected buildings within the planning area (Kiruna Council 2009). This was supported by the local authority's value assessment of buildings within the planning area, which was a part of the environmental impact assessment associated with the detailed development plan. This investigation suggested that most of the historic buildings should be relocated and, in most cases, restored to their original condition (Kiruna Council 2010b). However, this proposal was withdrawn, and the adopted detailed development plan stipulated that only five of the protected buildings originally identified within the planning area will be relocated (Kiruna Council 2010a).

The detailed development plan was amended and adopted as a result of a civil law agreement between the local authority and LKAB, regulating the mining company's liability for the town's built heritage. The agreement identified which historic buildings would be kept and relocated, within the whole town – not only the current Mine Town Park area – and during the entire urban transformation process. According to the agreement, up to twenty-one buildings will be moved within the urban transformation process, which includes the church and a few of the *Bläckhorn* buildings (Figure 6) (Kiruna Council and Luossavaara-Kiirunavaara AB 2011). The detailed development plan or associated documents do not specify how these particular buildings were chosen; neither was the reason for so drastically limiting the number of buildings to move clearly stated. However, according to media reporting, LKAB had performed an internal investigation of the cost of moving a number of historic buildings, and concluded that it would be more expensive to move buildings than to construct new ones. A spokesperson of the mining company concluded that:

> Regarding the Town Hall, it is difficult to move even if everything actually is possible, but the costs of moving buildings will be incredibly high. We can tell based on the investigation we made where we looked at Hjalmar Lundbohmsgården, Bolagshotellet, Fjällvivan and Bläckhornen ... Based on that, we can see that the price of moving will be too high, with the exception of Hjalmar Lundbohmsgården and a few of the *Bläckhorn* buildings. (Bergmark 2009: 22)

There is also a wish, stressed by the local authority, to build new and sustainable housing, with technologies that are environmentally friendly, which is expressed as a contrast to the wish to conserve the historic buildings (Sjöholm 2015). The mayor assumed that '[t]here are surely those who want to save cultural buildings, but many *Kirunabor* [those people who identify themselves with the settlement of Kiruna] probably want us to build new [buildings] now when we have the opportunity'. (Naess 2011: 5)

The County Administrative Board of Norrbotten, which supervises the local authorities' planning at a regional level, found the detailed development plan to be inadequate in managing Kiruna as a heritage site of

FIGURE 6 *Map of the historic buildings that will be moved during the urban transformation, according to the 2011 civil law agreement between the local authority and the mining company. This includes the church, the church bell tower, Hjalmar Lundbohmsgården and up to twelve* Bläckhorn *buildings (precisely which ones are not specified and may not be the ones marked at the map). The shaded area comprises the area of the detailed development plan for the first stage of the Mine Town Park. Source: Jennie Sjöholm.*

national interest. The detailed development plan was not approved until it was decided to move two more buildings within the planning area, and the local authority had agreed to finalize a cultural heritage analysis.

The local interest groups Kirunas rötter (Kiruna Roots) and Hjalmar Lundbohmsgården ekonomiska förening (Hjalmar Lundbohmsgården Business Association) advocated relocation of a large number of historic buildings, assembled in a 'Kiruna Old Town'. They envisioned '*a new, living neighbourhood with local identity with buildings from the company area; housing, corner shops, Hjalmar Lundbohmsgården and the Company Hotel'* (Situation Kiruna 2012).

According to the current planning documents and decisions made, just over twenty historic buildings will be preserved through relocation during the urban transformation process. Most of these were built by the mining company and are currently located in the company area. There are two parallel approaches towards the relocation of these buildings. The local authority has outlined a development plan for the new town centre, in which it is stated that the buildings to be moved will be distributed throughout the new built areas, at approximately one building per block (Kiruna Council 2014). At the same time, LKAB is planning for a new company area north-west of today's settlement. Here, they will locate Hjalmar Lundbohmsgården along with some other historic buildings which they have agreed to move (LKAB 2013). Hjalmar Lundbohmsgården is the only listed building that will be relocated (County Administrative Board of Norrbotten 2011b). The Town Hall and the railway station had been listed, but this protection has now been repealed. The local authority and LKAB had agreed to demolish, rather than relocate, these buildings. The County Administrative Board agreed to repeal the protection of the railway station as its assessment was that the risk of moving the building outweighed its heritage values, but also because other, similar, railway stations are protected and therefore represented from a national perspective (County Administrative Board of Norrbotten 2011a). The Town Hall will be discussed in more detail below.

Re-evaluations of the built heritage

Within contemporary heritage studies, heritage values are often considered to be socially constructed rather than intrinsic to the objects of conservation (Smith 2006, Pendlebury 2009). Heritage may be designated if values and meanings are attached to it, and 'is thus a product of the present, purposefully developed in response to current needs or demands for it, and shaped by those requirements' (Tunbridge and Ashworth 1996: 6). This takes place within a heritagization process, which can be defined as 'the process by which objects and places are transformed from functional "things" into objects of display and exhibition' (Harrison 2013: 69). For example, built environments are recognized as heritage, and buildings and places might be added to lists and gain protection through legislation. Heritage can be contested and challenged; for instance, built environments and urban areas are normally continuously assessed and evaluated, especially during situations of change. This leads to new phases of heritagization: re-heritagization and de-heritagization (Sjöholm 2016). Re-heritagization refers to a process during which already-designated heritage is either reaffirmed as heritage, where the same historic buildings and environments are recognized and interpreted in the same way as before, or when new or additional meanings are attached to it. De-heritagization refers to a process during which previously designated heritage is rejected, and protection is repealed. This is caused by a loss of, or decrease in, architectural or societal value of its cultural significance.

In Kiruna, an initial heritagization took place in the 1980s, when large parts of the town's built environment were designated as built heritage through the local authority's conservation planning process and the designation of the town as a heritage site of national interest. The contemporary urban transformation process has challenged this appointed built heritage. As the urban transformation process has developed, re-heritagization and de-heritagization have taken place, sometimes as parallel processes and, at other times, historic buildings first underwent re-heritagization only to later experience de-heritagization.

Re-heritagization has mainly occurred through reaffirmation of already-designated heritage. This has been promoted by the internal logic within the planning processes, where planning documents refer back to previous planning documents and decisions. The local authority's detailed comprehensive plan from 2006 and detailed development plan from 2010 focused on already-designated and protected historic buildings, outlined in the conservation plan from 1984. The agreement in 2011 between the local authority and the mining company, defining which buildings to move, has further reaffirmed the status of these buildings as significant built heritage. Media reporting during the urban transformation process has also acknowledged already-designated built heritage as significant, where, in particular, the Town Hall, the church and the *Bläckhorn* workers' housing are mentioned.

The urban planning process has not encouraged the broadening of the conceptualization of the town's built heritage to include buildings outside the already-designated heritage. On the contrary, planning for the urban transformation has initiated de-heritagization processes. A defining event for this was the agreement in 2011 between the local authority and LKAB, specifying which buildings would be relocated with funding from the mining company. Prior to this agreement, the urban planning process was aiming for relocation as the main strategy when managing protected buildings. The twenty-one buildings specified in the agreement is a relatively small number compared to the number of historic buildings and environments previously identified for protection.

The most striking example of de-heritagization is the management of the Town Hall in the urban planning process. The local authority and the mining company made a joint application to the County Administrative Board of Norrbotten in 2010 to have the protection repealed (Kiruna Council, LKAB 2010). They had agreed that LKAB would pay for the building of a new town hall, but intended to reuse some artistic details of the building, such as the bell tower and the doorknobs of the main entrance, but otherwise the original building would be demolished. However, the County Administrative

Board dismissed the application. Instead, the regulations were amended to allow the building to be dismantled and rebuilt, with partially reconstructed materials, at a new location where 'the building's design as an idea and in its physical materials must be reused' (County Administrative Board of Norrbotten 2012: 1). The decision was based on an investigation initiated by the County Administrative Board, showing in which way, and to what extent, it would be possible to dismantle and rebuild the Town Hall, as well as a calculation of the cost (Gezelius 2011). The investigation also presented possible ways to modernize the building, for example, by upgrading technical systems, improving accessibility and increasing energy efficiency. The County Administrative Board found the relocation of the Town Hall reasonable when considering the building's significant heritage values and in relation to the estimated cost of dismantling and rebuilding. The Kiruna Council and LKAB opposed the County Administrative Board's decision, and appealed to the Administrative Court in Luleå. However, the court approved the decision to dismantle and rebuild parts of the building, although it rejected the stipulation of rebuilding to a specific design (Administrative Court in Luleå 2013). This decision was appealed by the local authority to the Administrative Court of Appeal, who judged in favour of the Kiruna Council (Administrative Court of Appeal in Sundsvall 2014). Thus the building lost its protection and will be demolished. During this process, organizations such as the Swedish Association for Building Preservation, Europa Nostra and ICOMOS made appeals to have the Town Hall conserved (Junkka 2011). DOCOMOMO (the international committee for documentation and conservation of buildings, sites and neighbourhoods of the modern movement) argued that the Town Hall should be reassembled, as 'moving Kiruna Town Hall could set an example of beneficial community spirit, skill and care of the cultural heritage' (Lander 2011: 22). The Royal Academy of Fine Arts stressed that the relocation of built heritage is essential to managing the town's built environment, and that given Kiruna's history and international significance, the integration of the Town Hall with the new town centre is central to maintaining continuity (Fries and Slöör 2011). The former Chief County Heritage Adviser, who was responsible for the listing of the Town Hall in 2001, claimed that demolishing the building would be a great loss to the town and to the county. She argued that 'Kiruna must not lose its soul and its identity through the town move – the most important buildings must move along' (Lagerstam 2011: 19). An architect stated in a debate article in the national newspaper *Svenska Dagbladet* that 'Kiruna's self-image is to no small extent based on its remarkable buildings' and emphasized that the Town Hall had been awarded the prestigious Kasper Salin architecture prize in 1964 by the organization Architects Sweden for its architectonic qualities; he suggested that the entire building should be rebuilt (Waern 2011: 6). All of this pleading, from architectural and heritage experts, was unsuccessful. Clearly the Administrative Court of Appeal placed greater emphasis on other factors.

Discussion

The key question in Kiruna is, therefore, how the relocation of the town is likely to affect the authenticity of the heritage site. Will the town, literally, be moved? Not as such. According to planning documents, a gradual transformation will take place over the coming twenty years or so. A new town centre will be established, but with a relocation of functions rather than of buildings.

The local authority has throughout the planning process stressed that reconstructions are undesirable. One argument has been that reconstructions would not be authentic; the reasons behind are not much dwelled upon, but seem to relate both to notions that buildings which have been moved lose authenticity at a new setting, and that new constructions, looking like existing buildings, would be pastiches. It is also clear that the authority prefers to build anew without references to Kiruna as a historic site, other than to continue a tradition of building what is new and innovative of the time. However, the long-term transformation process would enable conservation both through relocation and reconstruction of historic buildings. A well-planned relocation should have a high likelihood of meeting conservation criteria on reconstruction based on thorough documentation, for example, as stipulated in the Riga Charter on Authenticity and Historical Reconstruction in Relationship to Cultural Heritage (Stovel 2001). Investigations of how buildings would be moved, or dismantled and rebuilt, have not been presented, except for the Town Hall; so that actual conservation measures or consequences for authenticity have not been discussed for the historic buildings affected by the town relocation. The decision to build a new town hall was made early in the process by the Kiruna Council and LKAB, and there seems to have been a strong desire to have a new building, in many ways with a design contrasting with the existing Town Hall.

Only a small number of historic buildings will be relocated, although moving techniques have not yet been clarified. The approximately twenty buildings selected for relocation are representative of the town's architecture and are visually significant in the townscape, but one unresolved question is whether these are sufficient to retain the town's heritage values. The County Administrative Board has stated that a significantly larger number of buildings must be relocated in order to maintain Kiruna as a heritage site of national interest.

The urban planning process focuses on a few historic buildings, although overall structures such as the original town plan and the mine itself is part of the designated heritage site. The winning proposal of the urban design competition does not relate to the existing town plan and its designated values, and the replanning does not reflect the historic environments once – and relatively recently – designated as significant built heritage. The local authority's plan to scatter the historic buildings that are to be moved in the new town centre may provide some continuity and identity of the historic neighbourhoods, but these are likely to be designed, as are any new developments. LKAB's reconstruction of a new company area is more likely to be a linkage to the past, because it will contain a cluster of relocated historic buildings and it will re-establish the spatial relationship between the mining company and the civil municipality.

References

Administrative Court in Luleå (2013), *Länsstyrelsens i Norrbottens län beslut den 4 april 2012 [County Administrative Board of Norrbotten's Decision of 4 April 2012]*, 901–12, Luleå: Förvaltningsrätten [Administrative Court].

Administrative Court of Appeal in Sundsvall (2014), *Förvaltningsrätten i Luleås dom den 7 maj 2013 i mål nr 901–12 [Administrative Court in Luleå's Verdict 7 May 2013]*, 1505–13 edn, Sundsvall: Kammarrätten [Administrative Court of Appeal].

Ahnlund, M. and L. Brunnström (1987), 'Från Dawson till Pullman: Nordamerikanska bolagssamhällen – en översikt', *Bebyggelsehistorisk tidskrift*, 13: 7–54.

Bergmark, K. (2009), 'Flytt av gamla Kiruna prissatt', *Norrbottens-Kuriren*, 23 October: A22.

Bergström, I. (2002), *Tyckt om hus*, Karlskrona: Stadsmiljörådet: Boverket.

Book, T. and D. Bergman (2008), *Förgängelsens geografi: provisorier i kulturlandskapet*, Stockholm: Carlsson.

County Administrative Board of Norrbotten (2011a), *Beslut om att häva byggnadsminnesförklaringen av järnvägsstationen i Kiruna, Jukkasjärvi bandel 100:14, Kiruna stad och kommun, dnr 432–2679–11 [Decision to Repeal the Listing of the Railway Station in Kiruna]*, Luleå: Länsstyrelsen i Norrbottens län [County Administrative Board of Norrbotten].

County Administrative Board of Norrbotten (2011b), *Delbeslut om tillstånd till att flytta Hjalmar Lundbohmsgården inom Kiruna stad, i och med stadsomvandlingen, Fjällrosen 1, Kiruna stad och kommun, dnr 432–2679–11 [Decision on Permission to Move Hjalmar Lundbohmsgården within the Town of Kiruna Due to the Urban Transformation]*, Luleå: Länsstyrelsen i Norrbottens län [County Administrative Board of Norrbotten].

County Administrative Board of Norrbotten (2012), *Beslut om jämkning av skyddsbestämmelser och tillstånd till ändring av byggnadsminnet Kiruna stadshus, Tätörten 3, Kiruna stad och kommun, dnr 432–2679–11 [Decision to Adjust Protective Regulations and Permission to Alter the Listed Building the Town Hall in Kiruna]*, Luleå: Länsstyrelsen i Norrbottens län [County Administrative Board of Norrbotten].

Dahlström, H. (2015), 'Ullspiran i ny form', *Norrländska Socialdemokraten*, 24 November: 21.

Forsberg, M. (2015), 'Bostadsområdet Ullspiran blir till ett unikt minneslandskap', *Norrbottens-Kuriren*, 19 November: 26–7.

Fries, U. and S. Slöör (2011), 'Konstakademin: Riv inte – flytta Kiruna stadshus', debate article, *Norrländska Socialdemokraten*, 7 April: 19.

Garner, J. S. (ed) (1992), *Company Town: Architecture and Society in the Early Industrial Age*, New York: Oxford University Press.

Gezelius, L. (2011), *Stadshuset – demontering och återuppbyggnad*, Stockholm: Schlyter/Gezelius Arkitektkontor AB.

Harrison, R. (2013), *Heritage: Critical Approaches*, Abingdon: Routledge.

Junkka, Å. (2011), 'Debatten fortsätter', *Norrländska Socialdemokraten*, 23 April: 24.

Kiruna Council (1984), *Bevarandeplan Kiruna C. Antaget av kommunfullmäktige 1984–09–10, § 210 [Conservation Plan for the Town of Kiruna]*, Kiruna: Kiruna kommun.

Kiruna Council (2004), *Vi ska flytta en stad [We Will Move a Town]*, Press release, Kiruna: Kiruna kommun.

Kiruna Council (2006), *Fördjupad översiktsplan för Kiruna centralort [Detailed Comprehensive Plan for the Town of Kiruna]*, Kiruna: Kiruna kommun.

Kiruna Council (2008), *Kulturmiljöanalys Kiruna etapp 1 [Cultural Heritage Analysis Part 1]*, Kiruna: Kiruna kommun.

Kiruna Council (2009), *Samrådshandling detaljplan för Bolagsområdet, Gruvstadspark, Kiruna kommun [Draft Consultation Detailed Development Plan, the Company Area, Mine Town Park, in the Town of Kiruna]*, Kiruna: Kiruna kommun.

Kiruna Council (2010a), *Antagandehandling detaljplan för Bolagsområdet, Gruvstadspark, Kiruna kommun [Adopted Detailed Development Plan, the Company Area, Mine Town Park, in the Town of Kiruna]*, Kiruna: Kiruna kommun.

Kiruna Council (2010b), *Bedömning av kulturvärden för byggnader inom Gruvstadsparken: Del av miljökonsekvensbeskrivning till detaljplan för del av Bolaget, Gruvstadspark [Assessment of Heritage Values in Buildings within the Mine Town Park: Part of the Environmental Impact Assessment of the Detailed Development Plan for Part of the Company Area, the Town of Kiruna]*, Kiruna: Kiruna kommun.

Kiruna Council (2014), *Sammanfattning Utvecklingsplan [Summary of Development Plan]* [Homepage of Kiruna kommun [Kiruna Council]]. Available online: http://kiruna.se/Stadsomvandling/Nya-Kiruna/Utvecklingsplan-for-nya-Kiruna-/ (accessed 27 August 2014).

Kiruna Council and LKAB (2010), *Begäran om upphävande och förändring av byggnadsminnen [Request to Repeal and Change Listed Buildings]*, Letter to the County Administrative Board of Norrbotten, Kiruna: Kiruna kommun and LKAB.

Kiruna Council and Luossavaara-Kiirunavaara AB (2011), *Avtal angående Gruvstadsparken del 1 m.m. [Agreement Concerning Mine Town Park Part 1]*, Kiruna: Kiruna kommun.

Lagerstam, L. (2011), 'Rivet stadshus blir öppet sår', debate article, *Norrländska Socialdemokraten*, 16 September: 19.

Lander, L. (2011), 'DOCOMOMO vädjar: Riv inte Kiruna stadshus', debate article, *Norrländska Socialdemokraten*, 19 February: 22.

LKAB (2013), *Angående Hjalmar Lundbohmsgården, utgående brev till Kiruna kommun, beteckning 13–52 [Letter to Kiruna Council, Concerning Hjalmar Lundbohmsgården]*, LKAB, Kiruna: Samhällsomvandlingen.

LKAB (2014), *Års- och hållbarhetsredovisning 2013*, LKAB, Luleå.

LKAB, ÅF-Infraplan and Wilhelmson arkitekter (2006), *Nya Kiruna [New Kiruna]*, Kiruna: LKAB.

Naess, K. (2011), 'Storgräl om flytten', *Norrländska Socialdemokraten*, 26 August: 5.

National Heritage Board (2010), *Beslut om ändring av värdebeskrivningen gällande område av riksintresse för kulturmiljövården Kiruna – Kirunavaara [BD 33], Dnr 331–00556–2009 [Decision to Change Heritage Value Description of the Cultural Heritage Site of National Interest Kiruna-Kirunavaara]*, Stockholm: Riksantikvarieämbetet [National Heritage Board].

Pendlebury, J. R. (2009), *Conservation in the Age of Consensus*, London: Routledge.

Rentzhog, S. (2007), *Friluftsmuseerna: en skandinavisk idé erövrar världen*, Stockholm; Östersund: Carlsson; Jamtli förlag.

Schönbeck, B. (1994), *Stad i förvandling: uppbyggnadsepoker och rivningar i svenska städer från industrialismens början till idag*, Stockholm: Solna.

Situation Kiruna (2012), *Situation Kiruna: Ett blad om Kirunas stadsomvandling [Situation Kiruna: A Leaflet about Kiruna's Urban Transformation]*, Kiruna: Situation Kiruna.

Sjöholm, J. (2015), 'Att flytta en mönsterstad', *Fabrik og Bolig*, 1: 24–43.

Sjöholm, J. (2016), 'Heritagization, Re-heritagization and De-heritagization of Built Environments: The Urban Transformation of Kiruna, Sweden', PhD thesis, Luleå University of Technology, Luleå.

Smith, L. (2006), *Uses of Heritage*, New York: Routledge.

Stovel, H. (2001), 'The Riga Charter on Authenticity and Historical Reconstruction in Relationship to Cultural Heritage: Riga, Latvia, October 2000', *Conservation and Management of Archaeological Sites*, 4(4): 241–4.

Tunbridge, J. E. and G. J. Ashworth (1996), *Dissonant Heritage: The Management of the Past as a Resource in Conflict*, Chichester: Wiley.

Waern, R. (2011), 'En byggnad för värdefull för att rivas', *Svenska Dagbladet*, 7 February: 6.

PART 4

Political Dimensions and Image Building

Introduction

In many instances, the timing, nature, extent and form of reconstruction all have political implications. This is true for both natural disaster and that resulting from human activity, whether from warfare, fire or another. A most obvious initial point is that authorities are usually impelled by public opinion to promise swift reconstruction; although circumstances often lead to action being slower than is promised or desirable. The move from immediate post-disaster shelter to permanent reconstruction takes years, if not decades. The slow start of actual rebuilding in post–Second World War Britain, following a short but intense period of replanning, is but one example. The same example also demonstrates political implications in the form of central–local conflict, where municipalities argued for administrative and financial powers for reconstruction to apply to wider areas than central government was willing to allow; and local landowners often argued against the local plan, especially where powers of compulsory purchase were involved. The inevitable differences between ideal and reality in reconstruction are so often explained by such factors.

Image and the form of reconstruction can be equally important. Again, in post-war Britain, a plan, or even the process of replanning – let alone any completed rebuilding – were often tools in processes of reshaping place-identity, or civic boosterism. Even unbombed towns rapidly jumped on the replanning bandwagon. Elsewhere, though, the physical form of rebuilt buildings or areas could readily be edited to create, or reinforce, a desired political identity. This was the case in post-war Poland, where Soviet-led rebuilding erased many surviving traces of Germanic cultural influence; or Dresden, 'rebuilt with the programmatic aim of creating a new city shaped by the "socialist society" on the site of its old "feudalistic" and "bourgeois" predecessor' (Paul 1990: 172). In Nuremberg, though, it was felt desirable to recreate elements of the dominant pre-war city form: specifically the steeply pitched roof forms traditional in the region. According to Heinz Schmeissner, the city's chief planner, this was to preserve 'the concept of Nuremberg'. The reconstruction thus produced a significant number of pitched roofs, in contrast to the flat-roofed Modernism usually thought to dominate architecture in this period (Soane 1994: Figure 9.1). Although some of these dimensions clearly arise in the examples of reconstruction explored in earlier chapters, this section presents three specific explorations of such issues.

Martin Cherry examines post-war Britain, but focuses on a 'disaster' other than the wartime bombing: this is the large-scale and rapid change wrought by programmes of 'slum clearance', and the effect on, and impact of, public consultation. This is an unusual definition of 'disaster', but this is merited by the scale of action needed to address the problem of slum housing at a time of de-industrialization; some of the initiatives (especially the Housing Market Renewal – or 'Pathfinder' – Programme of 2002–11) have indeed been recognized as disastrous rather than merely ineffectual. Cherry explicitly brings to the forefront the political dimension of decision-making, and the interplay between government (at various levels), special interest groups and wider concepts of public participation. Professionalism, and elitist values, are in conflict with views of communities. Opposition is stifled. But changing political agendas over this period, of several decades, have placed more weight on 'localism', community values and priorities, and hence processes of heritage definition and management are challenged.

Julija Trichkovska discusses the rebuilding of Skopje through a single large-scale urban and architectural project, 'Skopje 2014'. She reminds us of the destruction caused by the 1963 earthquake, which devastated over 70 per cent of the city and attracted much international attention, including a UN-supported international competition for a reconstruction masterplan. This was won by Kenzo Tange, although his modernist plan was never fully implemented. Twenty years after the creation of the Republic of Macedonia, supported by the ruling right-wing Macedonian Party and in the context of political conflict with Greece, the fragmented state of

Skopje was addressed. Not only was this project a belated response to the earthquake, but it sought to reposition Skopje (and hence Macedonia) on the international stage, generate international investment and suppress the perceived 'communist-socialist' feel of the city centre. Deliberately nationalist features were created, including a statue of Alexander the Great, and the new Triumphal Arch. Baroque details were used, including through use of plaster and Styrofoam, to create a new visual identity not always supported by the public. In this and other aspects of the project, the political authorities exerted pressure on heritage protection services, and removed the protected status of part of the central area. This example of highly politicized and contested reconstruction creates huge challenges for the future, and Trichkovska argues that its negative impact is akin to another earthquake – the reconstruction itself has brought chaos.

Finally, Olivia Muñoz-Rojas deals with the politics of reconstruction after the Spanish Civil War. These circumstances were complicated by the nature of the victorious Franco regime, its interpretation of Spanish cultural values and its harsh repression of opponents. Eight decades later, it is still a contentious issue, difficult to research and still generating rifts in society. One party's legislation (the so-called Historic Memory Law) was virtually suspended by its opponents as it refers to the removal of features that refer positively to the Franco uprising and dictatorship. This is truly 'dissonant heritage'. The modernizing renewal of housing, agriculture and industry following the conflict was rooted in ideas that the working class would not become politically class conscious; and classical monumental (civic) and traditional (regional) styles dominated well into the 1950s: this was architecture and planning as manifestation of the dominant political order. Symbolism in form, style and even materials was important. However industrial prefabrication and slowly increasing international contacts did introduce new forms akin to international modernism. Following the transition to democracy this difficult heritage remained, and it has been particularly problematic to produce a rational policy towards dealing with the many remaining overt signs of the dictatorial regime. The fate of the Historic Memory Law inevitably questions whether such legal measures are appropriate or effective in such circumstances. A collective amnesia marked the reconstruction period, but reconciliation so many decades later might need a more nuanced approach to physical reconstruction, memory and memorials in the built landscape.

References

Paul, J. (1990), 'Reconstruction of the City Centre of Dresden: Planning and Building During the 1950s', in J. M. Diefendorf (ed), *The Rebuilding of Europe's Bombed Cities*, London: Macmillan.

Soane, J. V. (1994), 'The Renaissance of Cultural Vernacularism in Germany', in G. J. Ashworth and P. J. Larkham (eds), *Building a New Heritage*, London: Routledge.

Chapter 4.1

Historic Buildings Preservation and Public Opinion in England

Martin Cherry

This chapter examines the impact of public opinion on UK policy towards historic buildings and places during periods of major – and to many, catastrophic – change during peacetime, particularly systematic 'slum clearance' (in the 1960s and 1970s) and programmes to remedy the impact of de-industrialization on communities in the first decade of the twenty-first century. Wartime conditions and extensive bombing did not create a groundswell of opinion in favour of urban conservation. It was not until the mid- to late 1960s that local and central governments felt compelled to face up to the impact of comprehensive slum clearance, barely controlled commercial development and radical road schemes on both communities and historic fabric. Governments, wary of public opinion, chose to deal with special interest groups, mostly professional and sometimes elitist, that themselves remained generally aloof from day-to-day politics. The need actively to win wider public support for planning and conservation took time to gain traction. The concept of citizen and community participation, fashionable in academic circles in the late 1950s and 1960s, took decades to translate into a government commitment to full-blown participatory politics, if indeed it ever did. The tacit partnership between government and specialist pressure groups led to a widening interpretation of what constituted 'special interest', extending into new areas such as industrial archaeology (in the late 1970s and 1980s), twentieth-century and post-war architecture (from the 1980s and 1990s respectively). Conservation lobbies and government, while often finding themselves in tension over individual cases, in reality cohabited in a state of what might be termed 'conservation corporatism'. The combination of articulate and influential special interest groups, which constantly pushed at the frontiers of the politically acceptable, with an elaborate arsenal of heritage controls, made the regulatory system appear increasingly unassailable. But with increasing public participation have come challenges to establishment and specialist views about what is significant: as more weight is placed on community values and priorities, not least in the area of heritage grants, the state finds itself less and less in control of how heritage is defined.

Wartime and post-war attitudes to the historic environment

The statutory protection of historic buildings in its present form emerged in the United Kingdom from the ruins of cities blitzed in the Second World War. Various laws prior to the war made some provision for protecting important buildings, but the system – if it can be called that – was patchy and largely ineffective (Delafons 1997). It was enemy action (both real and anticipated) that resulted in the drawing up of lists of buildings of architectural and historical importance to provide a guide for the emergency services responsible for the demolition or stabilization of bomb-damaged buildings, as well as for planners contemplating the brave new post-war world. Protection of the 'national heritage' formed only a small subsection of the massive and far-reaching package of reforms in the late 1940s that saw the establishment of national parks and new towns, as well as a consolidated town and country planning regime. Safeguarding historic buildings was considered by many politicians to be an uncontroversial and non-partisan sideline: listing was not discussed at all by the House of Commons in the parliamentary debate on the pivotal 1947 Town and Country Planning bill, and only briefly in the House of Lords. Despite some lone voices, most politicians' experience of the prevailing legislation did not suggest that 'heritage protection' would ever grow to such a scale that it might impact on the public purse or on private property rights, considerations that would normally excite fierce passions.

In reality, the wartime and post-war years, right down to the mid-1960s, were characterized by a marked lack of any sense of urgency about historic buildings and towns on the part of government, either local or central. People wanted and expected change but were uncertain what change might look like. A view recorded by Mass Observation (M-O) in 1942 – 'I think I'd like a lot of changes.' 'What particularly?' 'I don't know' – summed up the bewilderment of many (quoted in Kynaston 2007: 41). There were bigger challenges to meet in the fields of housing, health, welfare and the economy and little public demand for reform in the heritage field. There was no overnight transformation of British towns and cities in the immediate post-war years. M-O found that 83 per cent of people interviewed were pessimistic about reconstruction plans. Tom Harrisson, the founder of M-O, thought that debates about planning went over the heads of 90 per cent of the population (Kynaston 2007: 42). Ironically, some of the urban environmental ills that planners struggled to ameliorate, such as traffic congestion, were considered by many to have their positive side and anecdotal evidence suggests that people preferred narrow streets with pavements and two-way traffic as being more convivial, easier to negotiate and safer than the segregation of people from cars that many of the new plans envisaged. It was to be another twenty years before sidewalks received a convincing apostle in Jane Jacobs (1961: chapters 1–3). Congestion might seem a tolerable price to pay since high-density development could facilitate the human tendency to socialize (Erten 2014: 47). A number of influential commentators believed that the encroachment of subtopia and ribbon development on the countryside and the erasure of the distinction between town and country to be the greater evils: 'at the end of the [twentieth] century Great Britain will consist of isolated oases of preserved monuments in a desert of wire, concrete roads, cosy plots and bungalows' (Nairn 1955: 5). Urban conservation and reconstruction were, in some ways, unfortunately placed in the debates of the time, when notions of national identity ('Englishness') were bound up more with the intrinsic value of the countryside, where urban dwellers felt alien (Sharp 1932: 5). The men behind the national parks legislation considered that only the educated and sensitive town dweller would be able to appreciate the raw beauty of these special places; seaside holidays would do for the masses, although some saw the value of Butlin's holiday camps as a sort of stepping stone towards a more rarefied sensibility, a form of 'interim canalisation' (C. E. M. Joad, quoted in Matless 2016: 342).

There were exceptions to the general state of official inertia regarding listed buildings and historic areas. A growing body of sensitive studies was produced in the 1940s, those of Thomas Sharp pre-eminent among them, which sought a contextually responsive approach to the reconstruction of historic towns. Broadly based around the concept of townscape, these studies sought to transform meaningless urban muddle into meaningful compositions, living environments for human beings (for example, Sharp 1946, Gibberd 1953, Cullen 1961). Peter Larkham has demonstrated that there is plenty of evidence in the post-war plans to indicate sensitivity to historic buildings, areas and character. Although, perhaps, not strong enough to indicate a generally held principle, it was sufficiently present to counter the view that the plans were, as a genre, overtly modernist (Larkham 2003: 306–12).

But, as the economy recovered in the early 1960s, official thinking around conservation was ill prepared to meet the challenges of large-scale redevelopment, often commercially led and speculative, that prevailed in most British cities. Progress on compiling the lists of buildings of special historic and architectural interest was slow and no systematic attempt was made to measure the rate of loss to the historic building stock. To get an idea of where things stood, the minister responsible for listing, Lord Kennet, asked his civil servants how many listed buildings disappeared each year.

> I was prepared for the shock of a high figure; a hundred a year? Even two hundred a year? I was not prepared, though, for the answer I got: 'We don't know; and this is because nobody tells us; and this is because we have never asked anybody to tell us'. I marveled at the willingness of Parliament to set up, and the Civil Service to operate, a system designed to have a certain effect without ever checking whether it was having that effect, or another, or none. (Kennet 1972: 53)

There were about 100,000 listed buildings in 1966. Kennet estimated that the rate of loss was in the region of 400 each year and that, if nothing were done, 'they would all be gone in two hundred and fifty years'. Nikolaus Pevsner, to be helpful, made some proposals that would speed up the rate at which the Royal Commission on Historical Monuments (England) published its county inventories, bringing the completion date forward from 500 to 200 years. 'Slowness', Kennet recognized, 'was the proper concomitant of excellence' but it would not meet the planning demands of the time, even though the Commission's remit was to single out structures worthy of protection (Kennet 1972: 85–6). It was hoped that listing, carried out by investigators attached to the relevant ministry, would make more rapid headway. Little more was required at first than to identify the buildings with the minimum amount of supporting material – little more indeed than an address. But the listing operation was not fully resourced: there were fourteen investigators in 1946; twenty-four in 1951; the complement was reduced by the new Conservative administration to twelve and then to nine; it was only in 1966–7 that the number of investigators rose again, to nineteen (Kennet 1972: 50, 103; Delafons 1997: 66). Even so, seven times more was spent by the government in 1966 on military bands than on historic buildings grants (Kennet 1972: 65). Michael Heseltine finally remedied the situation in the 1980s when the 'accelerated listing resurvey' doubled the numbers of listed buildings to over one-third of a million (Robertson 1993).

Official responses to public opinion

One of the reasons why officialdom was so patronizing towards public opinion is that it was considered to be uninformed. Howard Robertson, a former Director of the Architectural Association, believed that:

> The public in England is not stupid [but] it knows little of architecture ... what it is actually looking for is no doubt an architecture fresh yet

familiar, clean but not new-looking, purposeful yet homely, simple yet decorative, comfortable but not dull, convenient but not gadgety, an architecture reflecting in fact as far as possible the best characteristics of the British public; the backbone public, which includes the public that is in all the seats of the theatre except the most expensive ones, the public that buys the Penguin books. (Roberston 1944: 85–6)

Lord Kennet was of like mind and felt hopeful: 'the second quarter of the twentieth century was our low-water mark in visual consciousness', but with increasing post-war prosperity, the increasing number of stately homes open to the public, the growth of amenity societies, John Betjeman, Pevsner's 'Buildings of England' series and, above all, the impact of TV had 're-awakened our visual nostalgia' (Kennet 1972: 51–2). Thomas Sharp recognized that the public needed to be consulted on plans, but emphatically that they should not participate in their preparation. Public opinion, even that part of it made up of Penguin Books or 'Buildings of England' readers, was malleable: it could be formed but it should not form policy.

The anaemic state of democracy (as Kennet considered it to be) led to a heavy reliance being placed on expert opinion. The key writers on urban redevelopment, such as Abercrombie, Johnson-Marshall, Summerson and Sharp, allowed that the claims of conservation should not be discounted, but nor should they stand in the way: despite their different emphases, the plans they developed evinced 'a shared set of values and attitudes prevailing among their readers' – that is, specialists (Larkham 2003: 305). Special interest groups – some of them soon to be called 'statutory amenity societies' when they assumed a more central role in decision-making on heritage matters and, indeed, became the recipients of state funding for their casework – built on the sense of outrage that resulted from acts of vandalism such as the demolition (in 1962) of the Victorian Coal Exchange and the Euston Arch, both in London, and of much of Eldon Square, Newcastle (in 1966) to urge stronger safeguards for outstanding historical buildings and ensembles. The legislation of the late 1960s (notably the Civic Amenities Act, 1967 and the Town and Country Planning Act, 1968) emerged out of this shift in professional opinion. It also owed much to the lucky presence of politicians Richard Crossman and Wayland Kennet in positions of power as ministers (and Duncan Sandys as an active MP in constructive opposition): three champions in the right place at the right time. The Acts favoured a more holistic and sustainable approach to historic towns and recognized the contribution that setting and groups of modest buildings made to the overall character of places. They brought the protection of listed buildings into the modern world – for the first time there was a presumption in favour of preservation – and it gave certain amenity societies a statutory role in the process. Essential changes were made to rectify the balance of power between public authorities and private developers: the punishments for illegal demolition were increased so that they became a deterrent, red tape which made it well-nigh impossible for local authorities to contest a proposal to demolish was removed, and the playing field between local authorities and developers was levelled – or at least partly so. The 1969 Housing Act provided local authorities with the statutory tools to carry out conservation on a more holistic basis by providing state funding to support 'general development areas', in other words to build conservation and refurbishment into comprehensive housing improvement schemes.

Some prominent planners, such as London's chief strategic planner, David Eversley, fumed: 'Ruskin, 100 years ago, attempted to impress his code of aesthetics and morals on the working classes of his time through lectures and pamphlets. Now his successors [such as the Victorian Society or the Georgian Group] use the force of law to *impose* their minority viewpoint on the community' (the emphasis is Eversley's, 1973: 186). Even so, there was a sea change in professional attitudes towards historic places, not just outstanding individual buildings. Thoughtful ministers, such as Kennet, were anxious to find ways to allow local authorities to combat the monolithic bulldozer approach and 'to pick their way green-fingered through a part of their town, redeveloping here, improving there, all on a really sensitive, fine mesh' (Kennet 1972: 90). Roy Worskett, an influential practitioner and thinker, was a strong advocate of the dynamic relationship between historic fabric, use and reuse, planning and design. He recognized what he took to be a growing sense of post-war nostalgia among those who had experienced the war and now lived under the shadow of a final nuclear catastrophe. But it is possible that what Worskett was really observing was more a reaction to the widespread destruction of historic buildings and places on the part of a 'second generation', the sons and daughters of those whom M-O had found to be so bewildered when interviewed in 1942 (Worskett 1969: 9). The influence of planners' and architects' views was beginning to be contested by community protest groups, who were more direct in their methods and prepared to get involved in local politics. These tended to be led by activists who were born in the 1930s or soon after the Second World War. Pendlebury perceptively identifies the balance of forces that was taking shape in the late 1960s and early 1970s. Of the four famous urban 'conservation' studies (for York, Chester, Chichester and Bath) commissioned in 1966 by Lord Kennet, it is Esher's low-intervention approach that 'is still considered a major benchmark in conservation planning in York whereas in Bath it is the reaction to [Buchanan's] modernist planning, *The Sack of Bath*, that is the touchstone' (Pendlebury 2006: 164).

The Sack of Bath, published in 1973, was a reaction to the 'cultural blindness' that brought about the destruction of large areas of Georgian artisan housing in the city, a book that expressed 'the simmering, bursting indignation of those who cared about it' (Fergusson 1973: 1). The Bath protests were among the first in a notable trend towards direct action. It inspired the project to save Spitalfields, an outstanding area of eighteenth-century housing, market and workshops that had escaped most of the bombing directed on the nearby docks and City of London, but now itself threatened with redevelopment. This required tenacity, squats, sit-ins and the establishment of an historic buildings trust, all of which, despite losses along the way, led to the retention of much that was of architectural value. The Spitalfields Trust's growing success finally won the support of the local authority, which provided improvement grants, and this in turn encouraged investors in search of quality character properties. The threat to the social fabric of the community by the commercialization and gentrification of the area, movingly described by historian Raphael Samuel, a resident, was a risk that faced all of these protest projects over the coming years. Conservation and the rise in property values eased out poorer residents and changed the whole social character of a district. In conservation circles, Samuel's was a dissenting voice: 'The effect, though not the intention, of the Trust's intervention has been ... to destabilize the local population and invite the attention of private speculators' (1989: 168). The problem was recognized by the national amenity societies. In a major report by all the societies on Spitalfields's big neighbour, the City of London, the danger was anticipated that the conservation of historic buildings and the fabric of neighbourhoods might displace communities but, short of identifying corners of the city where low-cost housing might be built, it was sensitive but fatalistic about the chances of retaining working people (SPAB et al. 1976).

That this period (c. 1966–73) is critical in the history of the protection of historic buildings and areas is widely recognized. The legislation was strengthened and made increasingly coherent and the key national amenity groups became locked into the conservation establishment and underpinned by statute. But concentration on the physical fabric of historic buildings and areas, their 'special architectural or historic interest', diverted the focus of attention away from the communities that occupied them and did so at precisely the same time as the government was becoming agitated about the role of the public in planning matters and about how best to respond to growing demands for greater participation in planning decisions.

The following section looks at the tensions this created – a recognition for the need to involve the public combined with a resistance actually to do so – with special reference to historic housing, which was generally unprotected and in poor condition, and an area the main conservation bodies entered only very late in the day. Where there is a threat to housing, it is normally large scale and disruptive to many families and whole communities.

Participatory politics, community values and the historic housing stock

The Skeffington report and organized groups

The lack of public involvement in planning matters came increasingly to be seen as problematic. Edward Carter, sometime Director of the Architectural Association, was of the view that a proposal for a new building, however bad, was almost certain to go ahead 'if it conforms to the general rules established by the local authority for site coverage, height, set-back, provision of car parking, and so on ... and the general public has little chance of expressing an opinion until everything is agreed'. His point was that while the public was technically permitted to inspect plans, few individuals did, and of those most were members of the amenity societies. Leaks excited public protests and caused delays (Carter 1962: 175–6). Robert Moyle MP voiced misgivings in parliament that, even though the general public had developed 'very powerful views' about development plans, 'we often find that public inquiries held to settle the issues pass completely unnoticed, especially in larger towns and cities' (Moyle 1968). In 1968, the government commissioned Arthur Skeffington MP, a politician and economist, to consider the best methods 'of securing the participation of the public at the formative stages in the making of development plans for their area'. One of the drivers behind this was the desire to shift a greater part of the load for expediting plans onto local authorities and speed up public planning enquiries. The assumption was that greater transparency would take the antagonisms out of planning and make things happen faster. It was urgent to do something, since planning proposals 'were affecting a more random selection of sectors than had been the case previously, when the main effect had been felt in inner city slum districts. Consequently, larger numbers of articulate social groups were being affected and they protested vigorously' (Damer and Hague 1971: 222). While Skeffington delivered more than the government had bargained for – his recommendations to encourage public meetings and appoint community development officers were considered overly enthusiastic and were not adopted – the major thrust of his report was to develop a dialogue with the articulate middle class groups that were mobilizing in the face of highway and improvement schemes. He recognized that the public was made up of 'passives' and 'actives' and, understanding that 'actives' made more waves, he favoured targeting organizations since these 'contain the active minority, the yeast of the community'. The report did not, therefore, have the impact many had hoped for. As Peter Shapely suggests in his introduction to the newest edition of the report, the notion of public participation, a concept 'still in its infancy', remained 'largely undetermined and vague' and at best it was seen as a more efficient system of convincing people of the virtues of planning. 'Technocrats and local authorities simply subverted the ambiguities of the Report for their own purposes' (Shapely 2014: 29; see also Parry et al. 1992: 29). To local authorities and technocrats, one might add amenity societies. Although the 1968 Town and Country Planning Act required public participation, it did not prescribe how this might be achieved and, throughout the 1970s and 1980s, many local planning authorities interpreted it as being discretionary and 'adopted minimal interpretations of the legislation' (Hampton 1990: 21). The 1971 Town and Country Planning Act skilfully mixed the mandatory and the discretionary: planning authorities were required to take steps 'as will *in their opinion*' ensure that people 'who *may* be expected to want an opportunity to make representations' were made aware of their rights and were given adequate opportunities to make representations' (my emphasis) (Fagence 1977: 268).

Historic housing and 'Voiceless' communities

Shortly after Lord Kennet was appointed parliamentary secretary at the Ministry of Housing and Local Government in 1966, he visited France and Italy to see how things were done there. He was impressed with the reforms of André Malraux, but considered his approach to regeneration in conservation areas too *dirigiste*, involving powers of expropriation and the displacement of local communities with little say in the matter, and with no intention of 'repatriating' them. One of the priorities, he noted, was to encourage middle- to high-income groups to move in, along with the traditional accompaniments of cultural facilities and upper-crust patisseries, a process that was supported by the conservation societies, which were growing in number and influence (Kennet 1972: 54–62; for Malraux see Poirrier 2003). Kennet considered that such methods would be politically unacceptable in Britain. Yet, as Raphael Samuel observed, the same forces were in fact at work in Spitalfields and the situation there was replicated wherever distinctive, old districts were renovated (Anson 1981). Similarly, with comprehensive housing clearance schemes, many of them targeting architecturally and historically significant places, all of them threatening somebody's home, communities were similarly displaced but there were no specialist societies to champion them. Part of the problem was community fragmentation. Community attitudes surveys, carried out as part of the Redcliffe-Maud report (1969) showed that only 6 per cent of those polled were interested in the wider issues of local government; most people were concerned with only the very small areas in which they lived, a street or a group of streets, seldom as large as an electoral ward. Opposition to the construction of London's orbital box motorway in the 1960s, which threatened the demolition of over 10,000 houses, took off only when organized at a strategic level: the 'Homes Before Roads' organization could attract 100,000 votes at Greater London Council elections (Hart 1976: 159–60).

There is much moving and persuasive evidence to suggest that at times of extreme stress, it is family, friends and home that constitute the most meaningful bonds. Social scientists in the 1950s and 1960s focused on family, friends and home in the context of class and community. More recently, what has come to be known as 'place theory', influenced by social anthropology and the experience of aboriginal societies and minority groups, has shifted attention to the attachment people feel to specific, physical sites. The pull of such sites may prove very strong, even if there is nothing left there (Read 1996: 22–3). The social tensions caused by wholesale housing renewal and slum clearance in Britain after the Second World War resulted in part from official failure to take attachment to place seriously – or even to think about it at all. What was known was anecdotal and fuzzy, not hard enough to form a basis for policy. The oral history of planning still remains a 'little explored field' (Adams and Larkham 2013: 147). Between 1955 and 1985, around 1.5 million inadequate houses were cleared, including 25 per cent of the pre-1914 housing stock and involved about 3.7 million people – that is around 15 per cent of the population. Yet the justification for this national policy, its impact on community cohesion and the quality of life was based on a narrow evidence base and many sources used were methodologically weak (Tunstall and Lowe 2013). Even the most influential studies, such as Young and Willmott's survey of the rich community networks in Bethnal Green that were threatened by displacement in the 1950s, a study which pioneered a sociological discipline that was new to Britain, were, as the authors acknowledged, substantially impressionistic, largely eschewing detailed statistical analysis (Young and Willmott 1962).

The evidential base for assessing the *physical* state of working class housing earmarked for clearance was even weaker than that for measuring the social impact of demolition. Norman Dennis's important work in the 1960s on Sunderland (in the industrial north-east of England) went some way to measure attitudes to clearance – in some areas 62 per cent were opposed (especially where existing housing was fit for purpose: Johnson 2015: 52–7) – but found the assessments of the physical state of the housing to be parlous: 'No written criteria [for assessing the houses] had been prepared, and the classification of each particular dwelling was the result of a visual external inspection, frequently from a moving vehicle, by personnel with little formal training in the relevant housing legislation and with only a layman's knowledge of building materials and structures' (Dennis 1970: 323) To make matters worse, there was no redress since 'the unsatisfactory factual basis of the original (and repeated) blighting announcements' could not be taken into account during any subsequent public enquiry (Dennis 1972: 158–9).

Sunderland still possesses distinctive areas of Victorian housing that have attracted scholarly attention as innovative solutions to the 'perennial problem of housing the working classes' (Johnson 2010) (Figure 1). Only two short rows of the distinctive 'Sunderland cottage' are listed although the number of conservation areas UK-wide featuring Victorian and early

FIGURE 1, A and B *Many late nineteenth-century working class houses in the city of Sunderland (Tyne & Wear, N. E. England) were owner-occupied and financed by small community banks, resulting in the distinctive 'Sunderland cottage' (1A). The threat of 'slum clearance' resulted in two short terraces being listed in 1978 but the lack of conservation areas means that the wider townscape remains unprotected. Planning policy has favoured rehabilitation rather than demolition, and such houses have become popular with first-time buyers. This has resulted in accretive changes that provide more living space but also obscure the original form (1B). Source:* © *Michael Johnson (see Johnson 2015).*

twentieth-century worker's housing increased substantially during the 1990s (Larkham 1996: 205) and has continued to do so. Conservation lobbies were quite slow to enter the field of housing of this sort, not least because it was a political minefield. Without champions, residents of nineteenth-century housing threatened with demolition sometimes sought to use listing to protect their communities – usually without success if the buildings themselves did not fulfil the selection criteria, which do not allow community considerations to be taken into account (author's conversations with Barrow-in-Furness residents, 1993). Each home may be unique to those who live there, but to be protected under listing or historic buildings rules, it must not just be special to somebody but be representative or outstanding: 'mere uniqueness is insufficient' (Read 1996: 142). The protection of Victorian and Edwardian mass housing has always been a challenge in terms of statutory protection, even though its importance was recognized by John Summerson in 1960: too big an issue to tackle then, he warned that at some point the nettle would need to be grasped. Area controls would always be the preferred option since it was difficult to apply listing to repetitive units that might be replicated in their thousands across the country, however subtle the regional variation of plan and decoration might be (Muthesius 1984). The question of what to do with areas containing defective and substandard housing was always going to be a high-voltage one, politically: areas were large; local feelings went deep on the part of both communities and planning authorities; and solutions ranged from clearance to refurbishment – these were common denominators when dealing with the post-war legacy and were to be so again in the early 2000s, when policymakers turned their attention to the crisis of the depressed housing market in the old industrial regions of northern England, the so-called Pathfinder Programme, to which, in conclusion, we now turn.

What catastrophe hit this place? Attending to everyone's past

As knowledge and appreciation of the historic environment grew during the 1970s and 1980s – and with it public toleration of listing and the constraints it imposed – so the criteria for protecting historic buildings broadened to encompass an ever-wider range of structures. From the 1990s, English Heritage (the government-funded national body responsible for the historic environment) ventured into areas quite remote from most people's comfort zones – coal mines, textile mills, aircraft hangars and post-war architecture. To retain public confidence, this necessitated an opening up of the listing system that, hitherto, had been secretive and resistant to debate: the listing selection criteria were refined and published and the public widely consulted on general policy and individual cases (Cherry 2007). The step to engaging with the sort of housing threatened by demolition or radical refurbishment was a natural, if potentially contentious, one to take. To some it would confirm the drift of conservationists towards conserving everything; to others it would fulfil a sort of social contract: 'Private citizens are of course entitled to save their own past, but when preservation becomes a public act, supported with public funds, it must attend to everyone's past' (Herbert Gans, quoted in Hayden 1997: 3). Failure to do so leads to exclusion (Hall 1999). Increasingly, as they move into areas where cultural value is defined by others – residents, non-specialists, children and community leaders – specialist conservation bodies find that the 'authorized heritage discourse' carries less weight: in heritage situations, while still bringing much to the party, they are no longer even first among equals (Smith 2006: 29–35 and *passim*).

The notion of 'everyone's past' is encapsulated in housing, in everyone's home. It was housing, and especially social (public-funded) housing, that caused the greatest controversy in the post-war listing programme (carried out by English Heritage) – especially when it involved large-scale developments such as Churchill Gardens in Pimlico (London) or megastructures such as Park Hill (Sheffield). The study of nineteenth- and twentieth-century housing for the working class had been a respectable subject of academic research since the 1970s (Hinchcliffe 2016). The listing of concrete high-rise touched a raw nerve among some, although English Heritage's selection of post-war housing for listing was even handed and included much that was low density and traditional in style (Saint 1992). Even that caused outrage among some who saw the inclusion of the comfortable and quirky as being part of a conservative hidden agenda (Whiteley 1995). A MORI poll found (much even to English Heritage's surprise) that a large majority of people favoured the protection of the best buildings of the post-war period (a majority that rose to 85 per cent of young adults) and where residents were hostile to the listing of their homes, it was generally a reflection of poor management and declining levels of maintenance, rather than the intrinsic architectural quality of the buildings themselves (Cherry 1996, While 2007).

The fact that people respond more positively to places that are well maintained and cared for – well-managed housing, for instance – long ago provided heritage bodies with an incentive to tackle the causes of social and economic decline, as well as physical deterioration, and to focus more on regeneration. There was considerable debate about the various options for the management of post-war housing as part of the public consultation that preceded its being listed. More problematic for a national conservation body was transferring this approach – combining the assessment of architectural and historic interest with planning for a sustainable future – to mass housing that, while significant, came nowhere near satisfying the national listing selection criteria: this was to happen with the Pathfinder Programme. This initiative (2002–11, properly called the Housing Market Renewal Programme) was a response to the crisis of de-industrialization. Set up to rebuild housing markets and communities in the deprived old industrial heartlands of England that had suffered from depopulation, environmental decay and run-down social services, the programme polarized opinion. It was abruptly cancelled in 2011: during its nine years it 'secured the refurbishment of 108,000 dwellings, 15,000 new properties and the clearance of 31,000 dwellings' (Leather et al. 2012: 1). If it had run its course, 'it would have brought about the most extensive change to the [urban] historic environment since the slum clearance programmes of the 1960s' (Menuge 2005–6: 34–5). This was not a natural territory for heritage bodies to enter, but English Heritage did so and developed a rapid assessment methodology, a sort of tool kit to help residents articulate what they considered to be the special historic and visual character of the places where they lived, precisely the element missing in the 1960s for neighbourhoods such as those in Sunderland discussed above (Samuels and Clark 2008).

The rapid 'character and identity' assessments of Pathfinder renewal areas – aids to support, even to empower, local communities – inevitably got caught up in the heated debate about the renewal initiative, especially around the time it was terminated. 'The performance of individual Pathfinders was closely aligned to the performance of the local economy' and there was always the expectation that 'the worst neighbourhoods [would suffer] increased dereliction and an outflow of private investment': in other words some areas lay beyond the reach of public/private renewal partnerships (Leather et al. 2012: 3). At its worst, the programme was condemned as social cleansing resulting in destruction, dereliction and waste that would force the question: 'what catastrophe hit this place?' (Hatherley 2013). Where nineteenth-century housing stood derelict, its demolition opposed by conservation bodies, gentrification might be seen as the only solution, 'des-res' neighbourhoods just waiting to happen. The involvement of conservation bodies in programmes where communities are viewed as markets carries with it enormous dangers – and has done since the Sack of Bath – in that such programmes can 'embed powerful networks of institutional and economic players, privilege partial expertise and stifle opposition' (Webb 2010).

The involvement of the lead national conservation body in a programme designed to ameliorate the effects of what was essentially an economic and social crisis did not take place in a cultural vacuum. The emphasis on developing tools to help non-specialists define what it was that made their own homes and neighbourhoods special to them mirrored policy shifts within other organizations. The Heritage Lottery Fund (HLF) that dispenses £300m each year to heritage-based projects 'remains steadfast in the refusal to give a potentially limiting definition to the word "heritage" ... moving away from what appeared to its critics in the 1980s to be a patrician, backward-looking and object-based set of values towards something much more dynamic and democratic, with a firm commitment to addressing social and economic deprivation' (Hewison and Holden 2014: 21). The HLF asks applicants for grant aid to identify *all* the different ways in which people value the place, building or object for which funding is being sought. At the time of writing, the most recent HLF initiative (the 'Great Place Scheme') focuses entirely on 'local context and flavour'; the scheme's purpose is to respond to 'individual needs and desires' while at the same time contributing to the local economy – successful projects 'must provide a "return" ' (HLF 2016). The specialist conservation voice becomes one of several, all bidding for equal attention, all seemingly equally valid and authoritative. The Culture Minister (2001–07) recognized the role of the specialist as one of many equals: 'Instead of experts making all the decisions, [they] would share their knowledge with the public, and facilitate people making more of their own informed judgments' (Jowell 2004). The state of 'corporate conservation' that has prevailed for most of the post-war period was born at a time when the assessment of national heritage was considered to be safe in the hands of connoisseurs. Now the assessment of cultural value is a partnership between specialists, public institutions and local communities and depends on trust and mutual respect for its success, especially in situations where change is driven by a sense of crisis, as is often the case with housing renewal, with developments under the glare of publicity. Perhaps the most immediate challenge to the sustainable management of the historic environment, however defined, is the pernicious anti-intellectualism and the derision meted out to experts and the notion of expertise that characterized the Brexit campaign in the 2016 referendum on the UK's EU membership: this genie, now out of the bottle, threatens the delicate web of mutual trust that is a prerequisite for attending to everyone's past.

References

Adams, D. and P. J. Larkham (2013), 'Bold Planning, Mixed Experiences: The Diverse Fortunes of Post-war Birmingham', in M. Clapson and P. J. Larkham (eds), *The Blitz and Its Legacy: Wartime Destruction to Post-war Reconstruction*, Farnham: Ashgate.

Anson, B. (1981), *I'll Fight You for It: Behind the Struggle for Covent Garden*, London: Cape.

Carter, E. (1962), *The Future of London*, Harmondsworth: Penguin.

Cherry, M. (1996), 'Listing Twentieth-Century Buildings: The Present Situation', in S. MacDonald (ed), *Modern Matters. Principles and Practice in Conserving Recent Architecture*, London: Routledge for English Heritage.

Cherry, M. (2007), 'Architectural History and Conservation', in M. Forsyth (ed), *Understanding Historic Building Conservation*, Oxford: Blackwell.

Cullen, G. (1961), *Townscape*, London: Architectural Press.

Damer, S. and C. Hague (1971), 'Public Participation in Planning: A Review', *Town Planning Review*, 42 (3): 217–32.

Delafons, J. (1997), *Politics and Preservation: A Policy History of the Built Heritage, 1882–1996*, London: Spon.

Dennis, N. (1970), *People and Planning: The Sociology of Housing in Sunderland*, London: Faber & Faber.

Dennis, N. (1972), *Public Participation and Planners' Blight*, London: Faber & Faber.

Erten, E. (2014), 'Townscape as a Project and Strategy of Cultural Continuity', in J. Pendlebury, E. Erten and P. J. Larkham (eds), *Alternative Visions of Post-war Reconstruction: Creating the Modern Townscape*, London: Routledge.

Eversley, D. (1973), *The Planner in Society: The Changing Role of a Profession*, London: Faber & Faber.

Fagence, M. (1977), *Citizen Participation in Planning*, Oxford: Pergamon.

Fergusson, A. (1973), *The Sack of Bath; A Record and an Indictment*, London: Compton Russell.

Gibberd, F. (1953), *Town Design*, London: Architectural Press.

Hall, S. (1999), 'Un-settling "The Heritage", Re-imagining the Post-nation', *Third Text* 49, 3–13.

Hampton, W. (1990), 'Planning', in N. Deakin and A. Wright (eds), *Consuming Public Services*, London: Routledge.

Hart, D. A. (1976), *Strategic Planning in London: The Rise and Fall of the Primary Road Network*, Oxford: Pergamon.

Hatherley, O. (2013), 'Liverpool's Rotting, Shocking "Housing Renewal": How Did It Come to This?', *The Guardian* 27 March. Available online: https://www.theguardian.com/commentisfree/2013/mar/27/liverpool-rotting-housing-renewal-pathfinder (accessed 30 August 2016).

Hayden, D. (1997), *The Power of Place: Urban Landscape as Public History*, Cambridge, MA: MIT Press.

Hewison, R. and J. Holden (2014), *Challenge and Change: HLF and Cultural Value*, London: DEMOS for the Heritage Lottery Fund.

Hinchcliffe, T. (2016), 'Pandora's Box: Forty Years of Housing History', *The London Journal*, 41 (1): 1–16.

Heritage Lottery Fund (2016), *Great Place Scheme*, guidance for applicants. Available online: http://www.greatplacescheme.org.uk/sites/default/files/pdfs/GreatPlaceScheme_applicationguidance_0.pdf (accessed 1 September 2016).

Jacobs, J. (1965 [originally 1961]), *The Death and Life of Great American Cities: The Failure of Town Planning*, Harmondsworth: Penguin.

Johnson, M. A. (2010), 'The Sunderland Cottage: "The Favourite and Typical Dwelling of the Skilled Mechanic"', *Vernacular Architecture* 41: 59–74.

Johnson, M. A. (2015) *The Sunderland Cottage. A History of Wearside's 'Little Palaces,'* Stroud: Amberley Publishing.

Jowell, T. (2004), Press release. Available online: www.culture.gov.uk/global/press notice/archives-2006 (accessed 20 June 2016).

Kennet, W. (1972), *Preservation*, London: Temple Smith.

Kynaston, D. (2007), *Austerity Britain 1945–1951*, London: Bloomsbury.

Larkham, P. J. (1996), *Conservation and the City*, London: Routledge.

Larkham, P. J. (2003), 'The Place of Urban Conservation in the Reconstruction Plans of 1942–1952', *Planning Perspectives* 18/3: 295–324.

Leather, P., B. Nevin, I. Cole and W. Eadson (Nevin Leather Associates/Centre for Regional, Economic and Social Research, Sheffield Hallam University) (2012),

The Housing Market Renewal Programme in England: Development, Impact and Legacy. Available online: https://www.inta-aivn.org/images/cc/Habitat/ background%20documents/HMR%20legacy%20paper%201%2012.pdf (accessed 1 September 2016).

Matless, D. (2016), *Landscape and Englishness*, 2nd expanded edition, London: Reaktion.

Menuge, A. (2005–6), 'Housing Market Renewal Initiative (Pathfinder)', *English Heritage Research News*, 2: 34–5.

Menuge, A. (2008), *Ordinary Landscapes, Special Places: Anfield, Breckfield and the Growth of Liverpool's Suburbs*, Swindon: English Heritage.

Moyle, R. (1968), Contribution to Parliamentary debate. Available online: http:// hansard.millbanksystems.com/commons/1968/jan/31/town-and-country-planning-bill#S5CV0757P0_19680131_HOC_300 (accessed 1 September 2016).

Muthesius, S. (1984), *The English Terraced House*, New Haven, CT: Yale University Press.

Nairn, I. (1955), *Outrage*, London: Architectural Press.

Parry, G., G. Moyser and N. Day (1992), *Political Participation in Democracy in Britain*, Cambridge: Cambridge University Press.

Pendlebury, J. (2006), 'Planning the Historic City: 1960s Plans for Bath and York', in J. Monclús and M. Guàrdia (eds), *Culture, Urbanism and Planning*, Aldershot: Ashgate.

Poirrier, P. (2003), 'Heritage and Cultural Policy in France under the Fifth Republic', *International Journal of Cultural Policy*, 9 (2): 215–25.

Read, P. (1996), *Returning to Nothing: The Meaning of Lost Places*, Cambridge: Cambridge University Press.

Roberston, H. (1944), *Architecture Arising*, London: Faber & Faber.

Robertson, M. (1993), 'Listed Buildings: The National Resurvey of England', *Transactions of the Ancient Monuments Society*, 37: 21–94.

Saint, A. (1992), *A Change of Heart. English Architecture since the War: A Policy for Protection*, London: English Heritage.

Samuel, R. (1989), 'The Pathos of Conservation', in M. Girouard, D. Cruickshank and R. Samuel (eds), *The Saving of Spitalfields*, London: The Spitalfields Historic Buildings Trust.

Samuels, I. and J. Clark (2008), *Character and Identity. Townscape and Heritage Appraisals in Housing Market Renewal Areas*, London: English Heritage and Commission for the Built Environment.

Shapeley, P. (ed) (2014), *People and Planning: Report of the Committee on Public Participation in Planning (The Skeffington Committee Report)*, Abingdon: Routledge.

Sharp, T. (1932), *Town and Countryside: Some Aspects of Urban and Rural Development*, Oxford: Oxford University Press.

Sharp, T. (1946), *Exeter Phoenix: A Plan for Rebuilding*, London: Architectural Press.

Smith, L. (2006), *Uses of Heritage*, London: Routledge.

Society for the Protection of Ancient Buildings, Georgian Group, Victorian Society, and Ancient Monuments Society (1976), *Save the City: A Conservation Study of the City of London*, London: SPAB.

Tunstall, R. and S. Lowe, for Connected Communities (2013), 'Breaking up
    Communities? The Social Impact of Housing Demolition in the Late Twentieth
    Century'. Available online: http://www.ahrc.ac.uk/documents/project-reports-
    and-reviews/connected-communities/breaking-up-communities-the-social-
    impact-of-housing-demolition-in-the-late-twentieth-century (accessed 1
    September 2016).
Webb, D. (2010), 'Rethinking the Role of Markets in Urban Renewal: The Housing
    Market Renewal Initiative in England', Housing, Theory and Society, 27 (4):
    313–31.
While, A. (2007), 'The State and the Controversial Demands of Cultural Built
    Heritage: Modernism, Dirty Concrete, and Postwar Listing in England',
    Environment and Planning B Planning and Design, 34 (4): 645–63.
Whiteley, N. (1995), 'Modern Architecture, Heritage and Englishness', Architectural
    History, 38: 220–37.
Worskett, R. (1969), The Character of Towns: An Approach to Conservation,
    London: Architectural Press.
Young, M. and P. Willmott (1962), Family and Kinship in East London,
    Harmondsworth: Penguin.

Chapter 4.2

Politicized Reconstruction – the Project 'Skopje 2014'

Julija Trichkovska

*Those who have the possibility to control and design space have
an important instrument to reproduce and enlarge their power.*
(Lechler 2010: 47; see also Harvey 1990)

The tale of Skopje, the city that underwent many transformations in the
Balkans throughout its history and where today many aspire to build an
image of a capital with historic gravitas, has been permeated with many
controversies that also follow the fate of the state – the Republic of
Macedonia – itself.

This retrospective account of certain events that mark the development
of the city is a contribution to the ongoing discussions on the socio-political
and cultural genesis of the Project 'Skopje 2014', an urban and architectural
initiative that has been implemented in the past several years in the central
city area and which has brought very dramatic and, for many of its residents
controversial, transformations. Our stance regarding these changes is related
to the heritage protection system, since it is relevant to the provision of
conditions for the planning strategy of the living space that breathes with the
ideas and works of many generations of diverse political, ethnic, religious
and other social groups.

Historical overview

Skopje is divided into two halves by the River Vardar: this has profoundly
influenced its urban and architectural development. The modern

orientation of the central urban space was begun after the five centuries of Ottoman rule, during which the settlement was concentrated on the left bank of the river.

As an important geostrategic gate of the Ottoman Empire in its expansion towards the other parts of the Balkans and Central Europe from the end of the fifteenth century, Skopje began developing according to the oriental urban plans of the central Ottoman towns (Anatolia), which brought about the change in the image of this former centre of the Byzantine Empire and the medieval Serbian state.[1] As the most frequented administrative-trading zone of the Ottoman Empire, Skopje (in Turkish, Ushkup), the so-called *charshiya* (bazaar), featured many impressive sacral and other public facilities of Islamic provenance. A fortification was erected in the immediate vicinity of the settlement (today known as the Kale heritage site), using the remains of the Roman city Scupi, as well as the structures from the medieval Christian centre. It is not much of a feat to 'reconstruct' the settlement from that time, since an important part of its urban structure as well as numerous monumental edifices still testify to one of the oldest and largest oriental bazaars in the Balkans (see Богојевиќ 2014 for Ottoman architecture in Skopje).

The city began rapidly to expand on the right bank of the river in the 1930s, on the eve of the Second World War, when Skopje became the administrative and political centre of the so-called 'Vardar Governorship' within the Kingdom of Yugoslavia. Through the implementation of urban development projects and construction of several public edifices from the time of Joseph Mihajlovich, city mayor from 1929 and an architect by vocation, the central area of Skopje had undergone its 'modern age' makeover that was commensurate with its role as one of the regional, economic, political and cultural centres of pre–Second World War Yugoslavia. (More detailed characteristics of the architecture and monumental art in the Ante-Bellum Skopje are given in Петковски and Томовски 2003, Грчев 2003).

The historical sources testify to a large number of published advertisements for the construction of public buildings at that time (Грчев 2003). It was expected that the key role in the establishment of the criteria for the selection of the projects, as well as for the scope of their implementation, was in the hands of the ruling regime following the official policy of the newly formed state (Грчев 2003: 191–8). Most of them, masterpieces of architects of Russian, Czech and Serbian origin educated in Western Europe, represent

---

[1]Skopje, the Roman settlement Scupi, is mentioned as a metropolitan seat of the Dardanian Province as early as 493 (cf. Lilčiќ 1995: 60). It is well known that in the Middle Ages, Skopje was an important ecclesiastical and political centre of the Serbian medieval state, in particular, at the time of the reign of King Dushan, who, in 1346, was crowned as the 'Tzar of the Serbs and the Romans (Greeks)' in Skopje, that rose the Serbian Autocephalous Church to the rank of a patriarchy (Ђирковиќ 1969: 47).

strands of the (post-) academicism of eclectic expression, including elements of Byzantine architecture in certain cases (Грчев 2003).

The older residents of Skopje still remember the monumental edifices situated on the Macedonia Square (at that time known as King Peter Square), such as the Army Hall,[2] the National Bank,[3] the Railway Station[4] (whose remains most poignantly capture and commemorate the tragedy that struck the city in 1963), as well as the Public Theatre,[5] one of the few edifices located on the other side of the Vardar river. The only remaining representative administrative building from that time is the Parliament of the Republic of Macedonia, the former seat of the Vardar Governorship, the so-called Banovina Palace.[6] It is noteworthy that, although its original exterior is fairly well preserved, this building has recently undergone 'reconstruction' with the addition of glass domes. This intervention was justified by the government as being needed to answer the ever-increasing demand for more functioning spaces within the Parliament, while the conceptual design was likened to 'similar' examples in other European metropolises, most frequently the Reichstag, Berlin, restored with a new dome by Foster and Partners. Today we can say that the very idea of intervention on such a historical monument was a segue into the strategy for the great 'reconstruction' of architectural monuments located in the central city area implemented through the Project 'Skopje 2014'.

Recovering from a natural disaster

From today's perspective, it is difficult to imagine what the development of the city of Skopje would have been like had the earthquake of 26 July 1963 not occurred, since this natural disaster completely changed the city's image. This dire event, in which 2,000 residents of Skopje lost their lives, and the homes of 200,000 (the population of Skopje at that time) were totally wrecked or significantly damaged, was the prerequisite for a fundamentally new masterplan in which making provision for the normalization of society in the spirit of the time represented both a necessity and a huge challenge.

---

[2]According to William Baumgarten, a Russian emigrant, this was built in 1929 in Academic style (Грчев 2003: 211, 215–7).

[3]According to the awarded project of the Serbian architect Bogdan Nestorovich. Construction began in 1931 in the classic variant of the European 'monumental Academicism, with pure geometric forms and calm and symmetric façade composition' (Грчев 2003: 217–8).

[4]Built in 1940 according to the project of the architect Velimir Gavrilovich from Belgrade (Грчев 2003: 258–63).

[5]Torn down in the earthquake of 1963. Construction began in 1921 according to the project of architect Josip Bukovac and, because of many interventions in the original project, it was completed in 1929 in a specific variant of European Academism (Грчев 2003: 220–3).

[6]The project of the Czech architect Vjeceslav J. Hudak implemented in 1938, with pure geometric forms on the basic composition of the façades (Грчев 2003: 201–5).

Many countries extended solidarity and aid; renowned domestic and foreign urban planners and architects created a new image for the city that was more than 70 per cent devastated.

An international competition for a reconstruction masterplan, launched in 1965 with the support of the United Nations, was won by the well-known Japanese architect Kenzo Tange.[7] According to the panel jury, it was Tange's 'integrating approach towards the urban reconstruction of the old and the new Skopje' which was one of the decisive factors in its acceptance. The jury's explanation was that 'instead of rebuilding the city, Tange tried to preserve the remaining structures in Skopje and used the City Wall to frame the historic areas. He also treated the city's geographical characteristics in a delicate manner'.[8]

Even though the vision of Kenzo Tange was not fully implemented, what he offered has been recorded as an avant-garde model of modern urban architecture and planning. However, that which was implemented in the key urban areas – the residential complex, the City Wall and the City Gate (the new Railway Station) – gives an impression of a 'wayward' project, ripped away from the original concept and context when seen from today's perspective of the city's development.

It is not an accident that Kenzo Tange's plan for the reconstruction of the central city area was not implemented. A less important issue to be discussed in this review would be to consider the funding needed for such a 'mega' project; something that, needless to say, an economically weak state could not afford. What does lend itself to a more in-depth analysis of the underlying reasons and what, almost fate-like, haunts the development of the city throughout history, is of a social and political nature. For the governing regime of the Socialist Republic of Macedonia, formed in the spirit of the ideological matrix of the Socialist Federal Republic of Yugoslavia, it seemed that an avant-garde project of such proportions was an overly ambitious enterprise. Without attempting to evaluate Kenzo Tange's project itself, it nevertheless should be noted that what he himself felt constituted a 'problem' at one time turned out to be one of the important aspects of the success – or the failure, if you will – of such a model: the lack of an analytical discourse on the collective memory and the mentality of Skopje's citizens.[9]

---

[7]Available online: http://tststsss.tumblr.com/post/8342830969/kenzo-tange-reconstruction-plan-for-skopje (accessed 28 August 2016).
[8]'The competition jury applauded Tange's scheme for its successful incorporation of Kale Hill into the composition of the centre and the integration of the left and right banks of the Vardar [River] by their development with public buildings, shops, bridges, and pedestrian squares and platforms'. Available online: http://tststsss.tumblr.com/post/8342830969/kenzo-tange-reconstruction-plan-for-skopje (accessed 28 August 2016).
[9]Chausidis points out that Tange's 'ideal city' was meant to change the aesthetics of living for the newly arrived residents of Skopje city in the post-earthquake period, who had fled the poverty-stricken villages, and to bring them closer to the 'futuristic objects' of his project. It was an unrealistic expectation at the time (Чаусидис 2013: 33–4).

Facing the challenges of the new age and burdened with the socialist parameters on the attainment of simple spatial concepts and clean-line, functionalist architecture, those who participated in the design of the city's development plans in subsequent decades made compromises which were not always attuned to the state-of-the-art capacities inherent in modern urban planning. So, very often the mere infilling of empty space in order to correspond with existing built-up space sufficed to justify the integrating principle in the planning of the city neighbourhoods.

However, at the same time, it is noteworthy that some of the implemented architectural projects, most of which were the designs of renowned Macedonian architects from the time of (post-) modernism, became the landmark axes of the post-earthquake Skopje. They included, among others, the Skopje City Mall (1973, by the architect Professor Zhivko Popovski); the seat of the Central Committee of the Federation of the Communists of Macedonia, today the government seat (1970, by the architect Petar Mulichkovski); and the University Campus 'SS. Cyril and Methodius' (1974, by the architect Marko Musich). All of these were built on large 'open' spaces, so that they neither represented a replacement of something that had previously existed nor posed a 'threat' to something still existing in their immediate vicinity.

Enforced reconstruction – project 'Skopje 2014'

Skopje's central urban area, particularly around the spacious square, remained vacant at the time of the commencement of the pluralist political system in the Republic of Macedonia, after it gained independence in 1991. In that decade, the urban planning of that part of the city did not offer any models that could be followed. Twenty years later, this shortcoming encouraged the new regime to devise a huge project, the so-called 'Skopje 2014'. Euphoric in its attempt to provide a voice for the expression of the national sensibility of the young politicians from the ruling conservative Macedonian Party, VMRO-DPMNE, at the same time the project was instigated as part of a response to the long and strained atmosphere which loomed over the citizens of the Republic of Macedonia because of the antagonism with its southern neighbour, the Republic of Greece, with its policy of denial of the Macedonian identity and constitutional name.

Project 'Skopje 2014' was officially promoted by the Government of the Republic of Macedonia at a press conference at the beginning of 2010 with a video presentation (3D animation); at the time, it also became omnipresent in the domestic and foreign media. The implementation of every successive stage of the still-ongoing project stirs the emotions of every social stratum and reignites debates among intellectuals from all walks of life. Behind the stated aim of the project, promoted as a 'creation of infrastructure for international investments, for the purpose of which a functional and recognizable place is needed, commensurate with other European metropolises' (Manca 2014), was, in fact, the need of the new ideologues to suppress (in some cases, even, deface) the 'communist-socialist' ambience of the central city area. This they wished to replace with the symbolism of selected elements from national history rendered in sculpture-like forms, as well as with architectural components taken out of the ideological matrix of European culture from the time of the Counter-Reformation, as expressed through baroque art.

The idea of the Project 'Skopje 2014' had been foreshadowed through some decisions of the ruling regime several years prior to its official promotion, when ancient Roman sculptures taken from the collections of national museums were placed in front of the Government building. In fact, the term 'antiquization', that has followed the project since its commencement, originates from this very decision, which, at the same time, represented an unprecedented breach of the general principles of presentation and protection of historical monuments. This resiting of ancient statues signalled the desire of its commissioners to express the 'antique' as opposed to the 'Slavic' ethnic background of the Macedonian people. Later, in the Project 'Skopje 2014', the national narrative of antique history would be implemented still more prominently with the placement in Macedonia Square of a fountain featuring the figure of Alexander the Great mounted on a horse on a high-towering pedestal, surrounded by reliefs and sculptures expressive of his life and exploits (Figure 1). The equivalent on the other side of the Vardar is the statue of his father, Phillip II. The conceptual course of this action was followed by the newly built edifices in the classical manner with some baroque decorative motifs – the Triumphal Arch (the so-called 'Macedonia Gate'), at the entrance to Macedonia Square (Figure 2), and the buildings of the Museum of Archaeology, the Public Prosecution Office, the Ministry of Foreign Affairs and the Museum of VMRO and the Museum of the Victims of Communism, all located on the left bank of the river.

Almost simultaneously with the placement of the antique sculptures in front of the Government building, and just within a short walking distance on the left side of the Vardar, a sculpture of Skender Bey (the Albanian fifteenth-century national hero) was placed at the very entrance to the protected zone of the Old Skopje Bazaar. This was done by the largest Albanian political party, DUI (the holder of the local authority in the municipality 'Chair', which borders the municipality 'Centre' wherein the bulk of Project 'Skopje 2014' has been implemented) and the coalition partner of VMRO-DPMNE – thereby giving voice to the expression of their own national/ethnic identity. It is likely that this act was a response to Project 'Skopje 2014', which had been implemented without the consent of the second-largest ethnic community in the Republic of Macedonia. This case, too, triggered many public debates, first and foremost among the experts on cultural heritage protection. The

FIGURE 1 *Macedonia Square. Source: Julija Trichkovska.*

FIGURE 2 *Macedonia Gate during the coloured revolution. Source: Julija Trichkovska.*

state had demonstrated some respect for the preserved heritage in this part of Skopje by putting the so called 'Historical Site – the Old Skopje Bazaar' under special legal protection (Republic of Macedonia 2008), thereby alleviating the politically sanctioned pressure from the contemporary planners upon the built heritage. However, understanding cultural heritage protection more as a legislative procedure for the control of the façades of the oriental shops and determining measures for permissible dimensions and street view, rather than as an active relationship with the relevant historical structure for the purpose of its sustainable development, took its toll a long time ago.[10] Instead of focusing on the developmental component of this cultural heritage unit, the local authorities have recently plunged into expansive construction activities in the buffer zone towards the River Vardar, for which conceptual solutions for the new Skender Bey Square were made.[11]

The support of the government of the Republic of Macedonia for this project was expressed through the statement that 'it would represent a well suited transition from the modern to the traditional part of the city' (Трпковска 2010: 16). It is an undisputable fact that the space deserves to be distinctly landscaped and, within that context, the solutions offered are a positive step forward. Without attempting critically to review those which have been presented (in particular, bearing in mind that, at the time of writing, we still do not know what was chosen to be implemented, even though we can witness the beginnings of construction works), we cannot help but imagine the political dimension of this decision. We perceive the articulation of the newly formed Skender Bey Square as a counter to the landscaping of Macedonia Square, that is, the Project 'Skopje 2014', thereby somewhat balancing the desires and needs of the two largest ethnic communities in the Republic of Macedonia.

The cases preceding the Project 'Skopje 2014' were seminal in preparing the ground for the 'historical-cultural' justification for the landscaping of the city centre according to the concept of the political élite of the VMRO-DPMNE and crucial also to its implementation, carried out with the intellectual and professional expertise and assessments of the selected planners and architects. To make a comprehensive analysis of the Project itself from the urban, architectural, aesthetic, artistic, cultural and social points of view in order to meet the criteria of an all-encompassing multidisciplinary approach is beyond the scope of this chapter. Moreover, to some extent during all

---

[10]According to the Special Law (Republic of Macedonia 2008, Articles 10 and 11) a Programme for Revitalization of the Old Skopje Bazaar was drafted and updated several times. However, since there is no strategy for its implementation, what can be seen today is reduced to the painting of façades and the opening of several souvenir shops of traditional handcraft items.
[11]The two conceptual solutions were submitted by four architects from the Skopje Studio for Architecture 'Arhigrup'. It encompassed a space ranging from 13,000 m² to more than 28,000 m², in order to redefine the plateau around the sculpture of Skender Bey to the Boulevard Gotse Delchev (Трпковска 2010: 14–17).

these years, such observations have been made by architects, urban planners, art historians and archaeologists.[12] The divided opinions of the experts on the issues surrounding the many layers of the project also reflect the divided opinions of the citizens about what is happening in their immediate environment; on a few occasions, there have been physical altercations and affrays among the people with radically opposed opinions.[13]

This chapter instead addresses the issue of legislative changes on the planning of urban blocks, imposed on the cultural heritage protection services by the political authorities. In order to accommodate new projects, the aim was to justify the conceptual solutions set forth by modifying the established parameters for the protection of the monuments and their integration in the city development plans.[14] The result was the termination in 2012 of the cultural heritage protection status of the 'Central City Area II' which had been in operation since 1998,[15] after which just a few single monuments retained legal protection; they were not included in the suggested reconstruction activities of the Project 'Skopje 2014'.

As a continuation of this orchestrated process, and with the aim of imposing the obligation on the state and local authorities continuously to fund the functioning of the new 'monuments' by the state and local authorities, some were proclaimed in 2013 as *ex lege* protected cultural assets. These included the Macedonia Gate (built in neoclassical style, that functions as a museum-like tourist point and a temporary Registry Office), the Memorial House of Mother Theresa (a building of ambiguous and mixed stylistic elements of unknown origin, located in the pedestrian zone of Macedonia Street), the Museum of VMRO-DMPNE and the Museum of

---

[12]Here I would like to emphasize the works of the archaeologist Professor Nikos Chausidis (Чаусидис 2013); the art historian Valentino Dimitrovski (Димитровски 2010); and the architects Milan Mijalkovich and Katarina Urbanek (Мијалковиќ and Урбанек 2011). These, although using different approaches, cover the key components of the development of the city throughout history, with a critical review of the latest project. No less interesting are the perceptions of the German and Macedonian students of architecture and urban planning presented in their common project (Herold 2010), and Katerina Mojanchevska (Mojanchevska and van Dijk 2013). In particular, the observations of the architect and urban planner Professor Miroslav Grchev are critical (Грчев 2014: 45–9, 97–100, 140–56, 170–6, 281–5).

[13]The first conflict (2010) among the civilians took place after the announcement of the building of a Christian temple on the main city square between 'the defenders of the Christian faith' and the students of architecture and urban planning from the Faculty of Architecture and Construction Engineering at the University SS. Cyril and Methodius who expressed their professional opinion against the idea of such a facility being constructed in that particular area.

[14]Since 1998, the 'Central Urban Area II' has been under legal protection (Decision No. 0804–259/1, 6 June 1998, made by the Institute for the Protection of Monuments of the City of Skopje).

[15]An act enforced by the Cultural Heritage Protection Office (within the Ministry of Culture of the Republic of Macedonia) in 2012, based on the Case Study on the Re-evaluation of the 'Central Urban Area II', drafted by the Conservation Center – Skopje (Decision No. 07–101/1/, 17 February 2012).

the Victims of Communism (built in neoclassical style, located on the left bank of the River Vardar).[16]

Throughout the campaign immediately preceding it and, in particular, during the implementation of the Project 'Skopje 2014', it was pointed out that the funds already, and still being, spent on its implementation are exorbitant. The information pertaining to the problematic public bidding procedures, the frequently increased expenditure on every single project[17] and the exorbitant funds paid to a few selected participants by the authorities (unknown to the audience at large)[18] certainly stoke suspicions about the propriety of the procedures for the allocation and the spending of public funds.

The general image of the new Skopje ('Skopje 2014') may be epitomized in the well-known adage: 'Much was wanted ... many things were started'. The main leitmotif of the planned interventions was borrowed from the conceptual background of European Baroque, which aspires towards opulence, ornamentation, embellishment and glorification. Hence, the commonly used term 'baroquization' by those who have derided the project is not a random appellation, especially when we consider that the conglomerate of stylistic and structural solutions of 'Skopje 2014' does not reflect the generic features of European Baroque art. This is more problematic because such obsolete styles (no matter if they are neoclassical or baroque), never intrinsic to this region, look grotesque when infiltrated into the historical discourse and the contemporary context of urban living.

Among the most characteristic enterprises is a 'baroque' façade makeover, 'covering' the recognizable edifices from the period of Socialist Realism by using new material (plaster/Styrofoam) to create, albeit superficially and temporarily, the new, desired visual effect. This mimicry is especially conspicuous in the recent façade makeover of the building of the Government.[19] In addition, the buildings of EVN Macedonia (Power

---

[16]Two decisions made by the Cultural Heritage Protection Office (No. 18–451, 5 June 2013, and No. 18–452, 8 June 2013). By virtue of Law on the Cultural Heritage Protection, Article 37, section (1) and referring to Article 12 (2) and Article 13, section (2), *ex lege* protected facilities are those in which valuable collections of moveable cultural heritage are housed, regardless whether the edifices themselves possess historic and architectural values. Such collections have not been registered in the recently protected edifices *ex lege*.

[17]There is no official data presented to the public about the budget spent for this project. The latest data, taken from the research of civil associations on 136 sculptural structures, involving 32 investors, 125 companies, 9 foundries, as well as for honoraria to around 140 authors, indicate that the funds spent exceed 700,000,000 euros (http://skopje2014.prizma. mk, accessed 28 August 2016).

[18]By way of example, only the name of the then-unknown sculptor Valentina Stevanovska is mentioned with regard to seven implemented projects (among which is the fountain with the sculpture of Alexander the Great), for which she received about three million Euros (based on the research of the NGO: http://skopje 2014.prizma.mk accessed 28 August 2016).

[19]The author of the project, the still professionally active architect Petar Mamuchevski, was not consulted about the proposed changes to his own project.

Supply Company), the former shopping mall (the so called 'NA-MA') and the trading and residential complex 'Pelister' – the buildings flanking the eastern part of the city square – have already been, or are currently being, transformed in this way. A similar tendency was announced with the design for the 'baroque' façade of the City Shopping Mall, which ran against the strongly negative responses of the experts and the public at large.

The state's pursuit of a new national image through the production of lavish architectural edifices and the glorification of important persons and events from national history was intended in part to engender a feeling of exhilaration and pride in the common citizens. Reactions have been mixed: the procurement of economic benefits by a few selected domestic companies, participants in the expansive construction activities, has been especially beneficial in times of recession and heightened competition for markets and capital.

As an oddity in this brief review of the Project 'Skopje 2014', we will highlight the solutions presented that have no connection whatsoever even with the projects 'drawn' from the national history, whether implemented on Western European and/or the Balkan soil, as well as no association imaginable with any contemporary architectural or urban concept. The most prominent examples of those are the two concrete 'pirate' ships, dug into the shallow Vardar river bed (Figure 3); the weeping willows 'planted' (into concrete pedestals) and the fountains in the river itself; the 'Panoramic

FIGURE 3 *New buildings on the left side of the Vardar river and one of the ships.* Source: *Julija Trichkovska.*

Wheel' (in the process of construction on the right bank quay of the Vardar), as well as the two bridges with innumerable sculptures that lead directly to the entrances of the Archaeological Museum and the Public Prosecution Office. They are the finishing touches in the fabricated narrative of the contemporary manuscript on the development of the city that could earn the epithet 'Macedonian version of Las Vegas'.

Conclusion

In brief, the central city area of Skopje represents a 'construction site' that does not cease to shock the experts, instigate polarization of its citizens and dumbfound the visitors/tourists.

With the passage of time, the retrograde solutions freighted with a socio-political agenda channelled through the Project 'Skopje 2014' will receive comprehensive evaluation. This should be offered to the citizens transparently but this will happen only if any future administration makes provision for a thorough critical evaluation of the project and, at the same time, shows the courage to make decisions on how the chaos wreaked in the urban and architectural development of the city of Skopje can be overcome. That certainly will be a huge challenge for future generations. For the time being, most of the concerned intellectuals and citizens of Skopje have been left with a dilemma: has this city experienced another 'earthquake' whose devastating power we could (or could not) have predicted and prevented?

The latest developments in the country (April–May 2016), that is experiencing its deepest political crisis, directly affected the buildings constructed through the project 'Skopje 2014'. The act of painting the new façades undertaken by the people that participated in the demonstrations against the ruling regime became a leitmotif of the so-called 'Colour Revolution'. This authentic expression of civil resistance gives a specific dimension to the project's future.

References

Богојевиќ, Л. К. (2014), *Османлиски споменици во Скопје*, Скопје: Табернакул.
Чаусидис, Н. (2013), *Проектот Скопје 2014 – скици за едно наредно истражување*, 33–4, Скопје: Никос Чаусидис.
Димитровски, в. (2010), 'Панаѓур на фарсатаќ', *Порта*, 3: 6–7.
Ђирковић, С. (1969), 'Православна црква у средњовековној српској држави', *Српска православна црква, 1219–1969*, Београд: Свети Архијерејски синод Српске православне цркве.
Грчев, К. (2003), *Архитектонските стилови во македонската архитектура од крајот на 19 век и периодот меѓу двете светски војни*, 198–230, Скопје: Институт за фолклор 'Марко Цепенков'.

Грчев, К. (2014), *Името на злото*, Скопје: Темплум.

Harvey, D. (1990), 'Flexible Akkumulation durch Unrbanisierung – Reflectionen über "Postmodernismus" in Americanischen Städten', in R. Borst and S. Krätke (eds), *Das neue Gesicht der Städte – Theorethische Ansätze und empirische Befunde us der Internationalen Debatte (Basel, etc.)*, Basel/Berlin: Birkhäuser.

Herold, S. (ed) (2010), *Reading the City: Urban Space and Memory in Skopje*, Berlin: Sonderpublikation des Institutes für Stadt- und Regionalplanung Technische Universität Berlin.

Lechler, J. (2010), 'Reading Skopje 2009: A City between Amnesia and Phantasia Architecture, Urban Space, Memory and Identity', in S. Herold (ed), *Reading the City: Urban Space and Memory in Skopje*, Berlin: Sonderpublikation des Institutes für Stadt- und Regionalplanung Technische Universität Berlin.

Lilčiќ, V. (1995), 'Antiquity', in N. Čausidis and L. Ugrinovska (eds), *Macedonia Cultural Heritage*, Skopje: Misla.

Manca, F. (2014), 'Project Skopje 2014'. Available online: https://antroponovicke. wordpres.com/tag/project-skopje-2014 (accessed 28 August 2016).

Macedonia, Republic of (2008), *The Special Law on Protection of the Old Skopje Bazaar*, Official Gazette of the Republic of Macedonia No. 130, 15 October.

Мијалковиќ, М. and Урбанек, К. (2011), *Скопје, светското копиле – архитектурата на поделениот град*, Skopje: Готен.

Mojanchevska, K. and P. van Dijk (2013), 'A Future of the Past' – Disjuncture Between Urban and Cultural Policy Planners in the City of Skopje', The Hague: International Institute of Social Studies. Available online: https://www. researchgate.net/publication/284187074_Disjuncture_between_urban_and_ cultural_policy_planners_in_the_city_of_Skopje (Accessed 28 August 2016).

Петковски, Б. and Томовски, К. (2003), *Архитектурата и монументалната уметност во Скопје меѓу двете светски војни*, Скопје: Музеј на град Скопје.

Трпковска, К. С. (2010), 'Алка помеѓу минатото и сегашноста', *Порта* 3 (142): 14.

Chapter 4.3

The Future of Post-Civil War Reconstruction: Lessons from Spain

Olivia Muñoz-Rojas

Introduction

The main lesson one may draw from the case of contemporary Spain with regard to post-war reconstruction is the long-term, deep challenges posed by a civil war followed by an exclusionary regime, which not only exerted physical and psychological repression on the defeated side, but enforced an understanding of national authenticity that left out the *vanquished*, i.e. one half of the nation. After the proclamation of General Franco's dictatorship in the aftermath of the Spanish Civil War (1936–39), those who had fought on the Republican side were silenced and repressed, and a rigid, reductionist image of Spain and Spanish values was (re)constructed by the regime in discourse and literally in stone (Colmeiro 2005: 44). Once Franco died and Spain transited to democracy in the mid-1970s, the memory of the war and the ensuing dictatorial domination was once more repressed to avoid further conflict at a socio-politically delicate juncture. Collective amnesia and amnesty for those responsible for decades of repression were the price paid for democracy (Erice 2009: 352–7; Morán 2015).

Today, eight decades after the outbreak of the civil war and four after Spain's transition to democracy, it has still not been possible to persuade all relevant actors to negotiate a common approach to the multiple legacies of

Francoism, including its built heritage. The so-called Historic Memory Law,[1] passed in 2007 under a socialist government, was opposed in parliament by the conservative right, who virtually suspended it while in government (2011–15). The Law does not pay excessive attention to the built heritage of the Francoist period, if by that we mean its architecture and infrastructures. However, Article 15 does envisage the removal of monuments and insignias that refer positively to the 1936 military uprising and the dictatorship (1939–75), and demands a solution to the presence of the *Valle de los Caídos* (Valley of the Fallen), the monumental burial compound that Franco had political prisoners build north-west of Madrid.

The first part of this chapter looks back at the reconstruction process in post–civil war Spain, with an emphasis on its symbolic and ideological dimension, including the aspiration to rebuild a New Spain, the search for an authentically Spanish architectural and planning style, the prioritization of rural, over urban, reconstruction, but also less obviously symbolic aspects such as the use of forced labour. The second part of the chapter analyses the situation of this heritage after the transition to democracy, in particular after the approval of the Historic Memory Law and the different initiatives taken under its umbrella.

Post–civil war reconstruction in Spain: Towards a new social and political order

National reconstruction in post–civil war Spain was understood as physical rebuilding, moral regeneration and economic renewal (Casares 1940). It was deemed that one of the reasons for the spread of 'bolshevism' and the outbreak of the civil war had been the increasing class resentment experienced in the cities, where workers were concentrated in marginal, poor and unhealthy districts. Many believed that the construction of clean, larger homes for workers in socially mixed neighbourhoods, adequately serviced by the municipality and the Church, would prevent the danger of these workers becoming politically class conscious and ensure the harmonious yet hierarchical coexistence of Spaniards of different social backgrounds in the cities. Simultaneously, the construction of modern, rational agricultural units in the countryside would anchor potential new rural migrants in non-urban environments, reinforcing the traditionally more conservative values and aspirations of rural Spain.

---

[1]The actual name of the law is *Proyecto de Ley por la que se reconocen y amplían derechos y se establecen medidas en favor de quienes padecieron persecución o violencia durante la Guerra Civil y la Dictadura* (Draft Law to recognize and broaden rights and measures in favour of those who suffered persecution or violence during the Civil War and the Dictatorship).

Economic renewal would build on agricultural modernization and state-sponsored industrialization (Muguruza Otaño 1940). Spain lacked a significant entrepreneurial, capitalist class to which industrialization could be entrusted. Having rejected foreign investment, the regime's only choice was to continue relying on the traditional financial oligarchy, which had backed the military coup and financed the military rebels throughout the war. This financial aristocracy was hardly bent on risk-taking, but ready to place money in state-sponsored industrializing ventures in exchange for the regime's protection of social privilege and traditional values. Towards the end of the 1950s, the regime's autarchic programme had failed, and Spain was plunged into economic stagnation, which no longer favoured even the financial aristocracy. The regime was forced to catch up with reality. Dogmatic discourses and heavy bureaucracy were eventually transmuted into technocratic language and managerial practices. This was the beginning of Spain's 1960s economic boom.

By then, the physical reconstruction of the country was deemed accomplished. The process began in early 1938 when the Servicio Nacional de Regiones Devastadas y Reparaciones (National Service for Devastated Regions and Reparations) was created by Franco's wartime government in Burgos. Every reconstruction project, regardless of its volume and cost, had to receive the approval of Regiones Devastadas (Llanos 1987: 43). Destruction was deemed an unfortunate result of 'the holy and victorious liberation Crusade', when it was not viewed as the direct outcome of 'the barbarous and merciless violence deployed by the hordes, who, instructed by Russia, showed all their hatred towards everything representing the basic and secular principles of the Christian and Spanish spirit' (*Reconstrucción* 1940: 2). The Department's fundamental commitment was to *orientate and facilitate* the reconstruction process, and only in certain cases was it responsible for carrying out the works. In all other cases, the initiative was left to local authorities and private owners, who still had to comply with Regiones Devastadas' regulations. Sympathetic 'entities, companies or private individuals' wishing to reconstruct their property were guaranteed at least partial funding through the loans system set up by the Instituto de Crédito para la Reconstrucción Nacional (Credit Institute for National Reconstruction), the financial branch of Regiones Devastadas (Jefatura del Estado 1939: 1642–3).

Consistent with the regime's autarchic programme, the Credit Institute extracted its funds from exclusively 'national sources' (*Reconstrucción* 1940), including the income brought by the confiscations and economic sanctions imposed on individuals who had remained on the Republican side during the war and were now being summarily tried for their political responsibilities, and the revenues that private companies paid the state for hiring war and political prisoners to be employed in construction work (Jefatura del Estado 1939: 1642–3). The term *prestaciones personales* or payment in kind was used euphemistically to refer to these exceptional sources (*Reconstrucción* 1940). In the end, reparations *were* exacted, not from another nation, but from the other half of the Spanish nation.

Forced labour became an extensive and well-developed officially coordinated practice after the war. The use of political prisoners as forced labour, and their inhumane living and working conditions, was given a legal and even charitable façade through the so-called scheme of cancellation of penalties by work (Lafuente 2002). The arrangement proved extremely efficient for the state from an economic point of view. The authorities openly argued that the construction of many of the dams, for example, would have been almost impossible without the scheme (Lafuente 2002: 77–8). Private companies were soon allowed, if not encouraged, to hire prisoners, mainly for construction work.

Regiones Devastadas stepped in directly and carried out reconstruction works in those towns and villages that had lost more than two-thirds of their built-up area. Formally, it was the Head of State, General Franco, who 'adopted' these towns and villages (*Reconstrucción* 1940, Moreno Torres 1948). The system proved an excellent propaganda tool for the regime, even though very often the adopted villages were inaugurated without having been finished, and sometimes they never were (Blanco 1987: 19).

The priority of Regiones Devastadas was the restoration of town halls, *casas cuartel* (the Civil Guard barracks), religious buildings and houses in smaller towns and villages. The regime's preference for rural environments, religious buildings and traditional architecture is apparent in *Reconstrucción*, the monthly magazine published by Regiones Devastadas between 1940 and 1953 as well as in the series of projects that its director, José Moreno Torres, reported as accomplished works in the first illustrated summary of reconstruction achievements published in 1946 (Moreno Torres 1946).

Finding an authentic Spanish national style

Discussions about which architectural style should be the specific brand of the new regime were intense during the initial post-war years. Architecture and planning were conceived as state arts, and the built order ultimately as a manifestation of the political order. Until the 1950s various stylistic practices coexisted and sometimes overlapped; fundamentally, *fachadismo* (façadism),[2] classical monumentalism, folkloric traditionalism and rationalism.

---

[2]*Fachadismo*, or the early rebel propaganda architecture, consisted of the vast settings in wood and *papier mâché* that were installed in squares and open places for military parades and mass gatherings around the Caudillo. Conceptually similar to the scenarios from where Hitler and Mussolini captivated their audiences, they also took inspiration from the Baroque Catholic liturgy tradition. Not to be confused with façadism in the sense of developing a new structure behind a retained historic front wall. See Sambricio 1977: 28.

The Falange's[3] preference for sober, classical monumentalism, specifically seventeenth-century Spanish architecture, is most visible in the largely unaccomplished projects for the recreation of Imperial Madrid. The architect Luis Moya referred to the colonization of America and the successful building enterprise that Spain had engaged in at the time through the prolific construction of towns in the newly conquered lands (Moya 1940: 15). To Moya, a devoted Catholic, who understood architecture as a true reflection of the social order (Capitel 1977: 10), the secret of Spain's success in the sixteenth and seventeenth centuries lay in its capacity to appropriate diverse influences and produce something genuinely Spanish and imperial. In his view, it was mainly through the mediation of Juan de Herrera, the architect of the Palace of the Escorial, that Spanish golden-age architecture had been successful in becoming 'a true Imperial architecture, like that of ancient Rome' (Moya 1940). Commissioned in the sixteenth century by Philip II, son of the German Emperor Charles V, the Escorial was acclaimed as the culminating point of Spanish architecture by the leading group of Falangist architects and intellectuals. The symbolic value of the Escorial was exploited in interesting ways. Not only was it presented as a product of the Renaissance and, hence, indirectly of Greece and Rome, but German purity and rectitude were said to be impregnated in its solid granite walls by way of its royal commissioner – maybe a convenient nod to the Third Reich (Sánchez Mazas 1939).

The preference for certain construction materials because of their close symbolic and material association with the perceived historical sources of the New Spain – the Roman and Hapsburg Empires – and the focus on their visual appearance and texture contain disturbing racialized connotations. Although the importance of race in the ideological structure of the Franco regime should not be overestimated, in this case buildings made of particular materials were invested with certain morals and ideals in a similar fashion to racist discourses which attribute particular virtues and defects to human bodies that share similar physical characteristics.[4] The Falangist intellectual Ernesto Giménez Caballero, for example, suggested, 'the fight between stone and brick (Christian and infidels in the past, Nationalists and Reds in the present)' had lasted for many centuries 'in the architectural frontline of Spain' without reaching an ending (Giménez Caballero 1944). This stereotypical identification of narrow streets and brick architecture of poor quality with the Moorish and Jewish legacies as well as with popular, working class architecture, was not uncommon during this period (García

---

[3]The Falange was the Spanish fascist party. It was part of the *Movimiento Nacional*, the larger state party/movement that Franco created, which included other ideological 'families' such as the monarchists and the national Catholics.
[4]In fact, it is often both the buildings and the bodies that inhabit them that become essentialized or stigmatized in this way.

FIGURE 1 *The Air Ministry, designed by José Gutiérrez Soto, echoing the Palace of the Escorial, with Madrid's Victory Arch in the foreground to the right. Source: Enrique Dans (Wikimedia Commons).*

Cortés 1940). One of the few official buildings that was erected in the 'new' monumentalist style was the architect José Gutiérrez Soto's Air Ministry in Madrid's Moncloa district (Figure 1).

If classical monumentalism was reserved for the capital city, official buildings and commemorative crosses and arches, folkloric traditionalism and regionalism inspired the reconstruction of the adopted towns and villages. In most cases, it was impossible to restore the villages to their exact former appearance since there were no plans and drawings available (Blanco Lage 1984: 68, 69). The architects of Regiones Devastadas tried to find a balance between the new national style and local and regional specificities. Traditional, often handcrafted materials were used, and simple and sober lines predominated in the new constructions (Pérez Rodríguez-Urrutia 2002: 160). Despite the emphasis on regional diversity and the actual incorporation of local elements in the designs, the buildings that Regiones Devastadas constructed across Spain have a common, distinct flavour, which makes them easily recognizable, and indeed reminiscent of the colonial constructions in former Spanish America (Otero 1987: 94).

The architects of Regiones Devastadas proved quite successful at adapting to the ideological requirements of the regime while dealing with the severe scarcity of materials that Spain suffered at the time. As it turns out, behind the traditionalist façades of the buildings often hid surprisingly rationalist solutions. It could be argued that the post-war circumstances favoured an undeclared rationalist response to the building needs in the devastated towns and villages (Figure 2).

FIGURE 2 *Main square in the 'adopted' town of Brunete. Source: author's collection, original photographer unknown.*

From the 1950s, more and more architects deemed the national, monumentalist style obsolete and unrealistic. And the folkloric traditionalism fostered by Regiones Devastadas, despite its proto-rationalist elements, was not so apt for the urban context. Many architects refused to continue to ignore foreign modernist architecture. Although still conditioned by post-war Spain's material scarcity, a more eclectic architectural panorama started to take shape (Pozo 2004).[5] Gradually Spain began to have access to industrially prefabricated construction materials used in Europe and the United States in the aftermath of the Second World War. These materials opened up new possibilities, especially for housing construction. In 1957, reconstruction proper officially ended. The equivalent of 1,426 million euros had been spent by Regiones Devastadas on reconstruction between 1939 and 1957,[6] and more than 150 technicians, 108 architects, 46 engineers and 180 experts had worked for the Department across thirty regional offices (Otero 1987: 93). Regiones Devastadas was dismantled, and its remaining functions were absorbed by the new Ministry of Housing.

The earliest period of isolated experimentation during which the regime's architects sought to produce a genuine, uncorrupted Spanish style was fairly short, but it is instructive because it reflects the struggle to define the regime ideologically. It can be characterized as modern in its aim to develop a national architectural programme based on functional, serialized and vernacular structures, but it was reactionary in its conception of the urban *versus* the rural and the kind of aesthetics it sought to establish, including the profuse 'marking' of public space with fascist and National-Catholic symbols. Hence, in spite of what could be termed as modest results in relation to the grandiose rhetoric deployed by the regime,[7] a large number of Spanish towns and cities do bear the physical mark of both the civil war and the dictatorship. How has and how should this material presence be dealt with in a democratic context?

Francoist heritage after the transition to democracy

Although there is little research on the topic, there is almost no indication that a systematic approach to Francoist buildings and monuments during and immediately after the transition to democracy was taken at national, regional or municipal levels. In the heat (or joy) of the moment, the newly

---

[5]There has recently been significant interest in the Spanish architecture of the 1950s, which includes the work (mostly public projects) of architects Luis Cubillo, Rafael de la Hoz, José Luis Romany and many others. See Pozo 2004.

[6]This is the updated (June 2016) equivalent of the figure given by Gloria Otero (1987): 96,000 million pesetas. The figure has been calculated on the webpage of the Instituo Nacional de Estadística, see http://www.ine.es/calcula/calcula.do.

[7]As an example of the contrast between rhetoric and reality, note the state's plans to build 1.4 million new homes between 1944 and 1954, of which an average of 16,000 per year were actually built.

democratically elected local councils removed some of the more obvious Francoist elements such as busts, plaques, crosses to the fallen and statues, and changed the names of the streets that honoured the rebel heroes (Martín Pallín 2009: 63). As in other cases, such as the Italian after Mussolini, more than the buildings themselves, it was the explicit signs and symbols of the dictatorship adorning the buildings that people wanted removed.

In contrast, two exhibitions contributed to identifying and revaluing the post-war architectural legacy and reconstruction efforts. The first, 'Arquitectura para después de una Guerra, 1939–1949' ('Architecture for the aftermath of War, 1939–1949'), was held in Barcelona in 1977. While acknowledging the ideologized environment in which this architecture was produced, the exhibition and its catalogue avoided imposing any conclusion, leaving it to the viewer to meditate on the binomial ideology-aesthetics (Amado Cercos and Domenech Girbau 1977, Viejo-Rose 2011: 155–6). Ten years later, another exhibition, 'Arquitectura en Regiones Devastadas', focusing on the reconstruction work carried out by Regiones Devastadas, was organized in Madrid. Neither these exhibitions nor the interest in this period that a series of renowned architectural historians have shown has resulted in the design of specific policies that deal with Francoist heritage.

By the time that the Historic Memory Law was approved in 2007, thirty years after the transition to democracy, a significant number of monuments and statues, including of General Franco himself, were still in place in many towns and cities. To many, the continued existence of such explicit signs of the dictatorship in a democratic context was an aberration. Far from exceptional, the Historic Memory Law is a representative example of the process of memory institutionalization as well as of the widening of the concept of heritage witnessed in many countries over recent decades.[8] It should also be seen as the result of changes in Spanish society, in particular the arrival of a new generation with sufficient emotional distance from the events: it is the grandchildren of the killed and the repressed that have taken the lead in the process of memory recovery (Yusta Rodrigo 2011).

The Historic Memory Law includes several measures, fairly different in nature, ranging from victim indemnifications, exhumations, removal of insignias and monuments that refer positively to the military uprising of 18 July 1936, recovery and conservation of historical documentation to granting of Spanish citizenship to former members of the International Brigades (who fought with the Spanish Republicans) and descendants of Spanish political exiles. Article 15 regulates 'public symbols and monuments', and establishes that 'the Public administrations [...] will take appropriate measures to remove coats of arms, insignias, plaques and other objects or commemorative mentions of personal or collective

---

[8]On memorialization, see, among others, Williams 2007. On the widening of the concept of heritage, see San Martín Calvo 2014: 212–24.

exaltation of the military uprising, the Civil War and the repression of the Dictatorship'. These measures may include taking away subsidies or public grants from public institutions and private owners who do not proceed accordingly. The article also establishes that removal 'will not be applicable when the mentions are for private remembrance strictly, when they do not exalt the rebels, or in the event of artistic, architectural or artistic-religious circumstances protected by law'.

What kind of constructions does article 15 aim at? To date, and despite plans for both, there is neither an official catalogue of existing Francoist symbols nor specific rules on how to classify them. Many town councils are reluctant to inventory local symbols, the first step towards a national catalogue (Gómez 2015). Nevertheless, a look at the press coverage in recent years reveals that statues of Franco, crosses to the fallen on the rebel/ Nationalist side, pre-democratic coats of arms on the façades of public buildings and metal plaques of the Francoist Housing Institute on public housing façades have been removed most frequently. In quantitative terms, between 2006 and 2010, 642 projects related to the removal of monuments and insignias took place (Figure 3). More than one million euros were spent on these initiatives (Junquera 2010a).[9]

FIGURE 3 *Francoist plaque that was originally placed on the façade of the General Command Headquarters in Ceuta. Source: Xemenendura (Wikimedia Commons).*

---

[9]These figures have not changed substantially since, given that the conservative right in government 2011–15 virtually suspended the law.

The technical commission in charge of deciding on the potential historical or artistic value of particular symbols was approved in March 2009, and included five permanent members and fourteen scholarly advisors: ten historians, two art historians and two architects (*EcoDiario.es* 2009). Such distribution suggests the prevalence of the historic over the artistic criterion.

Autonomous communities with strong nationalist traditions such as Catalonia, the Basque Country and Galicia have generally been more active in applying the Law. In Catalonia, for example, there were 7,700 Francoist symbols left in September 2010, according to the figures of Memorial Democràtic, the official Catalan platform for the recovery of historical memory. At the same time, Barcelona stands out for being one of the cities that has applied itself the most in the removal of Francoist symbols. The Victory statue, at a prominent intersection in central Barcelona, was the last Francoist monument to disappear from the Catalan capital in January 2011. It has become part of Barcelona's History Museum collection (*ABC* 2011).

The continued presence of the Valle de los Caídos – Franco's memorial and burial compound, close to the Escorial – is exceptionally polemical, and little progress has been made towards an acceptable solution. In their final report, the special committee that was created in 2011 to assess the situation, proposed, among others, treating the building as regular public heritage, removing Franco's remains, exhuming the bodies of the hundreds of Republicans that were buried there without their families' consent and creating a memory museum. The report soon fell into oblivion as the conservative right came into power that same year (Junquera 2015). But the Valle de los Caídos is not the only controversial case. The removal of the O Castro cross in Vigo, dominating the Galician town from a hill top, was recently ruled out by the High Court of Galicia with the argument that, once stripped of its fascist ornamentation, the cross does not evoke the values of the dictatorship, but serves as a reminder of political prosecution on both sides of the conflict (Coco 2015). More than two-thirds of the residents of Tortosa who participated in a binding public poll in spring 2016 voted for maintaining the town's monument to the Nationalists' victory in the Ebro battle. Partly because 'they have grown used to it', but mostly because they consider the cost of pulling it down 'superfluous', considering current local budget cuts (Rovira 2016). The fate of the statue of General Franco as commander of the Legion, at the foot of the wall of Old Melilla, the only statue of the dictator left in public space, is once more on the table after the party Podemos publicly advocated its removal in summer 2015 (*20minutos* 2015).

Judging from the press, the application of article 15 can turn into a veritable hot potato for many town councils. The decision to remove a cross or a headstone with the names of the fallen on the Nationalist side is often a source of significant tension among local political groups and the local citizenry. This is not necessarily a negative outcome: conflict around the permanence or otherwise of a monument or memorial forces citizens to confront their past instead of repress it (Dolff-Bonekämper 2003).

Alternatives to a law

The discomfort that certain constructions stir apparently has an expiry date. However, as we know, a society may revise its heritage at any moment, deciding to eradicate those elements that it considers uncomfortable or illegitimate because they belong to a past which it wishes to erase from collective remembrance – we may think only of the recent destruction of Palmyra at the hands of the ISIS.

The question here is to what extent do future generations have the right to know their past, including the darkest? It is a complex query. Regardless of how much we want to think in terms of *longue durée* and be responsible towards future generations, we cannot ignore the needs and concerns of the present ones. Still, it is legitimate to ask if the law, as such, is the best instrument to address issues that affect the symbolic order of a society, changing collective sensitivities, and contradictory experiences of the present and the past in the present. Perhaps other sociocultural forms are more adequate to address and resolve the material presence of a traumatic past?

Resolution 2057, issued by the Parliamentary Assembly of the Council of Europe in May 2015 and specifically devoted to cultural heritage in crisis and post-crisis situations, states, 'conflict resolution and reconciliation are complex processes which may take several generations'. The Resolution also concludes that 'the process of reconstruction of cultural heritage has a strong potential for reconciliation and building of social cohesion, but it can also be misused to reignite division and hatred'.[10] Clearly, this is what happened during the post–civil war reconstruction process in Spain, when monuments were erected to honour only one side of the conflict. Only one particular understanding of Spain, including its architecture and built heritage, was celebrated, and everyday public space was profusely marked by the vanquishers. Is there a risk now, in a democratic context, that the sheer removal of Francoist monuments and symbols may reignite division, jeopardizing once more the possibility of achieving social and cultural cohesion in Spain? Is there a risk after such removal that collective amnesia will be the definitive response to a difficult past?

Echoing Walter Benjamin's urge to recover the memory of the vanquished, but also his preference for the techniques of collage, montage and urban palimpsests, I am tempted to ask: Are there more creative and engaging ways of dealing with the uncomfortable legacy of Francoism? What about encouraging collaborative projects in which artists work

---

[10]Resolution 2057 on 'Cultural heritage in crisis and post-crisis situations' was issued by the Parliamentary Assembly of the Council of Europe in May 2015 based on a previous report (Document 13758, produced by the Committee on Culture, Science, Education and Media) and recommendation (Recommendation 2071).

together with political representatives, historians, urbanists, other experts and ordinary citizens? These projects, or processes, are not expected to be straightforward, but the process itself of debating, deciding and generating responses would have a democratic and socially cathartic value.[11] As the Faro Convention on the Value of Cultural Heritage for Society argues, everyone in society needs to be involved in the ongoing process of defining and managing cultural heritage (Council of Europe 2005).

Some initiatives under the Spanish Historic Memory Law arguably show this greater sensitivity towards the plural, changing and conflicting nature of public memory. The memory route that was inaugurated in the cemetery of Zaragoza in 2010 is an attempt to conciliate opposed memories and interpretations of the past (Elorza 2007): along with the spiral of metal plaques with the 3,543 names of Republicans shot in this place during the civil war and its aftermath, the cross to the fallen on the Nationalist side, erected in the cemetery in 1941, was preserved (*ABC* 2010, Junquera 2010b). In the municipality of Amoeiro in Galicia, the mayor successfully launched a crowdfunding campaign in 2015 to place explanatory/ denunciatory plaques on remaining Francoist symbols, instead of removing them. The mayor argued that using crowdfunding instead of public funding added legitimacy to the initiative, making it more participatory as well (L.F. 2014). In 2014, a memory park was inaugurated in Málaga's former San Rafael cemetery, where more than 4,100 Republicans were executed and buried in collective graves on site by the rebels. In the middle of the park, a pyramid covered in white marble with the names of those killed inscribed contains the remains of the close to 3,000 bodies identified to date. The same inclination towards creating a place of retreat and reflection can be found in the Sartaguda Memory Park, inaugurated in 2008 and dedicated to the Navarran victims of the civil war and Francoism.[12]

More such initiatives would arguably contribute to overcoming the persistent trauma of the civil war and Franco's dictatorship. It should be possible to generate a superposition of legacies which despite their dissonance reflect and do not avoid the complexity of Spain's (increasingly less) recent past. Furthermore, the brutal, painful work of the hundreds of thousands of political prisoners that lies behind many buildings and infrastructures constructed under the dictatorship should be publicly documented and visible, be that through plaques, memorials, museums or artistic projects. Not to say the numerous buildings and spaces where torture was practised systematically. Instead of simply eliminating the uncomfortable presence of crosses and inscriptions, it would be more valuable perhaps to stress their presence, contrasting it with the symbolic absence of the vanquished by

---

[11]For a critical appraisal of the role of art in memorialization processes, see Huyssen 1995, 2003. See also Young 2000 and Zelizer 2001.
[12]See http://www.parquedelamemoria.org/

rendering visible their slave work, torture and death in the everyday built environment.

Concluding remarks

The Spanish case highlights a number of aspects that may be relevant to other cases of post–civil war reconstruction, transitions to dictatorship, transitions to democracy after dictatorship and different combinations of these experiences. First, there is the notion of collective amnesia that can be more or less deliberately applied in the (re)construction of a country, including its heritage, after a war or a regime change. Like the Francoist dictatorship, which systematically erased the memory of the Republican side and all that it stood for, other dictatorial regimes across the world do and have done the same. If at all, in these cases the vanquished side is only referred to as the incarnation of the enemy of the true nation in stark contrast with the vanquishers, representing the *authentic* nation. Post-war reconstruction is an unparalleled opportunity for dictatorial regimes to aesthetically recreate what they believe to be the authentic nation. However, regime branding does not necessarily require reconstructing a country from scratch: the same goal can be reached by highlighting particular heritage and neglecting other. As important as the actual physical reconstruction and management of heritage is the discourse that accompanies these endeavours. In Francoist Spain, such discourse was, among others, based on a moral understanding of construction materials, different materials representing different values, echoing a wider trend among architects at the time, including Mies van der Rohe (Mozas 2011: 121).

Collective amnesia may also be induced or openly agreed in democratic contexts. Some would argue that such peaceful transitions to democracy as the one in Spain in the 1970s or South Africa in the 1990s would not have been possible without collectively agreeing to put the past behind. The stakes are always higher for the defeated or previously repressed side which is the one having to accept forgetting past injustices in order to embrace a common, non-violent future. The Spanish case shows that such collective amnesia may only be a temporary solution. Sooner or later, it seems, the past catches up, and those who apparently forgot at one point, or rather often their descendants, demand justice, that is, fair acknowledgement of the suffering of their parents and grandparents and condemnation of those who caused it. In Spain, this demand has taken the form of a Historic Memory Law, which also envisions revising the physical heritage of Francoism. The question, as discussed above, is whether it should be left to a particular government alone to legislate this matter. If we take Ashworth and Tunbridge's (1996) view that heritage – and certainly the heritage of a dictatorship into which some of the present generations were born – is intrinsically dissonant (i.e. different groups interpret its objects and buildings differently), there should be more room for a long-term, collaborative approach, where different social actors are involved and a variety of memorialization techniques deployed. In a democracy, the aim should not be to find a universal and definite solution to the way the past, especially a past of conflict and repression, is handled.

Acknowledgement

This chapter draws on ideas researched over many years, some of which have been discussed previously by the author in work such as *Ashes and Granite: Destruction and Reconstruction in the Spanish Civil War and Its Aftermath* (Brighton: Sussex Academic Press, 2011) and 'Granite remains: Francoist monuments today', *Public Art Dialogue* 2, 2 (2012): 147–57.

References

20minutos (2015), 'Podemos pide la retirada de la estatua de Franco ubicada en Melilla', *20minutos*, 27 July.

ABC (2010), 'Zaragoza inaugura el miércoles el primer memorial a los fusilados de guerra', *ABC*, 22 October.

ABC (2011), 'Barcelona retira de sus calles el último monumento franquista', *ABC*, 30 January.

Amado Cercos, R. and Ll. Domenech Girbau (1977), 'Arquitectura para después de una guerra', *El País*, 4 October.

Ashworth, G. J. and J. E. Tunbridge (1996), *Dissonant Heritage: The Management of the Past as a Resource in Conflict*, Chichester: Wiley.

Blanco, M. (1987), 'España Una', in M. Blanco et al. (eds), *Arquitectura en Regiones Devastadas*, Madrid: MOPU.

Blanco Lage, M. (1984), 'La Gran Reconstrucción', *Revista MOPU* 310: 66–71.

Capitel, A. (1977), 'Madrid, los años 40. Ante una moderna arquitectura', *Cuadernos de Arquitectura y Urbanismo* (Arquitectura para después de una guerra) 121: 8–13.

Casares, F. (1940), 'Significado moral de la reconstrucción de España', *La Vanguardia Española*, 26 July, reprinted in G. Ureña (1979), *Arquitectura y urbanística civil y militar en el período de la autarquía (1936–1945): Análisis, cronología y textos*, Madrid: Istmo.

Coco, A. (2015), 'La Cruz do Castro de Vigo ya no se tira', *ABC*, 10 February.

Colmeiro, J. F. (2005), *Memoria histórica e identidad cultural: de la postguerra a la postmodernidad*, Barcelona: Anthropos Editorial.

Council of Europe (2005), *Framework Convention on the Value of Cultural Heritage for Society* (The Faro Convention), Strasbourg: Council of Europe.

Council of Europe (2015), 'Cultural Heritage in Crisis and Post-Crisis Situations', Resolution 2057, Strasbourg: Parliamentary Assembly of the Council of Europe.

Dolff-Bonekämper, G. (2003), 'Le Forum de la Culture à Berlin, Monument d'histoire contemporaine', in M. Gravari-Barbas and S. Guichard-Anguis (eds),

Regards croisés sur le patrimoine dans le monde à l'aube du XXIe siècle, Paris: Presses Universitaires Paris-Sorbonne.

EcoDiario.es (2009), 'Memoria. Dos catedráticos de Arte, dos arquitectos y 10 historiadores asesorarán al Gobierno sobre retirada de símbolos', *EcoDiario.es*, 3 March. Available online: http://ecodiario.eleconomista.es/politica/noticias/1074317/03/09/Memoria-Dos-catedraticos-de-Arte-dos-arquitectos-y-10-historiadores-asesoraran-al-Gobierno-sobre-retirada-de-simbolos.html (accessed 17 June 2016).

Elorza, A. (2007), 'Memorias históricas', *El País*, 20 October.

Erice, F. (2009), *Guerras de la memoria y fantasmas del pasado: Usos y abusos de la memoria*, Oviedo: Editorial Eikaisa.

García Cortés, M. (1940), 'El "Madrid histórico" debe evocar y el genio y poder de nuestro pueblo', *Reconstrucción 7*.

Giménez Caballero, E. (1944), *Madrid nuestro*, Madrid: Ediciones de la Vicesecretaría de Educación Popular.

Gómez, A. (2015), 'La cruzada de un sólo abogado contra los símbolos franquistas en calles e iglesias', *El Confidencial*, 17 July.

Huyssen, A. (1995), *Twilight Memories. Marking Time in a Culture of Amnesia*, New York and London: Routledge.

Huyssen, A. (2003), *Present Pasts: Urban Palimpsests and the Politics of Memory*, Palo Alto, CA: Stanford University Press.

Jefatura del Estado (1939), 'Ley de 16 de marzo creando el Instituto de Crédito para la Reconstrucción Nacional', *BOE* 81 (22 March): 1642–3.

Junquera, N. (2010a), '1.821 de las 2.052 fosas comunes del franquismo están todavía por abrir', *El País*, 23 October.

Junquera, N. (2010b), 'Una ruta de la memoria une en Zaragoza a vencidos y vencedores', *El País*, 22 October.

Junquera, N. (2015), '¿Quién pone flores frescas en la tumba de Franco?', *El País*, 20 November.

Lafuente, I. (2002), *Esclavos por la patria. La explotación de los presos bajo el franquismo*, Madrid: Ediciones Temas de Hoy, S.A.

L.F. (2014), 'Amoeiro coloca las primeras placas de la Memoria Histórica', *Faro de Vigo*, 11 June.

Llanos, E. (1987), 'La Dirección General de Regiones Devastadas: su organización administrativa', in M. Blanco et al. (eds), *Arquitectura en Regiones Devastadas*, Madrid: MOPU.

Martín Pallín, J.A. (2009), 'Eliminación de los símbolos y monumentos de la Dictadura', *Patrimonio cultural de España*, 1: 61–82.

Morán, G. (2015), *El precio de la Transición*, Madrid: Akal.

Moreno Torres, J. (1946), *El Estado en la reconstrucción de las ciudades y pueblos españoles*, Madrid: Instituto de Estudios de Administración Local.

Moreno Torres, J. (1948), *La reconstrucción urbana en España/Urban Reconstruction in Spain*, Madrid: Ministerio de la Gobernación, Dirección General de Regiones Devastadas.

Moya, L. (1940), 'Orientaciones de arquitectura en Madrid', *Reconstrucción 7*: 10–15.

Mozas, J. (2011), *Rashomon. La triple verdad de la arquitectura*, Vitoria-Gasteiz: a+t architecture publishers.

Muguruza Otaño, P. (1940), 'Sistematización técnica en un Plan Nacional de Resurgimiento', *Instituto Técnico de la Construcción y Edificación*, 17: 3.

Otero, G. (1987), 'La Reconstrucción de Regiones Devastadas, en la Sala de Exposiciones del M.O.P.U. Arquitectura para después de una guerra', *Revista MOPU* 94.

Pérez Rodríguez-Urrutia, F. (2002), 'Las nuevas formas de colonización de la arquitectura de postguerra en la obra de Fernando de Urrutia Usaola: Arquitectura para Regiones Devastadas, los poblados hidroeléctricos y ciudades-jardín en la periferia', paper presented at the Arquitectura, ciudad e ideología antiurbana conference, Pamplona.

Pozo, J. M. (ed) (2004), *Los brillantes 50: 35 proyectos*, Pamplona: T6.

Reconstrucción (1940), 'Organismos del Nuevo Estado. La Dirección General de Regiones Devastadas y Reparaciones', *Reconstrucción*, 1: 2.

Rovira, M. (2016), 'Tortosa vota conservar el mayor monumento franquista', *El País*, 28 May.

Sambricio, C. (1977), '... "¡Que coman República!" Introducción a un estudio sobre la reconstrucción en la España de la posguerra', *Cuadernos de Arquitectura y Urbanismo* (Arquitectura para después de una guerra), 121: 21–33.

San Martín Calvo, M. (2014), *Bienes culturales y conflictos armados: Nuevas perspectivas de Derecho Internacional*, Navarra: Thomson Reuters Aranzadi.

Sánchez Mazas, R. (1939), 'Herrera Viviente', *Arriba*, 2 July, reprinted in G. Ureña (1979), *Arquitectura y urbanística civil y militar en el período de la autarquía (1936–1945): Análisis, cronología y textos*, Madrid: Istmo.

Viejo-Rose, D. (2011), *Reconstructing Spain. Cultural Heritage and Memory After Civil War*, Brighton: Sussex Academic Press.

Williams, P. (2007), *Memorial Museums: The Global Rush to Commemorate Atrocities*, Oxford: Berg.

Young, J. E. (2000), *At Memory's Edge: After-Images of the Holocaust in Contemporary Art and Architecture*, New Haven, CT: Yale University Press.

Yusta Rodrigo, M. (2011), '¿ "Memoria versus justicia"? La "recuperación de la memoria histórica" en la España actual', *Amnis* 2, 27 October. Available online: http://amnis.revues.org/1482;DOI:10.4000/amnis.1482 (accessed 10 March 2016).

Zelizer, B. (ed) (2001), *Visual Culture and the Holocaust*, New York: Rutgers.

Conclusions, Guidelines and Looking Forward

John Bold, Robert Pickard and Peter J. Larkham

There are right and wrong ways of carrying out building works but the question of how to reconstruct buildings or areas after disaster, whether man-made or natural, is not capable of a simple, binary answer. Although we live in a period in which feelings and outraged moral judgements have become the default position in an interconnected digital world of instant responses, the chapters in this volume suggest that a more dispassionate and nuanced approach to the exceptional, though distressingly frequent, requirements for post-disaster reconstruction would be desirable. In looking closely at particular cases, the contributors have shown the need for individual approaches, tailored to national and local requirements which are influenced by a number of factors, some of which may be in conflict with each other: these include the need to reinstate functions within an overall development plan, the need to create a recognizable place, to assert identity and respect memory, the need to modernize buildings and upgrade living conditions, the need to reflect political or ideological standpoints, the need to reflect contemporary or historicist paradigms, the need to attract investment and tourism, and the need to provide a platform for future growth. There are no generic approaches and no simple answers to complex questions. Whether we rebuild in a new form for a new age, or try to replicate what was there before the disaster, or resurrect an image on the same scale as before with upgraded infrastructure and modified detailing, will all require site-specific consideration. This is not to say that there is no point in having any guidelines for post-disaster reconstruction since every case is individual, rather that guidelines are required so that each individual case might be considered within an agreed, advisory framework which does not need constant reinvention.

The chapters have shown the recurrent nature of discussions across Europe and North America on the notion of authenticity and on the tensions between conscious conservation and contemporary design, tradition and modernity, but when we look more closely at the examples we see that these apparently straightforward categories are not mutually exclusive. It is only at the two extremes of modernist or historicist polemics where, as ever, the extremes (Le Corbusier and John Ruskin) have more in common with each other, not least in their righteous indignation, than a superficial reading of the mainstream thought of either tendency would allow. So much is clear, but the chapters have also raised or implied important questions about authority, political and institutional, and wherein lies the power to determine outcomes. So in assessing what should happen after a disaster, a question which in the case of natural disaster has been shown here to have been peculiarly omitted in disaster guidance which has concentrated on preparedness rather than recovery, who decides? Are the choices to be political or economic, made by an elite (the 'authorized heritage discourse') or through citizen or community collaboration? If by the latter, then who decides which values might condition which responses? Are some values more acceptable than others? Is this an issue for a democratic majority decision? Such questions beg the larger question of who is in charge of the process. This too is not capable of simple answers since it will be conditioned by culture, history, politics, economics and circumstance.

In looking back to examples of reconstruction and some of the discussions which underpinned them, we should also, in so far as it is possible, attempt to have an eye on the future and its potential view of the memorialization which reconstruction may imply. Perhaps reconstruction should take its cue from sustainable development, defined as development which responds to the needs of the present without compromising the capacity of future generations to respond to their own needs. To some extent, the contemporary philosophy of restoration and conservation, with an emphasis on new interventions being reversible, already subscribes to such an approach. But might such a desire to avoid constraining future interventions be a function of cowardice and lack of confidence in our own judgement? Might it also invite the architectural blandness which has characterized those developments in which the architect, wishing to leave options open for later expansion, avoided strong statements? Perhaps we can do no more than be true to the fulfilment of our current needs, not least since heritage is about present purposes, rather than attempting somewhat hubristically to predict future requirements and perceptions.

A further issue, raised or implied, is that of terminology. Some short notes on terminology at the beginning of this volume are offered as a rudimentary guide rather than a definitive set of inalienable definitions. They are mere scratches on the surface of the problem, not least since they are in English only, with no attempt made to express the variations in interpretation of already complex concepts into other languages which may, as several contributors note, assign different meaning and weighting within an apparently direct translation. So 'completely destroyed' and rebuilding something to 'look the same', both phrases which appear to be unambiguously clear, are likely to become unclear and arguable in translation to other languages and other circumstances in which, for example, the idea of 'completely destroyed' may be an ascription which is politically or emotively charged rather than a precise descriptor, and the notion of 'looking the same' may be a function of pragmatic, optimistic recovery rather than a consequence of perfect vision.

Overall, the message from the chapters in this book is that cultural heritage, defended, celebrated, restored and reconstructed, is fundamental to sustainable conflict resolution and the well-being of society. Reconstruction of that heritage after crisis is a political act, but is not solely the responsibility or concern of politicians – they are, or should be, acting on behalf of, and in concert with, civil society as a whole. This is a joint, social responsibility, as the Faro Framework Convention on the Value of Cultural Heritage for Society (2005) affirms in its endorsement of the role of cultural heritage in supporting the principles of human rights and democratic society, managing diversity, increasing democratic participation and improving the living environment and quality of life. But in our unstable world of climate change, globalized economic disruption, scarcity, targeted destruction and consequent social disintegration and despair, it may be difficult to be optimistic. It is unfortunate but inevitable that people will continue having to reconstruct after disaster. Steps should be taken to help them through increasing the collaboration of the international bodies, pooling expertise, giving a greater force and authority to conventions and pronouncements, and greater weight to international and domestic courts of law. Coordination of activities is required since, in times of diminishing resources, duplication of activity is an indulgence. This is an area in which the Council of Europe, the European Union, UNESCO, ICOMOS and other national and international agencies could surely work together on improving the instruments required for crisis and post-crisis heritage management and reconstruction.

Since cultural heritage has become a target both of assault and misrepresentation, as well as mere neglect, we surely need clearer guidelines for addressing policies and practice relating to the heritage in crisis and post-crisis situations and stronger affirmation of principles, particularly those relating to reconstruction as part of the post-crisis development process. There have been many charters and conventions over the last twenty years which have recommended a more pragmatic approach to heritage management, but we must continue to argue against a certain heritage orthodoxy rooted in the long-established preserve-as-found view of those who wish to argue for an inalienable authenticity – the view underpinning the restrictions imposed in the enormously influential ICOMOS Venice Charter (1964) on the conservation and restoration of monuments and sites which ruled out *a priori* the reconstruction of archaeological sites, and by implication, buildings as well. Now, as ICOMOS is itself considering its position on reconstruction, and as the Parliamentary Assembly of the Council of Europe has recommended the production of guidelines for the protection and reconstruction of damaged or destroyed cultural heritage (Council of Europe 2015), we need new guidelines which reflect a world which has changed. Reconstruction is going to happen anyway and sometimes it will be in a manner inimical to established notions of good practice. So those notions need an admixture of flexibility to enable a more appropriate response to individual circumstances.

Although many of the chapters in this book, and recent international initiatives, have focused on the question of how to reconstruct after war or natural disaster, we should consider also the transferability of methodologies to potentially analogous situations. The strategies adopted for post-crisis modernization and reconstruction may also be deployed in response to the demands of large-scale urban renewal. The modernization of old centres of population, accompanied by removal and rehousing, creating a place which no longer looks like home, may be as cathartic as recovery from crisis – indeed for some it may be read as another sort of disaster, requiring comparable strategies for recovery including the involvement of the local population and the clear communication of rationale and intent. The process has much in common with other more obviously disastrous situations and ideally should be treated with a comparable sensitivity to feelings about place as well as to the demands of modernization and renewal.

Guidelines

The preparation of international Guidelines for Reconstruction will require further detailed consideration and consultation. They might, however, take a form which begins with a discussion of existing charters, terminology, principles and concepts, followed by considerations of typology and procedures. This approach has been described in detail elsewhere by two of the editors of this volume (Bold and Pickard 2013). In the present context, it will suffice to offer a summary account of the typological and procedural considerations to be borne in mind, when faced with the need for post-crisis reconstruction.

Typology

Objectives of the intervention

There are many reasons for intervention and many categories of possible reconstruction, as the chapters in this volume have shown. It is clearly important in embarking upon reconstruction to have an understanding of why it is being attempted. Reconstruction may take the form of an authentic spiritual and ritual repetition, as in dismantling and rebuilding Japanese temples, or to affirm religious and architectural continuity at a holy site. Reconstruction may be for political or dynastic reasons, or as an optimistic symbol of national identity and unity, peace and stability following war. It may be viewed as part of a healing process, encouraging the return of those displaced by war to a place which looks familiar. It may be necessary to restore a missing unit or space in an ensemble to restore coherence, or to recreate an entire historic urban landscape, particularly if that landscape has significant resonance for the population. Reconstruction may be carried out at archaeological sites for purposes of explanation or to serve modern functions. It may be a strategy in the memorialization of people or events. It may be for leisure, consumption or tourism. It may be in traditional materials, expressive of the continuity of the past, or in modern materials when the intention is to express the idea of a building, recapturing the spirit of place. Reconstruction may be carried out for education and research – there are many reconstructions of timber buildings, for example, based on archaeological evidence which exemplify the combined research and popular education roles of reconstructions. Reconstruction may also be achieved through digital or virtual means for purposes of interpretation (see below). This list is long but not exhaustive.

What are the exceptional cases?

Since reconstruction is regarded as an exceptional circumstance in heritage management, although this is, in fact, highly arguable since it has happened frequently, a number of charters and guiding documents have sought to specify those exceptional circumstances in which reconstruction may be allowed. The Declaration of Dresden (1982) made an exceptional case for the 'complete reconstruction of severely damaged monuments' by war, but also noted that this must be based on reliable documentation of their condition before destruction. The Krakow Charter (2000) further stated that reconstruction of an entire building, destroyed by armed conflict or natural disaster, may be acceptable if there are exceptional social or cultural motives that are related to the identity of the entire community. The Riga Charter (2000) stated that exceptional circumstances arising from 'tragic loss through disasters whether of natural or human origin' may pertain when 'the monument concerned has outstanding artistic, symbolic or environmental ... significance ... [and] provided that appropriate survey and historical documentation is available'. Further provisions included the avoidance of falsification of context or damage to significant historic fabric, and the need for reconstruction to be established through full and open consultation among national and local authorities and the community. The World Heritage Convention Operational Guidelines (2015) state that the reconstruction of archaeological remains or historic buildings or districts is justifiable only in exceptional circumstances, without detailing those circumstances. There is an element here of St Augustine – 'make me holy, but not yet'.

Context/wider vision

The Ename Charter (2008) is concerned with the interpretation and presentation of sites and refers to those being considered for reconstruction: sites should relate to their wider social, cultural, historical and natural contexts and settings, including multifaceted historical, political, spiritual and artistic contexts. All aspects of a site's cultural, social and environmental significance should be considered. Interpretation should take into account all groups that have contributed to the historical and cultural significance of the site; the surrounding landscape, natural environment and geographical setting; the intangible elements of a site's heritage (local customs, cultural and spiritual traditions, stories, visual arts, etc.); and the cross-cultural significance of the site including the range of perspectives based on scholarly research, ancient records and living traditions which could be used in interpretation. In such a remarkably comprehensive formulation the usefulness of such a document, determined to be inclusive and not to offend by being exclusive, becomes questionable: easier simply to assert that everything is significant rather than attempting to specify. Issues of context and environment are also raised in the Declaration of San Antonio (1996) which identifies 'context' as one of several possible indicators of authenticity – in terms of whether it corresponds to the original or other periods of significance and whether it enhances or diminishes the significance of the site.

Procedures

Assessment

The building, site or ensemble must be clearly identified and its history and evolution researched, enabling an assessment of significance and possible options. It is important to consider the building or site in its context, rather than seeing it as an isolated phenomenon. The reconstruction may well be part of a wider development plan. The separation of professional responsibilities into institutional bunkers – heritage, environment and town planning – often militates against integrated planning which should draw on a wide range of specialisms and cut across narrow departmental and ministerial responsibilities.

The range of possible interventions within the proposed development, including reconstruction, should be itemized. This may result in the preparation of various options about which choices will need to be made. The possibility of reconstruction should be considered alongside other strategies which may include a new building or stabilization and preservation as found. Making choices will require an assessment of the degree of survival of the original fabric, the extent of available documentation (a recurrent mantra in all heritage conventions) and the preparation of evidence of significance. The latter is particularly complex since there is a range of levels and types: historical, architectural, technological, aesthetic, religious, spiritual, symbolic, physical context, the spirit of place and value to the community. In assessing options for reconstruction, an assessment of exceptional significance may outweigh the usual requirements for the survival of the major part of the fabric and the fullest documentation.

Choices should also be informed by an assessment of the sustainability of the project. This will include the management of the process, the longer-term functions and management of the buildings or site after completion, the economic and social benefits and potential contribution to the well-being of the community.

Conservation statement/management plan checklist

In documenting the site and the proposal there is a long list of potential topics to be covered and the range of expertise required. These include: technical condition, historical background, vulnerability, site significance, original design and evolution, landscape, archaeology, ecology, social aspects, recent works, management of the site and of the project, monitoring of works, conservation and management policies and formulating a long-term maintenance plan.

Consultation and communication

Consultation with local stakeholders, community and amenity groups is crucial. Development planning, including reconstruction, is not just a task for the professionals involved in the technical aspects. The provision of physical and intellectual access by the public to cultural heritage sites, and the vital part played by interpretation and presentation, are fundamental to the Ename Charter on Interpretation, but the desirability of public engagement at the earlier planning and decision-making stages must also be stressed. This is emphasized in the Deschambault Declaration on the Preservation of the Heritage of Quebec (1982): 'the public has a legitimate right to participate in any decision in regard to actions to preserve the national heritage'.

In all cases of reconstruction and renewal the views of as many potential stakeholders as possible must be canvassed, meetings held, participation encouraged and options discussed. The creation of a project website will facilitate this process. Procedures must be transparent to ensure the maintenance of public trust, with decisions clearly explained, communicated, documented and published.

Technical requirements

The assessment of technical requirements includes the consideration of the extent of survival of fabric, the presence of appropriate documentation, the availability of suitable materials for new work, the availability of expertise, the skills of the potential workforce and the availability of funding. The assessment of surviving fabric will, in certain cases, be an assessment of original fabric, but in others it may be the assessment of layers of fabric over longer periods of time, revealing a historical development which should be preserved. The approach should be sustainably and pragmatically driven rather than being driven by the pursuit of a lost, irrecoverable ideal.

Decisions on the technical approach should consider whether the intention is to produce a wholly new building or a reconstruction which looks so far as possible the same as the building which has gone, or whether the reconstruction should be in the spirit of the time, style and materials of the original, but adapted to contemporary needs. A phased programme of works, with finite components which can be individually signed off and assessed, is recommended, particularly when funding is spasmodic.

Labelling/identification of the new

Good restoration practice enables new work to be distinguished from the old or original, and it also allows for future reversibility. More extensive reconstruction may not be so legible, so a discreet sign on or near the building or site should state the circumstances, extent and date of the work.

Documenting the process and results

All work on the project should be fully documented. A project monitoring system is required to ensure the maintenance of quality, compliance with national standards, adherence to time and budget requirements. This will also require the establishment of an expert advisory board responsible for monitoring the project progress and reporting as necessary. Such a board may on occasion have delegated directive powers.

When work has been completed, documentation of what has been done, with reasons where appropriate, should be made available on a website as well as deposited with the owners and managers of the building or site, the local planning department, or the local library or archive, using appropriate digital records. A post-implementation review should consider and document the lessons learned during the process of planning and carrying out the works. It should also consider the successes and failures of the intervention, for future reference. This consideration involves a further consultation process to take into account the views of users of the building and other stakeholders. This process also should be fully documented.

Looking forward: Digital technology

The use of three-dimensional (3D) digital technology has developed very quickly over the last fifteen years, augmenting such traditional recording techniques for historic buildings as hand measurement and photogrammetry, assisting the documentation and analysis of buildings and places for recording purposes and for guiding works of repair and restoration, with increasing potential in the field of architectural reconstruction. The existence of a digital 3D model of a building makes it possible to perform several tasks that would be difficult to conduct on site, including the analysis of surfaces and the identification of potential structural problems. A digital model allows for the rotation and visualization of a building from artificially created positions, not simply from the ground level.

Laser scanning can provide a great number of measurements relatively quickly which is useful when assessing large or complex buildings or sites, creating 3D images from 'point clouds' to map objects (English Heritage 2011). Building information modelling (BIM) allows the production of 3D geometric models usually based on previously acquired 3D information, which can be supplied by laser scanning and photogrammetry, although other 2D survey sources can also be used, enabling digital representation of the structure and an understanding of how the architectural components fit together (Andrews et al. 2015). Other methods are now being researched and developed for their potential for mapping, such as multiple light imaging, through Reflectance Transformation Imaging (RTI) techniques, with Polynomial Texture Mapping (PTM) being the most common type of RTI used in the context of cultural heritage (English Heritage 2013, Payne 2013). It is used to create texture maps of objects and is composed from multiple digital photographic images.

Indeed, it is now possible to acquire, store, process and present many different kinds of information in digital form to support work on historic buildings and sites. One very good example of this is the creation of the open access Million Image Database by the Institute of Digital Archaeology (IDA) as a comprehensive library of 3D imagery of threatened sites in the conflict areas of the Middle East, North Africa and Asia developed through crowdsourcing by the distribution of low-cost, high-tech cameras, to volunteer photographers who can donate their images using social media, email or more conventional means. The use of BIM for historic structures, as Historic BIM (HBIM), is in its infancy, but such a record for a heritage asset could readily enhance post-disaster decision-making (Maxwell 2014).

Digital technologies have enabled the *virtual* reconstruction of buildings, which may be presented at sites, in museums or events. Use of the imaging techniques to create models for exhibition can be useful for presenting destroyed structures after conflict or natural disaster. For example, the recent computer-generated reconstruction of Coventry Cathedral in the United Kingdom, which was destroyed by incendiary bombs in 1940, will allow visitors to the ruins to have an enhanced awareness of the original building, while understanding the devastation of war. Smart technology in the form of tablets, smartphones and virtual reality headsets can be used to visualize the reconstructed building, including the art work of the original stained glass windows (Bridge 2016).

It is now evident that 3D virtual reconstructions could significantly support studies for the eventual real reconstruction of damaged or destroyed structures. The IDA, as an extension to its Million Image Database, has investigated the idea of 3D replication in full scale, using proprietary cement, sandstone or marble-based 3D printing and machining techniques (Institute of Digital Archaeology 2016). The potential of 3D printing to replicate sites generated worldwide headlines in April 2016 when a two-thirds scale model of the 2,000 year-old Arch of Triumph in the ancient city of Palmyra, Syria, destroyed by ISIS in October 2015, was erected in Trafalgar Square, London, and subsequently re-erected in Manhattan's City Hall Park, New York, in September 2016. The model was recreated from about 100 pre-war photographs taken mainly by tourists over a five-year period and was programmed to drive a massive stonecutting machine at a quarry at Carrara in northern Italy to reproduce the elements of the arch.

Digital imaging techniques could have a significant role in the future for reconstructing architectural heritage, although the potential to reconstruct sites with digital accuracy should not be used as a justification for their demolition or for allowing physical fabric to fall into disrepair. The increasing ease, speed and relatively low cost of this high-tech technology will need to be checked against the appropriateness of wholesale and full-scale replacement of damaged or destroyed sites. In fact the physical replication of the Palmyra arch resulted in much media attention with different views about whether destroyed heritage should be replicated (see, for example, Al Bustani 2015, Abrahams 2016, Clammer 2016, Hadingham 2016, Ruiz 2016). While there may be a case to argue for reconstruction on the same grounds as for other conflict-damaged monuments such as the reconstruction of the war-damaged historic centre of Warsaw, with similar arguments for the importance of the site in terms of the local and international community and symbolism, it remains important to bear in mind the words of the Riga Charter (2000) that 'replication of cultural heritage is in general a misrepresentation of evidence of the past ... but that in exceptional circumstances, reconstruction of cultural heritage, lost through disaster … may be acceptable, when the monument concerned has outstanding artistic, symbolic or environmental … significance for regional history and cultures'.

Advances in digital technology offer new possibilities for improving the standard of reconstruction, bearing in mind that Warsaw was rebuilt largely on the basis of drawings, simple photographs and Bellotto's eighteenth-century *vedute* rescued during the war. The Historic England draft *Advisory Note on the Reconstruction of Heritage Assets* published in 2016 refers to the fact that international charters and documents place great weight on having accurate evidence on which to base reconstruction, noting that the 'recent exponential growth of digital recording technologies offers great opportunities for significant places to be recorded comprehensively in an increasingly cost effective way' (Historic England 2016).While it is important to recognize the value of technological developments, which could create almost perfect copies, it is important to maintain the criterion that replication is to be contemplated only in exceptional circumstances. Technological development will also require clear guidelines on approaches since it may be possible to be very selective in terms of how a reconstruction is carried out: one of the technicians who modelled the Palmyra arch explained at the launch of the project that the digital model was edited so that the final version excluded bullet damage, thereby removing the record of war (Abrahams 2016).

Authentic reconstruction

Consideration of digital technologies which may so easily replicate lost appearances brings us back to the apparently oxymoronic notion of authentic reconstruction, discussed in the introductory chapter. Authenticity has lost the absolute quality which it used to enjoy and has become, through redefinition and refinement, a contingent quality. It is a slippery and elusive notion, and its application to digitally based replication should be reconsidered since a closer, more symbiotic authenticity may now be contemplated. Do we mean in this context that the reproduction is authentic to the spirit of the original and accurate in the minute detail but not original in terms of facture? If so, does this matter – is it real facture or the appearance of facture that counts? Have we come so far in teasing out the meaning and application of definitions that we have obscured any understanding of the practical applications of technological advances? Authenticity is surely an arguable, mutable value rather than an absolute quality and unlike uniqueness may have relative qualities and attributes. If guidelines for heritage reconstruction could move away from the notion of absolute, binary, right or wrong answers to difficult questions, based on the notion of a really absolute authenticity, towards a culturally relative, pragmatic approach in which the notion of authenticity is a negotiable rather than an absolute concept, then we might feel that this book has been a worthwhile exercise. Authentic reconstruction in such circumstances would come to be regarded as a relative concept which in a contingent world not ruled by moral imperatives is no more than an acknowledgement that almost everything in life is negotiable, even the implementation of the Venice Charter, so long as we allow each individual situation its particularity as we work towards non-generic, case-specific, site-specific outcomes.

References

Abrahams, T. (2016), 'Palmyra Arch Lives Again (Again): The Latest Version of the Destroyed Arch Raises Interesting Questions About Protecting and Recreating Antiquities', *RIBA Journal*, 26 May. Available online: https://www.ribaj.com/culture/palmyra-arch-venice (accessed 26 November 2016).

Al Bustani, H. (2015), 'Can and Should ISIL's Destruction at Palmyra be Undone?', *The National*, 2 September. Available online: http://www.thenational.ae/world/middle-east/can-and-should-isils-destruction-at-palmyra-be-undone (accessed 26 November 2016).

Andrews, D., J. Bedford and P. Bryan (2015), *Metric Survey Specifications for Cultural Heritage* (third edition), Swindon: Historic England.

Bold, J. and R. Pickard (2013), 'Reconstructing Europe: the Need for Guidelines', *The Historic Environment*, 4 (2): 105–28.

Bridge, M. (2016). 'Coventry Cathedral is Virtually Rebuilt', *The Times*, 25 October. Available online: http://www.thetimes.co.uk/article/coventry-cathedral-rises-again-in-virtual-reality-3lwgt3x25 (accessed 22 November 2016).

Clammer, P. (2016), 'Erasing Isis: How 3D Technology Now Lets Us Copy and Rebuild Entire Cities', *The Guardian*, 27 May. Available online: https://www.theguardian.com/cities/2016/may/27/isis-palmyra-3d-technology-copy-rebuild-city-venice-biennale (accessed 26 November 2016).

Council of Europe (2015), 'Parliamentary Assembly', *Cultural Heritage in Crisis and Post-Crisis Situations*, Recommendation 2071(2015).

English Heritage (2011), *3D Laser Scanning for Heritage: Advice and Guidance to Users on Laser Scanning in Archaeology and Architecture* (second edition). Available online: https://www.historicengland.org.uk/images-books/publications/3d-laser-scanning-heritage2/ (accessed 22 November 2016).

English Heritage (2013), *Multi-light Imaging for Heritage Applications*. Available online: https://content.historicengland.org.uk/images-books/publications/multi-light-imaging-heritage-applications/Multi-light_Imaging_FINAL_low-res.pdf/ (accessed 22 November 2016).

Hadingham, E. (2016), 'The Technology That Will Resurrect ISIS-Destroyed Antiquities', *NOVA Next*, 9 Jun 2016. Available online: http://www.pbs.org/wgbh/nova/next/ancient/digital-preservation-syria/ (accessed 22 November 2016).

Historic England (2016), *Historic England Advisory Note on the Reconstruction of Heritage Assets* (Draft, 1 April 2016). Available online: https://content.historicengland.org.uk/content/docs/guidance/draft-reconstruction-of-heritage-assets-apr16.pdf (accessed 26 November 2016).

Institute of Digital Archaeology (2016), *The Future of Digital Archaeology: The Importance of Preserving and Restoring Ancient Objects.* Available online: https://static1.squarespace.com/static/54d141f5e4b032ab36c35a29/t/56c6234a 2b8ddedda8543765/1455825741243/IDA+World+Government+Summit+Repo rt.pdf (accessed 22 November 2016).

Maxwell, I. (2014), *Integrating Digital Technologies in Support of Historic Building Information Modelling: BIM4Conservation (HBIM)*, London: Conference on Training in Architectural Conservation (COTAC).

Payne, E. M. (2013), 'Imaging Techniques in Conservation', *Journal of Conservation and Museum Studies*, 10 (2): 17–29.

Ruiz, C. (2016), 'Fake It Till You Remake It: The Lost Masterpieces That Are Returning – Digitally', *The Times*, 26 May. Available online: http://www. thetimes.co.uk/article/fake-it-till-you-remake-it-the-lost-masterpieces-that-are-returning-digitally-9j685780f (accessed 26 November 2016).

INDEX